W9-CHF-550

EMOTION AND CULTURE

EMPIRICAL
STUDIES OF
MUTUAL
INFLUENCE

EMOTION AND CULTURE

EMPIRICAL STUDIES OF MUTUAL INFLUENCE

edited by

shinobu kitayama and

hazel rose markus

American Psychological Association

Washington, DC

Copyright @ 1994 by the American Psychological Association. All rights reserved. Except as permitted under the United States Copyright Act of 1976, no part of this publication may be reproduced or distributed in any form or by any means, or stored in a database or retrieval system, without the prior written permission of the publisher.

First printing May 1994
Third printing November 1997

Published by
American Psychological Association
750 First Street, NE
Washington, DC 20002

Copies may be ordered from
APA Order Department
P.O. Box 92984
Washington, DC 20090-2984

In the UK and Europe, copies may be ordered from
American Psychological Association
3 Henrietta Street
Covent Garden, London
WC2E 8LU England

Typeset in Century Book by Techna Type, Inc., York, PA
Printer: United Book Press, Baltimore, MD
Cover Designer: Grafik Communications, Ltd., Alexandria, VA
Technical/Production Editor: Miria Liliana Riahi

Library of Congress Cataloging-in-Publication Data
Emotion and culture: empirical studies of mutual influence / edited
  by Shinobu Kitayama and Hazel Rose Markus.
     p.   cm.
  Based on papers presented at the International Conference on
Emotion and Culture held at the University of Oregon in Eugene in
June, 1992.
  Includes bibliographical references and index.
  ISBN 1-55798-487-5 (acid-free paper)
  1. Emotions—Cross-cultural studies—Congresses.
2. Ethnopsychology—Congresses.   I. Markus, Hazel.
II. Kitayama, Shinobu.   III. International Conference on
Emotion and Culture (1992 : University of Oregon)
BF531.E517 1994
152.4—dc20   94-2570
                                                   CIP

British Library Cataloguing-in-Publication Data
A CIP record is available from the British Library.

Printed in the United States of America

APA Science Volumes

Best Methods for the Analysis of Change: Recent Advances, Unanswered Questions, Future Directions

Cardiovascular Reactivity to Psychological Stress and Disease

The Challenge in Mathematics and Science Education: Psychology's Response

Cognition: Conceptual and Methodological Issues

Cognitive Bases of Musical Communication

Conceptualization and Measurement of Organism–Environment Interaction

Developmental Psychoacoustics

Emotion and Culture: Empirical Studies of Mutual Influence

Hostility, Coping, and Health

Organ Donation and Transplantation: Psychological and Behavioral Factors

The Perception of Structure

Perspectives on Socially Shared Cognition

Psychological Testing of Hispanics

Researching Community Psychology: Issues of Theory and Methods

Sleep and Cognition

Studying Lives Through Time: Personality and Development

The Suggestibility of Children's Recollections: Implications for Eyewitness Testimony

Taste, Experience, and Feeding: Development and Learning

Temperament: Individual Differences at the Interface of Biology and Behavior

Through the Looking Glass: Issues of Psychological Well-Being in Captive Nonhuman Primates

A PA expects to publish volumes on the following conference topics:

Changing Ecological Approaches to Development: Organism–Environment Mutualities
Converging Operations in the Study of Visual Selective Attention
Psychology of Industrial Relations
Maintaining and Promoting Integrity in Behavioral Science Research
Measuring Changes in Patients Following Psychological and Pharmacological Interventions
Perspectives on the Ecology of Human Development
Sleep Onset: Normal and Abnormal Processes
Stereotypes: Brain–Behavior Relationships
Women's Psychological and Physical Health

As part of its continuing and expanding commitment to enhance the dissemination of scientific psychological knowledge, the Science Directorate of the APA established a Scientific Conferences Program. A series of volumes resulting from these conferences is jointly produced by the Science Directorate and the Office of Communications. A call for proposals is issued several times annually by the Science Directorate, which, collaboratively with the APA Board of Scientific Affairs, evaluates the proposals and selects several conferences for funding. This important effort has resulted in an exceptional series of meetings and scholarly volumes, each of which individually has contributed to the dissemination of research and dialogue in these topical areas.

The APA Science Directorate's conferences funding program has supported 29 conferences since its inception in 1988. To date, 20 volumes resulting from conferences have been published.

Contents

Part Three: Emotion as Moral Category and Phenomenon

Conclusion

Contributors

Phoebe C. Ellsworth, University of Michigan
Nico H. Frijda, University of Amsterdam
Catherine Harman, University of Oregon
Janis H. Jenkins, Case Western Reserve University
Shinobu Kitayama, Kyoto University
Hazel Rose Markus, University of Michigan
Usha Menon, University of Chicago
Batja Mesquita, University of Amsterdam
Michael I. Posner, University of Oregon
Mary K. Rothbart, University of Oregon
Richard A. Shweder, University of Chicago
Harry C. Triandis, University of Illinois
Geoffrey M. White, East–West Center, Honolulu
Anna Wierzbicka, The Australian National University

Preface

The chapters in this volume examine the mutual influence of emotion and culture. From various perspectives, they focus on how feelings—good, prideful, shameful, angry—are shaped and personalized in the recurrent episodes of everyday social and cultural life. Together, they can be read as an initial response to Lutz's (1988) challenge to social scientists in her provocative book *Unnatural Emotions* "to explore the neglected ways in which social and cultural forces help to give emotions their observed character" (p. 210).[1] Both individually and collectively, the investigators in this book attempt to establish a cultural approach to emotion research, understand current data and theories, and advance fruitful agendas for future research.

The contributors to this volume represent a number of different nationalities and social science disciplines, including cultural, social, and developmental psychology; psychopathology; psychological anthropology; and linguistics. Their diverse approaches are brought to bear on a variety of issues surrounding this single topic: How does culture come into play in a scientific understanding of human emotions?

The impetus for this book was the International Conference on Emotion and Culture, held at the University of Oregon (in Eugene) in June, 1992. In addition to the authors of this volume, 11 other specialists on emotion or culture participated. They include

Hiroko Akiyama, University of Michigan
Michael Bond, Chinese University of Hong Kong
Joseph J. Campos, University of California, Berkeley
Steve Cousins, Rikkyo University, Japan

[1]Lutz, C. (1988). *Unnatural emotions: Everyday sentiments on a Micronesion atoll and their challenge to Western theory.* Chicago: University of Chicago Press.

Susan E. Cross, Iowa State University
Robert Mauro, University of Oregon
Joan C. Miller, Yale University
James A. Russell, University of British Columbia, Canada
Shalom H. Schwartz, Hebrew University of Jerusalem
Toshitake Takata, Nara University, Japan
Robert B. Zajonc, University of Michigan.

Their collegial enthusiasm, support, and contribution both during and after the conference have been indispensable. Even where no explicit mention is made of their names, they have contributed and, in many cases, altered the arguments found in many of the chapters. Although unable to participate in the meeting for urgent personal reasons, Alan Fiske at the University of Pennsylvania has also encouraged us throughout this project. Finally, several faculty members at the University of Oregon, most notably Marian Friestad, Lewis Goldberg, and Hill Goldsmith also provided indispensable support by being present throughout the conference and by sharing their professional opinions and judgments.

Much of the funding for the conference came from the scientific conference program of the American Psychological Association's Science Directorate. Our thanks go to Virginia Holt of the Science Directorate for her help in shaping this project. Additional financial support was provided by the Psychology Department, Institute of Cognitive and Decision Sciences of the University of Oregon, and by the Institute for Social Research of the University of Michigan. A grant from the Committee on Culture, Health, and Human Development of the Social Science Research Council enabled us to invite graduate students from six countries to attend the conference. In addition, the conceptual framework of this book benefited from many conversations with the members of this Committee. We also received support from the Culture and Cognition Program of the University of Michigan and were encouraged in our efforts to prepare this book by the members of the program, particularly by Richard E. Nisbett and Lawrence Hirschfeld. Both editors were funded by Grant BNS-9010754 from the National Science Foundation during the period of the conference and the preparation of this book. We thank all these organizations for their generous support.

We would also like to acknowledge many individuals who handled with skill and wit a variety of logistic aspects of the meeting, including two secretarial staff members, Vonda Evens and Colleen Vande Voorde; two postdoctoral fellows, Stephen Ahadi and Angela Simon; and several students, Mara Cadinu, Michael Crowley, Carene Davis-Stitt, Joseph Dien, Carl Hayashi, Amy Hayes, Shuyeu Lin, Hisaya Matsumoto, and Leslie Smith. Finally, our heartfelt thanks go to Debbie Apsley, who has provided outstanding administrative, secretarial, and emotional support throughout every phase of the conference and of this book project.

Shinobu Kitayama
Hazel Rose Markus

CHAPTER 1

Introduction to Cultural Psychology and Emotion Research

Shinobu Kitayama and Hazel Rose Markus

R ecently, anthropologists and psychologists, reviving a set of long-standing interests, have begun to examine the divergent, dynamic, yet systematic ways in which cultural beliefs, values, or construals of one's self and of the world give shape to psychological processes and to the ensuing conscious experience. Drawing on this newly emerging literature, this book focuses on the cultural factors that contribute to the shaping and the working of human emotions. Specifically, we wish to establish that emotion can be fruitfully conceptualized as being social in nature or, in Lutz's (1988) words, as being "anything but natural." No doubt, emotions are comprised of a myriad of physiological, neurological, and psychological components. Many of these component processes may be demonstrably hardwired. Nevertheless, by themselves, these processes are not emotions. Rather, the components may be combined and accorded their divergent functions and forms through social and cultural processes by which individuals try to accomplish, collectively and personally, a form of adaptation and adjustment to their own immediate sociocultural, semiotic environment. Through this pursuit of adaptation and adjustment to one's cultural and social environment, the component processes are organized and enabled to become emotions.

Despite earlier approaches emphasizing culture as a primary determinant of emotional experience (e.g., Ekman, 1973, chapter 1), many social scientists have long been comfortable with the assumption that emotions are biologically prewired internal processes for the homeostatic maintenance and regulation of behavior (e.g., Buck, 1988; Ekman, 1984; LeDoux, 1987). However, the idea that emotions are not purely natural or biological events, but are influenced and shaped through social and cultural processes, has received considerable attention in recent years (e.g., Campos, Campos, & Barrett, 1989; Frijda, 1986; Lutz, 1988; Ortony & Turner, 1990; Rosaldo, 1984). Research directly relevant to the present interest in emotion and culture is currently underway in a variety of substantive domains of social science including social psychology, developmental psychology, cultural psychology, medical anthropology, and psychopathology. This book seeks to integrate these diverse approaches to emotion and culture within a common theme, thus setting an agenda for the view that emotion and culture are mutually and reciprocally related.

The present emphasis on culture does not presume that biological or physiological processes are unimportant in emotion. On the contrary, extensive research on the biological aspects of emotion has amply demonstrated that these processes are pivotal and crucial in emotional processes. What is proposed here is that the development and organization of emotional processes and experience, with all their biological underpinnings, is significantly influenced, sustained, or modified by the systems of meanings in which the self, others, and other social events or objects are made significant. The extent of this cultural influence may be greater than previously assumed in psychology. This view of emotion from a cultural perspective highlights aspects of emotion that have not been well captured by the current universalistic, and mostly biological, perspective on emotion and thus promises to engender controversy, excitement, and new theory and research. As the editors of this book, we had in mind the following three specific agendas:

1. to outline the ways in which cultural processes organize emotional processes and emotional experience,
2. to outline the ways in which emotional processes and emotional experience foster and enhance sociocultural processes, and
3. to integrate cross-cultural descriptions of emotion within contemporary theories of the human emotion.

Exploring the interdependence between culture and emotion is all the more significant and timely in conjunction with the recent reemergence of an interdisciplinary field of cultural psychology. In the last decade, provocative publications examine the ways in which sociocultural processes are implicated in the workings of the human mind. Some of the edited volumes from anthropology that mark this confluence of interest and theoretical approach include Shweder and LeVine's (1984) *Culture Theory*; White and Kirkpatrick's (1985) *Person, Self, and Experience*; Marsella, DeVos, and Hsu's (1985) *Culture and Self*; Stigler, Shweder, and Herdt's (1990) *Cultural Psychology*; and most recently, Schwartz, White, and Lutz's (1992) *New Directions in Psychological Anthropology*. Some of psychology's contributions to this growing field include Berman's (1990) *Cross-Cultural Perspectives*; Bond's (1988) *The Cross-Cultural Challenge to Social Psychology*; Moghaddam, Taylor, and Wright's (1993) *Social Psychology in Cross-Cultural Perspectives*; Smith and Bond's (1993) *Social Psychology Across Cultures*; Stevenson, Azuma, and Hakuta's (1986) *Child Development and Education in Japan*; a variety of cross-cultural investigations published in the *Journal of Personality and Social Psychology*; and theoretical analyses by Triandis (1989), by Markus and Kitayama (1991), and by Miller (in press) on the role of the self as a mediator between culture and behavior, and by Wierzbicka (1986) and Russell (1991) on linguistic categories of emotion (see also Hunt & Agnoli, 1991). Also, there have been several notable contributions on the topic of culture and emotion at recent meetings of the International Society of Research on Emotion, the Society of Experimental Social Psychology, and the Society of Psychological Anthropology.

These publications converge in their approach and suggest that a renewed focus on cultural influence can be quite productive in enriching psychological theories of emotion. Yet, there has not been any book addressing cultural influence on the processes and experience of emotion from multiple, interdisciplinary perspectives. Hence, many provocative ideas and intriguing data have yet to be brought together. We believe that this volume will be instrumental in consolidating and extending the cultural perspective on emotion.

Conceptual Focus of This Book

The biological approach to emotion in the past two or three decades has revealed a great deal about emotional processes (see Ekman, 1984, and LeDoux, 1987, for reviews). Ironically, however, the remarkable accomplishments of this approach have highlighted how much remains to be understood about the development and organization of human emotions. For example, no neuroanatomical analysis is, at the moment, capable of distinguishing shame from guilt or of explaining why Chinese and Americans differ dramatically in their psychological and psychosomatic symptoms when faced with significant life difficulties.

Emotion as Fully Encultured

A number of analyses of emotion from a cross-cultural perspective (e.g., de Riviera, 1984; Kitayama & Markus, in press; Kleinman, 1988; Lutz, 1988; Markus & Kitayama, 1991; Russell, 1991), along with investigations on human socioemotional development (e.g., Barrett & Campos, 1987; Zahn-Waxler & Kochanska, 1990), imply that emotion processes, and thus the ensuing conscious experience of emotion, may be drastically different depending on the surrounding sociocultural environment. Many of the emotions observed in everyday life seem to depend on the dominant cultural frame in which specific social situations are constructed and, therefore, cannot be separated from culture-specific patterns of thinking, acting, and interacting.

To date, the interdependence between emotion and cultural environment has been examined without challenging the core assumptions of the biological approach. Yet, as Barrett and Campos (1987) observed, a paradigm shift is underway in the field of emotion. An emotion may be conceptualized more usefully and perhaps more accurately as a fuzzy set of component processes, such as facial expressions, patterns of cognitive appraisals, and action tendencies (Ortony & Turner, 1990). Not one of these components is either necessary or sufficient to define the emotion. Yet as a whole, they form a cluster that retains certain characteristic functions vis-à-vis a pertinent social (or nonsocial) situation.

From the functionalist point of view, emotions may be seen as an assortment of socially shared scripts composed of physiological, subjective, and behavioral processes. These emotion scripts develop as individuals actively, personally, and collectively adapt and adjust to their immediate sociocultural, semiotic environment. Emotion scripts are obviously afforded by a number of biologically hardwired component processes, but they also reflect the cultural environment to which they are adjusted and tuned. We may find similar emotion scripts across seemingly divergent cultures to the extent that these cultures share common elements, such as ecological conditions and prototypic models of social relationships (Fiske, 1991). At the same time, to the extent that the cultures vary in some other important regards, emotion scripts may also take correspondingly divergent forms.

Once existent, emotion scripts will organize and modulate the workings of the biological component processes themselves. The currently emerging literature on local biologies has begun to suggest the extent to which human physiology (for example, some hormonal and metabolic functions) are markedly influenced by cultural and social processes (e.g., Worthman, in press). Thus, the cultural approach to emotion calls into question "the traditional dualist idea that the closer we come to the body, the farther away we must be from culture" (Jenkins, chapter 10, this volume). Instead, the body can be fully encultured itself and can supply the immediate experience of emotion, which is "anything but natural" (Lutz, 1988).

In short, according to the current cultural perspective on emotion, culture can penetrate deeply into virtually every component process of emotion, not only the cognitive or linguistic elements that are directly provided by the culturally shared pool of knowledge, but also physiological and neurochemical elements, which need to be adjusted or tuned for the individual to accomplish a reasonable degree of adaptation and adjustment to the pertinent cultural environment. Furthermore, if emotions are literally formed through individuals' active pursuit of adaptation to their cultural environment, the emotions will in turn function to maintain and regulate or, in some cases, to challenge the very cultural environment to which they have been tuned. Thus, we may expect a degree of fit between the specific nature of the cultural environment (e.g., widely shared values, practices, and social systems) and the members' emotional organization.

Critique of Basic Emotions Theories

Unlike the functionalist view of emotion, some theorists have explicitly assumed several basic emotions that are considered to be biologically hardwired and, thus, cannot be decomposed into distinct elements. However, this essentialist position can be contested and challenged. On purely logical grounds, simply because a certain emotion (e.g., anger) can be identified across divergent cultures, it does not necessarily mean that the configuration of a variety of components (which as a whole constitute this emotion of anger) is fully represented as a unified neuronal program of the brain. Instead, it may be more accurate and more fruitful for social science research to hypothesize that the commonality of emotional configuration reflects, at least in part, the commonality of social and cultural processes in which the workings of the psychological component processes are situated. Far from inherent in the biological heritage of the human animal, the psychological organization called anger may reflect social and cultural processes. By extending the same line of reasoning, it is easy to see why some other emotions are relatively culture specific. Different cultural frames may highlight divergent modes of social interaction and appraisal patterns and thus may give rise to culture-specific emotional organizations.

Furthermore, even when a claim is made that anger exists in both Cultures A and B, there is no firm reason to believe that the two forms of anger, as observed therein, are identical. The claim should be construed more reasonably as a claim of family resemblance rather than of exact identity. That is to say, even though the same label (anger) is used in referring to a given cluster of component processes, both the exact set of the components that participate in the cluster and their interconnections can vary with the nature of the immediate situation, the developmental stage of the individual, and the culture in which he or she has been embedded and socialized. This argument can be illustrated readily in a developmental context. For example, even though some common components (such as autonomic arousal and the involvement of certain facial muscles) can be identified both in the anger of infants and in the anger of adults and thus share a degree of family resemblance, other participating components (e.g., instrumental responses, inhibitory tendencies) may be very different. Thus, the resulting organization of anger processes and anger experience may, in some cases, be different to the point at which the label of anger is no longer seen as appropriate.

Likewise, anger in the United States and its translation equivalent in Japanese, *ikari*, may well share important elements and resemble each other (otherwise, the quality of the translation would be suspect), yet the exact set of participating components and their organization, as well as the entailing conscious experience, may also vary widely across the two cultures. The essentialist claim of anger as a basic psychological or neuronal entity tends to mask this and other issues that may be crucial to a better understanding of the interaction between emotion and culture. Furthermore, by using anger in English as an anchor and standard of cross-cultural comparison and of generalization, the basic emotions theorists may have furthered an ethnocentric understanding of emotion.

New Questions and Issues

All in all, then, the current focus on cross-cultural variation in emotional processes and emotional experience may reveal a far greater impact of sociocultural processes on emotion than imagined within the traditional biological approach. To illustrate this point with concrete examples, selected questions that can be addressed from the current cultural perspective are listed below:

1. Anger is highly pervasive and natural in Western cultures. However, the experience and the organization of anger may depend crucially

on the beliefs, values, or construals of the social life unique to a given cultural group. Thus, anger, as manifested and embedded in Western cultures and as experienced by those in these cultures, may be understood best by analyzing the Western cultures themselves. If so, is anger a central and natural emotion in Western cultures primarily because these cultures stress independence and the expression of one's internal attributes such as rights, goals, or needs and because anger is most closely associated with the blocking of these rights, goals, or needs (e.g., I was treated unfairly)?

2. Many Asian or Eastern cultures stress interdependence (instead of independence) among individuals and insist on the importance of attending to others' needs or goals and of making connections with others (instead of emphasizing the significance of protecting one's intrinsic rights, needs, or goals and of separating the self from others; Markus & Kitayama, 1991). Is it possible, then, that anger is less common, less natural, and less integrated into the social life of the people of non-Western cultures? If so, can we still insist on an identity between anger as experienced in the West and anger as experienced in the East? Is it perhaps more prudent to consider the possibility that the two forms of anger are distinct in some important ways?

3. The close scrutiny of culture and emotion raises another set of important issues. Emotion may play a pivotal role in sustaining and bolstering cultural construals. Referring again to the example of anger, is it possible that, within the Western cultural frame, construals of one's intrinsic rights, needs, and goals are perceived as real and authentic and the pursuit of them as God given and natural because of the pervasive occurrence of anger when these needs or rights are infringed upon or blocked?

4. Can this perspective on culture and emotion account for those Chinese who are reported to complain about chest pains and fatigue instead of expressing despondent moods or aggressive feelings when faced with difficulties in life (Kleinman, 1988)? Can these phenomena of *somatization* be grasped by understanding how Asian construals of the individual and of the social world differ from those of their Western counterparts?

5. If we have somatization, can we meaningfully define *emotionalization* as well (Shweder, in press)? In other words, can emotion be viewed as a specific type of interpretive schema or as a script that locates internal sensations within a dynamically changing pattern of interaction with the social and nonsocial environment? Emotion scripts or schemas may be applicable to internal sensations and bodily experience and to the external realities in which the internal processes are embedded. These scripts or schemas will thus integrate the internal sensations with the external realities to yield simultaneously both a "deeply felt or moving" perception of the external realities and a "personally and socially meaningful" construal or experience of the internal sensations. Here may arise the very moral (i.e., moving) force of emotional experience. There is no reason to suppose, however, that emotionalizing is the only way of either social perception or bodily experience. Is it reasonable, for example, to suppose that, although emotion scripts or schemas are prevalent and common in Western culture today, some other schemas (like those of soma) are more common in other cultures and in other historical times? Soma or state of the physical body, as an interpretive frame, appears to allow the person to detach internal sensations from external realities rather than connecting them to the latter. Therefore, it may be seen as less dynamic, more static, and less moral (i.e., relatively detached from one's social relations with external realities). In analyzing these issues, we cannot proceed without considering a formidable issue of emotion lexicon. How can we conceptualize the interdependence between linguistic categories of emotion or soma, on the one hand, and emotional or somatic processes and experience on the other (Levy, 1984; Russell, 1991)?

6. We may also raise questions about non-Western emotions that have no obvious counterparts in the West, or what anthropologists have called *indigenous emotions*. Is it possible that such indigenous emotions (e.g., *amae* in Japan; Doi, 1986, 1990) are as natural and as basic within the cultural frame of interdependence as anger is natural and basic within the Western frame of individual independence and autonomy? If so, what does it tell us about the origin and the nature of human emotion?

Overview

This book contains 11 chapters that focus on issues surrounding the interdependence between emotion and culture. Taken as a whole, these chapters make a strong case that emotions are socially and culturally shaped and maintained, especially by means of collective knowledge that is represented in linguistic convention, everyday practice, and social structure and, furthermore, once existent, they serve as a significant moral force in maintaining the very social and cultural processes from which they are derived. While in agreement with this general theme, however, each of the chapters has its own, somewhat different emphasis. Therefore, the chapters are divided into four groups: (a) emotion as a social product; (b) emotion, language, and cognition; (c) emotion as a moral category and a moral phenomenon; and (d) the cultural shaping of emotion.

Emotion as a Social Product

The first three chapters (by Ellsworth, Frijda & Mesquita, and Markus & Kitayama) address how emotions are constructed and experienced within a social and cultural context. Although considerably different in the details, these chapters have in common a commitment to what might be called the componential approach to emotion. Following the functionalist perspective sketched above, this approach assumes that emotions are best seen as an assortment of socially shared scripts made up of physiological, subjective, and behavioral processes. Some of these processes are mental, confined mostly to the boundary of an individual person (e.g., physiological responses, sensory feelings of pleasure and pain), but many others are intermental (Wertsch & Tulviste, 1992), afforded or enabled in interpersonal communications and interactions (e.g., habitual interaction pattern such as attack or praise, socially shared feelings of intimacy or antagonism). One promising way of describing the multifaceted and social nature of the emotions is to specify the appraisal patterns associated with the current situation on a number of cognitive dimensions.

Ellsworth raises the important question of how we may seek to integrate both cross-cultural commonalities and divergences of emotion within a unified theoretical framework. In reviewing the research in this area, she notes that neither the universalist position nor the cultural constructionist position is acceptable in its extreme forms. Her solution to this often unproductive antagonism within the theoretical camps is to analyze emotions in terms of a limited number of dimensions that individuals use to appraise the nature of the impinging situation. Some of these appraisal dimensions (e.g., novelty and pleasantness of the situation) can be pervasive and may well be universal, but some others (e.g., responsibility and control) may not be or may be entirely culture specific. In both cases individuals are believed to analyze, perhaps subconsciously and spontaneously, the nature of the impinging event in terms of these appraisal dimensions supposedly provided by their culture.

Frijda and Mesquita follow a similar path, but provide additional considerations that may be significant in emotion and culture research. They suggest the notion of event focality as being central in analyzing cross-cultural variation in emotional processes. Some emotional event categories (e.g., terrorist attacks, damage to one's honor and dignity, disturbance of group harmony) may be widely shared and cognitively elaborated or *hypercognized* in certain cultural groups. These elaborated event categories are said to be *focal* in the culture. Each of these categories represents a number of appraisals, bodily reactions, and action tendencies packaged densely into a relatively coherent whole. Thus, the relevant appraisals are "precomputed" and stored in the form of a culturally shared emotion script. Insofar as any concrete, real-life situation resembles such a focal event category sufficiently, the actual situation may be treated as a specific instance of the focal event category. There is no need to analyze, in Ellsworth's sense, the nature of the impinging event. Rather, emotions may arise from similarity matching between the impinging situation and a culturally focal and collectively shared event category. Once an actual event ensues, such a focal event may then be readily accessed collectively (i.e., in the minds of all the participants at the same moment) and, once so collectively accessed, may play pivotal roles in guiding the reaction of the participants to the actual social situation.

In the last chapter of part 1, Markus and Kitayama elaborate on how cultural norms and values can be transformed into each member's psychological needs and suggest that an analysis of emotion socialization is the key to understanding the embodiment of the cultural and the social.

They suggest that it is the Western cultural imperative to separate the self from others and to seek, find, and express one's own internal attributes. However, many non-Western individuals see themselves as being fundamentally connected with other people. In this contrasting perspective, the cultural imperative is to fit in with the others, to seek and fulfill interpersonal obligations, and to become part of an ongoing relationship. Markus and Kitayama suggest, with empirical evidence, that these cultural imperatives can be incorporated into each person's emotion systems so that it "feels good" to behave in accordance with the respective imperative and it "feels bad" to behave against it. Then, they use this analysis to review cultural variations in social behaviors including conformity, stereotyping, and coping.

Emotion, Language, and Cognition

The chapters by Wierzbicka and by Posner, Rothbart, and Harman are more cognitive in orientation. Wierzbicka pursues the same componential approach to emotion from a perspective in linguistics. The linguistic analysis of emotion is significant because one primary nexus of the cultural approach is to advance a critique of the current and mostly unicultural psychological theories of emotion. This critique has revolved around the nagging question of whether or not one can identify a translation equivalent of any given English emotion term in other, non-Western languages. With a small set of semantic primitives as her primary tool, Wierzbicka provides linguistic evidence that the notion of *feel* is likely to be pancultural, but other emotion terms, including those traditionally considered basic by many psychological theorists, can be defined only by combinations of the act of *feeling* something and of a specific set of culturally defined features of the pertinent social situation. The necessary conclusion from this line of analysis is that *basic* emotions cannot be basic; otherwise other nonbasic emotions (such as *lek*, *fago*, and *amae*) would be equally basic because they can be decomposed readily into their constituting elements.

Whereas Wierzbicka makes an important contribution to the study of culture and emotion from a linguistic point of view, Posner, Rothbart, and Harman contribute important ideas, methodological points, and evidence of the developmental time course of mental systems from a perspective of cognitive science. They suggest, in detail, how biologically prepared elements of involuntary and voluntary attention processes might interact with culturally divergent socialization practices to form systems of mental control, especially of regulation of emotional responses. Extensive research on the interaction between biology and socialization throughout human development has just begun. This chapter illustrates the promise of and the urgent need for further research in this area.

Emotion as a Moral Category and a Moral Phenomenon

The chapters in this section pursue, in three different domains, the central question of cultural psychology, that is, how culture and emotion constitute each other. Earlier chapters suggest that whereas culture provides the semiotic grid in which emotion is defined and constructed, emotion embodies the culture's normative system so that *feel* and *ought* correspond closely and reinforce each other. As a result, cultural beliefs, values, and construals are rarely questioned by those within the culture. Although every culture has some deviances, for the most part, these beliefs, values, and construals are simply enacted and practiced. When there is deviance from these construals, pressures for conformity arise. In many cases, the deviants are subsequently treated as less than normal or even as mentally ill. The cultural construals, then, are experienced frequently as morally right and as representing a "normal" state of affairs: Adhering to them *feels* right or departing from them *feels* wrong. Where does the moral force of these construals come from? What makes them so unquestionable and natural? What is the source of the subjective authenticity of the cultural construals? Does emotion have anything to do with the moral character of cultural beliefs, values, and construals? The four chapters in this section, as a whole, provide some answers to these central questions.

From the perspective of an anthropologist, White describes how cultural norms and rules (the moral categories) can be transformed into emotional experience. He argues that "at the core of most emotion words are social and moral entailments capable of shaping social realities and of directing social behavior" (p. 217). Emotion is a scriptlike structure that functions as a mediator between the inside and the outside. Emotion serves to organize and to allow the actor to perceive his or her internal bodily processes. On the other hand, emotion is also used by the actor to define the nature of the outside social reality, to negotiate this reality with others, and to construct socially this very reality. Thus, emotion can be understood best in actual communicative context. For example, if someone asserts that he or she is angry, this will evoke in the partner of the social interaction a sequence of *backward inferences* to the effect that someone must have infringed on the person's right, goal, or desire in an unjustifiable way. Moral connotation and actual moral force are built into the very usage of emotion words and of emotion knowledge.

In pursuing this same notion of emotion as a culturally situated and shared phenomenon of moral entailment, Menon and Shweder analyze, in detail, an emotion narrative widely shared among the residents of the Hindu temple town of Bhubaneswar, Orissa, India—a narrative represented by the linguistic idiom "to bite your tongue" and the corresponding icon of Kali with her tongue extended between the teeth and her eyes wide open in excitement. In an ethnographically thorough and methodologically careful analysis, they demonstrate that the emotion narrative underlying the icon of Kali situates the idea of *lajya* in the particular Hindu culture as a shamelike state that functions to inhibit women's uncontrollable, yet fully justifiable, rage. Furthermore, this knowledge of emotion is widely shared among educated and uneducated, high and low in social class, old and young, and men and women and is hierarchically organized so that its core meanings are shared most widely among the Orissa residents. Only a subset of those who know the core meanings can show deeper narrative reach. The authors interpret this sense of *lajya* to arise from the tension between female power and male social authority characteristic of the Orissa society. Therefore, the culturally elaborated and hypercognized emotion of *lajya* brings to the very heart of an Oriya woman's emotional experience the socially enforced restraint on her justifiable anger. The icon of Kali, then, forcefully illustrates the notion of a focal emotion event discussed by Frijda and Mesquita, in which cultural knowledge, practices, bodily experience, and the like are densely packaged and collectively shared. As such, it serves as a mediator between the inside and the outside with the ultimate function of bringing about the embodiment of the social order in the form of an immediate experience of emotion.

Triandis pursues the same theme of transforming cultural norms and rules into emotional experience with regard to overarching ideological schemes of individualism and collectivism. According to his analysis, emergence of these ideological schemes depend on many macro-level factors, such as ecology, population density, and the form and wealth of the economy. This analysis complements those of a limited number of cultures and places these in a broader perspective. Then, Triandis reviews a large body of literature demonstrating that many aspects of social thinking, social behavior, and emotional experience can vary systematically with individualism and collectivism. In so doing, he suggests a heuristic value of the cognitive appraisal dimensions put forth by Ellsworth and others.

Finally, Jenkins reviews the pertinent literature in medical anthropology and seeks to reconceptualize psychological disorders critically and centrally as constituted by culturally shared idioms and practices. Several large-scale studies, especially one sponsored by the World Health Organization (1979), have revealed that even what many consider to be biogenetic disorders, such as schizophrenia, can be influenced and transformed by cultural factors. Evidence such as this urgently invites this reconceptualization.

Among the important points made by Jenkins, several complement those suggested by other authors of this volume. First, she warns us of the danger of *category fallacy* in cross-cultural diagnosis of mental disorders (Good, 1992; Kleinman, 1988). The category fallacy is implicated when a nosological category established in one cultural group, often in a Euro-American culture, is reified and applied to members of another culture in which the category no longer retains any coherence or validity. This criticism applies equally well to the essentialist theories of emotion, which also seek to establish emotion categories existent in a Euro-American culture as canonical and inherent in human nature. Another important point revolves around the notion of embodiment, which is raised as a critique of many cognitivist theories of culture that locates culture "from the neck up" (Csordas, 1993). Instead, along with some others in this book, Jenkins urges an analysis of how cultural systems of norms, values, and ideas are reflected in sensual experiences, bodily habits, and everyday practices. Finally, she emphasizes the need to situate any emotional phenomenon in general and any psychopathology in particular within a larger sociopolitical context. On the basis of these theoretical considerations, she describes *el calor* (the heat) as an embodied experience of suffering among Salvadoran refugees in the United States. Her vivid ethnographic account of this heat experienced as spreading throughout the body by many of the individuals in this cultural group calls into question the validity of *DSM–III* as applied to non-Western populations and suggests a need to reconceptualize the body as a primary medium by which culture is sensed and experienced.

The Cultural Shaping of Emotion

In the concluding chapter, Markus and Kitayama develop a conceptual framework that draws together many of the theoretical assumptions and empirical findings from the preceding chapters. The model spells out how core cultural ideas can structure individual emotional experience, and how this individual emotional behavior can, in turn, influence cultural meanings and practices.

Conclusion

This volume represents cultural psychology's attempt to reconstitute emotion as fully social and to understand all the strata of emotion—social, cultural, psychological, physiological, and neurochemical—from the top down. Rather than starting from the bottom, with physiological, neurochemical, and even psychological components as fixed givens, we seek to establish emotion primarily as a social, dynamically interactive process of self, culture, and the body, within which the person seeks to achieve a degree of adaptation to the cultural, semiotic environment.

    The components of emotion, many of which could be demonstrably hardwired, may be accorded functions and exact shapes as a result of the individual's active pursuit of adaptation to his or her cultural environment; and the component processes thus arranged through the person's interaction with his or her cultural environment, in turn, affords an immediate sensuous experience that responds closely to or reinforces the very cultural environment to which they are tuned.

Following the sociocultural theories of Mead (1934) and Vygotsky (1978), we may further suggest that this entire process of adaptation creates, consolidates, and holds in place the very meaning and significance of a myriad of "culturally constructed things" (D'Andrade, 1984) such as self, others, justice, honor, and many emotion categories cross-culturally common (e.g., anger and joy) and culture specific (e.g., *fago, amae, lajya, lek*, and many others). Although prepared and afforded by many biological processes and components, human emotions are actually shaped and formed by culture. Thus, taken in its entirety, emotion as a psychological process may be seen primarily as social and cultural. A better understanding of emotion would require far more research on specific characteristics of different cultures in which body and psychological processes are situated and allowed to function. We believe that the following 10 chapters suggest promising avenues of future research on emotion from this cultural perspective.

References

Barrett, K. C., & Campos, J. J. (1987). Perspectives on emotional development: Part 2. A functionalist approach to emotions. In J. D. Osofsky (Ed.), *Handbook of infant development* (pp. 555–578). New York: Wiley.

Berman, J. J. (Ed.). (1990). *Cross-cultural perspectives: Nebraska Symposium on Motivation, 1989.* Lincoln: University of Nebraska Press.

Bond, M. H. (Ed.). (1988). *The cross-cultural challenge to social psychology.* Beverly Hills, CA: Sage.

Buck, R. (1988). *Human motivation and emotion* (2nd ed.). New York: Wiley.

Campos, J. J., Campos, R. G., & Barrett, K. C. (1989). Emergent themes in the study of emotional development and emotion regulation. *Developmental Psychology, 25*, 394–402.

Csordas, T. J. (1993). *The sacred self: Cultural phenomenology of a charismatic world.* Berkeley: University of California Press.

D'Andrade, R. (1984). Cultural meaning systems. In R. A. Shweder & R. A. LeVine (Eds.), *Cultural theories: Essays on mind, self, and emotion* (pp. 88–119). Cambridge, England: Cambridge University Press.

de Riviera, G. (1984). The structure of emotional relationships. In P. Shaver (Ed.), *Review of personality and social psychology: Vol. 5. Emotions, relationships, and health* (pp. 116–145). Beverly Hills, CA: Sage.

Doi, T. (1986). *The anatomy of self: The individual versus society.* Tokyo: Kodansha.

Doi, T. (1990). The cultural assumptions of psychoanalysis. In J. W. Stigler, R. A. Shweder, & G. Herdt (Eds.), *Cultural psychology: The Chicago Symposia on Culture and Human Development* (pp. 446–453). Cambridge, England: Cambridge University Press.

Ekman, P. (1973). *Darwin and facial expression: A century of research in review.* San Diego, CA: Academic Press.

Ekman, P. (1984). Expression and the nature of emotion. In K. Scherer & P. Ekman (Eds.), *Approaches to emotion* (pp. 319–343). Hillsdale, NJ: Erlbaum.

Fiske, A. P. (1991). *Making up society: The four basic relational studies.* New York: Free Press.

Frijda, N. (1986). *The emotions.* Cambridge, England: Cambridge University Press.

Good, B. (1992). Culture, diagnosis, and comorbidity. *Culture, Medicine, and Psychiatry, 16,* 1–20.

Hunt, E., & Agnoli, F. (1991). The Whorfian hypothesis: A cognitive psychology perspective. *Psychologial Review, 98,* 377–389.

Kitayama, S., & Markus, H. R. (in press). A cultural perspective on self-conscious emotions. In J. P. Tangney & K. W. Fisher (Eds.), *Shame, guilt, embarrassment, and pride: Empirical studies of self-conscious emotions.* New York: Guilford Press.

Kleinman, A. (1988). *Rethinking psychiatry: From cultural category to personal experience.* New York: Free Press.

LeDoux, J. E. (1987). Emotion. In F. Plum (Ed.), *Handbook of physiology: Section 1. The nervous system: Vol. 5. Higher functions of the brain* (pp. 419–460). Bethesda, MD: American Physiological Society.

Levy, R. I. (1984). Emotions in comparative perspective. In K. R. Scherer & P. Ekman (Eds.), *Approaches to emotion: A book of readings* (pp. 397–412). Hillsdale, NJ: Erlbaum.

Lutz, C. (1988). *Unnatural emotions: Everyday sentiments on a Micronesian atoll and their challenge to Western theory.* Chicago: University of Chicago Press.

Markus, H., & Kitayama, S. (1991). Culture and the self: Implications for cognition, motivation, and emotion. *Psychological Review, 98,* 224–253.

Marsella, A., DeVos, G., & Hsu, F. (1985). *Culture and self.* London: Tavistock.

Mead, G. H. (1934). *Mind, self and society.* Chicago: University of Chicago Press.

Moghaddam, F. M., Taylor, D. M., & Wright, S. C. (1993). *Social psychology in cross-cultural perspective.* New York: Freeman.

Ortony, A., & Turner, T. J. (1990). What's basic about basic emotions? *Psychological Review, 97,* 315–331.

Rosaldo, M. Z. (1984). Toward an anthropology of self and feeling. In R. A. Shweder & R. A. LeVine (Ed.), *Culture theory: Essays on mind, self, and emotion* (pp. 137–157). Cambridge, England: Cambridge University Press.

Russell, J. A. (1991). Culture and the categorization of emotions. *Psychological Bulletin, 110,* 426–450.

Schwartz, T., White, G. M., & Lutz, C. A. (Eds.). (1992). *New directions in psychological anthropology*. Cambridge, England: Cambridge University Press.

Shweder, R. A. (in press). You're not sick, you're just in love. In P. Ekman & R. Davidson (Eds.), *Questions about emotion*. New York: Oxford University.

Shweder, R. A., & LeVine, R. A. (1984). *Culture theory: Essays on mind, self, and emotion*. Cambridge, England: Cambridge University Press.

Smith, P. B., & Bond, M. B. (1993). *Social psychology across cultures*. New York: Harvester Wheatsheaf.

Stevenson, H., Azuma, H., & Hakuta, K. (1986). *Child development and education in Japan*. New York: Freeman.

Stigler, J. W., Shweder, R. A., & Herdt, G. (Eds.). (1990). *Cultural psychology: Essays on comparative human development*. Cambridge, England: Cambridge University Press.

Triandis, H. C. (1989). The self and social behavior in differing cultural contexts. *Psychological Review, 96*, 506–520.

Vygotsky, L. S. (1978). Mind in society: The development of higher psychological processes. Cambridge, MA: Harvard University Press.

Wertsch, J. V., & Tulviste, P. (1992). L. S. Vygotsky and contemporary developmental psychology. *Developmental Pyschology, 28*, 548–557.

White, G. M., & Kirkpatrick, J. (Eds.). (1985). *Person, self, and experience: Exploring Pacific ethnopsychologies*. Los Angeles: University of California Press.

Wierzbicka, A. (1984). Human emotions: Universal or culture specific? *American Anthropologist, 88*, 584–594.

World Health Organization. (1979). *Schizophrenia: An international follow-up study*. New York: Wiley.

Worthman, C. M. (in press). Bio-cultural interactions in human development. In M. E. Pereira & L. A. Fairbanks (Eds.), *Juvenile primates: Life history, development and behavior*. Oxford, England: Oxford University Press.

Zahn-Waxler, C., & Kochanska, G. (1990). The origins of guilt. In R. A. Thompson (Ed.), *The 36th Annual Nebraska Symposium on Motivation: Socioemotional development* (pp. 183–258). Lincoln: University of Nebraska Press.

PART ONE

Emotion as Social Product

CHAPTER 2

Sense, Culture, and Sensibility

Phoebe C. Ellsworth

A genuine appreciation of the intricate relations between emotion and culture must involve consideration both of similarities across cultures and of cultural differences. By now, it should be abundantly clear that some aspects of emotion are very general across cultures, and possibly universal, and that people's emotional lives are profoundly influenced by the culture to which they belong. It seems to me that the interesting questions begin with the assumption that nearly all emotional experiences, everywhere, reflect both human nature and cultural context. The questions are these: "What is shared?", "*How* do cultures shape emo-

Beginning at least a decade ago, several people have encouraged me to broaden my thinking about emotion to include the role of culture, and this chapter is, in large part, a result of their persistence. Beatrice B. Whiting was the first; her influence on me began in my childhood, and I am only just waking up to its importance. In addition, Michael Bond, Richard Shweder, and Hazel Rose Markus have challenged and tempted me to move in this direction, and I am grateful to them. William I. Miller provided valuable information and advice while I was writing the manuscript, and both he and Colin W. Leach gave me helpful comments on an earlier draft.

tional experiences, expression, behavior, understanding?", "How do people go about the difficult task of understanding the feelings of someone from a different culture, and in what ways are they likely to succeed or fail?"

In some ways, the statement that emotional experience reflects both nature and culture seems like a shallow platitude; nonetheless, very little research has been informed by this assumption. Researchers have been far more likely to take sides and to argue that emotions are basically innate and universal or that emotions are basically constructed by one's culture. In part, this tendency toward oversimplification reflects disciplinary preferences, with psychologists and biologists tending to overlook the cultural differences that anthropologists emphasize, whereas the anthropologists' interest in documenting human variability leads them to overlook similarities (cf. Lutz & White, 1986). In part, it reflects the pendulum swings of intellectual trends and the tendency for each new generation of scholars to discredit the ideas of their parents, often by rediscovering the forgotten ideas of their grandparents.

When I began my study of emotion in the 1960s, the prevalent point of view in psychology was that, aside from a general undifferentiated physiological arousal, there were no emotional universals; emotional experience was socially or culturally constructed in particular contexts (Birdwhistell, 1970; LaBarre, 1947; Lindsley, 1951; Schachter & Singer, 1962). As a graduate student, I worked in Paul Ekman's lab on studies of the cross-cultural recognizability of certain facial expressions of emotion (Ekman, Friesen, & Ellsworth, 1972). From my point of view, this research was done partly in an attempt to temper the excesses of the dominant one-sided cultural relativism of the time; I saw myself as a revolutionary.

The revolution was largely successful. The old textbook demonstrations of the meaninglessness of facial expressions were eventually replaced by reproductions of the photographs used by Ekman, Sorenson, and Friesen (1969) in their research on "pan-cultural" facial expressions. Now, a new generation of psychologists (e.g., Fridlund, 1991; Russell, in press), in rebellion against the establishment point of view that many aspects of emotional experience are universal, is attempting to correct *our* oversimplifications by returning to cultural relativism under the post-modern rubric of *social constructionism*. If this means a return to the view that there are no similarities across cultures, it will be a regrettable distraction from the ever-neglected interesting questions, as well as a distortion of the evidence. Recently, Mesquita and Frijda (1992) conducted a comprehensive review and analysis of cross-cultural research on emotion and, finding abundant evidence for both culturally specific and universal emotional processes, concluded that "global statements about cross-cultural universality of emotion, or about their cultural determination, are inappropriate" (p. 198). In an exhaustive examination of one particular domain of emotional phenomena, humiliation, Miller (1993) concluded that "different cultures share more than the social constructionist orthodoxy would allow, but ... we surely share a lot less than the constraining and complacent univeralism of the positivist sciences unquestioningly assumes" (p. 196).

It makes sense that there should be similarities across cultures. Human beings belong to the same species; our brains, our bodies, our autonomic nervous systems, our hormones, and our sense organs are similarly constructed, and our consciousness is shaped by the constraints and opportunities that they provide. At a general level, human environments also resemble each other; they include novelty, hazard, opportunity, attack, gratification, and loss, which people must perceive with some accuracy and respond to appropriately. These are the kinds of events that generate emotion, and many scholars believe that the primary function of emotion is to move the organism to appropriate action in circumstances consequential for its well-being (e.g., Arnold, 1960; Lazarus, 1968; Plutchik, 1980; Scherer, 1984, and many others).

It makes sense that there should be differences across cultures. Cultures differ in their definitions of novelty, hazard, opportunity, attack, gratification, and loss, and in their definitions of appropriate responses. They differ in their definitions of significant events and in their beliefs about the causes of significant events, and these differences affect their emotional responses. Illness, for example, may be seen as caused by germs, God, chance, witchcraft, or one's own moral failure, and a person's emotional response to illness will reflect these beliefs. Finally, cultures differ in their beliefs about the meaning of emotional experiences, expressions, and behaviors.

Thus, it is obviously fatuous to assume that emotional responses to significant events are the same the world over, to mindlessly invoke "human nature" or "inclusive fitness" to explain and homogenize emotional experience, to assume and privilege sameness. It is no better to assume that the apparent similarity of emotional events in different cultures, such as the smiles of a mother and child when they are reunited, is necessarily misleading, to mindlessly invoke "culturally constructed meanings" to explain and fragment emotional experience, to assume and privilege difference. What is needed is a framework that allows consideration of the general and the particular at the same time. In this chapter, I suggest the appraisal perspective as one possible framework, and I explore some of the implications of the application of this perspective to questions about the role of culture in emotion.

Appraisal Theories

In the 1980s, a number of psychologists, working independently, came up with rather similar theories about cognition and emotion (Frijda, 1986; Ortony, Clore, & Collins, 1988; Roseman, 1984; Scherer, 1984; Smith & Ellsworth, 1985; Stein & Levine, 1989; Weiner, 1985). None of these theories were particularly focused on cross-cultural issues. The basic premise is simple and commonsensical: It is that emotions result from the way in which people interpret or appraise their environment and, consequently, that differences in emotions result from differences in the way people interpret or appraise their environment. Sorrow is different from anger because people who feel sad see their situation, and themselves in relation to their situation, differently from people who feel angry. Two people observing the same situation may feel very differently if they interpret the situation differently.

Without further specification, this proposition does not lead to much. But these researchers have tried to provide further specification by defining the kinds of appraisals that are fundamental in generating and differentiating emotions, and to describe the combinations of appraisals that correspond to emotions such as joy, fear, sorrow, and other commonly studied emotions. Most of these theories propose a small number of dimensions of appraisal (more than 2 but typically fewer than 10) that account for major differences among emotions, and there is now a good deal of evidence that emotions such as joy, fear, and sorrow are characterized by different patterns of appraisals (Mesquita & Frijda, 1992; Scherer, 1988). For example, in our initial study of appraisals, Craig Smith and I (1985) found that each of 13 different emotions has a distinctive pattern of appraisals that reliably differentiates it from the others. Table 1 gives examples of the appraisal dimensions that have commonly been found to be most important. It is illustrative only. Different theorists propose slightly different lists; nonetheless, there is an encouraging consensus at the core.

As an example of the differentiation of emotions by means of appraisal dimensions, consider fear, anger, sorrow, and guilt. They are all unpleasant, but they differ on other dimensions. In our research, fear is

TABLE 1

Examples of Proposed Appraisal Dimensions

Dimension	Smith and Ellsworth (1985)	Scherer (1984)	Frijda (1986)	Ortony et al. (1988)
Attention/ Novelty	X	X	X	X
Pleasantness/ Valence	X	X	X	X
Certainty	X	X	X	X (likelihood)
Effort/ Obstacle	X	X	X (open/closed)	X
Control/Coping potential	X	X	X	X
Agency	X	X (secondary dimension)	X	X
Norm/Self- compatibility		X	X (value) plus others	plus others

associated with moderately high levels of anticipated effort and very high levels of uncertainty; anger is associated with similarly high effort but much more certainty, and with a very strong perception that some other human being is responsible for one's adversity; sorrow is associated with a somewhat lower anticipated effort, lower attention, an intermediate level of certainty, and a very strong perception that one's misfortune is the result of circumstances beyond anyone's control. Guilt resembles sadness in anticipated effort and relative lack of attention, and anger in relatively high certainty, but it was the only negative emotion to be characterized by high levels of self-responsibility. Appraisal theories may be seen as an elaboration of Schachter and Singer's (1962) claim that differences in emotions are due to differences in the perceiver's interpretation of the environment. They go beyond Schachter and Singer in that they attempt to define the kinds of interpretations that contribute most fundamentally to emotional differentiation.

Appraisal theories are particularly compatible with a view of emotions as processes that develop in time, because the component appraisals of an emotional experience need not be simultaneous. In many instances, they cannot be simultaneous because the situation is not immediately clear to the perceiver; as new information is incorporated, the emotional experience changes. An infinity of emotional states and nuances is possible, and steady states are rare or possibly nonexistent.

Most appraisal theories, then, are fundamentally different in their assumptions and implications from categorical theories, which propose a limited number of discrete, innate, universal emotions. The most common of these hypothesized "basic emotions" are fear, sadness, happiness, and anger; beyond these, each theorist has a slightly different list (Ekman, 1972; Izard, 1971; Tomkins, 1962, 1963). In the strongest statements of this point of view, these basic emotions are described as hardwired, holistic neural programs, built into the species, which cannot be broken down into meaningful components and which cannot be modified except by the person's subsequent learned response to the firing of the program.[1]

---

[1]A theory that combines the idea of appraisals as components of emotions with the idea of basic, categorically distinct emotions is that of Roseman (1984). In his theory, appraisals are dichotomous rather than continuous judgments and the combined outcomes of these judgments constitute the basic emotion categories.

Categorical models, then, imply the existence of several culturally universal emotions. Given that the program fires in the same way always and everywhere, the major mechanism available to the categorical theorist to account for cross-cultural differences in emotion is the *display rule* (Ekman, 1972).[2] Although the basic emotions are universal, cultures differ in their beliefs about the meaning of these emotions and about the appropriateness or inappropriateness of emotional expressions and emotional behaviors in different social contexts. It is not only a matter of visible behaviors; cultures also differ in their beliefs about the appropriateness of even feeling certain emotions in certain contexts. Among the Utku Eskimos, feelings of anger are strongly condemned (Briggs, 1970), but among certain Arab groups, a man's failure to respond with anger is seen as dishonorable (Abu-Lughod, 1986). In any case, in theories that consider basic emotions to be innate and universal, the regulation of emotion is the major mechanism invoked to explain cultural differences.

There can be no doubt that emotional regulation is an extremely important source of cultural variation. Emotions are socially significant events, often potentially disruptive, and it is not surprising that most cultures have developed fairly complex theories about desirable and undesirable feelings and displays, and more-or-less elaborate sets of prescriptions and restrictions in the emotional domain. The socialization of emotions is one of the major tasks in raising children to be culturally acceptable adults.

Appraisal theories suggest an additional source of cultural differences, one that provides some specification of cultural variation in the elicitation of emotions, and that also provides a framework for understanding culturally general emotional phenomena without postulating the existence of basic universal emotions. The hypothesis is that the dimensions of appraisal identified in studies of Westerners are culturally general, that similar patterns of appraisal will result in similar emotions across cultures. Cultural differences in emotion are a result of cultural differences in the perception and interpretation of events: Cultures differ in

---

[2]Categorical theorists also agree that there can be widespread cultural variation in the kinds of event that elicit different emotions, but there is very little theory on the processes or mechanisms by which an elicitor becomes attached to one of the neural programs.

the kinds of events that attract attention; arouse immediate pleasant or unpleasant feelings; are seen as one's own fault, or someone else's, or no one's; or are perceived as obstacles. If people from two different cultures have different appraisals of an event, they will also feel different emotions. But if they appraise an event (the "same" kind or a "different" kind of event) in the same way—for example, as bad, irreparable, and produced by uncontrollable circumstances—people from both cultures will feel a similar emotion: in this case, sorrow.

Evidence is accumulating that suggests that several dimensions of emotional appraisal are consistent across cultures ([Gehm & Scherer, 1988] 27 countries, mostly European; [Matsumoto, Kudoh, Scherer, & Wallbott, 1988] Japan and the United States; [Mauro, Sato, & Tucker, 1992] the United States, Japan, Hong Kong, and the People's Republic of China; [Frijda & Mesquita, chapter 3, this volume] Dutch, Surinamese, and Turks in the Netherlands; and [Roseman, Rettek, Dhawan, Naidu, & Thapa, 1991] the United States and India). Attention to changing conditions; a sense of pleasure or distaste; a sense of uncertainty (or certainty); the perception of an obstacle; the sense of being in control or out of control; the attribution of agency; a sense of the likely praise, censure, or ridicule of one's group; and an ultimate judgment of the value or fitness of what has happened—these turn up with remarkable consistency in the emotional worlds of different cultures (Mesquita & Frijda, 1992).

Attention/Novelty

Probably the simplest and most inevitable appraisal is that of novelty, of a change in the environment (or, occasionally, in one's stream of consciousness) that deflects one's attention. This is the appraisal that commonly initiates the emotion process. LeDoux (1987) found that novel events trigger an identifiable neural circuit, activating something like a state of readiness for emotion, and, on many grounds, we would expect this activation to be universal. This initial, orienting attentional response probably corresponds to the posterior attention network described by Posner (Posner & Peterson, 1990; Posner & Rothbart, 1991). Arousal of this network does not necessarily lead to emotion. Often, a novel stimulus—an odd noise, a faint tickling sensation—is easily explained: a helicopter flew over, a dog's tail brushed your skin under the table. The person's attention returns to the conversation, and no particular emotion is aroused. Although such a change in attention is not a sufficient condition for emotion, it is possible that it is a necessary one. Emotion without such an attentional focus may correspond to what we typically call *mood*.

The stimulus that attracts attention need not be an external event; it can be the intrusion of a thought ("Did I turn off the stove?") or a memory (in reading a research report on sexual abuse, a scientist recalls an episode from her own past). Although some researchers define emotion-eliciting events as those that have significance for a person's present well-being (Lazarus, 1968), it is plausible that similar processes operate for memories of events that affected one's well-being in the past, for events that suggest previously unconsidered eventualities in one's future, or even for fictional events that trigger the emotion system before a woman can coolly remind herself that the cinematic killer is only an image on the screen.

It seems likely, then, that the basic orienting response—the uncontrollable kindling of attention by novel stimuli—is general across cultures. Of course, what is novel or worthy of attention in the physical or psychological milieu of one culture may be commonplace in another. In modern suburban America, physical stimuli such as snakes, leeches, people who are badly disfigured, and the starry sky are rarely seen and attract attention—apprehension or awe; in other cultures, the noise of a power mower, flashing neon signs, a talking toy, or a mall may seem equally awesome. The same is true for psychological stimuli. A broad grin or an immediate answer to a question may be noteworthy in some cultures; their omission may be equally noteworthy in others. In providing the background of the familiar, culture defines the unfamiliar.

Valence/Pleasantness

An immediate, unthinking response to stimuli as positive or negative is common to many, perhaps most, emotional experiences, and it too is very likely general across cultures (Zajonc, 1980). Most theories of emotion include valence as a fundamental attribute[3] and typically valence accounts for more variance than any other dimension in research designed to discover the underlying dimensions of emotional experience. From a psychoevolutionary point of view, the timely evaluation of a stimulus as "good for me" or "bad for me" is as crucial as the initial appraisal that it is worth noticing at all (Arnold, 1960).

As in the case of novelty, however, there is wide latitude for variability in what members of different cultures consider good or bad, benign or malevolent, beautiful or ugly. Even at the most primitive "biological" level, foods that are considered delicious in some cultures are considered repulsive or even deadly in others. In the realm of social behavior and social relationships, the potential for variability is enormous. The receipt of a valuable gift may elicit joy, shame, fear, or rage (Miller, 1993). What is common across cultures, according to the appraisal hypothesis, is that events are rapidly appraised as good or bad, and that this appraisal is an essential component of the emotional experience.

That valence is of fundamental importance does not imply that the perceiver always knows immediately whether a novel event is good or bad. If an event is unfamiliar or complex, the person may initially be uncertain whether the event is good or bad; the appraisal of uncertainty is salient. However, valence is still central to the experience of emotion because even in these situations, the person is uncertain *about* the valence of the event; the event is emotionally significant because it *might* be good or bad.

Agency/Control

We have consistently found that the attribution of agency is important in differentiating among the negative emotions of anger, sorrow, and shame/guilt. Furthermore, in describing these emotions, people commonly include their perceptions of agency as part of the experience. In part this may reflect a general tendency among human beings to make causal

---

[3]General arousal theories such as those of Lindsley (1951) and Schachter and Singer (1962) are one sort of exception.

attributions for events (Jones et al., 1972). In part, it may reflect a more specific motive to understand negative events so as to be able to cope with them (Ellsworth & Smith, 1988; Rozin & Fallon, 1987). In our American subjects, negative events seen as caused by other people evoke anger; negative events seen as caused by oneself evoke guilt (or regret, if no one else is hurt); negative events seen as caused by fate, or chance, or circumstances beyond anyone's control evoke sorrow (see also Frijda, 1986; Ortony et al., 1988; Roseman, 1984; Scherer, 1984).

Cultural belief systems provide a framework for understanding the causal structure of one's universe and especially for interpreting the forces that control human endeavor. The relative importance of one's own efforts, the behavior of other people, the laws of physics, fate, and the supernatural, as influences on significant events, varies enormously across cultures. Some cultures, such as our own, emphasize human agency and individual enterprise (Markus & Kitayama, 1991; Triandis, chapter 9, this volume), and we might predict that in such cultures anger would be a prevalent emotion readily experienced and readily recognized. Other societies assign greater power to destiny or to supernatural forces not easily controlled by human efforts, and we might hypothesize that in these cultures sorrow and resignation would be more common emotions. Still others, the collectivist or interdependent cultures (Markus & Kitayama, 1991; Triandis, chapter 9, this volume), emphasize the social reference group, and in these cultures, shame is far more salient than it is in America, where our research subjects often use the term synonymously with guilt and tend to provide rather trivial and impoverished accounts of their experiences with shame.

There is little relevant research, and the evidence for these hypotheses is mixed. Roseman et al. (1991) compared American subjects (from New York City and Long Island) with Indian subjects (from Allahabad) and found that the Americans more commonly appraised negative events as the work of other people and experienced higher levels of anger than the Indian subjects. Matsumoto et al. (1988) found that, compared with American subjects, Japanese subjects were reluctant to assign responsibility for emotional events (positive as well as negative) and simply responded "not applicable" to questions asking about responsibility.

Borke and Su (1972) found more disagreement between Chinese and American children about sad and angry stories than about happiness and fear stories; however, they found that the Chinese children were *more* likely to categorize stories as anger eliciting than were the American children. A similar pattern appeared when the children were asked to describe situations that produce different emotions. Mauro et al. (1992), studying Americans and three Asian groups, found high levels of cross-cultural generality for most of the appraisal dimensions they examined, but the greatest cultural differences were found on the dimensions of responsibility, control, and anticipated effort. (Their responsibility and control dimensions are both aspects of what I refer to here as agency.) Studies that have touched on the relation of perceptions of agency and negative emotions in single cultures generally support the idea that where there is little blame, there is little anger (Mesquita & Frijda, 1992).

Thinking about agency in cross-cultural terms suggests major causal influences that have been neglected in American research, potentially distorting our view of human emotions. In particular, American psychologists have little to say about the supernatural. Although a substantial number of Americans, including the American college students who provide so much of our data, believe in God, attend religious services, and pray regularly, they do not refer to Him in describing their emotional experiences. Neither positive nor negative events are attributed to divine intervention. We do not know whether this is because they really do not consider supernatural forces as a significant influence in their emotional lives or because they feel that reference to God is taboo in the at-best-agnostic atmosphere of a university laboratory.

In many cultures, supernatural forces matter much more, and members of the culture are much more willing to attribute emotional events to supernatural causes, but we (at least we psychologists) have little understanding of their role. From an appraisal point of view, various roles are possible, and perceptions of agency and perceptions of control need not vary together. In some cases, supernatural agents may show a great deal of resemblance to human agents (e.g., fairies, some witches, and the Gods of the ancient Greeks and Romans, who often seemed barely distinguishable from the worshippers and, indeed, could interbreed with them). Such supernatural beings might evoke an anger similar to that evoked by a powerful neighbor or boss. In some societies, supernatural forces are relatively impersonal, as in religions that emphasize fate, predestination, or the movements of the stars. Sorrow and resignation might be more common in such societies. Or a religious belief system may place special emphasis on the behavior of the worshippers themselves so that misfortune is seen as the consequence of one's own sin, failure to observe a taboo, or mistake in carrying out a religious ritual. In these cultures, guilt or shame might be expected to be common, depending in part on the publicity of the transgression. It is possible that supernatural forces elicit appraisals and emotions that are similar to those based on natural causes.

Norm/Self-Concept Compatibility

Scherer (1984) proposed an additional appraisal (or "stimulus evaluation check," as he called it) that he labeled "norm/self-concept compatibility." He defined it as a "comparison of stimuli, particularly one's own actions or the actions of others and their results, with external and internal standards such as social norms and various aspects of the real or ideal self-concept" (p. 308). In simpler language, a person sees that he or she (or someone else) has lived up to, surpassed, or fallen short of some standard defined by the community or the self. In the initial formulation of the Smith and Ellsworth (1985) version of appraisal theory, I assumed, without giving the matter much thought, that seeing onself as the cause of a negative outcome was sufficient to cover the situations that Scherer had in mind when he proposed this appraisal: situations eliciting guilt, shame, and embarrassment. I am now considering the possibility that this was a somewhat ethnocentric omission, reflecting contemporary Americans' relative lack of engagement with these emotions.[4] My recently renewed acquaintance with works by anthropologists has served as a useful reminder of the extraordinary importance of living up to the standards

---

[4]Even in contemporary America, there may be groups for which the peer-group collectivity is intensely important and shame occupies a central role in emotional life. In junior high school and the early years of high school, for example, the perils of nonconformity may be far more salient than they are earlier or later.

of the socially and morally correct behavior expected by one's reference group, and it may well be that failing to do so is a negative outcome that is different in kind from others and that is general cross culturally. The threat of ostracism from one's group, Gray (1971) suggested, may universally elicit fear, and behavior that risks such rejection may be a universal elicitor or emotion as well. Mauro et al. (1992) found considerable generality for the dimension of norm/self-concept compatibility. Whether the emotions elicited by behavior that violates shared *group* standards and the emotions elicited by failure to live up to one's *own* idiosyncratic standards are in fact similar is an open question. I expect that often they are not.

Other Dimensions

Other dimensions for which some evidence of cross-cultural generality has been found include certainty–uncertainty, perception of a goal obstacle, and perceptions of one's own ability to cope with the situation (or of the amount of effort required). There may be a correspondence between these and other attentional networks described by Posner and Rothbart (1991), the posterior attentional network and the vigilance network, but again, a common brain structure does not imply identity of experience. Understanding cultural similarities and differences in these dimensions follows the model we laid out for the others: Uncertainty, the perception of obstacles, and the sense of one's power to cope are important dimensions of emotion in most cultures, but what shakes one's certainty, what seems like an obstacle, and which obstacles one sees as surmountable are affected by one's cultural belief system. The same reasoning that we developed in relation to attention, valence, and agency applies to these other dimensions.

Evidence for the cross-cultural generality of these appraisals and for their relation to emotional experience continues to accumulate. There is no particular reason to believe, however, that these are the only appraisal dimensions that are significant in differentiating among emotions. One cannot discover anything about a possibly important dimension unless one asks about it and, so far, most research has been restricted to six or eight dimensions or fewer. Asking about six or eight dimensions allows us a richer, more differentiated picture than the traditional (and current) circular or conical models derived from research that only asked about two or three dimensions (Russell, 1980; Woodworth & Schlosberg, 1954; Wundt, 1903), but there is no reason to believe that even six or eight dimensions represent an exhaustive list.[5] There may be other dimensions of appraisal that play an important role in differentiating emotions, and some of these may also prove to be broadly general across cultures.

On the other hand, there may be dimensions of appraisal that play a powerful role in defining emotional experience in some cultures but not in others, and possibly even some that are unique to a single culture. A Westerner might study this possibility by taking an emotion term from another culture that has no close analogue in our own, such as *amae* (Japan; Kumagai & Kumagai, 1985), *liget* (Ilongot [Philippines]; Rosaldo, 1980), or *watjilpa* (Australia; Morice, 1977), and by trying to find out whether it can be understood in terms of the appraisal dimensions that have emerged from Western research or whether something else is needed.

One can imagine several possible outcomes of such a study. The "new" emotion might be described in terms of the dimensions already discovered, but might occupy a region of dimensional space that is relatively empty in Western cultures. For example, in our American subjects, we have not so far found any emotions that are very high on uncertainty but very low on attention. It seems "natural" to us that any situation that is fraught with uncertainty must compel attention. Yet, according to Bateson and Mead (1942), when faced with intense uncertainty about consequential events, Balinese people frequently fall asleep. Their emotion resembles our fear in some ways (negative, highly uncertain) but differs in that the drive to attend closely to the situation is replaced by a drive to shut it out entirely.

Another possible outcome might be that previously discovered dimensions cannot provide a satisfactory account of the new emotion and

---

[5]There are also some differences in the lists of appraisals generated by different appraisal theorists. I consider these to be minor and, in any case, my purpose here is to speculate about the implications of the general appraisal point of view for the cross-cultural study of emotion.

that some other dimension is relevant. Markus and Kitayama (1991) described a dimensional study of several Japanese emotion terms: *amae*, the sense of being accepted and cared for by others in a passive relationship of reciprocal dependence; *fureai*, feeling closely linked with someone; *oime*, feeling indebted to someone; and others. They found that an appraisal dimension of *engagement with others* was necessary to discriminate among these emotions: "the Japanese respondents clearly and reliably discriminated between ego-focused emotions and other-focused emotions on the dimension of interpersonal engagement" (p. 238).

Markus and Kitayama (1991) did not claim that this new dimension is culture specific, unique to Japan. The fact that it has not emerged in studies of Americans may simply reflect the fact that no one has looked for it. *Amae* is a difficult concept for Americans to grasp, but it is not a completely bewildering one. Very close friends, or siblings, or couples (perhaps particularly the females) may find the sense of reciprocal acceptance and dependence familiar. *Oime*, the unpleasant sense of indebtedness, is certainly recognizable. Although, relative to people from many other cultures, Americans consistently underplay the role of honor and obligation in their lives and (aided by the advertising industry) speak of gifts and favors as kindnesses that brighten the lives of the recipients, according to Miller (1993), we also understand that a gift or an invitation makes a claim on us, particularly if it is too large. We do not feel unalloyed pleasure when we receive an unexpected Christmas present from a colleague who is not a close friend. A neighbor may give us a jar of homemade preserves if she is giving them to other neighbors as well or a bag of tomatoes if it is clear that she needs to get rid of them, but if she shows up uninvited with a sweater that she has bought for us or even a jar of fancy preserves that came from a store, we feel awkward. The very fact that we have such a fine sense of what is and it not appropriate is an indication that gifts and favors have grim implications of reciprocal obligation and we do not like to feel beholden (*oime*). Words like "beholden," "indebted," and "obliged" have an archaic ring in late twentieth-century America, particularly in reference to emotions; they are not central to our lives, as they are in Japan, but they are by no means unknown. As a general dimension, the dimension of engagement may be unique to Japan, but it may not be; it may simply be much more salient and publicly acknowledged in Japanese culture than in ours. A Japanese can explain what the rules are; we can only tell if they have been broken. By looking for analogues of other cultural emotions and dimensions in our own society, whether or not we find them in any particular instance, we may extend our capacity to understand our own culture as well as the other.

Focal Events

Cultural differences in the centrality or availability of different appraisal dimensions may also reflect differences in what Mesquita and Frijda (1992) referred to as *focal events*: "Event types are called focal when they represent socially defined and shared concerns . . . . Focal events may be expected to be highly available. This implies, first, that focal events never remain unnoticed to the individual or his environment. When they do occur the individual can hardly escape being emotionally affected" (p. 184). That is, focal events are events that automatically arouse attention and imply valence within a particular culture: They are entry points to the emotions. In Japan, if a social exchange is such a focal event, even a small casual favor—one that might go unnoticed in America—may cause a person to appraise the situation considerably more extensively and elaborately than most Americans would, and to experience a considerably more finely nuanced set of emotional responses.

To complicate matters further, external events such as social exchanges or competitive interactions are not the only kinds of events that may be considered focal by a culture. An emotion itself is also an event to be appraised, and cultures vary in their beliefs about which emotions are most significant or revealing, which emotions are good or bad, and which emotions are appropriate to particular social roles or social settings. In many American subcultures, for example, to feel and express interest in other people's lives and problems is regarded as appropriate, normal, and not especially noticeable. In other cultures, such interest may be regarded as a highly inappropriate invasion of privacy. To some extent, the process of socialization is a process of teaching children by precept or example how to feel about feelings.

Tomkins (1962, 1963) argued that these evaluations of emotions become part of the emotional experience itself, creating complex emotional scripts that are developed and maintained within the context of the family. His argument applies as well or better to the development and maintenance of emotional scripts within the context of a culture. As I mentioned before, in appraisal theories, emotional experience is a continually changing process, and the evaluation of the emotion itself is a part of that process. The appraisals are perceptions that initiate or elaborate emotional processes or change their course, not stimuli that trigger a fully articulated experience corresponding to a categorically distinct "basic" emotion (cf. Ortony & Turner, 1990). An emotional experience may frequently begin with simple appraisals such as attention, valence, or uncertainty, but as the person responds to the situation, several things happen. First, the person's behavior may change the situation, thereby changing the appraisals of the situation, thereby changing the emotion itself. For example, if the person gains a sense of control over a threatening situation, frustration may turn into interest or into an affectively positive sense of challenge. Second, the person's emotional response becomes part of the situation. When an admired teacher seriously criticizes a student's work as falling short of his ability, the student may feel disappointed and frustrated; but if he then starts to cry in the professor's office, he may respond to his own display of emotion with shame.

I have made this student a male because, in American culture, it is considered inappropriate for a man to cry in most social contexts. But it is not simply the expression that is inappropriate—by extension, it is seen as inappropriate for men to be as deeply moved as women, to feel grief as strongly or as frequently. If boys are trained in this ideology, they may come to experience shame whenever they feel close to tears, so that their actual experience is different and more complex than it was when they were younger. This particular emotional experience may be comparatively rare in women. Each culture's values about emotions and their expression may come to affect the essential experience (and the expression and, ultimately, the definition) of that emotion.

The extreme rarity of anger among the Utku (Briggs, 1970) is often cited as the test case of cultural values resulting in the nearly complete suppression of an emotion. A slightly different explanation is that the lack of anger reflects a failure to appraise negative events as the fault of other people in the first place. By one interpretation, the emotion is aroused and then suppressed; by the other, the process of cultural suppression has gone on for so long that the appraisals necessary to arouse the emotion in the first place have atrophied.

Cultural values about emotions need not always be negative values resulting in shame or denial. Cultures also favor certain emotions as particularly admirable or suitable. Such cultural esteem may lead to the exaggeration of the expression and of the feeling of the valued emotions in different cultures or in different historical periods within a culture, as in the following exquisitely subtle example of an early nineteenth-century woman:

> But whatever might be the particulars of their separation, her sister's af-
> fliction was indubitable; and she thought with the tenderest compassion of
> that violent sorrow which Marianne was in all probability not merely giving
> way to as a relief but feeding and encouraging as a duty (Austen, 1811/
> 1961, p. 64).

Caveats and Epicycles

The example of Marianne's grief should alert us to several issues that have so far been set aside in this chapter, not because they are unimportant, but because a certain amount of initial oversimplification is necessary in order to get the basic theoretical position laid out.

First, cultures are not static. Focal events, beliefs, and value systems change over time, and we may expect corresponding changes in the emotional lives of the members of the culture. Lebra (1983) spoke of the high value placed on modesty in Japan where situations that threaten one's modesty are viewed as emotionally charged focal events: Ideally, a person should be as undemonstrative and inconspicuous as possible. An undemonstrative, inconspicuous demeanor is far from the ideal in late twentieth-century America: It is labeled as shyness, and therapy is sometimes recommended to correct the "problem." Assertiveness and extraversion are valued; to go unnoticed is a sign of weakness; and introversion is regarded as a sign of neurosis (Larsen, 1991). In the nineteenth century, however, these same qualities of retiring modesty were highly valued, particularly among upper-class women, but also among men. To be demonstrative and conspicuous was to be "shameless."

Cultures can change in many ways. Circumstances can change, for example, when a society is conquered; the people are likely to experience deprivation, discrimination, and various other hardships that have profound effects on their emotional lives. They may be forced to experience new and painful kinds of interactions with the conquerors, interactions that will rapidly be defined as *focal events*. Natural disasters—plagues, famine, and cataclysms of earth, sea, or sky—or profound economic changes may also restructure the world and, hence, the emotional world.

Appraisals can change—as a culture comes to appraise illness as a consequence of bacteria rather than of the evil intentions of other people, emotional responses to illness will change. As the views of the role of God (or of the gods) in everyday life change, so will the emotional lives of the people.

Finally, as different emotions become fashionable, the emotional lives of the people change, as is illustrated by Marianne's grief. Such fashions are particularly salient, at least in American culture, for emotions that are regarded as mildly pathological. In the 1950s, as any reader of Jules Feiffer knows, Americans suffered from paralyzing anxiety; a decade or so later, anxiety was replaced by depression; currently, people are visited by a variety of debilitating "syndromes" caused by past abuses and victimizations. A general sense of unhappiness is labeled differently as emotional fashions change. This is not to say that the feeling of unhappiness actually is the same—the changing cultural definition modifies the feeling itself and the significant physical symptoms.

These within-culture changes suggest that the intractable problem of translation, of trying to find equivalent words to describe emotions, is not unique to cross-cultural research; it may also confound the social historian who studies a single culture over time. The English word *sad*, a basic emotion label in most categorical theories, originally meant "satisfied," came to mean "sober" or "serious" (a state of mind highly esteemed by the Puritans in the 17th century) and only much later took on a meaning closer to "grieved." The term *shame*, which once implied grace, now implies disgrace. Several scholars, such as Wierzbicka (1992), have appropriately criticized psychologists for their simple-minded tendency to take English emotion words such as *fear, happiness*, and *anger* as representing basic emotional universals rather than as one culture's way of categorizing the world of feelings: "By using English emotion words as their basic analytical tools scholars are imposing on their subject matter an ethnocentric, Anglocentric perspective" (p. 287). Her solution resembles an appraisal model in that she analyzes Western and non-Western emotions into combinations of simpler components involving valence, control, uncertainty, and so on. Rather than taking appraisals as her primitives, she looks for semantic primitives with universal or near-universal meanings in all languages; rather than on complex, culture-dependent terms such as *gratitude, happiness*, and *grief*, she relies on simple, "culture-free" terms such as *want, think*, and *feel*. Whereas this approach may reduce the problems of variability in linguistic terms, it certainly does not eliminate them. Even within English and within the last three or four hundred years, the usage of these terms has changed enormously. For example, the term *feel* was not generally used to refer to emotional states ("feel sad", "feel ashamed") until the nineteenth century. Before that, one simply *was* sad or ashamed and "to feel something" typically meant to touch it (Miller, 1993). Thus, the phrase that Wierzbicka commonly uses in her prototypical scenarios—"X feels something"—was not emotionally meaningful in English until recently.

Second, even at a given point in time, cultures are not uniform. One of the dangers of cultural psychology is that the welcome focus on differences among cultures may distract us from the differences within cultures. The characterization of Japanese as collectivist and Americans as individualist, while illuminating, can also come perilously close to stereotyping. Some Americans fit the individualistic stereotype beautifully; many do not. The culture of men is not identical to the culture of women: Males and females are expected to differ in their sensitivity to different sorts of events, and they do. Likewise, differences in social status, ethnic background, and region are accompanied by differences in belief systems and emotions. Members of different groups within the same culture may appraise events differently and respond with different emotions, and the consequences of these within-culture variations may be especially insidious, because the people involved are less likely to think of cultural explanations and therefore more likely to make pejorative dispositional attributions (Jones & Nisbett, 1972), underestimating the role of culture and instead attributing others' "irrational" behavior to biological differences in race or gender, or to character flaws.

Likewise, differences in power create different cultural worlds within a culture. The experience of discrimination may be a dominant theme in the daily emotional lives of groups who suffer it and an organizing principle of their emotional lives. The group at the top, the group that ignores, slights, interrupts, and insults, may be oblivious to an entire range of emotions that go with being ignored, slighted, interrupted, and insulted.

Finally, there are individual differences. As human beings, if not as cultural psychologists, we are acutely aware of differences in the emotional responses of our friends, relatives, and colleagues: Some are cheerful, some melancholy, some anxious, some explosive. Differences in emotional style are one of the major bases for our classification of our acquaintances. People's sensitivity to the emotional idiosyncrasies of members of their own culture undoubtedly blinds them to cultural commonalities and to the role of culture itself. People's appreciation of individual differences within their own culture is probably a major resource to draw on in interpreting the emotional responses of people from other cultures, one that may lead to both understanding and misunderstanding. An American who meets a Japanese who is behaving with deferential modesty may be reminded of a friend who is particularly shy and may "understand" the Japanese person's perceptions and feelings by drawing on knowledge of that friend. Often this process will ultimately result in mistakes, for example, if the American decides that the Japanese needs encouragement to overcome the "problem." Whether such matching helps at all as a useful first step in cross-cultural understanding is an interesting question. Logically, it seems possible that a somewhat deviant member of one culture may resemble a more mainstream member of another culture, and that an understanding of the one could facilitate an understanding of the other. That it could not possibly lead to a thorough understanding is obvious, because the state of being deviant colors the emotional life of one person but not the other.

Third, the situation becomes immensely more complicated when we recognize that the initial emotional response to an event is in itself a significant event to be appraised, leading to the possibility of exponentially expanding cultural and individual nuances as the emotion develops over time.

Summary and Future Directions

According to appraisal theories of emotion, emotions consist of patterned processes of appraisal of one's relation to the environment along specified dimensions, such as novelty, valence, certainty, control, attribution of agency, and consistency with social norms, along with associated physiological responses and action tendencies. The appraisal perspective may provide a useful approach to the problem of accounting both for cross-cultural similarities and for cross-cultural differences in emotion. The basic premise is that the major dimensions of appraisal that make up emotion are general across cultures, and that similar patterns of appraisal along these dimensions will produce similar emotions across cultures. Thus, for example, if someone has lost something beloved, and if the loss is seen as due to circumstances beyond anyone's control, then the person will feel sad. However, one must know something about the belief system of a particular culture in order to know whether these preconditions are met.

Cultural belief systems define events as due to circumstances, or to a person's own efforts, or to the behavior of others; as good or bad; as controllable or uncontrollable; as certain or uncertain; and differences in these kinds of cultural appraisals affect people's emotional responses to events. Thus, an American who wins a coveted prize may attribute it to his or her own efforts and feel pride, whereas a member of another culture may attribute it to the support and encouragement of his or her mentors and feel gratitude.

No claim is made that the appraisal dimensions suggested here constitute a complete list. Indeed, one promising avenue for future research is to search for new appraisal dimensions that may be especially significant within a particular culture and to look for analogues in other cultures.

Another line of research that is desperately needed (regardless of one's theoretical point of view) is a series of studies replicating the highly influential but sketchily reported study of Japanese and American responses to emotionally arousing films (Ekman, 1972; Friesen, 1992). Ekman reported that the facial expressions of the subjects from the two cultures were indistinguishable when they believed that they were watching the films alone and unobserved, but were very different when they were in the company of others (muted for the Japanese, exaggerated for the Americans). Studies using this format, comparing members of various cultural groups and measuring appraisals and self-reported emotions as well as facial and physiological responses, would be immensely useful in beginning to assess the role of appraisal in actual experience and to distinguish the role of appraisal from the role of display rules.

Appraisal models suggest that emotional experiences become more complex over time, both episodically and ontogenetically. One implication of this idea is that one is more likely to find universals during the first few moments of people's responses to emotional stimuli, early in the sequence of appraisals than later on when more complex appraisals of agency and social propriety, and appraisals of one's own initial emotional response have entered the picture. The choice of emotional stimulus situations hypothesized to elicit similar or dissimilar patterns of appraisals in members of different cultures presents troublesome problems very likely requiring collaboration among researchers of different cultures and different disciplines. Nonetheless, so little has been done that even the discovery of unexpected problems may contribute substantially to our knowledge of emotion and culture. Despite the methodological problems, the hypothesis that emotions are cross culturally similar in their early stages and become more differentiated as they develop in time is worth studying, and whether there is ever a point of identity is an intriguing question. Psychologists like Posner, LeDoux, and Zajonc would probably say yes; many anthropologists would probably say no.

The capacity to recognize novel events and to appraise them as positive or negative is present at birth, presumably universal in normal babies. The capacity to make other appraisals, such as the perception of an obstacle or the attribution of agency, emerges later (cf. Scherer, 1984), and, of course, the early sensitivities to novelty and pleasantness become much more elaborated as well. A newborn will orient to a noise or a change in visual or auditory pattern (and will often show a facial expression of intense interest); but with development, the baby begins to have expectations, allowing new occasions for novelty when the expectations are violated. As infants mature, they learn how people in their culture appraise events. Thus, one would expect to find more obvious evidence of cross-cultural universals in newborn than in older children and in older children than in adults.

Campos (1992) quite rightly pointed out that babies from different cultures are not entirely free of cultural conditioning even at birth: They may have different intrauterine experiences and different experiences during the birth itself. I am happy to grant the point, though it could be argued that the salient features of wombs and passage through the birth canal have a lot more cultural similarities than cultural idiosyncrasies. All I am arguing is that members of different cultures are more alike at birth than they will ever be again. A systematic cross-cultural study of the emergence of the different appraisals and their correlation with the emergence of emotional responses (both those that are labeled as such by the culture and those that are not) would be an enormous contribution.

To return to the beginning, I do not think that we will be able to reach the interesting questions about how culture is related to emotion until we get beyond the idea that the statement "emotion is culturally constituted" is fundamentally incompatible with the statement "emotion is biologically based." Both statements are obviously true, and our goal should be to develop ideas, theories, models, and guesses that encompass both diversity and similarity. Theories of appraisal, though none was designed for the purpose, provide one promising approach.

References

Abu-Lughod, L. (1986). *Veiled sentiments*. Berkeley: University of California Press.

Arnold, M. B. (1960). *Emotion and personality*. New York: Columbia University Press.

Austen, J. (1961). *Sense and sensibility*. New York: Signet. (Original work published 1811)

Bateson, G., & Mead, M. (1942). *Balinese character*. New York: Academy of Sciences.

Birdwhistell, R. L. (1970). *Kinesics and context*. Philadelphia: University of Pennsylvania Press.

Borke, H., & Su, S. (1972). Perception of emotional responses to social interactions by Chinese and American children. *Journal of Cross-Cultural Psychology, 3*, 309–314.

Briggs, J. L. (1970). *Never in anger: Portrait of an Eskimo family*. Cambridge, MA: Harvard University Press.

Campos, J. (1992, June). Comment at the International Conference on Emotion and Culture, University of Oregon.

Ekman, P. (1972). Universals and cultural differences in facial expressions of emotions. In J. Cole (Ed.), *Nebraska Symposium on Motivation* (pp. 207–283). Lincoln: University of Nebraska Press.

Ekman, P., Friesen, W. V., & Ellsworth, P. C. (1972). *Emotion in the human face: Guidelines for research and a review of the findings*. Elmsford, NY: Pergamon Press.

Ekman, P., Sorenson, E. R., & Friesen, W. V. (1969). Pan-cultural elements in facial displays of emotion. *Science, 164*, 86–88.

Ellsworth, P. C., & Smith, C. (1988). From appraisal to emotion: Differences among unpleasant feelings. *Motivation and Emotion, 12*, 271–302.

Fridlund, A. J. (1991). Evolution and facial action in reflex, social motive, and paralanguage. *Biological Psychology, 32*, 1–96.

Friesen, W. V. (1992). *Cultural differences in facial expressions in a social situation: An experimental test of the concept of display rules*. Unpublished doctoral dissertation, University of California, San Francisco.

Frijda, N. H. (1986). *The emotions*. Cambridge, England: Cambridge University Press.

Gehm, T. L., & Scherer, K. R. (1988). Relating situation evaluation to emotion differentiation: Nonmetric analysis of cross-cultural questionnaire data. In K. R. Scherer (Ed.), *Facets of emotion* (pp. 61–78). Hillsdale, NJ: Erlbaum.

Gray, J. A. (1971). *The psychology of fear and stress*. London: Weidenfeld & Nicholson.

Izard, C. E. (1971). *The face of emotion*. New York: Appleton-Century-Crofts.

Jones, E. E., Kanouse, D. E., Kelley, H. H., Nisbett, R. E., Valins, S., & Weiner, B. (Eds.). (1972). *Attribution: Perceiving the causes of behavior*. Morristown, NJ: General Learning Press.

Jones, E. E., & Nisbett, R. E. (1972). The actor and the observer: Divergent perceptions of the causes of behavior. In E. E. Jones, D. E. Kanouse, H. H. Kelley, R. E. Nisbett, S. Valins, & B. Weiner (Eds.), *Attribution: Perceiving the causes of behavior*. Morristown, NJ: General Learning Press.

Kumagai, H. A., & Kumagai, A. K. (1985). The hidden "I" in *amae*: "Passive love" and Japanese social perception. *Ethos, 14*, 305–321.

LaBarre, W. (1947). The cultural basis of emotions and gestures. *Journal of Personality, 16*, 49–68.

Larsen, R. (1991). Personality and emotion. In V. Derlega, B. Winstead, & W. Jones (Eds.), *Contemporary research in personality* (pp. 407–432). Chicago: Nelson-Hall.

Lazarus, R. S. (1968). Emotions and adaptation: Conceptual and empirical relations. In W. J. Arnold (Ed.), *Nebraska Symposium on Motivation* (pp. 175–266). Lincoln: University of Nebraska Press.

Lebra, T. S. (1983). Shame and guilt: A psychocultural view of the Japanese self. *Ethos, 11,* 192–209.

LeDoux, J. E. (1987). Emotion. In F. Plum (Ed.), *Handbook of physiology: Part 1. The nervous system: Vol. 5. Higher functions of the brain* (pp. 419–460). Bethesda, MD: American Physiological Society.

Lindsley, D. B. (1951). Emotion. In S. S. Stevens (Ed.), *Handbook of experimental psychology* (pp. 473–516). New York: Wiley.

Lutz, C., & White, G. M. L. (1986). The anthropology of emotions. *Annual Review of Anthropology, 15,* 405–436.

Markus, H. R., & Kitayama, S. (1991). Culture and the self: Implications for cognition, emotion, and motivation. *Psychological Review, 98,* 224–253.

Matsumoto, D., Kudoh, T., Scherer, K., & Wallbott, H. (1988). Antecedents of and reactions to emotions in the United States and Japan. *Journal of Cross-Cultural Psychology, 19,* 267–286.

Mauro, R., Sato, K., & Tucker, J. (1992). The role of appraisal in human emotions: A cross-cultural study. *Journal of Personality and Social Psychology, 62,* 301–317.

Mesquita, B., & Frijda, N. H. (1992). Cultural variations in emotions: A review. *Psychological Bulletin, 412,* 179–204.

Miller, W. I. (1993). *Humiliation.* Ithaca, NY: Cornell University Press.

Morice, R. D. (1977). Know your speech community. *Aboriginal Health Worker, 1,* 4–9.

Ortony, A., Clore, G., & Collins, A. (1988). *The cognitive structure of emotions.* New York: Cambridge University Press.

Ortony, A., & Turner, T. J. (1990). What's basic about basic emotions? *Psychological Review, 97,* 315–331.

Plutchik, R. (1980). *Emotion: A psychoevolutionary synthesis.* New York: Harper & Row.

Posner, M. I., & Peterson, S. E. (1990). The attention system of the human brain. *Annual Review of Neuroscience, 13,* 25–42.

Posner, M. I., & Rothbart, M. K. (1991). Attentional mechanisms and conscious experience. *The Neuropsychology of consciousness* (pp. 93–111). San Diego, CA: Academic Press.

Rosaldo, M. Z. (1980). *Knowledge and passion: Ilongot notions of self and social life.* Cambridge, England: Cambridge University Press.

Roseman, I. J. (1984). Cognitive determinants of emotion: A structural theory. In P. Shaver (Ed.), *Review of personality and social psychology: Vol. 5. Emotions, relationships, and health* (pp. 11–36). Beverly Hills, CA: Sage.

Roseman, I. J., Rettek, I., Dhawan, N., Naidu, R. K., & Thapa, K. (1991). *Cross-cultural similarities in relationships between cognitive appraisals and emotional responses.* Unpublished manuscript.

Rozin, P., & Fallon, A. E. (1987). A perspective on disgust. *Psychological Review, 94,* 23–41.

Russell, J. A. (1980). A circumplex model of affect. *Journal of Personality and Social Psychology, 39,* 1161–1178.

Russell, J. A. (in press). Is there universal recognition of emotion from facial expression? A review of methods and studies. *Psychological Bulletin.*

Schachter, S., & Singer, J. (1962). Cognitive, social, and physiological determinants of emotional state. *Psychological Review, 63,* 379–399.

Scherer, K. R. (1984). On the nature and function of emotion: A component process approach. In P. Ekman & K. Scherer (Eds.), *Approaches to emotion* (pp. 293–317). Hillsdale, NJ: Erlbaum.

Scherer, K. R. (Ed.). (1988). *Facets of emotion.* Hillsdale, NJ: Erlbaum.

Smith, C. A., & Ellsworth, P. C. (1985). Patterns of cognitive appraisal in emotion. *Journal of Personality and Social Psychology, 48,* 813–838.

Stein, N., & Levine, L. L. (1989). Thinking about feelings: The development and organization of emotional knowledge. In R. E. Shaw & M. Farr (Eds.), *Aptitude, learning, and instructions: Cognition, conation, and affect* (Vol. 3, pp. 165–198). Hillsdale, NJ: Erlbaum.

Tomkins, S. S. (1962). *Affect, imagery and consciousness: Vol. 1. The positive affects.* New York: Springer.

Tomkins, S. S. (1963). *Affect, imagery and consciousness: Vol. 2. The negative affects.* New York: Springer.

Weiner, B. (1985). An attributional theory of achievement motivation and emotion. *Psychological Review, 92,* 548–573.

Wierzbicka, A. (1992). Talking about emotions: Semantics, culture, and cognition. *Cognition and Emotion, 6,* 285–319.

Woodworth, R. S., & Schlosberg, H. (1954). *Experimental psychology* (rev. ed.). New York: Holt.

Wundt, W. (1903). *Grundriss der Psychologie* [Compendium of psychology]. Stuttgart, Germany: Engelmann.

Zajonc, R. B. (1980). Feeling and thinking: Preferences need no inferences. *American Psychologist, 35,* 151–175.

CHAPTER 3

The Social Roles and Functions of Emotions

Nico H. Frijda and Batja Mesquita

E motions are complex, structured phenomena. They are not mere feeling states, that is, intraindividual states of conscious awareness that might as well remain within the confines of the individual's mind. They are parts of the very process of interacting with the environment. They are affective responses to what happens in the environment and cognitive representations of the event's meaning for the individual. They are, first and foremost, modes of relating to the environment: states of readiness for engaging, or not engaging, in interaction with that environment. It will be difficult to understand the social role of emotions if these are not, from the outset, viewed as dynamically changing, structured elements in ongoing interchanges, which both influence and are influenced by the other elements in these interchanges, such as the external events and the attitudes and actions of the other individuals involved.

Emphasizing the composite and structured nature of emotions is important because it implies that emotions can be described and not merely labeled. Emotions (i.e., these descriptions) thus can be compared with one another without much concern for the labels used. When looking at the literature (see Mesquita & Frijda, 1992, for review), one is struck by the extent to which cross-cultural emotion psychology is plagued by a preoccupation with emotion labels. True enough, emotion taxonomies differ (Russell, 1991). However, focus on categories and labels tends to obscure the structural similarity of processes that are labeled or categorized differently in various societies. Differences in labeling may be due solely to the fact that a given emotional process can be labeled or categorized in many ways, depending upon which of its several components is taken as the basis for categorizing. Therefore, to assess social factors in emotions themselves, the emotional phenomena should be discussed as structures described analytically.

In this chapter, we discuss the ways in which the sociocultural environment can be expected to influence the emotion processes, the roles and functions of these processes in social interaction, and the influences of the sociocultural environment upon those roles and functions. That is, we discuss the modes of influence on emotions of the immediate context of social interaction in which emotions arise and of the values, norms, and cognitive customs prevalent in a given culture. Before doing that, we briefly outline the conception of emotions that guides our analysis.

Emotion Theory

The Emotion Process

Emotions occur when an event is appraised by the individual as relevant to his or her concerns. The process by which this takes place may be represented as a sequence of steps, each involving one or several components. The sequence is illustrated in Figure 1. Events are encountered and coded in terms of the knowledge and event categories available to the individual. Appraisal processes scan whether the events are relevant to one of the individual's concerns. The emotion process proper begins when an event is indeed appraised as relevant—as favorable or harm-

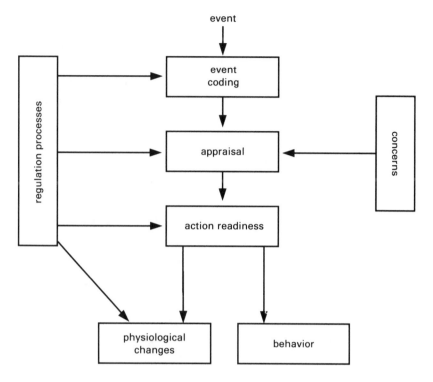

FIGURE 1. Emotion process.

ful—to one or to several concerns. Particular patterns of appraisal then lead to particular changes in action readiness and to concomitant physiological changes, which form the core of the emotional responses. However, regulation processes modify the outcomes of the various subprocesses and, thus, may attenuate, inhibit, or enhance the resulting responses in an event.

Two additional processes may occur that bear as a whole on the process as described. First, the emotion may become a focus of a higher order evaluation with regard to its individual or social desirability, which is one of the inputs for the regulation processes. We refer to the resulting evaluation as the emotion's *significance*. Second, the individual may categorize his or her emotion process, or any of its elements, and label it with an emotion term such as "anger," "sorrow," or "jealousy." The categorizing and labeling process does not necessarily take all the components of the sequence into account; hence, a given emotion process can be labeled in different fashions. Labeling is considered to be important in the emotion process because how we label our emotions may influence our evaluation, and thus the emotion's significance and the regulation processes. In what follows, we examine in some detail each of the components.

Concerns

Emotional evaluations derive from an individual's concerns, that is, from his or her goals, motives, values, and sensitivities. *Concerns* is a convenient general term to denote an individual's (short- or long-term) dispositions to prefer particular states of the world or of the self. Emotions are elicited by events that are relevant to one or more of the individual's concerns.

Emotions can be considered to be processes that serve to monitor and safeguard the individual's concerns (Frijda, 1986; Lazarus, 1991; Ortony, Clore, & Collins, 1988; Scherer, 1984). That indicates their function. The emotion that we call *fear* signals a threat to the concern that is involved in the emotion-eliciting event: one's physical integrity, one's prospect of success, the stability of one's intimate relationship with a particular individual, a particular social goal one has identified with, and so forth. The emotion called *anger* signals (among other things) actual or impending offense to such a concern. *Joy* signals that an event means achievement of satisfaction with regard to a given concern or a promise that such achievements are within reach.

One may say that behind each occurrence of an emotion, there is a concern (or several concerns) giving to the event its meaning and its power to elicit emotion. A given event, such as walking around unveiled or unclothed, elicits shame because the individual subscribes to a value condemning such behaviors, or because he or she desires to belong to the group and not be rejected. Another event, one's national flag being torn down and trodden upon, causes indignation because this conflicts (and only when it conflicts) with the desire for respect for one's national grandeur and the symbols that symbolize that. Others may not have such a desire and thus lack that particular emotional sensitivity.

Appraisal and Action Readiness

Emotions signal the relevance of events for favoring or harming one or several of one's concerns. They signal such relevance to the cognitive apparatus and the action system. What is usually referred to as *emotions* are, primarily, processes of appraisal of events as relevant, leading to processes of changes in action readiness and eventually to behavior (often, to physiological arousal as the logistic support of such readiness and behavior). *Appraisal,* as used in this chapter, refers to the appraisal of an event as positively or negatively relevant (primary appraisal), as well as to the assessment of further aspects of the event that are relevant for dealing with it (secondary appraisal). *Action readiness* means the state of readiness (or unreadiness) for achieving a particular change in the subject–object interaction or for interacting with the environment in general.

The term *appraisal* applies to processes that occur during actual encounters with specific events and is related to the picking up (or having expectations of) specific features in the interaction with the specific event. Sensing, recognizing, or interpreting the event as a source of pleasure or pain, now or in the future, is what constitutes primary appraisal. Evaluating the event as an actual or potential threat, as signaling unalterable loss, as being caused by a responsible causal agent, or as due to one's failure or transgression of some norm, implies secondary appraisal. These appraisals involve assessing the event with regard to dimensions such as causal agency, uncertainty about the event's outcome or implications, controllability or uncontrollability, and effort required for dealing with the event. Supposedly, these dimensions of "secondary appraisal" are relevant to the emergence of the various forms of action readiness, so that the appraisal of blaming a responsible agent leads to arousal of hostile action tendencies, the appraisal of an event as a potential threat leads to avoidant or self-protective action tendencies, and so forth.

Appraisal implies these evaluative and cognitive processes and not necessarily their conscious results. Conscious appraisal may, in some cases, be at variance with the appraisal process that elicited the emotional response (Frijda, 1993b). Nevertheless, appraisal processes and the particular appraisal involved in particular emotions are usually inferred from subjective reports of how the encounter is experienced. However, another source of hypotheses concerning appraisals is the way in which a particular event is treated by the individual (e.g., as a source of threat to be avoided, as the cause of harm to be opposed, and so on).

The processes of appraisal can take various forms. Primary appraisal, the evaluation of an event as positive or negative, extends from the automatic processes involved in primary affective responses to tastes, smells, pain, familiarity, and so on, to the no less automatic processes of anticipation through previous experience, and to the complex interpretative processes involved in understanding the implications of a given situation (e.g., interpreting a found handkerchief as a sign of possible infidelity, or understanding a certain behavior as showing a lack of respect that, in turn, is felt to imply a loss of one's social status, as it would be in Bali; Keeler, 1983). In many cases, the affective valence of the event is implied by the concept in terms of which the event is understood, and primary appraisal follows directly from the way in which the event is coded. We return to this in the next subsection.

Action readiness in emotion consists of readiness for relating or not relating to the environment. Basically, emotions are phenomena of readiness or unreadiness for interaction. The various forms that action readiness can take demonstrate this. They include general activation and deactivation that have interest and disinterest in the environment as one of their major aspects; exuberance in joy, depressed apathy and anomie, and generalized inhibition in anxiety provide illustrations. The variations in action readiness also include action tendencies, distinguished by their relational intent, and the modification of the subject–object relationship that they imply: acceptance or rejection of stimulation (as in joy or interest and in aversion), change in the power relationship with a given person (as in anger and guilt), self-protection from a source of threat (as in fear), or maintaining or breaking proximity with a person or object (as in affection or anger).

Modes of action readiness, too, are inferred from self-report, from behavior, or from both. They are constructs derived from (the lack of) impulses and inclinations felt as well as from the constructs advanced to account for the variety of behaviors having a similar relational sense. For instance, hypoactivation is a plausible inference from avowed disinclination to act, from expressed or manifest disinterest in one's surroundings, from hypotonic facial expression, and from behavioral apathy.

Under the appropriate circumstances, action readiness gives rise to overt behavior: expressive, instrumental, and verbal behavior of diverse kinds. The hostile impulse of anger can be expressed by violent movements and a fierce glance, by shouting, by fighting or poisoning, by blackmail or black magic, or by breaking contact. It can also give rise to cognitive behaviors, such as ruminating and thinking hostile thoughts, and to enhanced tendencies for particular modes of appraisal, such as the tendency for causal attribution (Gallagher & Clore, 1985). Which modes of behavior are shown depends supposedly on the precise circumstances and on the models for behavior found in the social environment. Whether or not any behavior is manifested depends on the reasons for and habits of inhibition and self-control.

Event Coding

Usually, appraisal processes are elicited by the particular meaning of an event rather than by the nature of the event per se. The majority of events that elicit emotions do so through their associated meanings, as grasped by the individual and as defined by the culture or the past history of the individual. Usually, associated meaning is what renders events relevant for some concern and, hence, gives it positive or negative valence. Understanding a particular remark as an insult renders it harmful for social prestige and, thereby, offensive; coding bodily contact as an instance of taboo makes such contact relevant for one's concerns regarding the avoidance of social, moral, or divine punishment.

We use the notion of *event coding* to recognize the fact that coding processes often intervene between events as such and their emotional appraisal. In particular, the notion serves to emphasize that cultures possess explicit verbal categories to identify classes of events with particular associated meanings and affective evaluations. Insult is one such category, personal loss is another, and success, a third; shameful behavior, affront to God's honor, magic spells, impure food, terrorist attacks, and actions of the "Great Satan America" are others. As Parkinson and Manstead (1992) indicated, such categories imply affective evaluations. Concern relevance is socially defined and embodied in the semantic network surrounding the concepts. Events coded as terrorist attacks or shameful behaviors are indubitably bad; events coded as actions of freedom fighters are indubitably good (Fisk, 1991). Concepts of this kind are represented by affective schemas, as analyzed by Fiske (1982) and Fiske and Pavelchak (1985).

Although event coding often implies appraisal of the event, it is useful to distinguish these two processes. First, not all appraisals result from event coding; the affective valence of physical pain is more primitive than that, even if event coding (pain interpreted as offense to self-esteem or as a threat to health) may drastically alter its emotional effects (Tursky, 1974). Second, event coding does not necessarily lead to actual emotional appraisal. One may be personally indifferent to the Great Satan and his actions, even when one knows these to be considered bad. One has to appraise the coded event as real and as actually involving one's interests to experience an emotion. As indicated, appraisal is tied to the specifics of the individual's encounter with a particular event: the insult as delivered here and now by a particular offender, or the specific context in which a terrorist attack is reported to have taken place. The notion of appraisal refers to the fact that, if an emotion is to occur, the event's goodness or badness, or pleasantness or unpleasantness has to be felt to engage the individual and to do so in the specific interaction (in fact, receiving an insult may be appraised as emotionally positive when it is felt to signal victory over the offender in a power struggle). Emotion, in the sense of change in action readiness or upset, is evoked only when such features, including those of secondary appraisal, are involved (Frijda, 1986, 1993b).

Be that as it may, event coding usually is an important phase in the emotion process. Event coding is highly dependent upon event categories distinguished in the language and upon socially elaborated, prescribed, or transmitted meanings. A given event (bodily contact between relatives, offense to social status, illness) may be coded differently in various cultures. Different codings may relate similar events to different concerns and, thus, give rise to different emotions.

Significance

Emotions include a further aspect, namely the emotion's *significance*. Significance is the meaning of the emotion itself for the individual, and this meaning may be of situational, individual, or social origin. Individuals often attach a particular significance to the emotion that they experience. The implications of having a particular emotion at a particular moment is itself an emotional event, relevant to other concerns than those that made the emotion arise in the first place. These other concerns include higher order concerns or principles, on the basis of which individuals monitor their behavior (Carver & Scheier, 1990). The emotion's significance forms part of a person's emotional experience and determines emotion regulation. Being proud of one's anger modifies the experience of that anger as well as its manifestations.

The significance of emotions is, we think, accessed largely through the emotion's label; to a large extent, it derives from the "emotion script" (Fischer, 1991) that is linked to the category under which the person subsumes his or her emotion. To an important extent, it is through emotion significance that cultural models and norms affect individual emotional experience.

Three kinds of significance may be distinguished, or three types of meanings that can accrue to particular emotions or emotion manifestations: meanings regarding the social effects of emotions, norm- and self-compatibility, and social cohesion.

First, emotions have social consequences. Certain emotion manifestations have direct social effects; the individual, by and large, knows this (Fischer, 1991), and it influences the tendencies to express or suppress. Anger provides the clearest example. Anger is meant to repulse or restrain others, and it often coerces or upsets (Kerkstra, 1984). Many of these effects are part of the culture's prevailing emotionology. Anger, for instance, may have effects that are more or less appropriate in a particular culture, in a given social environment, or in a particular interpersonal situation.

Social effects are not restricted to anger. Grief and weeping tend to elicit caretaking or compassion (Murray, 1979) and often even tolerance for slightly deviant behavior. Guilt emotion sometimes serves as an apology, and it often coerces others into feeling guilty in turn (Baumeister, Stillwell, & Heatherton, in press). In many circumstances, joy seems to invite participation of others and eagerness to share in the event. These effects are largely dependent on overt manifestation of the emotion, and they form the basis of the important self-presentational functions of emotional expressions: Emotional expressions may be enhanced, attenuated, or faked for self-presentational reasons (Laux, 1986; Laux & Weber, 1990). Self-presentation is one of the important shaping powers of emotional expression, in addition to general display rules. The social effects of emotions are not always or entirely dependent upon overt expression, though. A claim on other people's consideration may be made by the sheer loss and one's concomitant feelings of sorrow; guilt emotion can be used coercively by the verbal utterance "You make me feel guilty"; sorrow often carries the expectation that others should be compassionate or considerate, which sometimes is enough for the subject to feel abandoned or slighted when it is not forthcoming. These mechanics are known from family therapy (e.g., Pincus, 1973).

Second, norms exist with regard to having or not having particular emotions (e.g., anger in eighteenth-century New England; Stearns & Stearns, 1986), to having or not having particular emotions in particular situations (Hochschild's, 1983, feeling rules), and to showing or not showing the expression of particular emotions in either general or particular circumstances (e.g., weeping in intimate personal relationships; Ekman & Friesen's, 1971, display rules). Such norms can be assumed to be of both social and individual origin. In addition, and partly independently of the former, there are the individual's evaluations of whether or not his or her emotions or the expression of them are compatible with his or her self-image and self-ideal (Julien Sorel, in Stendhal's [1830/1991] *The Red and the Black*, wanted to be self-controlled and self-possessed; Lord Jim, in Joseph Conrad's [1900] book, expected himself to be fearless and courageous). An individual may be amazed by the indignation that one may find him or herself capable of.

What is interesting, both with regard to social effects and norm- and self-compatibility, is that these forms of significance can be assumed to depend both upon cultural emotion scripts (Fischer, 1991) and upon individual history and standards. The two may be at variance with one another. Also, individual norms and self-standards may cover emotions or emotion manifestations that cultural emotionology is silent about. Of course, here as elsewhere (cf. Frijda & Jahoda, 1966), the existence of recognized cultural scripts or norms does not preclude large interindividual variety within the group with regard to subscribing to the norms or adhering to them. It would be interesting and useful to obtain more insight into the varieties concerned.

The third form of significance relates to social cohesion. Emotions may separate individuals from others, or they may join them to others. They may be of a nature to keep them private, or to share with particular others, or to share them generally. In The Netherlands, shame tends to be an emotion that one shares only with intimate others and, at least in one of our studies, less frequently than other emotions (35.5% did not share shame before reporting it in the questionnaire study, as compared with 9.7% for the emotions of joy, anger, sadness, and fear; Moorkens, 1991). The cohesive effect of fear (Schachter, 1959) would appear to differ according to whether the others are or are not under the same threats. In Anglo-Saxon and Germanic cultures, grief upon loss is either moderately shared or kept mostly private. Cultures thus tend to differ in this regard, the classical illustration being Granet's (1922) analysis of mourning prescriptions in pre-World-War-I China. The expectation of difference leads to research that in part confirms and in part contradicts these expectations or, at least, leads to modifying them. Mesquita (1993), for instance, did not find so many clear-cut differences in sharing emotions as expected.

Emotion Labeling

Emotion labels may attach to any of the above components of the emotion process or to any combination of these. Major emotion labels, in English and in several other Western European languages, tend to be attached to combinations of appraisal and action readiness (Frijda, Kuipers, & Ter-schure, 1989). *Fear,* for instance, primarily categorizes the appraisal of threat. *Anger* would seem to categorize primarily the appraisal of an event as unpleasant and willfully caused by someone else, and as the action readiness to oppose or retaliate. *Furious* is defined almost solely by the action readiness for vehement overt expression. However, many emotion labels are based upon the particular type of eliciting event, as coded in the culture. *Jealousy* is an example in English (it cannot be defined other than by a threat-by-a-third-party kind of event coding). Bodily arousal may also on occasion be decisive for the labeling of an emotion. Such is the case for *pent-up,* in English, or *liget* in the language of the Philippine Ilongot that, to judge from Rosaldo's (1980) report, denotes diverse experiences of high arousal. Among the experiences so labeled is that which members of Western cultures would label as anger, or its equivalent. In other words, emotion labels may differ with regard to the components of the emotion process that they point to primarily, and which label is applied depends, perhaps, upon the aspect of the sequence that the subject or the onlooker focuses on. It also depends on the available labels and on the availability of those labels. English possesses jealousy that singles out the event, but other languages may not possess an equivalent and may have to be content with an equivalent of anger or upset (the Ilongot would have to settle for *liget*). As to the possibility of an emotion word involving primarily emotion significance, an emotion word denoting bad emotions is at least conceivable, and the Ifaluk word for justified anger (Lutz, 1988) explicitly has *significance* as one of its components.

It should be added that emotion labels tend to denote the various emotion components in a probabilistic, "prototypical" fashion (Fehr & Russell, 1984; Shaver, Schwartz, Kirson, & O'Connor, 1987). That is, if an emotion category is defined by several components, the label for this category may be considered applicable when any sign for any of these is present to a sufficient degree. An emotion is called *sorrow* when one responds with any sign of emotion to an unmodifiable loss of something valued, or when one feels the urge to cry, or when one is drawn into apathy (or when one sees someone else respond to an event likely to be appraised in this fashion, or sees him or her crying or apathetic), or when there is any combination of these.

Dimensions of Emotion Variation

Cultural differences may appear in any of the components mentioned above. People and cultures may also be highly similar in these regards. To illustrate these points, we describe some results from our own recent work (Mesquita, 1993) that compared respondents from Surinamese, Turkish, and autochthonous Dutch groups living in The Netherlands. First, we conducted an open-ended interview in which spontaneous reports of emotions were collected from the three groups of respondents. To control for different styles of spontaneous reporting, an emotion questionnaire was subsequently developed. The respondents were presented with five situations determined in previous research to be relevant to the emotional experience of the individuals in all three groups. Two situations were positive (Situation 1, compliment by others; Situation 2, social recognition), and three others were negative (Situation 3, personal offense by an acquaintance; Situation 4, personal offense by a close other; Situation 5, unfair treatment by a close other). For each of the situations, the questionnaire contained items designed to assess, among other things, (a) appraisals, (b) the perception of "obviousness" of the meaning of the relevant social situation, and (c) the extent of social sharing of the felt emotions. Respondents recalled their own personal experience that fitted the given description and answered these questions. For all questions, 3- or 5-point rating scales were provided. We interviewed about 90 respondents from each of the three groups. Interviewers were all women from the same cultural backgrounds as the respondents.

Appraisal Similarities and Differences

We mentioned that appraisals can be described as patterns of values on a limited set of appraisal dimensions: valence, certainty, controllability, agency, and so on. There is increasing evidence that many dimensions in this set are universal. Research on Western, Chinese, Indonesian, and

Japanese subjects suggest that the same dimensions are important, to about the same degree, to distinguish the various emotion categories (Markam, 1992; Mauro, Sato, & Tucker, 1992). In other words, whereas the emotional events that elicit emotions and the significance of emotions may differ appreciably from one culture to another, the elements of appraisal appear to be highly similar (Ellsworth, chapter 2, this volume). For instance, magical spells are elicitors of fear in certain cultures and not in others (Scherer, Wallbott, & Summerfield, 1986), and violent anger upon an insult is approved of in Albania, both by the individual and by society (Black-Michaud, 1975), and strongly rejected among the Utku Inuit (Briggs, 1970). The emergence of fear caused by a magic spell, like that of the announcement of dismissal from one's job, is due to the event's negative valence, the prospect of uncertain future harm, and the uncontrollability of the event. The anger in Albania as well as among the Utku (or in the perception of the Utku) is due to the experience of frustration or harm attributed to the action of a responsible other.

Not only do the dimensions of appraisal appear to be general, but major patterns of appraisal also do. The core meaning of most emotion terms in a given language can be reasonably explained in English; the explications, apart from describing event types, describe appraisals (and perhaps modes of action readiness). The emotions aroused by particular emotionally relevant situations (such as being insulted by a good friend or relative) tend to involve highly similar appraisal patterns in different cultural groups (for instance, Surinamese, Turks, and autochthonous Dutch in The Netherlands; Mesquita, 1993).

At the same time, there is evidence that cultures differ in the emphasis upon one or the other of the appraisal dimensions. Mauro et al. (1992) found such difference in the dimension of controllability: Controllability ratings of emotion incidents were significantly different between American and Chinese subjects, with Japanese subjects falling in between. Markus and Kitayama (1991) suggested that the implications of events for the relationship to close others, instead of only to the self, may be more pronounced in subjects from *interdependent* cultures. Solomon (1978) suggested that the much-mentioned low level of anger in the Utku

Eskimos is due to the low level of blaming others, that is, of causal agency attribution (see Mesquita & Frijda, 1992, for additional examples).

Differences in emphasis on particular appraisal dimensions have also emerged in our own research in The Netherlands (Mesquita, 1993). In open interviews with respondents of the Surinamese, Turkish, and autochthonous groups, spontaneous reports of emotions appeared to contain more frequent reference to social aspects of meaning in the Surinamese and Turkish groups than in the Dutch. This finding suggested that Turkish and Surinamese respondents appraise emotional situations more readily in terms of social dimensions. The results might also be explained, however, by different styles of spontaneous reporting. To reduce the possible effects of different reporting styles, emotion questionnaires were developed that included appraisal scales used successfully in cross-cultural research. This way the reported appraisals in different cultures would be more comparable, and the hypothesis of cultural differences in appraisal propensity could be tested more properly. To avoid problems of word equivalence, emotion instances were elicited by means of descriptions of types of situations. Respondents were asked to recall a situation that fitted the given type, and then gave answers to questions containing 3- or 5-point scales.

Some of the results pertaining to appraisal are given in Table 1, which summarizes the answers to three questions designed to assess the appraisal of intent by the others involved in negative emotional episodes (Situations 3, 4, and 5). These questions were not asked for positive emotional episodes (Situations 1 and 2). Respondents from the Surinamese and Turkish groups appeared to be more inclined to appraise the emotional events on their social dimensions. They appeared to evaluate other people's negative behaviors more in terms of power relationships than did the Dutch subjects. They attributed more intent to people who had hurt them and assumed more often that those people meant to better themselves by what they had done to the subject. Furthermore, other data indicated that both positive and negative events were assessed more readily as being relevant to their social prestige and to that of one's family and one's group. The cultural differences in the readiness to appraise

TABLE 1
Availability of Intent Appraisal

	Dutch	Surinamese	Turkish	
Situation 3: An acquaintance, a neighbor, or colleague offended you, did not take you seriously, or was inconsiderate toward you.	(n = 30)	(n = 30)	(n = 30)	F
Was the other person aware of what his/her behavior would mean to you?	1.2	2.2	3.1	**
Did the other person do it on purpose?	1.4	3.0	3.0	**
Did the other person do this to profit?	1.6	2.8	3.1	**
Situation 4: Your partner, an intimate friend, or a close relative offended you, did not take you seriously, or was inconsiderate toward you.	(n = 30)	(n = 29)	(n = 24)	F
Was the other person aware of what his/her behavior would mean to you?	1.1	2.4	1.8	*
Did the other person do it on purpose?	1.4	2.4	3.0	**
Did the other person do this to profit?	1.6	2.1	3.5	**
Situation 5: Your partner, an intimate friend, or a close relative treated you unfairly or improperly.	(n = 28)	(n = 30)	(n = 30)	F
Was the other person aware of what his/her behavior would mean to you?	1.2	2.2	2.1	
Did the other person do it on purpose?	2.6	2.2	2.5	
Did the other person do this to profit?	1.9	2.9	2.7	*

Note. Means of 4-point rating scales: 1 = not at all, 4 = entirely so.
*p < .05. **p < .01.

events along social dimensions may relate to differences in the degree of psychological independence and interdependence (Markus & Kitayama, 1991). There are indications that the Dutch have more independent selves, whereas the Surinamese and the Turks have more interdependent selves (Mesquita, 1993). Thus, the results suggest that in the two cultures in which the emphasis is on relationships with other people, emotional appraisals include social dimensions more readily, whereas appraisals in the culture in which independent selves are dominant are less likely to include social dimensions. The degree of psychological interdependence, supposedly significant to the readiness for social appraisals, may be a characteristic inherent in the different cultural backgrounds. It should be recalled, however, that the Turkish and Surinamese respondents were members of ethnic minority groups. Being an ethnic minority may in itself contribute to psychological interdependence (Rabbie, 1992).

Concern Differences

We stated the general notion that emotions are elicited because events are appraised as relevant to some concern. Concerns constitute another source of interindividual and intercultural variation in emotion. One may assume that individuals of all human groups share a number of basic concerns, such as those for physical health and the absence of pain, self-esteem, and the integrity of one's attachments. But differences, in intensity as well as in kind, are equally obvious. Social esteem would appear to be more of an issue in "honor" cultures, group harmony more so in inter-dependent cultures, and so on. Most noticeable are differences due to the concerns consisting of the presence and integrity of a particular object or symbol: one's God, the Flag, one's Leader, one's holy places, or ob-servance of given rituals.

Event coding and concerns obviously are closely related. Events involving objects of concern like those mentioned—the Leader, the Flag—are coded accordingly. Demeaning the Flag is coded as an insult, as is an attack on the Leader as a terrorist act, only because respecting the Flag and the Leader represent concerns.

The Notion of Focality

Events, as coded, differ in focality. Event types are supposed to become focal when they represent socially well-defined and generally shared con-cerns. Culturally focal events are events that are an important subject of daily discourse. An example of a focal event type in White American culture is that of situations involving success (D'Andrade, 1984): "In Amer-ican culture, success is a personal characteristic of great importance to most people. Such daily events as the organization of daily effort, the evaluation of task performance, and the marking of accomplishment through self-announcement and the congratulations of others are closely attended to and much discussed" (p. 95). Other examples of focal events are those involving honor or threats to honor in Bali or among the Bedouins, descriptions of which can be found in the ethnographic literature (Abu-Lughod, 1986; Black-Michaud, 1975; Keeler, 1983; Mesquita & Frijda, 1992).

Culturally, focal concerns are likely to draw attention to the events affecting them and to yield cultural "expertise" on such events. This may lead to less uncertainty and finer discriminations, the events may be represented in greater detail, and more different features may be distinguished with a high degree of availability. We thus assume that the representation of focal event types is well structured, which implies that in a given culture clear norms exist on how to interpret these events and how to respond to them. Focality would seem to be related to the degree to which emotions are socially embedded in the given culture; cultures appear to differ in this regard. It is likely that emotional events are more focal or that focal event types are more numerous when the culture considers emotions to be of social rather than of individual concern. Since focality implies that clear norms do exist about how to interpret relevant events, people in such cultures are likely to experience more certainty in their interpretations. An emotional reaction to a particular event is appraised as "obvious" if it seems to the subject to be imposed by the event rather than being the result of some subjective assessment or behavioral preference. Obviousness of particular components of emotions is likely to exclude their being reconsidered or put into question because alternative interpretations of the situation or alternative reactions are inconceivable. Thus, one would expect the focality of event types to enhance the obviousness of emotional situations.

This is in fact what we have found in our previously mentioned study (Mesquita, 1993). As alluded to, there is evidence that emotions are most socially embedded in the Turkish group and least so in the autochthonous Dutch group. Therefore, we expected that the meaning of emotional events would be perceived as most obvious by the Turkish respondents and least so by the Dutch, with the Surinamese lying between them. As described before, subjects were asked to report an emotional experience that fitted the description of a given type of situation and to answer questions about the emotional experience. Three questions referred to the obviousness of the situation's meaning. The first question asked whether another person would consider the situation as pleasant or as unpleasant, as the respondent had; the second question asked whether another person would think and feel in a similar way when in the respondent's position; and the third question asked whether another person would react as the respondent had. Subjects were offered three answer alternatives: no, somewhat, and yes. Because many of the respondents were unable to answer the question, we created a fourth, "don't know" answer category. Examples of answers in this category are "I don't know," "Every person is different," "It depends on the kind of person," "What a stupid question," and "How could I know?" Taking the different situation types together, such an answer was given by 16% of the Dutch, 10% of the Surinamese, and none of the Turkish respondents.

The answer categories were treated as points on an ordinal scale ranging from "I don't know" to "yes." We thus considered answers in the "don't know" category as standing for less obviousness than the "no" answers. The results, split out by type of situation, are presented in Table 2. As expected, we found the most obviousness in the Turkish group and the least in the Dutch group. Although the Dutch respondents did think, on the average, that other people would find the situations as pleasant or as unpleasant as they had, in three of the five situations, they thought so to a lesser extent than did those in the Surinamese and the Turkish groups. The Dutch respondents did not assume that another person would think, feel, or react as they had. The putative consequence of this lack of obviousness in the Dutch group is that there is more reconsideration and regulation of emotional responses. In another of our studies, which used structured interviews, Dutch respondents spontaneously reported, more frequently than respondents from the other two cultural groups, to have hesitated about the meaning of the situation (Mesquita, 1993). Similar hesitations may be expected with regard to other emotional components than appraisal.

The emotional situations appeared to have the largest number of "obvious" implications for the Turkish group. Not only did the Turkish respondents, on the average, expect other people to think and feel as they had under similar circumstances, they assumed that other people would also behave as they had. The answers of the Surinamese group fell in between the other two. Surinamese assumed obviousness with regard to

TABLE 2
Cultural Differences in the Felt "Obviousness" of the Situation's Meaning

	Dutch	Surinamese	Turkish	
Situation 1: People complimented you on something or showed admiration toward you.	(n = 30)	(n = 29)	(n = 24)	F
Another person would find it as pleasant as I did.	2.0	2.5	2.7	*
Another person would think and feel as I did.	1.4	2.0	2.6	**
Another person would react as I did.	1.8	1.4	2.4	**
Situation 2: You had success because of some socially recognized accomplishment or achievement.	(n = 27)	(n = 30)	(n = 30)	F
Another person would find it as pleasant as I did.	2.7	2.8	2.8	
Another person would think and feel as I did.	1.9	2.4	2.8	**
Another person would react as I did.	1.8	1.8	2.7	**
Situation 3: An acquaintance, a neighbor, or colleague offended you, did not take you seriously, or was inconsiderate toward you.	(n = 29)	(n = 27)	(n = 30)	F
Another person would find it as unpleasant as I did.	2.3	2.8	2.9	*
Another person would think and feel as I did.	1.6	2.5	2.8	**
Another person would react as I did.	1.6	1.6	2.4	**
Situation 4: Your partner, an intimate friend, or a close relative offended you, did not take you seriously, or was inconsiderate toward you.	(n = 30)	(n = 26)	(n = 22)	F
Another person would find it as unpleasant as I did.	2.4	2.9	2.8	*
Another person would think and feel as I did.	1.6	2.3	2.8	**
Another person would react as I did.	1.3	1.6	2.2	**
Situation 5: Your partner, an intimate friend, or a close relative treated you unfairly or improperly.	(n = 27)	(n = 30)	(n = 30)	F
Another person would find it as unpleasant as I did.	2.6	2.7	2.9	
Another person would think and feel as I did.	2.2	2.3	2.8	*
Another person would react as I did.	1.8	2.0	2.4	

Note. Means of 3-point rating scales: 1 = no, 2 = somewhat, 3 = yes.
*$p < .05$. **$p < .01$.

thoughts and feelings, but not with regard to the reactions elicited by an event. These results support the hypothesis that social embedding of emotions leads to an increased sense that the meaning and implications of particular events were more or less fixed, objective facts.

The focality of event types may have yet another effect. Focal event types may be expected to be highly available. This means that focal events never remain unnoticed by the individual. When such events occur, the individual can hardly escape being emotionally unaffected. It also means that events that affect the focal concern only remotely (events distant in space or time) are recognized as instances of the event type.

The anthropological literature provides evidence that supports these expectations. For instance, in some cultures, the danger of losing one's dignity or honor is of great concern. Thus, situations bearing upon one's dignity are focal, and emotions related to shame are likely to ensure in these situations. Not only are situations in which dignity or honor is actually offended considered to be shameful, but also situations that involve the possibility of such an offense. They motivate the individual to do whatever is needed to protect his or her dignity or honor from being compromised. For example, on Bali and Java, many situations are interpreted as threats to status and, thereby, as shame situations: "A person fears that he will compromise that status by proving incapable of demonstrating it in his own gestures and more importantly, in the gestures of others" (Keeler, 1983, p. 163). Because status is not a stable property, it has to be settled continuously in the encounters with other people. If others' gestures and speech are rude and demeaning, that fact signals the inadequacy of one's own status or the likelihood of such inadequacy, which gives rise to the emotion called *lek* on Bali and *isin* on Java. Both concepts are translated as falling within the shame or embarrassment domain (for more examples, see Mesquita & Frijda, 1992).

Emotions like *lek* and *isin* are present in Western culture as well. Self-exposure, other people's lack of respect, and encounters with more important persons elicit similar emotions of shyness, shame, or embarrassment. However, these eliciting situations are not focal ones in Western culture. They are less well-defined and are not consistently categorized as shame situations. Shame receives considerably less explicit attention and cultural recognition; it is, as Scheff (1988b, p. 400) called it, a "low visibility" emotion. Shame is not usually expressed in a conspicuous manner and has no extensive social consequences. Shame (or the existence of shame situations) is not much talked about; there is no clear script about what an ashamed person should do.

The high availability of focal event types does not necessarily imply that they or the concomitant emotions occur frequently. On the contrary, focal events may be so aversive that their anticipation arouses active avoidance behavior, as may be illustrated by the fear of assault in elderly people, which prevents them from going out at night, thus making such assaults infrequent. In fact, because the function of emotions like shame and guilt is to prevent them from occurring (see below), the instances of shame and guilt may be rare especially where they are important. Even mildly relevant situations may be recognized as instances of a particular focal event type and signal the possibility of a central issue of concern that, in turn, may lead to their avoidance. The anthropological literature provides pertinent examples. According to Briggs (1970), angry thoughts and acts are considered to be dangerous by the Utku Eskimos. It is felt that angry people are always likely to lose control; they may ultimately commit murder and, thus, are frightening. Anger situations appear to be extremely focal in Utku culture even though they are rare or absent. They are so rare that they do not even get the opportunity to elicit emotions.

In fact, the major emotional effect of the focality of emotionally charged event types may not be found in manifestations of the corresponding emotion at all, but it may be found in other aspects of emotionality. Insofar as negatively charged events are concerned, the phenomena can be expected to correspond to what is the usual result of emotion avoidance or suppression: emotional inhibition and unspontaneity in interpersonal interactions, anxiety and depression, and emotional outbursts. For example, the focality of shame or *isin* leads to the formality, reserve, or polite friendliness known from descriptions of the Awlad 'Ali (Abu-Lughod, 1986) or the Javanese (Keeler, 1983) and may be a contributor to the rage outbursts of *amok* (Averill, 1982); the abhorrence of bodily contact with menstruating Oriya women leads to reticence and occasional fear (Shweder, 1991). These are a few examples of how focality may be emotionally manifest in less direct or less immediate ways and places.

Emotions in Social Interaction

In our analysis, emotions are not only intraindividual states but also forms of subject–environment interaction. This interaction may remain latent when the emotion is only a state of readiness; but even then, it is readiness for engaging in or breaking off interaction. By this very nature of readiness for and actual form of interaction, emotions exert influence on social interaction. In addition, many emotions are social events because they tend to occur in a context of socially shared meanings. They are recognized by others, they shed light upon the emotional relevance of the environment, they affect interpersonal relationships, and they in turn evoke responses from others that also affect the relationship from their side.

Considering these pronounced social roles of emotions, one may expect considerable cultural differences with regard to the force of their expression, the focality of the events that may elicit them, and the frequency of their occurrence. Social structures and cultural values influence which social interactional effects are tolerated, expected, rewarded, or tabooed and, by consequence, to what extent corresponding emotions are discouraged, encouraged, or even shaped by the cultural environment. There is ample evidence in this regard and in particular with regard to emotions with the clearest social repercussions. Desire for revenge, shame, grief, and guilt emotion all show strong intercultural differences and are emotions for which certain cultures have elaborate rules or rituals. Revenge is an issue with an almost formalized place in the society of some Balkan countries and of the Berbers of North Africa (Black-Michaud, 1975); in Western cultures, it is almost entirely an individual, private, and mostly tabooed affair, except in subcultures of violence (Jacoby, 1983). Guilt emotion has been prominent in seventeenth-century Dutch Protestant and American Puritan society and has been important in those societies until recently (Stearns & Stearns, 1986). We have already mentioned shame as being focal in certain Muslim societies. Grief is an emotion that commands explicit rituals on Bali, as it did in precommunist China (Granet, 1922), whereas formalized occasions for expressing or stylizing grief are nearly absent in present-day Western societies (Aries, 1974; Elias, 1982).

Interactional Functions of Emotions

Emotions involve the subject's appraisal of particular events as positive or negative. Perceiving someone's emotion, therefore, indicates to the observer the presence of an object or event that is being so appraised. Usually, emotions involve additional aspects, and convey those to observers: the subject's power position with respect to the agent in the event, for instance; his or her self-assuredness with respect to his or her power to cope; his or her degree of being in control or of helplessness. Features such as these are part of the secondary appraisal structures and may be reflected in the emotional response. That emotion is picked up by observers, and that this includes important aspects of the subject's appraisals has several important social implications.

First, someone's emotion indicates to others the emotional potential of the situation. Emotions tend to define events to other individuals as emotionally valent ones, or they strengthen such a definition if it already existed. They show the event to possess emotion-arousing properties. My fear indicates to others the presence of something frightening; my disgust defines an object as potentially disgusting and may instigate in others a search for the disgusting attributes; my anger shows its object to be at least potentially offensive. Emotions in others may be considered to form major sources for learning the emotional valence of objects and events, in addition to the emotional outcomes of direct confrontations with objects and events; the work by Campos on social referencing in infancy showed how actively such emotional information can be sought (e.g., Klinnert, Campos, & Emde, 1986). Second, someone's emotions indicate to others whether the subject's appraisal conformed to the norms or deviated from them. Third, they are often of interest not merely in indicating the presence of a particular kind of event with a particular kind of emotional valence, but in defining the subject's social position and role within one's social structure. Grief defines one as a beaten or a bereft person, joy as a victorious and self-confident one. In many cultural contexts, we think, people's emotions are felt to define such roles and positions, both in the eyes of the subjects themselves, and in those of their environment. Emotions (i.e., many emotions) are social facts that continuously elaborate the network of social roles and relationships. The significance of emotions does not merely exist for the subject. It exists just as strongly for the social environment. A classical example, of course, was Jean Briggs being ostracized by her Utku group after a repeated show of anger (Briggs, 1970). A more detailed example comes from Schieffelin's (1983) study of the Papua New Guinea Kaluli:

> As anger is the extreme expression of the posture of assertion, grief is the extreme posture of vulnerability and appeal .... For our purpose, it is important to point out that though anger and grief show the greatest possible contrast in the projection of power versus vulnerability in the projection of self in a situation, they are alike in the context of reciprocity in that both are the result of loss and contain the implication that they are entitled to redress. Anger claims it with a demand for compensation or a move towards vengeance, while grief waits upon the compassion of others to provide it. (pp. 187–188)

As we said, an emotion shows the eliciting event as an emotion-consonant one. A particular remark is understood as an insult when heard in conjunction with the receiver's anger; the same remark may be understood in a different context as a joke. Children learn respect from the respect of their elders, as they do their hatreds, fears, and things to enjoy. Social transmission of animal fears has been demonstrated in the phobia literature (e.g., Rachman, 1990). Emotions are among the prime means for the transmission of socially shared meanings. They may even be the means of choice. Emotional charge has, of old, been one of the "laws of association" (Woodworth, 1938): Associations accompanied by emotion are assumed to be learned more rapidly. But in addition, emotional expressions of others involved in an emotionally significant incident may confer upon those incidents an emotional impact for the observer. It may be argued that expression of emotions in others is one of the major factors for rendering information emotionally salient (Frijda, 1993b).

However, the social functions of emotions go deeper and, in some cases, appear to be essential to the very existence of those emotions. Apart from signaling the relevance of events, emotions instigate socially relevant behavior: sharing and bonding behaviors, corrective behaviors, and the like. In some cases, instigating such behaviors appears to be the *raison d'être* of the emotions concerned. Many emotions appear to be basically social in nature, not so much because of what elicits them, but because of what they motivate the subject to do or not to do.

The clearest example again is anger. Anger is elicited primarily by social objects that are felt to act by wilful intent; and angry behavior is designed to act upon the offender by social means. The backbone of angry behavior consists of what animal studies call *bluffing behavior*, which is meant to intimidate. Shouting, foot-stamping, hair-raising, smashing objects, are all shows of power that effectively frighten conspecifics or others, although they may anger some of them. The facial display of anger contains a "fierce glance" (glowering, fixed stare with eyes widened and brows drawn downward; Ekman & Friesen, 1975) that again is best understood as a menace or an intimidation display, considering its effects on others, in humans as well as in subhuman primates (Van Hooff, 1972). Actual fighting is only one of the types of behavior elicited by the broad category of frustrative and harm-inducing conditions and is absent as a response to most of these (Averill, 1982).

Considering the eliciting conditions and subsequent behavior, most instances of anger do not have the ultimate aim to hurt the offender but to punish him or her, that is, to correct his or her behavior. Many instances of anger concern noncompeting group members, often close kin. Clearly, one of the functions of anger is that of social correction to ensure standard-conforming behavior (Averill, 1982).

This applies to animals as well as humans. Many chimpanzee-threats aim at keeping lower placed group members in their place (de Waal, 1982). This points to a second social function of anger, which is to regulate power relationships. Among humans, this latter function is most clearly noticeable in the desire for revenge. Vengeance and desire for revenge are widespread, if not universal, even in societies in which revenge is not institutionalized. As a deliberate strategy, it is a type of action designed to promote cooperation in situations that, in the short run, may favor competition (Axelrod, 1984). As an emotional urge, it seems to serve as a deterrent for the repetition of abuse of power and, thereby, at maintaining power superiority or at restoring the power balance (Frijda, 1993a).

There is an entire array of emotions that, in some way or other, serve as regulators of social relationships. Shyness is one of these. Recently, a proposal was made to consider shyness as a social distinctiveness display (Gomperts, 1992). That is, shyness can be considered as the emotion precipitated by the perception of superiority of others in social rank or of distinctiveness in a social role (e.g., formerly, in gender relationships). The manifestations of shyness, notably blushing, may serve to signal recognition of the social distinction and inhibitory control of interrank or interrole behavior. From that angle, even stage fright may not be just anxiety at being judged but a display controlling social presumption. Interestingly, some evidence has been adduced that, among social phobics, issues of social climbing are more pronounced than among agoraphobics or normal controls (Gomperts, 1992). Social shyness appears to be valued positively in societies that value social distinctions, and negatively where social distinctions are frowned upon (Gomperts, 1992; Shweder, in press). Another social-regulatory emotion is envy. Envy acts to equalize accumulated possessions among members of a closely knit group from the side of the envious; fear of envy does so from the side of the potential subject of envy.

Other emotions have different sorts of social functions. Their purpose seems to be mainly to prevent their occurrence; it is their anticipation that serves as a deterrent rather than their motivation of socially valuable action (although they may do that too).

One of these emotions is grief. Grief elicits giving off distress calls that motivate the lost object to come in search of the subject. In addition, as Averill (1968) and Bowlby (1969) argued, grief motivates search for the lost object by the subject. Anticipation of grief or the excitement that is its initial state motivates one to remain close to the attachment figure. Generally speaking, grief and its anticipation motivate bond-strengthening and bond-maintaining behavior.

Another emotion with an obvious social function is shame. As with grief and desire for revenge, the emotion is most powerful through one's efforts to prevent it from occurring. It motivates norm-conforming behavior under its low-intensity forms of embarrassment, uneasiness, or *gêne* as it is called in French (Scheff, 1988a). Norm conformity may not be the most general designation for the aim of shame. More generally, emotional discomfort is elicited by any signal of possible exclusion from the group that can be attributed to some of one's properties or ways of behavior (Frijda, 1993b; Terwijn, 1993). Such signals lead to hiding behavior or to efforts to hide the relevant property (Scheff, 1988b). Norm deviation is only one of such properties; being a boy called Christophorus may be a reason for shame when one's classmates single it out as being ridiculous; being a child having red hair often does, too, as it provides a target for teasing and mockery. One's own behavior that deviates from one's own norms, from the self scheme or from explicit group norms, is only a later development and, we assume, a culture-bound one. Of course, one may argue that, for true shame, some notion of the self and of norms is necessary; but this argues only about the definition of the concept and not about the condition for an emotion that involves misery because of actual, assumed, or feared rejection by the group, and the instigation of hiding behavior.

Shame stimulates behavior that leads to acceptance by the group, in addition to stimulating behavior that flees group rejection; agreeing with the group norm is one of these behaviors (Frijda, 1993b; Terwijn, 1993). Therefore, it may be viewed as stimulating group cohesion. The emotions governing animosity toward other groups (e.g., distrust, hatred, contempt, derision) and investing in group identity obviously do the same.

The dynamics of shame obviously reach further, but they are beyond the scope of this chapter. We may suggest that shame caused by the behavior of one's kin serves group cohesion by the repair behaviors that it motivates (e.g., making up for the debts incurred by a family member). Other forms of shame reflect loss of status and belong to the emotions regulating the power relationships discussed previously.

A final emotion to be discussed is guilt. Emotions exist that are caused by the awareness of having caused discomfort or harm in someone else. Subjects refer to that emotion as "feeling guilty." As an example of such a constellation, we mention the long-lasting distress caused by having accidentally killed a child who suddenly crossed the street in front of one's car. It is important to note that no guilt in a legal sense or actual sense of being to blame needs to be involved. In fact, in an interview study in which 42 subjects were asked to describe experiences of guilt feelings and to answer questions about these experiences, 58% of the subjects blamed themselves although they also knew that they did not directly; 35% considered someone else to have been the cause, and 46% the victim to have been responsible (the percentages refer to overlapping groups of subjects). Nearly half of the subjects (43%) felt guilty because of unintended harm done to others (e.g., feeling guilty because of mother's distress at the subject having left home to marry; Kroon, 1988). McGraw (1987) also found unintentional harm to lead to stronger guilt feelings than intentional harm. Rarely, in only 33% of Kroon's sample, was the guilt feeling caused by behavior that could be described as conflicting with moral norms or as neglect. Also, guilt emotion does not necessarily reflect awareness of having transgressed some norm but, rather, having behaved carelessly, or having caused loss of love, or both. Considering these data, guilt emotion appears indeed to follow from the mere fact of having unintentionally caused harm in someone else, in many cases combined with the fact of being submitted to reproaches from the victim or others or of having been left by the victim.

Guilt emotion in most cases leads to a desire to make up for the harm done (73%), to ask forgiveness (60%), to want to talk about it with the victim (73%), or to submit to the victim's wishes (54%; Kroon, 1988). The conclusion seems warranted that guilt emotion is not a mere feeling, but an interpersonal attitude motivating corrective behavior. Such an emotion appears to be highly functional socially (Baumeister et al., in press). Anticipation of the distress motivates carefulness in behavior involving others and, particularly, involving close relationships. Guilt emotion is a cautionary emotion. The moral guilt feelings that are usually considered paradigmatic would, as with shame, seem to be particular developments growing out of a much more elementary distress at having been the cause of unwanted distress (Hoffman, 1984).

Talking of the social functions of these emotions might seem to imply that the emotions exist *to fulfill* these regulatory social functions. We indeed believe that this is the case. One may say that certain forms of anger, shame, grief, and guilt emotion exist for the sake of ensuring or facilitating these social regulations. What this means is that particular emotional sensitivities exist for those purposes. Grief presupposes an emotional sensitivity to loss; socially corrective anger presupposes sensitivity for normal transgression in others; shame presupposes sensitivity for group exclusion; and guilt presupposes sensitivity for distress in close others and for one's causal role in that. All this is plausible (the sensitivities constitute concerns) and quite functional. The functions ultimately reside both in preventing punishment to the individual subject (such as retaliation by someone carelessly treated) and in maintaining the well-functioning and integrity of the group.

Social Sharing

There is one additional link between emotions and social interaction. Individuals often communicate their own emotional experiences and discuss them with others in a relationship and, as a consequence, these experiences become *socially shared*. Western European subjects were found to have discussed their emotional experiences with at least one other person in about 90% of the emotional incidents reported (Rimé, Mesquita, Philippot, & Boca, 1991). The social environment is thus quite often involved in the emotions of the individual.

To the extent that emotional events are felt to be of concern to the social group, we should expect social sharing to consist of more than just being receptive to the information conveyed. When emotional events are socially significant, other people are likely to feel affected by what has happened and to feel a common responsibility for coping with the situation. Thus, they may help to find solutions for problems or to join in the celebration of fortunate events. In "interdependent" cultures, therefore, one may expect the social environment to be more committed to the individual's emotions, and the character of social sharing may be expected to differ between cultures.

This is in fact what we found in our previously described research (Mesquita, 1993) in which we compared Dutch, Surinamese, and Turkish groups living in The Netherlands and confirmed that social sharing is more social in character in the more interdependent Turkish and Surinamese cultures than in the more independently oriented Dutch. Subjects were asked whether they had talked with other people about the reported emotion incident. They were provided with two lists of items to check: one list mentioning behaviors that they themselves might have shown, and another list mentioning possible behaviors of the sharing partner. Turkish and Surinamese respondents, much more frequently than the Dutch ones, indicated having asked for active involvement of the sharing partner or having behaved in a way that presupposed such active involvement. Also, on the whole, the Turkish and Surinamese sharing partners seemed to have lived up to these expectations of commitment; the Turkish and Surinamese subjects indicated more often than the Dutch that their sharing partners had in fact shown active involvement, in particular in situations in which someone else had behaved unpleasantly toward the subject.

The precise situation profiles are items 3, 4, and 5 from Table 2. In negative situations like these, all groups showed about equal frequencies of social sharing: 87% of the Dutch, 81% of the Surinamese, and 84% of the Turks. However, the character of sharing differed, as shown by the data in Table 3. Cultural differences appear in asking support, in asking favors, and in warning the sharing partner. As was expected, the Dutch respondents reported fewer such socially engaging behaviors. Parallel results were obtained with regard to the reported behaviors of the respondents' sharing partners. Few differences were found with regard to their showing understanding or sympathy. The most pronounced differences occurred in advice, in coping assistance, and in the sharing partner otherwise taking an active role. In the Dutch group, the sharing partner showed fewer signs of active commitment than those in the other two cultural groups. There were some other detailed findings indicating that the fine grain of emotion sharing behaviors is where cultural differences are found. The Turkish group, for instance, showed less understanding than the other two groups (66%, as compared with 94% and 87%; $\chi^2 <$ .01), but agreed somewhat more with the respondents' view of the event. Most likely, the difference is due to the more fixed, socially defined meanings of relevant events among the Turkish people than among the other groups.

TABLE 3

Sharing Behaviors During First Instances of Social Sharing

	Dutch (n = 85)	Surinamese (n = 69)	Turkish (n = 68)	χ^2
Providing information				
I told exactly what happened.	82	83	79	
I told how I felt.	76	81	84	
I told what I thought about the actor.	85	86	79	
Soliciting an opinion				
I asked the other person what I should do.	27	32	35	
I asked the other person's opinion about what had happened.	55	65	66	
Actively involving the other person				
I asked the other person to support me or side with me.	21	22	46	**
I asked the other person to do me a favor.	6	78	26	**
I warned the other person about the actor.	5	26	28	**

Note. Entries represent percentage of respondents who indicated to have behaved in the way mentioned.
$**p < .01$.

Conclusion

Emotions have a variety of social functions. These functions derive in part from their very nature as emotions, namely, that of involving states of action readiness and of readiness or unreadiness to engage in interaction with the environment: Joy tends to open up, grief to shut off, and anger to be antagonistic. Other functions derive from the fact that social partners recognize these states of action readiness, undergo the effects of the behaviors that spring from them or expect to do so, and are alerted by them to emotional meanings in the shared environment.

The major social functions of emotions, as we have seen, are (a) modifying interindividual interactions in accordance with what appears to be important at the moment: establishing or breaking contact, self-protecting, accepting, removing or rejecting, as this seems indicated by the meaning of the environmental (or imagined or conceived) events and the valence of other persons; (b) regulating the balance of power, by threats of retaliation (as in anger) or by submission and conformity (as through shame and guilt emotion); (c) determining general patterns of social interaction, such as help-seeking (as in grief), proximity seeking (as in affection or as in grief or its anticipation), and carefulness with regard to others (as in guilt emotion); and (d) representing and motivating social cohesion (as in the social sharing of emotion).

The emotions that emerge are, in large measure, influenced by the immediate social environment and the cultural context. The social environment presents feedback to one's emotions, causing or strengthening emotion regulation, in both the attenuating and the encouraging sense of the concept of regulation, apart of course from providing causes and targets for the emotions as such. It also provides emotional meanings of objects and events, by the manifestations of emotions by its members. The cultural context provides meanings of objects and types of events at a larger and more fixed scale, in rules of behavior, feeling rules, and the prefabricated concepts for coding these events. It does so in particular by establishing the focality of certain emotionally significant event types that represent recurrent themes in the social life of the cultural group concerned.

There are several ways in which emotions fulfill these social functions; emotions play different social roles. First, they ensure the social transmission of emotional interpretations of events. They convey to others the meaning that an individual perceives in these events; these meanings include one's relationship to the event and to relevant others. Emotions can be seen as social statements about the situation, about oneself, and about other people. These social statements may lead to transmission of the emotion itself and of the emotional reaction, as when anger spreads through a group of people. Second, as already indicated, emotions tend to lead to behavior that influences others and that may be meant to do so, either unwittingly, because evolution shapes some behavior for communicative purposes (as when crying, smiling, or looking angrily), or more strategically (as when a show of suffering elicits feelings of guilt in others). Third, emotions tend to elicit reactions in others, either the ones that are meant to be elicited or other ones, like retaliation or approval, that stem from the recipients' own standards, interests, and emotions. These reactions are among the sources of emotion regulation as well as among the instruments for learning emotional meanings. Fourth, emotions being based in part upon socially determined event codings help to maintain these codings and the common emotional definition of the environment.

The social functions of emotions are not added onto the emotions as a secondary consequence of primarily intraindividual events. We may say that emotions have become intraindividual events only secondarily, after having been turned into states of experienced readiness rather than being states of readiness ready to translate into action. Emotions are not only social; one interacts with the physical as well as with the social environment. The social environment, however, is the dominant one in present societies and probably has always been so for the human species.

References

Abu-Lughod, L. (1986). *Veiled sentiments*. Berkeley: University of California Press.

Aries, P. (1974). *Western attitudes towards death*. Baltimore: Johns Hopkins University Press.

Averill, J. R. (1968). Grief: Its nature and significance. *Psychological Bulletin, 70*, 721–748.

Averill, J. R. (1982). *Anger and aggression: An essay on emotion*. New York: Springer.

Axelrod, R. (1984). *The evolution of cooperation*. New York: Basic Books.

Baumeister, R., Stillwell, A. M., & Heatherton, T. F. (in press). Interpersonal aspects of guilt: Two studies using autobiographical narratives. In J. Tangney & K. Fischer (Eds.), *Self-conscious emotions*. New York: Guilford Press.

Black-Michaud, J. (1975). *Feuding societies*. Oxford, England: Basil Blackwell.

Bowlby, J. (1969). *Attachment: Vol. 1. Attachment and loss*. London: Hogarth Press.

Briggs, J. L. (1970). *Never in anger: Portrait of an Eskimo family*. Cambridge, MA: Harvard University Press.

Carver, C. S., & Scheier, M. F. (1990). Origins and functions of positive and negative affect: A control-process view. *Psychological Bulletin, 97*, 19–35.

Conrad, J. (1900). *Lord Jim*. London: Blackwood.

D'Andrade, R. (1984). Cultural meaning systems. In R. A. Shweder & R. A. LeVine (Eds.), *Culture theory: Essays on mind, self, and emotion* (pp. 88–119). Cambridge, England: Cambridge University Press.

Ekman, P., & Friesen, W. V. (1971). Constants across cultures in the face and emotion. *Journal of Personality and Social Psychology, 17*, 124–129.

Ekman, P., & Friesen, W. V. (1975). *Unmasking the face*. Englewood Cliffs, NJ: Prentice Hall.

Elias, N. (1982). *Über den Einsamkeit der Sterbenden in unserer Zeit [The Loneliness of the dying in contemporary times]*. Frankfurt, Germany: Suhr Kamp.

Fehr, B., & Russell, J. A. (1984). Concept of emotion viewed from a prototype perspective. *Journal of Experimental Psychology: General, 113*, 464–486.

Fischer, A. H. (1991). *Emotion scripts. A study of the social and cognitive facets of emotions.* Leiden, The Netherlands: DSWO-Press.

Fisk, R. (1991). *Pity the nation: Lebanon at war.* Oxford, England: Oxford University Press.

Fiske, S. T. (1982). Schema-triggered affect: Applications to social perception. In M. S. Clark & S. T. Fiske (Eds.), *Affect and cognition: The 17th Annual Carnegie Symposium on Cognition* (pp. 55–78). Hillsdale, NJ: Erlbaum.

Fiske, S. T., & Pavelchak, M. A. (1985). Category-based versus piecemeal-based affective responses: Developments in schema-triggered affect. In R. M. Sorrentino & E. T. Higgins (Eds.), *Handbook of motivation and cognition* (pp. 167–203). New York: Wiley.

Frijda, N. H. (1986). *The emotions.* Cambridge, England: Cambridge University Press.

Frijda, N. H. (1993). The place of appraisal in emotion. *Cognition and Emotion, 7*, 357–388.

Frijda, N. H. (1994). The Lex Talionis: On vengeance. In S. H. M. van Goozen, N. E. Van de Poll, & J. A. Sergeant (Eds.), *Emotions: Essays on emotion theory* (pp. 263–289). Hillsdale, NJ: Erlbaum.

Frijda, N. H., & Jahoda, G. (1966). On the scope and methods of cross-cultural research. *International Journal of Psychology, 1*, 109–127.

Frijda, N. H., Kuipers, P. & Terschure, E. (1989). Relations between emotion, appraisal, and emotional action readiness. *Journal of Personality and Social Psychology, 57*, 212–228.

Gallagher, D. J., & Clore, G. L. (1985, May). *Emotion and judgment: Effects of fear and anger on relevant and irrelevant cognitive tasks.* Paper presented at the meeting of the Midwestern Psychological Association, Chicago.

Gomperts, W. (1992). *The opkomst van de sociale phobie* [The rise of social phobias]. Amsterdam: Bert Bakker.

Granet, M. (1922). Le langage de la douleur en Chine [The language of grief in China]. *Journal de Psychologie, 19*, 97–118.

Hochschild, A. R. (1983). *The managed heart.* Berkeley: University of California Press.

Hoffman, M. L. (1984). Interaction of affect and cognition in empathy. In C. E. Izard, J. Kagan, & R. B. Zajonc (Eds.), *Emotions, cognition, and behavior* (pp. 103–131). Cambridge, England: Cambridge University Press.

Jacoby, S. (1983). *Wild justice.* New York: Harper & Row.

Keeler, W. (1983). Shame and stage fright in Java. *Ethos, 11*, 152–165.

Kerkstra, A. (1984). *Conflicthantering bij echtparen* [Conflict management in married couples]. Amsterdam, The Netherlands: Academisch proefschrift, Vrije Universiteit.

Klinnert, M. D., Emde, R. N., & Campos, J. J. (1986). Social referencing: The infant's use of emotional signals from a friendly adult with mother present. *Developmental Psychology, 22*, 427–432.

Kroon, R. M. (1988). *Aanleidingen en structuur van schuldgevoel* [Antecedents and structure of the emotion of guilt]. Unpublished master's thesis, Amsterdam University, The Netherlands.

Laux, L. (1986). A self-presentational view of coping with stress. In M. H. Appley & R. Trumbull (Eds.), *Dynamics of stress* (pp. 233–253). New York: Plenum.

Laux, L., & Weber, H. (1990). Presentation of self in coping with anger and anxiety. *Anxiety Research, 3*, 233–255.

Lazarus, R. S. (1991). *Emotion and adaptation.* New York: Oxford University Press.

Lutz, C. (1988). *Unnatural emotions: Everyday sentiments on a Micronesian atoll and their challenge to western theory.* Chicago: University of Chicago Press.

Markam, S. (1992). *Dimensi pengalaman emosi: Kajian deskriptif melalui rama-emosi berdasarka teori kogniif* [Dimension of emotional experience: Descriptive analysis of emotions according to cognitive theory]. Unpublished doctoral dissertation, University of Indonesia.

Markus, H. R., & Kitayama, S. (1991). Culture and the self: Implications for cognition, emotion, and motivation. *Psychological Review, 98*, 224–253.

Mauro, R., Sato, K., & Tucker, J. (1992). The role of appraisal in human emotions: A cross-cultural study. *Journal of Personality and Social Psychology, 62*, 301–317.

McGraw, K. M. (1987). Guilt following transgression: An attribution of responsibility approach. *Journal of Personality and Social Behavior, 53*, 247–256.

Mesquita, B., & Frijda, N. H. (1992). Cultural variations in emotion: A review. *Psychological Bulletin, 112*, 179–204.

Mesquita, B. Gomes de. (1993). *Cultural variations in emotions: A comparative study of Dutch, Surinamese and Turkish people in the Netherlands.* Unpublished doctoral dissertation, University of Amsterdam, The Netherlands.

Moorkens, P. (1991). *Rapport de stage effectué à l'Université d'Amsterdam concernant le partage social des emotions* [Training report at the University of Amsterdam on the social sharing of emotions]. Unpublished manuscript, Université Catholique de Louvain, Belgium.

Murray, A. D. (1979). Infant crying as an elicitor of parental behavior. An examination of two models. *Psychological Bulletin, 86*, 191–215.

Ortony, A., Clore, G., & Collins, A. (1988). *The cognitive structure of emotions.* Cambridge, England: Cambridge University Press.

Parkinson, B., & Manstead, A. S. R. (1992). Appraisal as a cause of emotion. In M. S. Clark (Ed.), *Emotion: Review of personality and social psychology* (Vol. 13, pp. 122–149). Newbury Park, CA: Sage.

Pincus, L. (1973). *Marriage studies in emotional conflict and growth.* London, England: Tavistock Institute.

Rabbie, J. M. (1992). Over het ontstaan van saamhorigheid en cohesie binnen groepen en van rivaliteit en vijandigheid tussen groepen [Development of solidarity and cohesion within groups, and of competition and hostility between group]. *Onze Alma Mater, 46*, 153–171.

Rachman, S. J. (1990). *Fear and courage* (2nd ed). New York: Freeman.

Rimé, B., Mesquita, B., Philippot, P., and Boca, S. (1991). Beyond the emotional event: Six studies on the social sharing of emotion. *Cognition and Emotion, 5*, 435–465.

Rosaldo, M. Z. (1980). *Knowledge and passion: Ilongot notions of self and social life.* Cambridge, England: Cambridge University Press.

Russell, J. A. (1991). Culture and the categorization of emotions. *Psychological Bulletin, 110*, 426–450.

Schachter, S. (1959). *The psychology of affiliation.* Stanford, CA: Stanford University Press.

Scheff, T. (1988a, April). *Hiding behavior: Toward resolving the shame controversy.* Paper presented at the Conference on Shame Research, Asilomar, CA.

Scheff, T. J. (1988b). Shame and conformity: The deference-emotion system. *American Sociological Review, 53*, 395–406.

Scherer, K. R. (1984). Emotion as a multicomponent process: A model and some cross-cultural data. In P. Shaver (Ed.), *Review of personality and social psychology* (Vol. 5, pp. 37–63). Beverly Hills, CA: Sage.

Scherer, K. R., Wallbott, H. G., & Summerfield, A. B. (Eds.). (1986). *Experiencing emotion: A cross-cultural study.* Cambridge, England: Cambridge University Press.

Schieffelin, E. D. (1983). Anger and shame in the tropical forest: An affect as a cultural system in Papua New Guinea. *Ethos, 11*, 181–191.

Shaver, P., Schwartz, J., Kirson, D. & O'Connor, C. (1987). Emotion knowledge: Further exploration of a prototype approach. *Journal of Personality and Social Behavior, 52*, 1061–1086.

Shweder, R. A. (1991). *Thinking through cultures.* Cambridge, MA: Harvard University Press.

Shweder, R. A. (in press). You're not sick, you're just in love: Emotion as an interpretative system. In P. Ekman & R. Davidson (Eds.), *Questions about emotion.*

Solomon, R. S. (1978). Emotions and anthropology: The logic of emotional world views. *Inquiry, 21*, 181–199.

Stendhal (1991). *Le rouge et le noir* [Red and black]. Paris, France: Editions Folio.

Stearns, C. Z., & Stearns, P. N. (1986). *Anger: The struggle for emotional control in America's history.* Chicago: University of Chicago Press.

Terwijn, H. (1993). *A study of shame experiences.* Unpublished master's thesis, University of Amsterdam, The Netherlands.

Tursky, B. (1974). Physical, physiological and psychological factors that affect pain reaction to electric shock. *Psychophysiology, 11*, 95–112.

Van Hooff, J. A. R. A. M. (1972). A structural analysis of the social behavior of a semi-captive group of chimpanzees. In M. van Cranach & J. Vine (Eds.), *Social communication and movement* (pp. 75–162). San Diego, CA: Academic Press.

Waal, F. de (1982). *Chimpanzee politics.* London, England: Jonathan Cape.

Woodworth, R. S. (1938). *Experimental psychology.* New York: Holt, Rinehart & Winston.

CHAPTER 4

The Cultural Construction of Self and Emotion: Implications for Social Behavior

Hazel Rose Markus and Shinobu Kitayama

In December 1992, the Japanese royal family announced that Crown Prince Naruhito had chosen Masako Owada, a bright, highly educated, fast-track member of the Foreign Ministry, to become the future Empress. Most Japanese were pleased at the prospect of having such a lively and accomplished Princess as part of their monarchy. But according to American press reports, many Americans, as well as many young Japanese women, could not begin to fathom how such a thoroughly modern, internationalized woman, even if she liked the Prince, could toss away a brilliant career to marry him and disappear into the conservative, humorless, controlling royal family where her life would never be her own again and her primary goal would be to produce a male heir to the throne.

As the June marriage approached, it seemed evident, according to analysts on both sides of the Pacific, that Masako Owada felt that it was her "duty" to marry the Prince. From an American perspective, the decision seemed to reflect forced compliance, self-denigration, and self-sacrifice. In giving up her hard-won career, she seemed, in the eyes of many, to be betraying the cause of individual determination, feminism in

Japan, and ultimately, herself. The local controversy surrounding this particular social event is unlikely to be remembered for long, but it illustrates a classic problem in the analysis of social behavior and one that is at the heart of this chapter. From many European–American perspectives, the Princess's decision was "obviously" self-sacrificing and "naturally" accompanied by the emotion of unhappiness at not being able to realize some important defining attribute of the self. However, what is not evident in this analysis is the multileveled, dynamic interdependency among socially appropriate behavior, the self, and emotion.

The American understanding of this Japanese behavior is anchored in a particular individualist approach to the self. From a different orientation, one in which the individual is cast not as an independent entity but as one fundamentally interdependent with others, the decision to marry the Prince could be understood differently. It is possible from this other perspective that the Princess may not have felt sacrifice or injury to the self, but rather affirmation of a more connected, obligation-fulfilling, social self. She may indeed have felt content or "good" as a result of her decision to respond to the desires and expectations of others and marry into the royal family. As is evident in this example and in studies from anthropology and cultural psychology (for recent reviews see Markus & Kitayama, 1991; Moghaddam, Taylor, & Wright, 1993; Shweder, 1991; Shweder & LeVine, 1984; Smith & Bond, 1993; Stigler, Shweder, & Herdt, 1990; Triandis, 1990), what is regarded as positive or negative normative social behavior can vary dramatically from one cultural group to another.

Emotions figure prominently in social behavior, although this is seldom explicitly acknowledged. Emotions are significant because they make possible the social regulation of behavior. Commonly observed social behavior, and its accounts, whether it is inclining naturally toward others and taking their expectancies into account when marrying in Japan, or distancing oneself just as naturally from the expectancies of others and relying on one's current, private, and personal feelings when marrying in the United States, is not merely the result of a blind adherence to powerful norms or of a principled holding fast to a system of values and beliefs. Normative behavior typically *feels* "good" or "right" (cf. D'Andrade, 1984; Spiro, 1961).

Good Feelings and Normative Behavior: The Role of the Self

We suggest that a cultural group's ways of feeling are shaped by the group's habitual and normative social behavior, and in turn, these ways of feeling influence the nature of this social behavior. Consequently, asking how the Princess might have made her decision and how she must have felt about it (whatever its merits or actual antecedents) and describing and analyzing any instance of a given social behavior—identity construction and maintenance, conformity to group pressure, stereotyping and intergroup behavior, or coping and adaptation—will be markedly enhanced by locating it within its dominant cultural frames. An analysis of the emotional responses that accompany various actions provides further access to the cultural and social meaning of these actions. At the same time, variation in normative social behavior provides a window on the interdependence between emotion and culture. Such variation implies that affective reactions, including what types of feeling states are commonly experienced and elaborated, as well as how, and under what conditions these states are experienced, may vary substantially.

Furthermore, we suggest that the nature of the "lock and key" arrangement between affective responses and the social order that has been of pervasive interest to psychologists, sociologists, and anthropologists alike (D'Andrade, 1984; Durkheim, 1953; James, 1890; Lutz, 1988; Radcliffe-Brown, 1952; Schieffelin, 1985; Shweder, 1993; Spiro, 1961) can be further understood with the idea of a self that provides a meeting point and a framework for the relation between the individual and the social world. Each person is embedded within a variety of sociocultural contexts or cultures (e.g., country or region of origin, ethnicity, religion, gender, family, birth cohort, profession). Each of these cultural contexts makes some claim on the person and is associated with a set of ideas and practices (i.e., a cultural framework or schema) about how to be a "good" person. A sense of the "good" is an integral part of one's sense of the self, and one's sense of self shapes what is "good" (e.g., of value, concern, appropriate, etc.) and what is not (Markus & Kitayama, in press; Oyserman & Markus, 1993).

The self, then, is an organized locus of the various, sometimes competing, understandings of how to be a person, and it functions as an individualized orienting, mediating, interpretive framework giving shape to what people notice and think about, to what they are motivated to do, and (the focus of this chapter) to how they feel and their ways of feeling. The self is not a special part of the person or of the brain, it is the entire person considered from particular points of view (Neisser, 1988), and it is the ways in which the person is made meaningful or given significance.

The concept of a self as the particularized locus of various sociocultural influences prevents an oversocialized conception of the person and helps to explain why two people, even those in similar sociocultural circumstances (e.g., twins in the same family) are unlikely to feel exactly the same way in a given set of circumstances. The self of any given individual is some organization of all the various influences of his or her individual social and developmental history. This organization, in which some sociocultural influences are elaborated and emphasized and others are resisted or ignored, affords the person considerable agency and idiosyncracy. The "I" who then feels an affective state or emotion has, as its referent, a particular configuration of self-representations and conceptions that reflect the individual's unique construction of experience. However, there are still ways of feeling that can be linked systematically to particular cultural frameworks, even though a given emotional state cannot be completely explained from these perspectives.[1]

---

[1]A specific focus on the nature of the self is an extension of the ideas of many emotion theorists. Frijda (1986) claimed that "emotions arise when events are relevant to the individual's concerns" (p. 359; see also Mowrer, 1960; Pribram, 1971). Lutz (1988) contended that emotions reflect commitment to seeing the world in particular ways and refer to "what is culturally defined and experienced as 'intensely meaningful'" (p. 8). These concerns and commitments converge in a view of self that structures ongoing experience and the very nature of emotional experience.

In the marriage decision described here, the self that is being sacrificed or affirmed, depending on one's perspective, can assume a variety of forms and functions, depending on the cultural frameworks that have shaped it. The shape of the self (i.e., its various meanings and practices) will, in turn, determine the nature of "good" feelings and of the social behavior that will promote and foster these good feelings. This means that what is experienced as joyful or happy or as sad or angering depends on the mediating self. Aside from the good affective reactions that accompany sweet tastes or smells, or the bad affective reactions that result from extremely loud sounds, bright lights, or hissing snakes, most "good" or "bad" feelings depend on extensive emotional socialization. Through this process, people come to "have" feelings of the shape and variety that reflect the specific value commitments of their significant social groups. Basic to this argument is the idea that being moral (i.e., proper, right, or appropriate) according to one's group, feeling good, and being a person are all intimately connected. As the philosopher Taylor (1989) claimed, "to know who you [are] is to be oriented in moral space, a space in which questions arise about what is good or bad, what is worth doing and what is not, what has meaning and importance for you, and what is trivial and secondary" (p. 28).[2, 3]

[2]The joint shaping of ways of being and ways of feeling can be differentiated from an emphasis on how certain patterns of appraisal, for example, is the event pleasurable, uncertain, or controllable (see Ellsworth, chapter 2, this volume, and Frijda & Mesquita, chapter 3, this volume), determine particular emotions. We are concerned here with questions such as what will feel "good," "proper," "pleasant," or "right," what will feel "bad," "unacceptable," or "unpleasant"; whether personal control and certainty will be experienced as part of feeling "good" or will, instead, be irrelevant to it; and why. The concern is with the mutual and reciprocal enculturation of self and emotions so that certain ways of being naturally feel good or positive, while others feel bad or negative.

[3]One might be tempted to conclude that if good feelings are those that promote or reinforce the self, and that bad feelings do the opposite, then the concept of the self is theoretically superfluous. Yet, the nature and course of social behavior (which includes the emotional experience and its instrumental consequences) will be pervasively influenced by whether good feelings are experienced, as in the example here, as realizing one's own attributes (e.g., ideas, motives, goals) or as fulfilling the expectations of significant others. The nature of the mediating self is thus significant. It is the self that is one of the personalized carriers of the social context. Many of the recent calls to "contextualize" psychological analyses (Gergen, 1992; Sampson, 1988) have gone largely unheeded because it is difficult to determine what is meant by the social context of a given behavior. However, the meanings and practices accorded to the self by a given cultural group are among the important features of the social context that can be localized, specified, and assessed.

Linking Emotions to Culture-Specific Patterns of Behavior

Emotions as Meaningful Social Processes

From a theoretical point of view, emotions may be seen as some amalgam of component processes organized according to the nature of the functional relationship between the person and the environment, and more specifically, according to the relationship of the self, with relevant other people and groups of people (de Riviera, 1984). Emotions connect individuals to their social world and thus are the key to social integration and regulation because they are the basis of the reinforcement and reproduction of behavior (e.g., Zajonc, 1980). As such, they hold in place a group's dominant cultural tendencies, or coordinates, or emphases. For example, D'Andrade (1984) contended that "through the process of socialization individuals come to find achieving culturally prescribed goals and following cultural directives to be motivationally satisfying, and to find not achieving culturally prescribed goals and not following cultural directives to be anxiety producing" (p. 98). Similarly, with socialization, social behavior that is in line with a given cultural imperative or norm and is regarded as "positive" eventually comes to feel "good" and is relatively easily maintained and fostered. Social behavior that is in conflict with the dominant cultural tendencies and is regarded as "negative" social behavior eventually comes to feel "bad" and is rejected and feared (see also Spiro, 1961).

In characterizing the pervasive nature of the cultural frame and its potential influence on emotion, we drew from a type of analysis set up by Bartlett (1932) where he characterized the precise role of the relationship between culture and memory. He wrote:

> Every social group is organized and held together by some specific psychological tendency ... , which gives the group a bias in its dealings with external circumstances. The bias constructs the special persistent features of the group culture and this immediately settles what the individual will observe in his environment. It does this markedly in two ways. First, by providing that setting of interest, excitement, and emotion which favors the development of specific images, and secondly, by providing a persistent

framework of institutions and customs which acts as a schematic basis for constructive memory. (p. 255)

Although Bartlett was not concerned with the source or the nature of a group's core psychological tendency, we suggest that this psychological tendency and the form of subjectivity that accompanies it derives from the cultural group's commitment to a particular meaning or approach to selfhood. We are interested here in charting the close relationship between this core tendency and emotional life. Taylor (1989) provided a useful starting point by sketching the nature of this interdependency:

> My self-definition is understood as an answer to the question Who I am. And this question finds its original sense in the interchange of speakers. I define who I am by defining where I speak from, in the family tree, in social space, in the geography of social status and functions. . . . We first learn our languages of moral and spiritual discernment by being brought into an ongoing conversation by those who bring us up. The meanings that the key words first had for me are the meanings they have for us, that is, for me and my conversation partners together. . . . So I can only learn what anger, love, anxiety, the aspiration to wholeness, etc. are through my and others' experience for us, in some common space. (p. 35)

Cultural Frameworks

Our analysis suggests that one reason for which different types of events make different groups of people happy, sad, or joyful, and for which some groups experience feeling states that are relatively incomprehensible to others is because of formidable differences in the underlying cultural frames of these groups. A cultural frame refers to an interpretive grid, or meaning system, or schema (see Bruner, 1990; D'Andrade, 1987; Shweder, 1993; Wierzbicka, chapter 5, this volume). It consists of language and a set of tacit social understandings, which Quinn and Holland (1987) labeled "vital understandings" (p. 12), as well as of the social representations and practices that reflect and enact these understandings in daily life (Bourdieu, 1972; D'Andrade, 1984; Giddens, 1984; Kitayama & Markus, in press-a; Quinn & Holland, 1987). Some of the elements of a shared cultural schema may be known and obvious to all (D'Andrade, 1987); other elements may be invisible, often taken for granted (Quinn & Holland, 1987), or may even be outside of conscious awareness (Moscovici, 1993).[4]

A Cultural Framework of Independence

In North America, a key element of the cultural framework is a set of beliefs about the self (Markus & Kitayama, 1991; Sampson, 1988; Shweder & LeVine, 1984; Triandis, 1990). These beliefs concern ways of being: what a self is and what to do with it. Such understandings as Taylor (1989) tried to draw out are not merely a metaphysical backdrop. Rather, they configure the nature of the fit between the individual and the cultural environment and structure the adaptive task and thus the nature of emotional reactions. Tied to an ideology of individualism, the self in North America and in much of Europe is defined as an independent, self-contained entity. Specifically, the model is that the self (a) comprises a unique configuration of internal attributes (e.g., traits, emotions, motives, values, and rights) and (b) behaves primarily as a consequence of these internal attributes (Markus & Kitayama, 1991). An explicit social goal from this perspective is to separate one's self from others and not to allow undue influence by others or connection to them.

Most North Americans, as well as many Europeans, particularly those in northern and central Europe, live within societies that are structured according to this perspective of what it means to be a person. Such a perspective is multiply rooted in Western philosophical tradition and is linked to a Cartesian view in which the goal of existence is to objectify the self. According to Lebra (1992), the ontological goal of this perspective is to highlight the division between the experiencer and what is experi-

---

[4]The term *cultural framework* is used because it seems to capture the central tendency of a large family of related terms. The dominant cultural framework includes the cultural group's ideas and ideals (e.g., its values, attitudes, beliefs, schemas, norms—its cultural software) and also its traditions, customs, and institutionalized social practices (e.g., its behavioral rituals, language, rules, legal practices—its cultural hardware) that codify and objectify these ideas and ideals and that make them relatively external, hard, obvious, and real (for a discussion of the importance of practices in cultural frames see Bourdieu, 1980; Gaskins, Miller, & Corsaro, 1992; and Miller, in press). We intend for this term to cover and include other similar terms that we might also have used, such as cultural imperative, normative imperative, design for living, ethos, cultural schema, mode of operation, core psychological tendency, and cultural construal. A variety of important distinctions can and have been made among these terms, but in our use of the term here, we emphasize that a cultural frame is not just a set of ideas, beliefs, or cognitive representations stored in memory.

enced or, in other terms, to separate the individual from the context. We have called the idea of a self as an entity containing significant dispositional attributes and detached from social context the *independent* view of self. It is an important part of the shared cultural frame of North America and Europe, and it is particularly characteristic of White, urban, male, middle-class, secularized, contemporary people.[5]

A Cultural Framework of Interdependence

Another model of the self that stands in significant contrast to the independent view is one that is characteristic of Japan, China, Korea, Southeast Asia, and much of South America and Africa. According to this perspective, the self is not and cannot be separate from others and the surrounding social context. The self is interdependent with the surrounding social context and it is the self-in-relation-to-other that is focal in individual experience (Markus & Kitayama, 1991). In fact, according to Kondo (1990), from the Japanese perspective, the self is fundamentally interrelated with others and to understand the Japanese sense of self requires dissolving the self/other or self/society boundary that is such an obvious starting point in all Western formulations of the self. The cultural press in this alternate model of the self is not to become separate and autonomous from others but to fit-in with others, to fulfill and create obligation, and, in general, to become part of various interpersonal relationships. We have called this view the *interdependent* view of self.

According to Lebra (1992), this interdependent view of self can be traced to Buddhist and, especially in Japan, to Shintoist philosophical traditions within which the very goal of existence is different from that

[5]There are, of course, other ideas about how to be a person, especially in a diverse society like the United States, some of which may even directly contradict the individualist or independent view, and many people may resist the dominant cultural frame in a variety of ways; but the general notion of the independence and autonomy of the individual from others is still influential in shaping social behavior because it is elaborated and given life in a broad net of social customs, practices, and institutions with a pervasive range of influence. This view of a cultural frame allows us to explain how a set of ideas or values can remain influential even when some individuals do not actively endorse them or behave accordingly (Kitayama & Markus, in press-a; Lave, Stepick, & Sailer, 1977). For example, many Americans would not claim that they are independent, autonomous entities; rather, they experience themselves as interdependent, highly social, and affiliative. Yet, they are constantly exposed to the individualist idea and its related practices because they live within a society created by and based on it.

assumed in the West. From this view, the core notion is not to "objectify the self" but to submerge the self and "gain freedom from the self." The emphasis is on downplaying the division between the experiencer and the object of experience, and it is connection with, rather than separation from others and the surrounding context that is highlighted.[6]

Much more could and must be said about these apparently startling differences in ontological emphasis (see Lebra, 1992; and Markus & Kitayama, 1991, for extended discussions of these differences), and the variety of other ontologies that must also exist should be drawn out, but our purpose here is simply to underscore that these divergent views of what the self should be are critical underpinnings of emotional experience. These ways of being are significant elements of the cultural frame, and as sketched by Bartlett (1932), they form the framework for individual experience of emotions and social behavior. If the self functions as an interpretive, integrative, or orienting framework for individual behavior, then whether one has a self that is shaped by a European–American ontological tradition or by an Asian one has the potential to make an enormous difference in how life is lived—what kinds of experiences will feel "good" and what social behavior will be coded as "positive," and what kinds of experiences will produce "bad" feelings and will accompany "negative" social behavior.

In our work, we compare cultural groups from different regions of origin (European–Americans and Asians). Although many other cultural comparisons are possible and interesting, there is now sufficient empirical work on this particular cultural comparison to begin to evaluate hypotheses about the nature of the connections among emotions, self, and

---

[6]In earlier papers (Kitayama & Markus, in press-a; Markus & Kitayama, 1991), we distinguished independence and interdependence as two broad sets of tasks that people need to perform in social life. Independence refers to a set of tasks or psychological tendencies to separate the self from the social context, encompassing goals of agency, autonomy, and disengagement from others. Interdependence, on the other hand, implies a set of tasks for psychological tendencies to connect the self with others, encompassing such goals as affiliation, communion, and engagement with others. We have suggested that these two tasks can be differently combined and incorporated into the definition and construction of the self, as well as into the pattern of cultural ideology, customs, and institutions. The two tasks—independence and interdependence—are assumed to be present in every culture, but cultures vary in the ways in which these tasks are weighted and organized in social life and manifest in individual thought and action.

social behavior. For example, when comparing American university students with Japanese university students, we do not assume that all individuals in a given cultural group are alike. We suggest only that members of a given group are more likely to have been exposed to and have operated within a given cultural frame than members of the contrasting group, and thus members of the same cultural group may share *some* similar behavioral tendencies or patterns. Thus, the Japanese, the Chinese, and the Koreans share a powerful philosophical tradition that is strikingly different from that of the West. But these three groups, as well as the individuals within each group, are obviously different from each other in numerous other ways.

Emotion and the Cultural Framework

A cultural framework includes a group's sense of and attitudes toward emotions, that is, what emotions or feelings are, why they are experienced, and what their significance is in social life, as well as the implicit answers to questions like *when* does one feel, *where* does one feel, and *how* does one feel. The cultural framework also includes an understanding of what kinds of events emotions are, for example, are they considered to be individual products that are agentically produced and experienced privately and corporeally, or are they considered to be communicative processes or interpersonal moods that define the relationships among two or more people (Jenkins, 1991).

Miller (in press) suggested that cultures can diverge even further in their understandings of emotions. Reviewing the anthropological evidence, she claimed that "many cultures do not share the concept of emotion assumed in psychological theory, with various cultures linking what might be considered to constitute emotional elicitors only to physical illness, making no distinction between thoughts and feelings or objectifying emotions" (p. 24; see also Gerber, 1975; Levy, 1973; Lutz, 1988; Lynch, 1990; Potter, 1988; Shweder, 1993). Lutz (1988) described an emotion concept as a confluence of cultural worldviews and scripts for social behavior. Specifically, she suggested that "to understand the meaning of an emotion is to be able to envisage (and perhaps to find oneself able to participate in) a complicated scene with actors, actions, interpersonal relationships in a particular state of repair, moral points of view, facial expressions, personal and social goals, and sequences of events" (p. 10).

Once it is acknowledged that emotions are more than just biologically prewired internal processes or bodily states (e.g., Kitayama & Markus, in press-b; Lutz, 1988; Rosaldo, 1984; White, chapter 7, this volume; Wierzbicka, chapter 5, this volume), it is evident that the very category of "emotion" can be constructed or assigned meaning in a variety of ways, and its very rank and standing among categories involved in the explanation of social behavior may vary dramatically.

Among those cultural groups that emphasize the importance of emotions in behavior, the answer given to the question "What *is* an emotion?" depends on how a group thinks about the nature of its functional relationship with the cultural environment. This understanding, in turn, will determine which aspect of the emotional experience or combination of aspects (e.g., the physiological, the subjective, the intersubjective, the instrumental action) will be emphasized and elaborated in experience as well as the role of these emotions in social behavior.

If an emotion is some amalgam of component processes that are organized by the nature of the functional relationship between the self and the cultural environment, then somewhat different sets of these components are highlighted and they are, in turn, combined in different ways depending on the pertinent cultural frame within which they are allowed to function. Specifically, given an independent frame for living and interacting with others, it may be the subjective part of one's emotional dynamics that is highlighted and elaborated; whereas given an alternative interdependent frame, it may be the interpersonal or intersubjective aspects of emotional experience that receive greater attention and elaboration. Furthermore, this divergent emphasis in emotional experience may in turn lead to correspondingly divergent definitions or emotion prototypes of *feeling good*. This means that outer or external cultural frames are inscribed into the inner or internal emotional experience. In this way, emotion may serve as the most proximate or experience-near carrier of cultural imperatives or assumptions about what constitutes the self, others, and the relationship between the two.

Emotion as Subjective Versus Intersubjective

From an independent view of the self, the most important features of the self are the internal and private ones, and thus the corresponding individual, subjective experience will receive an elaborated and privileged place in the behavioral process (Levy, 1984). Key features of this subjectivity are a heightened awareness of one's inner attributes and the tendency to organize one's reactions and actions according to these attributes. The goal is to realize and express these internal attributes. Subjective experience is a result of these efforts that, in turn, fosters these efforts.

For example, in the United States, it is the emotional states that have the individual's internal attributes (his or her needs, goals, desires, or abilities) as the primary referent that are most commonly manifest. They typically result from the blocking (e.g., "I was treated unfairly") or the satisfaction or the confirmation (e.g., "I performed better than others") of one's internal attributes. The emotion of anger, even when caused by the actions of another person, focuses one on the individual goal that has been blocked or on the individual right that has been abridged. Consequently, apparently negative emotions like anger or frustration are not entirely undesirable (certainly not as undesirable as in Japan) because such emotions highlight individual, private, internal attributes and signal that the imperative of the cultural framework—in this case independence—is being served.

For example, many North American self-help groups now work with victims of rape or incest to turn what is regarded within the cultural frame as the passive and negative emotion of shame into the more productive and desirable emotion of anger (see Kitayama & Markus, in press-b). The tendency toward independence of the self from the other requires and fosters the emotions that promote the felt independence and disengagement of self from others. Pleasant feelings or emotional states (like happiness or pride) and unpleasant feelings (like anger and frustration) highlight the fundamental separation of self from others and will feel "natural," "right," or "good." From the perspective in which emotions are private and internal phenomena, some reasonable intensity and some variability in emotional state are positive and promote the felt independence of self.

By contrast, from an interdependent view of the self, the most important features of the self are external and public: status, roles, and relationships. In contrast to individual, subjective experience, it is the intersubjectivity that results from interdependence and connection that receives a relatively elaborated and privileged place in the behavioral process. Key features of this intersubjectivity are a heightened sense of the other and of the nature of one's relation to the other and the expectation of some mutuality in this regard. The goal is not individual awareness, experience, and expression, but rather some attunement or alignment of one's reactions and actions with those of another, and intersubjective experience is a result of these efforts and, in turn, fosters these efforts.

Thus in Japan, it is the emotional states or feelings that accompany interdependence—friendly feelings, feelings of affiliation, calmness, smoothness, or connectedness—that are regarded as positive or desirable. The emotional state of anger experienced in an in-group setting is very troubling and regarded as extremely negative by the Japanese primarily because the manifestation of anger serves to break or disturb the relations producing interdependence.

The tendency toward interdependence of the self with others requires and fosters the relational, social emotions—sympathy, modesty (i.e., humility), agreeableness (i.e., harmony, balance, restraint). These emotions promote the felt interdependence of self with others and such engagement feels "natural," "right," and "good." The most common negative emotions are likely to be those that accompany a faltering of interdependence (anxiety, fear, shame) and a perceived disengagement of self from others. When these feelings are experienced, certain features of an interdependent relationship (e.g., harmony, tension, etc.) will be highlighted and the self will be perceived as being embedded and assimilated within the relationship. Thus, pleasant emotions (like feelings of closeness) highlight the unity and synchrony between the self and others in the relationship. Even unpleasant emotions in this category (feelings of indebtedness) focus attention not on the self, but on the relationship. These, then, are the emotions that have the most important social functions and the ones that will be promoted by "good" or "desirable" social behavior. From this perspective, relatively low levels of intensity and a relative constancy in an emotional state will be experienced as positive.

This difference in the definition of what constitutes an emotional experience or in how an emotional state is defined can be illustrated with a concrete recent empirical example. In a study comparing Americans with West Sumatrans (the Minangkabau), Levenson, Ekman, Heider, and Friesen (1992) found a remarkable cross-cultural divergence in the subjective experience of emotion along with an equally notable cross-cultural similarity in autonomic responses. Among Americans, they observed that posing the face to mimic positive and negative emotional expressions seems to cause systematic autonomic changes as well as the corresponding changes in subjective feelings. Thus, facial patterns that mimicked positive emotions resulted in positive subjective feelings, and those that mimicked negative emotions were linked with negative feelings. Among the Minangkabau respondents, the posed faces also caused similar autonomic changes, suggesting the presence of prewired and largely culture-free physiological and neurochemical networks connecting sensory signals from facial musculature with the functioning of autonomic nervous systems. However, among the Minangkabau respondents the posed faces did not produce any corresponding change in subjective feeling.

Later analysis of the cultural understandings of the Minangkabau by Levenson et al. (1992) revealed that these respondents may have had difficulty describing their emotional states because they were alone. Emotions for the Minangkabau, as with the Japanese, are typically experienced in the presence of others—relationally, interpersonally. By definition, an emotional event requires another person for its evocation, experience, and expression. To extend their initial analysis, one could argue that the subjectivity of the Minangkabau was keyed or tuned to the presence of others. So, in contrast with the Americans, the activity of the autonomic nervous system stemming from the configuration of the facial musculature did not constitute an emotion. Such results are consistent with the suggestion that Americans and Minangkabaus define emotions differently, and that they have different expectations about when and why an emotion will be experienced. This is one of the important ways in which a group's way of being structures emotional experience.

If groups differ in what they regard as an emotion and in their views of what gives rise to particular types of emotions, they are also likely to differ in what feelings they believe should properly accompany these antecedent events, and in what to do about these feelings (i.e., what sorts of instrumental responses are appropriate or how to express or manage these feelings). It is likely, then, that there will be systematic variation in some aspects of the emotional sequences or scripts that have been identified by emotion theorists (e.g., Frijda, 1986; Shweder, 1993).

In addition to determining what kind of an event an emotion is, cultural frames structure emotions in other, more specific ways. Specifically, many social events come "preappraised" in that there is no uncertainty or decision to be made about what kind of event has occurred. In such a case, the nature of the event has been collectively determined at a time prior to the actual eliciting event. The individual does not have to participate actively in the appraisal process. The cultural frame determines which dimensions of appraisal are most relevant and often elaborates only one of the endpoints of these dimensions. Frijda and Mesquita (chapter 3, this volume) call this preappraisal process *event-coding*. They contend that when cultures assign labels to events, such as a terrorist attack, they also determine the appropriate affective reaction. So for example, Americans are particularly tuned to positive social events, and many events are already coded as positive and likely to be associated with good feelings. They are also tuned to "see" events in terms of their own efforts and to perceive them as personally controllable. Thus, a good grade on an exam for an American student is preappraised as a positive, controllable event—the good feeling is automatic.

In terms of Frijda and Mesquita's (chapter 3, this volume) framework, cultural frames also shape emotion by inscribing in the self habitual domains of concern and also patterns of action readiness and behavior that are tightly linked to particular appraisals. The understanding that the self is fundamentally interdependent with others highlights domains of concern and emphasizes particular patterns of appraisal and action readiness. By contrast, an understanding of the self as autonomous sets up distinctly different concerns and behavioral patterns. In this manner, ways of feeling are specifically and continually enculturated in accordance with and commensurate with particular ways of being.

Divergent Ways of Being a Self and Feeling Good

In this section, we draw together studies conducted in different places for different purposes but that, together, begin to provide empirical support for the connections between self, emotion, and social behavior that have been hypothesized here. We illustrate the mutual and reciprocal relations between particular views of self, emotional experiences, and culture-specific patterns of thinking, acting, and interacting. The focus is on the simultaneous enculturation of independence and of pride and on individual happiness among North Americans and, similarly, on the simultaneous enculturation of interdependence and feelings of connection and relatedness among Asians. We illustrate how ways of being and ways of feeling good are interrelated and, together, part and parcel of the ideas and practices of the dominant cultural frames. We can see here the outlines of a process whereby the stances and commitments of a given cultural frame are incorporated into each individual's subjectivity and intersubjectivity.

In North America and in large parts of Europe, identity formation is most typically tied to the need and the ability to distinguish one's self from others: to individuate the self progressively. European–American psychologists have repeatedly demonstrated what appears to be an extremely powerful and, presumably, universal motive to believe that one is somewhat better than one's peers (Harter, 1990). It is among the most robust and well-documented findings of psychology. American children as young as four believe themselves to be better than their peers. American adults typically consider themselves to be more intelligent, friendlier, and more attractive than the average adult. A recent finding is that 70% of people in a national sample thought that they were above average in leadership ability and that they were smarter, more considerate, and more in control than their peers (Myers, 1989). Furthermore, American adults have more positive expectations for themselves and their futures than they have for other people. They believe that they are more likely to own their own home and earn a large salary and are less likely to contract a deadly disease or get divorced than other people.

This well-known, well-documented tendency to underestimate the commonality of one's desirable behaviors has been called the *false uniqueness effect* (Mullen & Riordan, 1988; Myers, 1989). It is believed to be one clear method of enhancing self-esteem. The reason that being positively different from others produces a good feeling about the self is seldom broached (see Josephs, Markus, & Tarafodi, 1992, for a discussion of this point). Typically, it is regarded as self-evident that being different in a positive sense produces a good feeling. One answer to such a question is that feeling positive about the self depends in part on realizing the approach to selfhood required by an independent culture. Realizing one's self as different in a positive sense validates, in Bartlett's (1932) terms, the group's core psychological tendency.

Yet, if a cultural group has a different core psychological tendency, as may be true of Asian cultural groups, then some very different social behavior may be associated with good feelings about the self. In this case, maintaining the self may assume a different form for more relational or interdependent selves. Positive feelings may not be linked with self-serving biases or with trying to see the self as positively unique. Good feelings may derive instead from realizing the approach to selfhood required by these interdependent cultures. Indeed, good feelings may be a function of good social relationships (i.e., fitting-in, belonging, maintaining harmony in one's relations, occupying one's proper place, engaging in appropriate action) while at the same time regulating one's inner personal thoughts and feelings so as to ensure interdependence. Such an interdependent perspective on the source and nature of good feelings may afford some understanding of why, on the occasion of her marriage to the Crown Prince of Japan, the Princess's mother could advise her daughter, "Be happy! Do the utmost to serve your country." From an independent perspective, happiness and serving one's country are not obvious partners.

In a study comparing a representative sample of Japanese college students in Japan and American college students in the United States, Markus and Kitayama (1991) found that it was the Americans who showed a distinct false uniqueness bias. When asked "What proportion of your peers is better than you are," in each of nine different domains, they believed that they were different from and better than others on all kinds of abilities (mathematics, athletics, language, memory) with regard to their independence and autonomy and even with regard to their sympathy and warmheartedness. On average, American college students reported that only 30% of their peers were better than they. In a representative sample, if people answer questions in an unbiased way, the group estimate should hover at 50%, which would indicate no bias in estimation.

The Japanese college students did not reveal such a false uniqueness bias. For these respondents, their estimates did hover around 50%. The departure from this estimate that did occur was found to be for women who believed that most other Japanese people were somewhat better than they. Takata (1987) has suggested that these results reflect what could be called a self-harmonizing bias among the Japanese—a reflection of the core psychological tendency of the interdependent cultural frame—to see one's self as part of a whole with others and thus like others in important ways.

Stigler, Smith, and Mao (1985), in a study of elementary school children in the United States and China, found a similar persistent tendency for Chinese children not to distinguish themselves on ratings of self-worth and competence. The Chinese children rated themselves significantly lower than the American children on the cognitive, physical, and general subscales of Harter's Perceived Competence Scale for Children, which specifically requires children to compare themselves with other children. This study also found that, for American children, there was a strong correlation between general self-esteem and esteem for particular domains of self (i.e., cognitive, social, physical) (rs $= .46–.53$). These correlations were low for the Chinese children (rs $= .23–.30$). Stigler et al. (1985) suggested that the scale may have activated what they called "strong self-effacing tendencies" among the Chinese.

Both false uniqueness and false modesty or self-effacement may be viewed as social judgment tendencies or habits of cognitive behavior that support and reflect their underlying cultural frames. Many Americans find the Japanese behavior in these circumstances difficult to understand or believe. Could it really be the case that some Asians actually prefer to believe that others are better than they are or, as has been shown in other studies, actually have more confidence in a test that showed them to be performing less well than their peers (Markus & Kitayama, 1991; Schwartz & Smith, 1976; Takata, 1987)? Could there actually be a concern that could rival good feelings about one's self and the continued pursuit of such positive self-feelings as a major life-organizing goal or motive (the Princess question again)?

Although there is probably little question that modesty is sometimes false, representing primarily an attempt at impression management, in many cases, self-effacement may follow naturally from a desire to maintain the self as an interdependent and respectable agent. Within an interdependent cultural frame, self-harmonizing can lead to a sense of fitting-in, the recognition of fully participating in a relationship, thereby meeting the criteria for positive social behavior and giving rise to a feeling of satisfaction that one is a worthy member of the community.

To answer questions regarding the authenticity of such social behavior requires understanding of the feeling states that accompany the self-serving, false uniqueness bias or the seemingly self-denying or self-harmonizing bias. In a recent study, Kitayama, Markus, and Kurokawa (1991) presented both Japanese college students in Japan and American college students in the United States with a number of labels for emotions, feelings, or sentiments—some indigenous to Americans and some indigenous to Japanese—and asked how frequently they experienced each of them in everyday life. The Americans reported an overwhelmingly greater frequency of experiencing positive than negative self-relevant feelings, but there was virtually no such effect among the Japanese.

Similarly, Akiyama (1992), in a national probability sample of 2,200 Japanese aged 60 years and older, found that the inverse correlation between negative affect and positive affect that characterized the American sample did not appear for the Japanese. There was virtually no correlation between negative and positive affect in the Japanese sample, and both positive and negative affect levels were considerably lower than those of American respondents. Akiyama suggested that because Japanese are not socialized to monitor, elaborate, or express their own self-feelings, such feelings are less likely to be encoded and recalled. Consistent with this suggestion, Matsumoto (1992) found that Americans are more accurate than the Japanese at recognizing four of Ekman's six basic emotions. Perceiving or experiencing an emotion may require, as in the Levenson et al. (1992) study described earlier, the participation of others. Feelings about the self—the core of emotion for those with independent selves—may not be sufficient to experience an emotion.

In contrast, Americans tied to an independent cultural framework will highlight and emphasize their individual feeling states precisely because such feelings are self-definitional. Self-relevant feelings are necessary, important, and the more the better. This fits with the culturally shared imperative to create, or define, or objectify the self. As Wierzbicka (chapter 5, this volume) pointed out, knowing that one feels, what one feels, and that one can instrumentally control one's emotions is extremely important in Anglo-American culture. Other observers have even claimed that Americans seem preoccupied with noting, registering, and in general, "working" on their emotions (e.g., Bellah, Madsen, Sullivan, Swidler, & Tipton, 1985). Positive self-feelings signal that a separate self or identity has been forged and will, in addition, function as an indicator of the adequacy and integrity of the self.

Positive *self* feelings are the basis of all good feeling. Self-esteem is typically operationalized as the total amount of good feelings directed toward the self (Epstein, 1973; Harter & Marold, 1991), and it is the basis of happiness American style, at least currently. Happiness indeed means "I feel good" and it plays a central role in American discourse and is the basis of psychological well-being (Wierzbicka, chapter 5, this volume). The American practice of smiling and being generally friendly is important because it is an indication that one has good self-feelings and such feelings reflect that one has the culturally required good inner self. That is, they indicate that the observed behavior is being directed by an autonomous self replete with positive attributes. Happiness and elation are apparently of a different nature in Japan and seem to require an awareness and assurance of connection and interdependence.

In a further exploration of the connection between general good feelings and more specific emotional experiences, we (Kitayama et al.,

1993) asked Japanese college students in Japan and American college students in the United States to indicate the frequency with which they had experienced a variety of feeling states. There was a high correlation between generic positive feelings (such as, relaxed, calm, happy, and elated—and feelings that can be applied to a range of situations) and positive feelings derived from interpersonally engaged emotional experiences (such as feelings of connection, friendly feelings—rs = .54–.81). The frequency of experiencing the general positive feelings correlated much less well with the frequency with which the respondents experienced positive feelings deriving from their own personal achievement (such as pride, feelings of superiority, and feeling "like being at the top of the world"—rs = .15–.39). These later feelings were, in fact, correlated highly with negative feelings: Those who felt good about their personal accomplishments were also those who felt the most negatively—not relaxed, not calm. These data on feelings are consistent with the Japanese belief that the "nail that sticks up gets pounded down."

The data from the American students were entirely different. General positive feelings were highly correlated with positive feelings rooted in personal achievements like pride (rs = .58–.66) and only moderately correlated with feelings rooted in interpersonal connection (rs = .06–.35), like friendly feelings toward others. These data suggest that beliefs in one's uniqueness and positive difference from others, as in the study by Kitayama, Markus, Kurokawa, and Negishi (1993), are likely to be associated with good feelings, self-esteem, and happiness, and people may indeed avoid pointed social comparison so as to maintain these positive self-feelings.

In a different type of study, Choi and Choi (1990) also explored the links between what it means to be a self and emotion. They asked Korean students in Korea and Canadian students in Canada what the word "we" signified. In the Korean group, 55% of the responses referred to affection, intimacy, comfort, and acceptance; among the Canadians only 15% of their responses of the meaning of "we" made reference to affective bonds. The most common "we" groups for the Koreans were family, friends, and groups of students, and when asked what were the essential factors for we-ness with others, affective responses were more important than responses relating to self-sacrifice or to submitting to group goals. Choi and Choi persuasively argued that North Americans think of groups primarily as collections of separate individuals and assume that feelings of we-ness are based on awareness of commonality or similarity. Such an analysis takes for granted the separation among individuals (cf. Kondo, 1990). Choi and Choi (1990) argued that we-ness for Koreans is rooted instead in affective, emotional forces (the connotative sense is of softness and comfort) and not in shared interest or similarity requiring first that A regard B as a separate entity and vice versa.

In another comparison of Koreans and Americans, Maday and Szalay (1976) asked respondents to free-associate to the label "me." For the Americans, the four most frequent categories were (a) I, person, individual; (b) other people; (c) physical appearance; and (d) good, friendly, sociable. The four most frequent themes for the Koreans were (a) family, love; (b) ideals, happiness, freedom; (c) hope, ambition, success; and (d) material goods. The notion that, for interdependent selves, the "me" includes important others is also implied by a study examining cultural variation in self-evaluation (Cross, Liao, & Josephs, 1992). Tesser (1988) has shown, with American respondents, that people feel good when a close other performs well in a non-self-relevant domain, but bad when a close other performs well in a highly relevant domain. Cross et al. (1992) reasoned that for those individuals that include others as part of the self or have an interdependent self in which relations with others are the self-defining units, self-evaluation maintenance may assume a different form. They found that in contrast with Americans, Chinese students in Taiwan did not feel threatened or bad when a close other performed well in relevant domains.

Overall, among those assumed to have independent selves, the positive feelings produced by personal achievement and the attendant tendencies to self-enhance seem genuinely positive, capable of alleviating other negative feelings or sentiments, and associated with a general sense of happiness. In contrast, among those assumed to have selves with a more interdependent cast, general happiness or satisfaction, is related most closely to the confirmation of the self as part of the unitary, ongoing relationship. From this point of view, the self-harmonizing or self-effacement observed in the studies of false uniqueness can be conducive, much more than self-enhancement, to positive feelings or satisfaction.

Without some attention to what the cultural frame of interdependence requires for selfhood and good feeling, one could be led to believe, as some earlier investigators were, that the interdependent selves have difficulty constructing a positive identity and show excessive amounts of fatalism, dependence, and anxiety. For example, Hartnack (1987) has shown how British psychoanalysts identified these and other negative attributes as basic to the Indian personality and then used their findings to justify continued British rule. It is evident that a consideration of self and self-processes must reflect the cultural framework or what it means to be a self. The construction and maintenance of the self as well as all the hypothesized self-processes (self-evaluation, self-esteem, self-presentation, self-consciousness, self-effacement) are all conditioned by the meaning or significance that is attached to the self.

These studies begin to delineate the role of the self in shaping emotion and suggest how differences in the behaviors associated with self-construction and maintenance (e.g., self-aggrandizing or self-harmonizing) can be reconciled when these practices are located within their relevant cultural frame. Positive emotions serve many global and specific interpersonal functions. Initially, and very important, they signal the accomplishment of the important cultural task of being a person in the prescribed way. Thus, for those with interdependent selves, feeling good requires a connection to others, and a connection to others produces good feelings. Similarly, for those with independent selves, feeling good and positive emotions necessitate a separation from others, and beliefs and practices that emphasize this separation feel good and are the basis of self-esteem.

Shaping the Ways of Feeling Good

Given the demonstrated interdependence between models of the self and the meaning and nature of emotion, we can ask how this powerful interdependence is created. If, as these data suggest, American children experience happiness and an entire range of general good feelings when they have reason to believe that they have some qualities or attributes that distinguish them from others in a positive manner, we can ask why it is that "standing-out," at least to some extent, feels good. Similarly, we can ask why Japanese children feel good when they fit-in. One preliminary answer might come from a detailed analysis of emotional socialization practices. For example, many American children are constantly praised and rewarded for work that they have done and projects that they have created. These children are habitually encouraged to identify attributes of the self that are unique in a positive manner. Initially, the child's caretakers help with this (e.g., "Sarah, you did such a great job on that painting, I am proud of you") regardless of what Sarah has actually done. A recent study by Little, Oettingen, Stetsenko, and Baltes (1994), comparing Russian, German (East and West), and American elementary school children for the relationship between estimates of self-efficacy and actual performance, showed this correlation to be lower among American children than among other groups.

Young children in the United States receive a great deal of positive reinforcement that is not particularly contingent on actual performance. For example, in sharp contrast with schoolchildren in most other parts of the world, American children are rarely given information about their relative rank in the classroom. Increasingly, in elementary schools, students receive no grades, and activities that foster competition and thus provide information about one's standing relative to others (even sports activities) are discouraged. These educational practices set up a situation in which students' beliefs about themselves and their abilities are relatively unconstrained. In the early grades at least, situations are constructed so that children can hold a set of positive beliefs about themselves. Obviously, it does not work in all cases. Many American children still feel negatively about themselves; but, in general, such practices are likely to lead to beliefs in one's relative uniqueness.

Similarly, many current child-rearing practices are geared toward helping the child develop a distinct sense of self that he or she can feel good about. A recent study (Chao, 1993b) found that 64% of European–American mothers in a California sample, as opposed to 8% of Chinese mothers in this sample, stressed building children's "sense of themselves" as an important goal of child rearing. Furthermore, criticism of children's actions was often explicitly avoided.

American children very quickly internalize the habit of identifying positive features in their own behavior, come to believe that they are better than others, and construct an identity that is built primarily around positive attributes. On average, the self-concepts of Americans contain about four to five times as many positive attributes as negative ones (Markus, Herzog, Holmberg, & Dielman, 1992). For North Americans, there is only one self, and it must be as positive as possible. In contrast, the Japanese self appears to be more fractionated, containing both a private self and a public self (Kuwayama, 1992; Rohlen, 1991). Given these two different aspects of self, there appears to be less concern among the Japanese in identifying and elaborating positive, personal attributes in the private self because it is the outside, public part of the self that makes contact with others and regulates social behavior. If one lives up to commitments, obligations, and responsibilities and their various roles, statuses and positions, it is decidedly less threatening to elaborate on shortcomings or negative aspects of the private self and to draw attention to them (Kim, 1992; Kim, Triandis, Kagitcibasi, Choi, Yoon, in press; Rohlen, 1989, 1991). In fact, self-criticism is valued, desired, and promoted in Japan. Schoolchildren are often instructed to think about what they did wrong and how to improve their performance the next day. Adults also engage in self-criticism: Professional baseball players, for example, are required to find publicly the flaws in their own playing (Whiting, 1989).

On the basis of this collection of findings, we can hypothesize that those with independent selves will develop self-evaluative schemas that are especially sensitive or "tuned in" to positive information. These people will be motivated to feel unique in a positive manner and, when they are able to construct or locate such information, they will feel good. Discussing and expressing positive, internal attributes of the self is the "right" thing to do. By contrast, those with interdependent selves are habitually motivated to fit-in with or align themselves with the group. When children fit and find their proper place, they become part of the whole and are not distinctive. This does not automatically imply learning how to give up or sacrifice one's own interest and wishes for the good of the group (Choi & Choi, 1990; Kim, 1992; Kim et al., in press). Rather, children learn that working together harmoniously is a way of creating and affirming the self. Kagitcibasi (1989) noted that whereas Canadian mothers are notable in efforts to "detach themselves" from their children, Japanese mothers do everything possible to convey a oneness between the mother and the child as the most desirable end state.

Peak (1991), in an examination of Japanese preschools, claimed that Japanese children are specifically taught about the "joy" of group life. In fact, Japanese mothers report that the primary reason for sending children to nursery school is to teach them how to fit in with their peers. It is the school's duty to teach group living (Peak, 1991; Rohlen, 1989). Recent studies reveal that Japanese teachers, in comparison with American teachers, direct their comments and questions to the group as a whole rather than to specific individuals (Hamilton, Blumenfeld, Akoh, & Miura, 1991). Similarly, Chinese children are encouraged to see the world as a network of relationships of which they are a part (Hsu, 1953). Chao (1993a) found that Chinese mothers explicitly stress fostering a happy, close, harmonious relationship with the child, as opposed to building self-esteem, as a goal of child rearing. When children learn to align their own goals with those of the group and find their proper place in a social network and "fit it," they are not distinctive.

The emphasis in interdependent child rearing is on attending to those circumstances in which the child is not aligned or does not fit-it. Deviations from the expectations of others need to be carefully monitored and, when detected, corrected. Here again, the caretaker plays a crucial role in helping the child find potential deficits or problems in his or her behavior. When a child is misbehaving, a caretaker might say "Kazuo, you are acting very strange; your friends may laugh at you if they see it." Attention is drawn to how the child is not behaving as expected, and the punishment involves being made to stand out, which poses a threat to the relationship between the child and the group. As a consequence, we can hypothesize that the self-evaluative schemas of those from interdependent cultures will eventually become especially sensitive and tuned not to positive but to negative, self-relevant information. If children begin at an early age to embody the cultural imperative in this way, it is not surprising that, by college, these students will be much more sensitive and responsive to events that may cause them to feel bad about themselves.

A focus on emotional socialization can also provide insight into why the Japanese are motivated to believe that they fit with others and are not at all distinctive from others (i.e., why they show self-harmonizing or self-effacement rather than false uniqueness), and why it is that the most frequently experienced negative emotion among the Japanese is a fear of causing trouble or of burdening someone else (i.e., as observed in Kitayama et al., 1991). Children of interdependent cultures, then, may become relative experts with regard to the negative or bad aspects of their behavior and, in every case, bad feelings result from disturbances or difficulties with social relations (Rohlen, 1989). All good affective responses involve the realization or expression of close, secure, harmonious relations (Azuma, 1986). Although the practices involved are likely to be somewhat different, Kim (1992; Kim et al., in press) reported that such socialization for interdependence has also been documented in Indian culture (Kakar, 1978; Sinha & Verma, 1987) and in Turkish culture (Kagitcibasi & Sunar, in press).

The data here are hardly sufficient or compelling, but they suggest the broad outlines of an enculturation process whereby the child comes to feel as his or her group does. The cultural framework is also created and reinforced through linguistic practices and through the artifacts, practices, and institutions of the society that reflect and promote this idea.[7] Although it may be difficult to fathom from an American viewpoint, within an interdependent cultural framework that what is labeled self-effacement can feel good, and an entire set of socialization practices works to ensure this link. Such apparently self-denying behavior is in the service of fitting-in. These practices reinforce the sense of being fully participating in a relationship and the ultimate sense of satisfaction as a worthy member of the community. Living up to this idea of being a person is then related to good feelings and to contentment or satisfaction in one's own life.

---

[7]For a discussion of some of these other practices, see Kitayama and Markus (in press-a) and Markus and Kitayama (in press).

Labeling such behavior as *self-effacement* is misleading, because although one's personal attributes may not be the focus of attention—indeed they may be relatively ignored—the interdependent self (i.e., the self as a member of a community) is very much promoted and affirmed. Obviously, a great deal more needs to be done to specify fully the transformation of the cultural imperative into individual subjectivity; but even at this initial point, we can understand how it is that the Japanese future Empress may feel good about her decision to marry into the royal family, and we can draw out some implications for future study of social behavior in cross-cultural perspectives.

Implications for Social Behavior

If we assume that the emotional experiences that affirm the cultural frame are those that will be highlighted and emphasized, then certain social behavior that elicits, fosters, or reflects the focal emotions should be relatively common. The social behavior of various cultural groups can be analyzed productively for the emotions that accompany it. Accordingly, certain emotional states that are difficult to accept as positive or desirable from an American point of view (being modest, humble, or full of shame, and the accompanying social behavior of withdrawing, conforming, remaining silent) can, when located within the appropriate cultural frame, be more readily appreciated as positive and as desirable.

An appreciation of the emotional concomitants of various kinds of social behavior is one key to fathoming otherwise unfathomable behavior. This is the general notion behind the extensive study of values (Rokeach, 1973; Schwartz & Bilsky, 1990). Yet in most studies, values are regarded primarily as cognitive representations or beliefs that guide behavior. With a focus on feeling states, we seek to add to this analysis and delineate yet another powerful domain of contact between the social world and individual subjectivity and intersubjectivity. Certain social behavior is not only believed to be good or proper, it also feels natural or right and is experienced as desirable and necessary.

Several reviews of social psychology in a cross-cultural perspective (Moghaddam et al., 1993; Smith & Bond, 1993) suggest very little generalizability of the basic social psychological findings across various cultural groups, and the patterns of conflicting findings have not yet been reconciled. One route of understanding these differences and avoiding despair over the impossibility of making generalizations may be a consideration of the relation between the behavior being observed and the underlying cultural frame. When studies of social behavior are conducted within a single culture, the ways in which psychological functioning and theories about psychological functioning are culture specific and are conditioned by particular models of the self and the world is typically not obvious. For example, when a given social behavior has been induced or observed, social psychologists have rarely asked whether the behavior experienced is good and whether it reflects culture's notion of how to be a self or whether the behavior in question goes against the cultural grain.

Conformity to Group Pressure

In considering the phenomenon of conformity, Smith and Bond (1993) reported 24 published nonreplications of Asch's (1952) findings. Of the several studies done with Japanese respondents, the one using strangers as confederates found very low levels of conformity (Frager, 1970), and another found a high rate of errors when intact social groups were used (Williams & Sogon, 1984). Across all the reported studies on conformity, more errors in the direction of the confederate (i.e., conforming responses) were made by respondents in collectivist societies (Smith & Bond, 1993).

An analysis of differential conformity rates would be facilitated by an understanding of the affective responses that accompany being influenced by or responsive to others. From the perspective of a cultural frame that is rooted in the idea of a fundamental human relatedness, it is necessary, important, and feels good or right to be sensitive and responsive to the expectations of others, at least to those others within the in-group. Personal thoughts and opinions are often withheld for the purpose of promoting group harmony. From the perspective of an independent cultural frame, conformity takes a very different cast. Although conforming is viewed as a necessary integrative mechanism, it is viewed most often as "yielding" to the collective; it is something to fear.

Research on conformity was undertaken primarily to determine ways of preventing conformity. Asch (1952), in the now classic studies, was most concerned with how people handle the pressures on them to act in ways that are contrary to their beliefs and values. He wrote that, in these studies, "the present task is to observe directly the interaction between individuals and groups when the paramount issue is that of remaining independent or submitting to social pressure" (p. 451). Here, the separation between the individual and the group is taken for granted, as is the importance of one's *own* beliefs and of holding fast to them.

Given this framework, one could assume that the affective response to group pressure felt by someone with an interdependent approach to self, even when the group pressure seems to be contrary to fact (as when a subject is pressured to agree that a long line is, in fact, a short line), might be strikingly different from that of an individual from a culture with an independent perspective on self. Conformity could be viewed more positively as the mutual negotiation of social reality or as an attempt at attunement with the others. Indeed, giving in to another could reflect tolerance, self-control, and maturity, as it often does in Japan. A recent study by Horike (1992) revealed that "conforming naturally to others" was the most important factor underlying humanness among Japanese respondents.

Currently, there are no data that reflect the relationship between normative pressures to conformity and affective responses. Yet, such data might further our understanding of differential rates of conforming in particular situations and allow the formulation of predictions about what levels of conformity to expect in particular cultural groups. A cultural group's ideas about how to be a self—such as the Japanese sense of self as submerged in a prior social world (Lebra, 1992; Rohlen, 1991)—is an important part of the interpretive framework that determines an individual's affective response to the influence of others and the likely behavioral response.

An exploration of the nature of the emotional experience during social influence situations could further our understanding of those affective states that involve a connection or a unity or synchrony among individuals. The nature of these socially engaging emotions have not been explored, especially as they unfold in the course of social interaction. The questions posed here for conformity could be similarly asked about a range of social influence phenomena—groupthink, obedience, deindividuation. In all of these cases, the behavior in question is, from an American perspective, problematic or negative and occurs when the exogenous group threatens the individual's independence. The influence of others is viewed as a weakness or a failure (see Markus & Kitayama [in press] for a discussion of these ideas). From a perspective of an interdependent cultural framework, the very experience of social influence is described, labeled, understood, and felt differently.

Stereotyping and Intergroup Behavior

Another important area of social behavior is stereotyping. The majority of research on stereotyping has been done with an independent cultural framework. From the point of view of the American melting pot ideology, all cultural differences should be submerged quickly (Moghaddam et al., 1993). Moreover, stereotyping is inherently negative from an independent perspective because it involves constructing people as group members and not as individuals. As Oakes and Turner (1990) noted, the idea that one is an exemplar of a social category or that individual freedom or agency is importantly configured by one's past or current group membership seems somehow undemocratic or un-American. Yet, from a framework in which people are taught from the earliest age about the joy of group life, a positive and distinctive group stereotype may well function for the group as a positive and unique self-concept does for the individual in North America.

When the group is the primary basis of self-definition, in-group membership takes on particular importance, the interdependent members of the group will evoke positive evaluations and the out-group members, negative evaluations (Jarymolvich, 1987; Reykowski, 1991). And if, as is often the case, among those in interdependent or collectivist cultural groups, self-interest is secondary and often subverted in the interest of the group (Triandis, chapter 9, this volume), then the desire to maintain a positive view of one's group may be extremely powerful.

Furthermore, if the notion of *we* is associated with strong positive affect, as indicated in the studies of Choi and Choi (1990), and if the group is considered to be a primary reality so that individuals seek to uncover their similarity or identity with others (as indicated by the earlier data on self-effacement), then the group may become a dominant category for organizing cognitive space (Reykowski, 1991). Perceiving others as part of a group and sharing the same qualities with them may be experienced as extremely positive and accompanied by "good" emotions. In fact, the positive emotions may well require an experience of collectivity. Here again, some empirical research on the affective responses associated with stereotyping or assigning others to groups may be instructive. Turner, Hogg, Oakes, Reicher, and Wetherell (1987) suggested that collectivists may habitually function at the group level and may well be more sensitive to group-related cues, and such functioning may well be associated with good feelings.

Given a perspective that privileges the group over the individual, current theorizing about the nature and functioning of stereotyping may need to be refined. If experiencing the world in relational or collective terms is typical and encouraged, then stereotyping can be examined for its potential positive consequences and for its negative and destructive ones. Furthermore, the concept of encouraging personal and individual friendly contact among members of different groups who are hostile to one another, in the belief that this contact will change attitudes toward the group as a whole, should be reevaluated (Amir & Sharon, 1987; Lopez, 1993) once it is realized that feeling as one's group feels may be sought after and valued. Exploring the nature of the emotional experiences that accompany the sense that one is fully participating in a relationship or an important group may be useful in examining unexplored assumptions of current theories of stereotyping. Such work fits in with the current reconsideration of the functionalist perspective of stereotyping (Katz, 1960; Snyder, 1993).

Coping and Adjustment

Another important area of social behavior concerns coping and adjustment. The burgeoning literature in health psychology has focused on trying to identify the features of good copers and bad copers. Good copers are those who maintain positive illusions about themselves, have high self-efficacy, focus on the problem rather than their own state, and have strong social support networks (Antonucci, 1990; Lazarus & Folkman, 1984; Taylor, 1989). People will be judged as good or as well-adjusted copers to the extent to which they can maintain this mode of operation after a crisis. However, successful coping is tied to a cultural group's view of how to be a self. With a view of how to be a self that differs from the independent view, effective coping may take a different form.

In North America, prolonged grieving over the loss of a loved one and the failure to return to an autonomous lifestyle can be considered pathological, but this perspective is tied to a view of the self as a bounded, autonomous whole. As Stroebe, Gergen, Gergen, and Stroebe (1992) pointed out, from an interdependent perspective, the loss of another means a breaking of bonds and can destroy one's interdependent identity. Consequently, the bonds, even with the deceased, must be maintained or the self is threatened. Such a connection is maintained in some Japanese homes with a commemorative altar that allows for paying continued respect to one's ancestors.

Cross (1992) looked directly at the role of the self in coping. In a study with Asian international students, she found that those with interdependent selves suffered the most stress in American graduate schools, a place in which an independent cultural frame is clearly dominant. Those Asian students who coped best during graduate school were those who took on characteristics of an independent self.

Within different cultural frameworks, coping, mental health, and well-being can take different forms and are likely to be associated with different ways of feeling. For example, the avoidance of suffering may seem to be a universal goal, but as the work of Kleinman (1988) and Das (in press) in China and India documented, even this assumption may be questioned. According to some perspectives, suffering is a part of being human and can even be ennobling and associated with good feelings. If the pursuit of well-being is indeed a universal goal, research in this domain will be furthered by relating normative coping practices and desirable feeling states to the relevant cultural frame.

We have outlined here some of the ways in which culture, self, emotion, and social behavior constrain and afford each other. Initially, such a framing may seem to enlarge the scope of these phenomena to the point at which they are no longer tractable, but we believe that the type of framework offered here has the potential to generate specific, testable hypotheses. As social psychologists, we have focused in this last section on the implications of this interdependency for the analysis and explanation of social behavior. An understanding of the potential for systematic variation in emotional experience is one key to making sense of the conflicting set of results and failures to replicate that are increasingly reported in social psychology as considered in cross-cultural perspective. Specifically, we have argued that one of the specific and powerful ways in which cultural context influences individual behavior is through its influence on the meanings and practices of the self.

Each cultural context provides some message about what it means to be a person. Through emotional socialization, ongoing social and linguistic processes, these cultural messages or imperatives are incorporated into the emotional system so that it feels "good" to behave in accordance with these imperative and it feels "bad" when one cannot or does not. In this way, the self shapes one's sense of the good by specifying one important set of criteria for what is "good" (and also how to feel good, when to feel good, why to feel good, etc.). As a consequence, the nature of the positive or good or the negative or bad emotions will depend on the supporting cultural frame. From a European–American cultural perspective, "good" emotions are experienced when one's own needs are met or one's own attributes are verified or expressed. From an Asian cultural perspective, "good" emotions entail fitting-in with others, seeking and fulfilling obligations, and becoming part of an ongoing relationship. This means that good feelings will be typically manifested as individual happiness from an independent perspective, but as sympathy or as feelings of similarity and connectedness from an interdependent perspective. These two different types of "good" feelings will be experienced differently—personally and subjectively in one case and interpersonally and intersubjectively in the other—and will be tied to different types of instrumental responses.

Out of this perspective comes a number of challenging ideas that are at odds with many current views on emotions and deserve further analysis (e.g., for some groups, sympathy is a basic emotion): that shame, or even humiliation, can be a desirable emotional experience for some groups (see Asad, 1987; Menon & Shweder, chap. 8, this volume), and that emotions are not experienced individually but relationally. This perspective also raises new questions about the functions of emotions, such as (a) do emotions serve the same cultural functions in all groups (Potter, 1988, argued that emotions are essentially unimportant for the Chinese in the regulation of everyday action); (b) what makes an emotion basic; (c) what does it mean to experience emotions intersubjectively or relationally; (d) how does variation in the criteria for the generalized "good" or "bad" feelings influence the emotions of fear, anger, and surprise; (e) which aspects of the "good" feelings may be similar and which may be different from one another across cultural groups; and (f) how does a group's understanding and experience of emotion influence how the emotions should be observed, manipulated, or assessed (e.g., the questionnaires requiring reflections on one's own emotional state may be appropriate and adequate for groups with a private property view of emotion, but altogether inappropriate for groups who have a more interpersonal view of the nature and experience of emotion). Pursuing these questions may eventually allow an integration of two views of emotions that have remained separate and that have been pursued in distinct literature, that is, the view of emotions as discrete internal, personal products, and the view of emotions as moral, social, historical, political, and cultural products.

References

Akiyama, H. (1992, June). *Measurement of depressive symptoms in cross-cultural research.* Paper presented at the International Conference on Emotion and Culture, University of Oregon, Eugene.

Amir, Y., & Sharon, I. (1987). Are social–psychological laws cross-culturally valid? *Journal of Cross-Cultural Psychology, 18,* 383–470.

Antonucci, T. C. (1990). Social supports and social relationships. In R. H. Binstock & L. K. George (Eds.), *The handbook of aging and the social sciences* (3rd ed., pp. 205–226). San Diego, CA: Academic Press.

Asad, T. (1987). On ritual and discipline in medieval Christian monasticism. *Economy and Society, 16*(2), 159–203.

Asch, S. E. (1952). *Social psychology.* Englewood Cliffs, NJ: Prentice Hall.

Azuma, H. (1986). Why study child development in Japan? In H. Stevenson, H. Azuma, & K. Hakuta (Eds.), *Child development and education in Japan* (pp. 3–12). San Francisco: Freeman.

Bartlett, F. A. (1932). *Remembering: A study in experimental psychology.* Cambridge, England: Cambridge University Press.

Bellah, R. N., Madsen, R., Sullivan, W. M., Swidler, A., & Tipton, S. M. (1985). *Habits of the heart: Individualism and commitment in American life.* Berkeley: University of California Press.

Bourdieu, P. (1972). *Outline of a theory of practice.* Cambridge, England: Cambridge University Press.

Bourdieu, P. (1980). *The logic of practice.* Stanford, CA: Stanford University Press.

Bruner, J. (1990). *Acts of meaning.* Cambridge, MA: Harvard University Press.

Chao, R. K. (1993a, March). *Clarification of the authoritarian parenting style and parental control: Cultural concepts of Chinese child rearing.* Paper presented at the 60th Anniversary Meeting of the Society for Research in Child Development, New Orleans, LA.

Chao, R. K. (1993b). *East and West concepts of the self reflecting in mothers' reports of their child rearing.* Unpublished manuscript, University of California, Los Angeles.

Choi, S. C., & Choi, S. H. (1990, July). *We-ness: A Korean discourse of collectivism.* Paper presented at the First International Conference on Individualism and Collectivism: Psychocultural Perspectives for East and West, Seoul, Korea.

Cross, S. E. (1992). *Cultural adaptation and the self: Self-construal, coping, and stress.* Unpublished doctoral dissertation, University of Michigan, Ann Arbor, MI.

Cross, S. E., Liao, M., & Josephs, R. (1992, August). *A cross-cultural test of the self-evaluation maintenance model.* Paper presented at the 100th Annual Convention of the American Psychological Association, Washington, DC.

D'Andrade, R. (1984). Cultural meaning systems. In R. A. Shweder & R. A. LeVine (Eds.), *Culture theory: Essays on mind, self, and emotion* (pp. 88–119). Cambridge, England: Cambridge University Press.

D'Andrade, R. (1987). A folk model of the mind. In D. Holland & N. Quinn (Eds.), *Cultural models in language and thought.* Cambridge, England: Cambridge University Press.

Das, V. (1992). Moral orientations to suffering: Litigimation, power and healing. In L. Chen, A. Kleinman, & N. Ware (Eds.), *Health and social change in international perspectives* (pp. 139–157). Boston: Harvard School of Public Health.

de Riviera, J. (1984). The structure of emotional relationships. In P. Shaver (Ed.), *Review of personality and social psychology: Vol. 5. Emotions, relationships, and health* (pp. 116–145). Beverly Hills, CA: Sage.

Durkheim, E. (1953). Individual representations and collective representations. In D. F. Pocock (Trans.), *Sociology and philosophy* (pp. 1–38). New York: Free Press. (Reprinted from *Revue de Métaphysique*, 1898, *6*, 274–302)

Epstein, S. (1973). The self-concept revisited or a theory of a theory. *American Psychologist, 28,* 405–416.

Frager, R. (1970). Conformity and anti-conformity in Japan. *Journal of Personality and Social Psychology, 15,* 203–210.

Frijda, N. (1986). *The emotions.* Cambridge, England: Cambridge University Press.

Gaskins, S., Miller, P. J., & Corsaro, W. A. (1992). Theoretical and methodological perspectives in the interpretive study of children. In W. A. Corsaro & P. J. Miller (Eds.), *Interpretive approaches in children's socialization* (pp. 5–23). San Francisco, CA: Jossey-Bass.

Gerber, E. (1975). *The cultural patterning of emotions in Samoa.* Unpublished doctoral dissertation, University of California, San Diego.

Gergen, K. J. (1992). Psychology in the postmodern era. *The General Psychologist, 28,* 10–15.

Giddens, A. (1984). *The constitution of society.* Oxford, England: Polity.

Hamilton, V. L., Blumenfeld, P. C., Akoh, H., & Miura, K. (1991). Group and gender in Japanese and American elementary classrooms. *Journal of Cross-Cultural Psychology, 22,* 3.

Harter, S. (1990). Causes, correlates and the functional role of global self-worth: A life span perspective. In R. J. Sternberg & J. Kolligian, Jr. (Eds.), *Competence considered* (pp. 67–97). New Haven, CT: Yale University Press.

Harter, S., & Marold, D. B. (1991). A model of the determinants and mediational role of self-worth: Implications for adolescent depression and suicidal ideation. In G. R. Goethals & J. Strauss (Eds.), *Multidisciplinary perspectives on the self* (pp. 66–92). New York: Springer-Verlag.

Hartnack, D. (1987). British psychoanalysts in colonial India. In M. G. Ash & W. R. Woodward (Eds.), *Psychology in twentieth-century thought and society* (pp. 233–253). Cambridge, England: Cambridge University Press.

Horike, K. (1992, July). *An investigation of the Japanese social skills what is called "hito-atari-no-yosa" (affability).* Paper presented at the 25th International Congress of Psychology, Brussels, Belgium.

Hsu, F. L. K. (1953). *Americans and Chinese: Two ways of life.* New York: H. Schuman.

James, W. (1890). *Principles of psychology.* New York: Holt.

Jarymolvich, M. (1987). Perceiving one's own individuality. The estimation and attractiveness of self-distinctness from others. *Warsaw Psychological Monographs.* Warsaw, Poland: University of Warsaw Press.

Jenkins, J. H. (1991). Anthropology, expressed emotion, and schizophrenia. *Ethos, 19,* 4.

Josephs, R. A., Markus, H., & Tarafodi, R. W. (1992). Gender and self-esteem. *Journal of Personality and Social Psychology, 63,* 391–402.

Kagitcibasi, C. (1989). Family and socialization in cross-cultural perspective: A model of change. In R. A. Dienstbier & J. J. Berman (Eds.), *Nebraska Symposium on Moti-*

vation, 1989: *Cross-cultural perspectives* (pp. 135–200). Lincoln: University of Nebraska Press.

Kagitcibasi, C., & Sunar, D. (in press). Family and socialization in Turkey. In J. P. Roopnarine & D. B. Carter (Eds.), *Parent child relations in diverse cultural settings: Socialization for instrumental competency*. Norwood, NJ: Ablex.

Kakar, S. (1978). *The inner world: A psychoanalytic study of childhood and society in India*. London: Oxford University Press.

Katz, D. (1960). The functional approach to the study of attitudes. *Public Opinion Quarterly, 24*, 163–204.

Kim, U. (in press-a). Introduction to individualism and collectivism: Conceptual clarification and elaboration. In U. Kim, H. C. Triandis, & C. Kagitcibasi (Eds.), *Individualism and collectivism: Theory, method, and applications*. Newbury Park, CA: Sage.

Kim, U., Triandis, H. C., Kagitcibasi, C., Choi, S. C., & Yoon, G. (in press-b). Introduction to individualism and collectivism: Social and applied issues. In U. Kim, H. C. Triandis, & C. Kagitcibasi (Eds.), *Individualism and collectivism: Theory, method, and applications*. Newbury Park, CA: Sage.

Kitayama, S., & Markus, H. R. (in press-a). Construal of the self as a cultural frame: Implications for internationalizing psychology. In J. D'Arms, R. G. Hastie, S. E. Hoelscher, & H. K. Jacobson (Eds.), *Becoming more international and global: Challenges for American higher education*.

Kitayama, S., & Markus, H. R. (in press-b). Culture, self, and emotion: A cultural perspective to "self-conscious" emotions. In J. P. Tangney & K. W. Fisher (Eds.), *Shame, guilt, embarrassment, and pride: Empirical studies of self-conscious emotions*. New York: Guilford Press.

Kitayama, S., Markus, H. R., & Kurokawa, M. (1991, October). *Culture, self, and emotion: The structure and frequency of emotional experience*. Paper presented at the biannual meeting of the Society for Psychological Anthropology, Chicago.

Kitayama, S., Markus, H., Kurokawa, M., & Negishi, K. (1993). *The interpersonal nature of emotion: Cross-cultural evidence and implications*. Unpublished manuscript.

Kleinman, A. (1988). *Rethinking psychiatry: From cultural category to personal experience*. New York: Free Press.

Kondo, D. (1990). *Crafting selves: Power, gender, and discourses of identity in a Japanese work place*. Chicago: University of Chicago Press.

Kuwayama, T. (1992). The reference other orientation. In N. R. Rosenberger (Ed.), *Japanese sense of self* (pp. 121–151). Cambridge, England: Cambridge University Press.

Lave, J., Stepick, A., & Sailer, L. (1977). Extending the scope of formal analysis. *American Ethnologist, 4*, 321–339.

Lazarus, R. S., & Folkman, S. (1984). *Stress, appraisal, and coping*. New York: Springer.

Lebra, T. S. (1992, June). *Culture, self, and communication*. Paper presented at the University of Michigan, Ann Arbor, Michigan.

Levenson, R. W., Ekman, P., Heider, K., & Friesen, W. V. (1992). Emotion and autonomic nervous system activity in the Minangkabau of West Sumatra. *Journal of Personality and Social Psychology, 62,* 972–988.

Levy, R. I. (1973). *The Tahitians.* Chicago: University of Chicago Press.

Levy, R. I. (1984). Emotions in comparative perspective. In K. R. Scherer & P. Ekman (Eds.), *Approaches to emotion* (pp. 397–412). Hillsdale, NJ: Erlbaum.

Little, T. O., Oettingen, G., Stetsenko, A., & Baltes, P. B. (in press). *Children's school performance-related beliefs: How do American children compare to German and Russian children.* Berlin: Max Planck Institute for Human Development and Education.

Lopez, G. (1993). *The effect of group contact and curriculum on White, Asian American, and African American students' attitudes.* Unpublished doctoral dissertation, University of Michigan, Ann Arbor.

Lutz, C. (1988). *Unnatural emotions: Everyday sentiments on a Micronesian atoll and their challenge to Western theory.* Chicago: University of Chicago Press.

Lynch, O. M. (1990). *Divine passions: The social construction of emotion in India.* Berkeley: University of California Press.

Maday, B. C., & Szalay, L. B. (1976). Psychological correlates of family socialization in the United States and Korea. In T. Williams (Ed.), *Psychological anthropology*. The Hague, Netherlands: Mouton.

Markus, H. R., Herzog, A. R., Holmberg, D. E., & Dielman, L. (1992). *Constructing the self across the life span.* Unpublished manuscript, University of Michigan, Ann Arbor.

Markus, H., & Kitayama, S. (1991). Culture and the self: Implications for cognition, emotion, and motivation. *Psychological Review, 98,* 224–253.

Markus, H. R., & Kitayama, S. (in press). A collective fear of the collective: Implications for selves and theories of selves. *Personality and Social Psychology Bulletin.*

Matsumoto, D. (1992). American–Japanese cultural differences in the recognition of universal facial expression. *Journal of Cross-Cultural Psychology, 23,* 1.

Miller, J. G. (in press). Cultural psychology: Bridging disciplinary boundaries in understanding the cultural grounding of self. In P. K. Bock (Ed.), *Handbook of psychological anthropology.* Westport, CT: Greenwood.

Moghaddam, F. M., Taylor, D. M., & Wright, S. C. (1993). *Social psychology in cross-cultural perspective.* San Francisco: Freeman.

Moscovici, S. (1993, Spring). The return of the unconscious. *Social Research, 60*(1).

Mowrer, O. H. (1960). *Learning theory and behavior.* New York: Wiley.

Mullen, B., & Riordan, C. A. (1988). Self-serving attributions in naturalistic settings: A meta-analytic review. *Journal of Applied Social Psychology, 18,* 3–22.

Myers, D. (1989). *Social psychology* (3rd ed.). New York: McGraw-Hill.

Neisser, U. (1988). Five kinds of self-knowledge. *Philosophical Psychology, 1,* 35–59.

Oakes, P. J., & Turner, J. C. (1990). Is limited information processing capacity the cause of social stereotyping? *European Review of Social Psychology, 1,* 111–135.

Oyserman, D., & Markus, H. R. (1993). The sociocultural self. In J. Suls (Ed.), *Psychological perspectives on the self* (Vol. 4, pp. 187–220). Hillsdale, NJ: Erlbaum.

Peak, L. (1991). *Learning to go to school in Japan: The transition from home to preschool life*. Berkeley: University of California Press.

Potter, S. H. (1988). The cultural construction of emotion in rural Chinese social life. *Ethos, 16*, 181–208.

Pribram, K. (1971). *Languages of the brain: Experimental paradoxes and principles of neuropsychology*. Englewood Cliffs, NJ: Prentice Hall.

Quinn, N., & Holland, D. (1987). Culture and cognition. In D. Holland & N. Quinn (Eds.), *Cultural models in language and thought* (pp. 3–40). Cambridge, England: Cambridge University Press.

Radcliffe-Brown, A. R. (1952). *Structure and function in primitive society*. New York: Free Press of Glencoe.

Reykowski, J. (1991). *The transition from collectivism: Introduction to a research project*. Unpublished manuscript, Polish Academy of Science, Warsaw.

Rohlen, T. P. (1989). Order in Japanese society: Attachment, authority, and routine. *Journal of Japanese Studies, 15*, 5–41.

Rohlen, T. P. (1991). *A developmental topography of self and society in Japan*. Paper presented at the Conference on Self and Society in India, China, and Japan, Honolulu, HI.

Rokeach, M. (1973). *The nature of human values*. New York: Free Press.

Rosaldo, M. Z. (1984). Toward an anthropology of self and feeling. In R. A. Shweder & R. A. LeVine (Eds.), *Culture theory: Essays on mind, self, and emotion* (pp. 137–157). Cambridge, England: Cambridge University Press.

Sampson, E. E. (1988). The debate on individualism: Indigenous psychologies of the individual and their role in personal and societal functioning. *American Psychologist, 43*, 15–22.

Schieffelin, E. L. (1985). The cultural analysis of depressive affect: An example from New Guinea. In A. Kleinman & B. Good (Eds.), *Culture and depression: Studies in the anthropology and cross-cultural psychiatry of affect and disorder* (pp. 101–133). Berkeley: University of California Press.

Schwartz, S. H., & Bilsky, W. (1990). Toward a theory of the universal content and structure of values: Extensions between cross-cultural replications. *Journal of Personality and Social Psychology, 58*, 878–891.

Schwartz, J. M., & Smith, W. P. (1976). Social comparison and the inference of ability difference. *Journal of Personality and Social Psychology, 34*, 1268–1275.

Shweder, R. A. (1991). *Thinking through cultures: Expeditions in cultural psychology*. Cambridge, MA: Harvard University Press.

Shweder, R. A. (1993). The cultural psychology of the emotions. In M. Lewis & J. M. Haviland (Eds.), *Handbook of emotions* (pp. 417–431). New York: Guilford Press.

Shweder, R. A., & LeVine, R. A. (Eds.). (1984). *Culture theory: Essays on mind, self, and emotion*. Cambridge, England: Cambridge University Press.

Sinha, J., & Verma, J. (1987). Structure of collectivism. In C. Kagitcibasi (Ed.), *Growth and progress in cross-cultural psychology* (pp. 201–203). New York: Swets North American.

Smith, P. B., & Bond, M. B. (1993). *Social psychology across cultures*. New York: Harvester Wheatsheaf.

Snyder, M. (1993, June). *Stereotypes, prejudice, and discrimination: A motivational inquiry*. Invited address presented at the Fifth Annual Convention of the American Psychological Society, Chicago.

Spiro, M. (1961). Social systems, personality, and functional analysis. In B. Kaplan (Ed.), *Studying personality cross-culturally* (pp. 93–127). New York: Harper & Row.

Stigler, J. W., Shweder, R. A., & Herdt, G. (Eds.). (1990). *Cultural psychology: Essays on comparative human development*. Cambridge, England: Cambridge University Press.

Stigler, J. W., Smith, S., & Mao, L. (1985). The self-perception of competence by Chinese children. *Child Development, 56*, 1259–1270.

Stroebe, M., Gergen, M. M., Gergen, K. J., & Stroebe, W. (1992). Broken hearts or broken bonds: Love and death in historical perspective. *American Psychologist, 47*, 1205–1212.

Takata, T. (1987). Self-deprecative tendencies in self-evaluation through social comparison. *Japanese Journal of Experimental Social Psychology, 27*, 27–36.

Taylor, C. (1989). *Sources of the self: The making of modern identities*. Cambridge, MA: Harvard University Press.

Tesser, A. (1988). Toward a self-evaluation maintenance model of social behavior. In L. Berkowitz (Ed.), *Advances in experimental social psychology* (Vol. 21, pp. 181–227). San Diego, CA: Academic Press.

Triandis, H. C. (1990). Cross-cultural studies of individualism and collectivism. In J. Berman (Ed.), *Nebraska Symposium on Motivation, 1989* (pp. 41–133). Lincoln: University of Nebraska Press.

Turner, J. C., Hogg, M. A., Oakes, P. J., Reicher, S. D., & Wetherell, S. M. (1987). *Rediscovering the social group: A self-categorization theory*. Oxford, England: Basil Blackwell.

Whiting, R. (1989). *You gotta have wa*. New York: Macmillan.

Williams, T. P., & Sogon, S. (1984). Group composition and conforming behavior in Japanese students. *Japanese Psychological Research, 26*, 231–234.

Zajonc, R. B. (1980). Feeling and thinking: Preferences need no inferences. *American Psychologist, 35*, 151–175.

PART TWO

Emotion,
Language,
and Cognition

CHAPTER 5

Emotion, Language, and Cultural Scripts

Anna Wierzbicka

In this chapter, I will explore the relationship between emotion and culture and that between emotion and cognition. I will examine the concept of emotion, and I will argue that this concept is culture specific and rooted in the semantics of the English language, as are also the names of specific emotions, such as sadness, joy, anger, or fear.

I will also show that both the concept of emotion and the language-specific names of particular emotions can be explicated and elucidated in terms of the *natural semantic metalanguage* developed over many years by myself and colleagues on the basis of comparative lexical research into many languages and based on three and a half dozen universal semantic primitives.

I will argue that different cultures encourage different attitudes toward emotions, and that these different attitudes are reflected in both the lexicon and the grammar of the languages associated with these cultures. I will try to show that the framework of universal semantic primitives provides a suitable basis for description and comparison of not only emotions and emotion concepts but also of cultural attitudes to emotions, and that the use of this framework provides a necessary counterbalance to the uncritical use of English words as conceptual tools widespread in the psychology, philosophy, and sociology of emotions.

The chapter is divided into two parts. The first part, on theoretical issues, discusses the language-specific character of emotion concepts and grammatical categories; the need for lexical universals as conceptual and descriptive tools; the doctrine of *basic emotions* and the issue of the discreteness of emotions; and the relationships among emotions, sensations, and feelings. The second part, on *cultural scripts* (with special reference to the Anglo and Polish cultures), explores attitudes toward emotions characteristic of different cultures (in particular, of the Anglo and Polish cultures) and shows how these attitudes can be expressed in the form of cultural scripts formulated within the framework of universal semantic primitives.

Theoretical Issues

In his book, *The Dance of Life*, Edward Hall (1983) noted wryly that "the American abroad—even when he is most successful—is likely to voice such sentiments as 'After all, when you get to know them, they are just like the folks back home'" (p. 103). Presumably, Hall was implying that, in some important respects, "they" (people from other cultures) are *not* like "the folks back home." But, of course, in some respects, "they" *are* like "the folks back home." The real question, then, is, In what respects are they similar, and in what respects are they different? Finding the line between shallow universalism and superficial relativism can be very difficult. Few areas of study exemplify this difficulty better than the area of emotion.

The Lexicon of Emotions

One common form of shallow universalism is that which posits that there is a finite set of discrete and universal basic human emotions that can be identified by English words such as *happiness, anger, fear, surprise, disgust*, or *shame* or by their corresponding adjectives (e.g., Ekman, 1980, 1989, 1992; Izard, 1969, 1977). Cross-cultural lexical research undertaken by linguists and anthropologists demonstrates that concepts such as happy or angry are not universal, but constitute cultural artifacts of Anglo culture reflected in, and continually reinforced by, the English language (e.g., Goddard, 1990, 1991, 1993; Harkins, 1990; Lutz, 1988b; M. Z. Rosaldo, 1980; Russell, 1991; Wierzbicka, 1991a, 1992b, 1992c, 1992e, 1993a). Another conclusion emerging from this research is that the set of emotion terms available in any given language is unique and reflects a culture's unique perspective on people's ways of feeling. It also reflects the links between feelings, cognition, moral norms, and social interaction.

To draw on my personal experience (as a bilingual and bicultural person), I would say that I tend to perceive my daily emotions in terms of lexical categories provided by Polish (my native language), such as those illustrated in the following sentences:

Przykro mi (To me, (it is) unpleasant/hurtful).
Denerwuję się (I am making myself upset/nervous/on edge).
Jestem zachwycona (I am euphoric with admiration/delight).
Jestem zła (literally, I am bad, i.e., I am displeased/angry/furious).
Wściekła jestem (I am enraged/furious/mad).
Strasznie się cieszę, że . . . ("I am rejoicing terribly that . . .").
Mam do ciebie żal (literally, I have regret to you, i.e., I hold something
     against you, and I am sad/sorry).
Tęsknię do ciebie (I miss you/I am homesick for you/I ache for you).
Bardzo mnie to boli (This hurts me very much, I ache because of this).
Serce mi się kraje (My heart is cutting itself).

None of the categories illustrated in these sentences has exact equivalents in English, and the sentences themselves cannot be adequately translated into English.

However, within an English-speaking context, I often talk—and sometimes think—about my daily subjective experience in terms of the lexical categories of the English language, such as *upset, frustrated, resentful, annoyed, disgusted, happy,* and so on. None of these categories has exact equivalents in Polish, and they suggest a different interpretation of emotional experience. I think that this different interpretation cannot be separated from the subjective experience itself.

Grammatical categories, too, provide precious insight into different modes of emotional experience (e.g., Ameka, 1990; Bugenhagen, 1990; Wierzbicka, 1992a). Polish grammar suggests three different ways of viewing one's emotions: active/volitional, passive/involuntary, and neutral. This colors, I believe, my own and other Poles' subjective experience. For example, there is a difference, for me, between the experience of *gniewać się* (roughly, to manufacture anger within oneself; no equivalent in English) and that of *być zła* (roughly, to be angry).

Clearly, it is language that creates the impression that ways of feeling differ from one another in a discrete and precisely identifiable way. As James (1890, quoted in Johnson-Laird & Oatley, 1989) observed:

> If one should seek to name each particular one of [the emotions] of which the human heart is the seat, it is plain that the limit to their number would lie in the introspective vocabulary of the seeker, each race of men having found names for some shade of feeling which other races have left undiscriminated. If we should seek to break the emotions, thus enumerated, into groups, according to their affinities, it is again plain that all sorts of groupings would be possible, according as we chose this character or that as a basis, and that all groupings would be equally real and true. (p. 81)

As James rightly observed, upon this largely (though, perhaps, not entirely) nebulous world of feelings, every language imposes its own interpretive grid, lexical or grammatical. Grammar may draw distinctions based on general semantic parameters, such as voluntariness, duration, or value (good or bad); whereas lexicon suggests particular cognitive structures (often, cognitive scenarios with built-in sequences of events, as in the case of the English word *disappointment*), encoded in single words or in larger phraseological units (e.g., in English, *to bear a grudge against someone* or *to feel sorry for someone*).

Languages differ enormously in the size and character of their *affective lexicon*. In particular, they differ enormously in the size of their sets of single words designating cognitively based feelings, such as *joy*, *distress*, *relief*, *surprise*, and so on. For English, *Roget's Thesaurus* (Lloyd, 1984) lists hundreds of such words (nouns, adjectives, and verbs), and even though not all of them are in common use, the number of those that are is no doubt well above 100. On the other hand, in the Chepang language of Malaysia, studied by Signe Howell (1981), the number of such words is, according to Howell, less than 10.

But it is not only the size of the affective lexicon that varies greatly from language to language; there is also no isomorphism among individual concepts. For example, English words such as *happy, angry, sad,* or *disgusted* do not mean the same as their closest equivalents in many other languages of the world (cf. Wierzbicka, 1992c, 1992e). Given this wide cross-linguistic variation, there is no reason to assume that some English words (e.g., *happy, angry, sad,* or *disgusted*) have a privileged status and offer access to psychological states of universal significance.

The Ifaluk language of Micronesia, described in a number of studies by Lutz (1982, 1985, 1987, 1988b) and in Wierzbicka (1992c), does not have a word for a concept like *anger*; instead, it has a word for the concept of *song*, described by Lutz as something like "justified anger." However, Lutz's discussion showed clearly that this word does not mean the same as the English word *anger*, and not only because *song* is supposed to be "justified." *Song* is a less aggressive feeling than *anger*, a feeling that is less likely to lead to physical violence. Typically, *song* manifests itself in reprimands, in refusal to eat, or in a pout. What is more, in some cases, *song* can lead to suicide or to an attempted suicide. The hidden goal of *song* is, according to Lutz (1987) "to change the situation by altering the behavior of the offending person" (p. 301), but the actions caused by *song* are often directed toward oneself rather than towards the guilty person (for example, an attempted suicide rather than an attempted murder). From an earlier article on the same subject (Lutz, 1982), we learn that *song* is regarded as "good for people (and especially parents) to feel and express when a wrongdoing has occurred. It is only through the observation of their parents' *song* in particular situations that children are said to learn the difference between right and wrong" (p. 121). Accordingly, people in a higher position, who are responsible for other people's behavior, can be expected to feel and to show *song* frequently. "An elder is more often *song* (justifiably angry) at a younger person than at a peer or at a higher-ranked individual. The chiefs are often said to be *song* at those who have broken rules or taboos" (Lutz, 1982, p. 122).

Using the language of universal semantic primitives (to be discussed later), one could say that both the concept of *song* and that of anger involve the thought that "this person did something bad." But in the case of anger, the negative judgment leads to an urge to do something bad to that person ("because of this, I would want to do something bad to this person"). In the case of *song*, the urge to do something is not oriented toward anyone, and it can express itself in a refusal to eat as much as in a reprimand ("because of this, I want to do something"). This does not mean that *song* can express itself in any action whatsoever. All the actions mentioned by Lutz (a reprimand, a refusal to eat, a pout, an attempted suicide) have a common denominator: *X* wants *Y* to know that *Y* has done something bad and to draw consequences from this (i.e., to do something because of this).

Lutz (1987) observed that the Ifaluk culture enjoins people to avoid aggression, and that in its hierarchy of values, it puts this injunction much higher than Western culture and, in particular, than American culture:

> Although both the Ifaluks and Americans may have the goal of avoiding violence, roles of physical aggression in the two societies and beliefs about those roles are in dramatic contrast, in part due to cultural differences in the importance attached to that goal. (p. 300)

The fact that the Ifaluk language has no word corresponding to the English word *anger* and that the closest Ifaluk counterpart of this concept is much softer and closer to *admonition* seems to constitute a lexical confirmation of this difference between the two cultures.

Another example is provided by the Polish concept of *złość* (adjective *zły, zła*), a much more basic word in Polish than *gniew* (roughly, anger but a somewhat dignified kind of anger, rather like wrath). For example, Ekman's (1975) photograph of a woman viciously baring her teeth as if she wanted to bite someone would bring to mind in Polish *złość* rather than *gniew*. Similarly, a child's tantrum would be linked with the word *złość* not with the word *gniew*. *Gniew* (like anger) implies a judgment ("this person did something bad") so it easily acquires intellectual and moral connotations, whereas *złość* is compatible with an almost animal aggression or with a childish rage. *Gniew* can be dignified and impressive, but *złość*—like *tantrum, temper,* or *aggro*—cannot.

Thus, it is an illusion to think that emotion terms can be matched across language boundaries or that English words, such as *happy*, *sad*, or *angry*, can provide a guide to universal human emotions. To compare human emotions and to elucidate the interplay of universal and cultural factors shaping them, we need a different kind of conceptual tool.

The Need for Lexical Universals

Psychologists writing about emotions and emotion concepts usually focus, understandably, on those that have been lexicalized in English (the language in which they are writing). But to understand human conceptualization of emotions, we also need to take an interest in the emotion concepts lexicalized in other languages of the world. We need to try to understand those concepts from a native's point of view (cf. Geertz, 1984), to try to enter the conceptual world of other peoples and abandon our Anglo perspective in interpreting that world. For example, as mentioned earlier, to the Ifaluks, *song* is not a kind of anger, just as to native speakers of English, anger is not a kind of *song*. To say that *song* is a justified anger means interpreting this concept through the prism of the English language (just as to say that anger is an aggressive *song* would mean interpreting this concept through the prism of the Ifaluk language).

Every language imposes its own classification upon human emotional experience, and English words such as *anger* or *sadness* are cultural artifacts of the English language, not culture-free analytical tools (cf. Russell, 1991). On the other hand, conceptual primitives such as good and bad, or want, know, say, and think, are not cultural artifacts of the English language but belong to the universal alphabet of human thoughts; they appear to have their semantic equivalents in all, or nearly all, languages of the world. By defining emotion concepts encoded in a given language in terms of lexical universals, we can free ourselves from the bias of our own language and we can see those concepts from a native's point of view, while at the same time making them comparable with the concepts encoded in any other language. Lutz (1985) stated:

> In the translation of ethnopsychologies, we rely heavily on our own and others' understanding of concepts such as "mind," "self," and "anger." ...
> If the terms of our description themselves are taken as nonproblematic ...,

we run the risk of reducing the emotional lives of others to the common denominator or intersection with our own. (pp. 68–69)

The point is well taken, but the problem is not insoluble: We can avoid this risk by explaining emotion concepts not in terms of Anglo concepts (mind, self, or anger) but in terms of lexical universals, that is, concepts encoded in distinct words in any human language (such as good or bad, know or want).

It is true that the identification of lexical universals is not a straightforward matter, and that the list assumed here[1] must be regarded as tentative. There are several thousand languages in the world, and it is impossible to check a hypothetical list against all of them and to determine whether a language has a word for a particular concept is a task that requires painstaking analysis. For example, it takes the larger part of an entire paper for Goddard (1990) to establish conclusively that the Australian Aboriginal language Yankunytjatjara does have an exact semantic equivalent of the English verb *want*.

Similarly, it is by no means easy to establish that *feel* is a true lexical universal. In fact, Lutz (1985) claimed that Ifaluk does not distinguish

---

[1]The natural semantic metalanguage (NSM) used in this chapter is the outcome of an extensive empirical study of a wide range of languages, undertaken over two decades by the author and colleagues. On the basis of this research, a set of lexical universals was identified tentatively (see Goddard & Wierzbicka, in press) and a universal metalanguage was developed. Because this metalanguage is carved out of natural language and can be understood directly via natural language, it has been called the NSM. The latest version of the lexicon of this metalanguage, arrived at by trial and error on the basis of more than two decades of cross-linguistic lexicographic research, includes the following elements:

[substantives] I, you, someone, something, people
[determiners, quantifiers] this, the same, other, one, two, many (much), all
[mental predicates] know, want, think, feel, say
[actions, events] do, happen
[evaluative] good, bad
[descriptors] big, small
[intensifier] very
[metapredicates] can, if, because, no (negation), like (how)
[time and place] when, where, after (before), under (above)
[taxonomy, partonymy] kind of, part of.

These elements have their own, language-independent syntax. For example, the verb-like elements *think, know, say, feel,* and *want* combine with nominal personal elements *I, you,* and *someone* and take complex, proposition-like complements (such as, I think or you did something bad). The nominal element *someone* combines with the determiner-like elements *this, the same, two,* and *all* (whereas *I* does not combine with them). For a fuller discussion, see Wierzbicka (1991c).

lexically between *feel* and *think*, and that the most relevant word in this area, *nunuwan*, "refers to mental events ranging from what we consider thought to what we consider emotion.... Thus, *nunuwan* may be translated ... as 'thought/emotion'" (p. 47). Lutz argued that

> it is not simply that thought evokes, or is accompanied by, an emotion; the two are inextricably linked. *Nunuwan* is included in the definitions of various words we would consider emotion words. For example, *yarofali* "longing/missing" is the state of "continually *nunuwan* about [for example] one's dead mother." (p. 48)

In fact, Lutz's careful and admirably presented data are compatible with a different analysis: namely, that *nunuwan* means *think* rather than *think* or *feel*, and that its frequent emotive connotations are due to context rather than to the word itself. For example, one of Lutz's (1985) informants says of a pregnant woman R. that she "has lots of *nunuwan* because the health aide is leaving on the next ship which is coming, and she [R.] *nunuwan* that there will be trouble with the delivery of the baby" (p. 47). This is compatible with the interpretation that *nunuwan* always means think, and that emotions are implied only by the word's context.

As for the primitive feel, it appears that it does have an exponent in Ifaluk, too, although in the form of a noun rather than of a verb. The word in question is *niferash*, and Lutz's primary gloss for it is our insides, but her data suggest that *niferash* may mean feel as well as insides, and that it can refer to physical as well as psychological feelings, just like the English verb *feel*:

> To say "My insides are bad" (*Ye ngaw niferai*) may mean either that one is feeling physically bad or experiencing bad thoughts and emotions, or both. The exact meaning, as with the English phrase "I feel bad," is determined by context. (Lutz, 1985, p. 47)

The suggestion that *nunuwan* can be linked (invariably) with the primitive think and *niferash* with feel is supported by informants' comments such as the following one, cited by Lutz (1985): "T. said that if we had bad *nunuwan*, we will have bad insides, and if we have good *nunuwan*, we will have good insides" (p. 47). This comment seems to mean that bad thoughts cause bad feelings. It is also supported by data from other languages (e.g., Australian Aboriginal languages) in which some words for internal body parts (stomach, heart, liver) can also mean feel, so that "I stomach good" means "I feel good," and "I stomach bad" means "I feel bad" (cf. Goddard & Wierzbicka, in press; see also the section, The Relationships Among Emotions, Sensations, and Feelings in this chapter).

The final identification of lexical universals is a long-term task of cross-cultural semantics. The decade or so that has been devoted to this task has produced a list that must be regarded as provisional and subject to amendments. However, this list is sufficient for use as the basis of a metalanguage in terms of which meanings in general and meanings of emotion words in particular can be effectively described and compared (for illustrations, see Wierzbicka, 1992b, 1992c, 1992e).

Basic Emotions and the Issue of Discreteness

Does the feeling of jealousy differ qualitatively from the feeling of envy? This is hard to tell. In the folk theory reflected in English lanugage, the two are different, but as Harré (1986) pointed out, the differential use of these words depends on assumptions about rights, duties, values, and so on. Whether these feelings are really different may be impossible to discover (even by introspection).

This example illustrates the general problem of the relationship between language and actual feelings. The categories of our language suggest to us a certain interpretation of our feelings, and it is difficult—perhaps impossible—for us to sort out our awareness of the feelings themselves from the interpretation imposed on them by language.

This difficulty may lie at the root of the theory that there are some discrete basic emotions, clearly differentiated from one another and associated with different genetic programs.

It goes without saying that concepts such as joy, sadness, fear, anger, surprise, or disgust differ discretely from one another (as can be shown by assigning to them distinct explications; e.g., Wierzbicka, 1990b, 1992b, 1992c, 1992e, in press-c). However, there is no evidence that the corresponding feelings (and the bodily disturbances associated with them) differ discretely from one another; there is no evidence that the feeling reported sometimes as sadness differs discretely from that reported sometimes as distress, or that the feeling reported sometimes as frustration differs discretely from that reported sometimes as anger.

Introspective evidence suggests that feelings tend to be nebulous, fluid, and difficult to compare without language, and that it is hard not to agree with Harré (1986) and others that if one were to stare internally at two feelings, one reported as envy and one as jealousy, it would be difficult to identify them as such or to distinguish them sharply from one another without all the assumptions embodied in these two words.

The feelings of sadness and anger are so different from one another that, when compared directly, they may both seem discrete. But a simple question, such as "Are you sad?", is not always easy to answer. To pigeonhole a feeling is usually an arbitrary interpretive decision. It is not at all like saying, "This is an apple, and that is an orange."

In fact, Ekman's (1992) statement that each of his basic emotions stands not for "a single affective state but a *family* of related states" (p. 172) seems to suggest a step in the direction of a nondiscrete view (and, presumably, a concession to the critics of the earlier versions of his theory). Ekman said that "there is robust, consistent evidence of a universal facial expression for anger, fear, enjoyment, sadness, and disgust" (p. 176). At the same time, he acknowledged that "for each emotion more than one universal expression has been identified" (p. 176). These different (facial) expressions of anger, for example, suggest different feelings. But if so, then what is the evidence that the family in question differs sharply from other families of feelings? And what do all the affective states within a family have in common?

In Ekman's (1992) view, "each emotion family can be considered to constitute a *theme* and *variations*. The theme is composed of the characteristics unique to that family" (p. 173). Contrasting his position with that of Rosch (1973), Ekman insisted that he was talking not merely of prototypes, but of invariants "to be found in all instances of an emotion," and he rejected the suggestion "that the boundaries between basic emotion families are are fuzzy" (p. 173). Yet, he failed to identify any such invariant themes and relegated the task to future research: "One of the major empirical tasks ahead is to isolate the theme and variations for each emotion family" (p. 173).

To illustrate his ideas of invariant themes, Ekman (1992) suggested that, "in all members of the anger family the brows are lowered and drawn together, the upper eyelid is raised and the muscle in the lips is tightened" (p. 172). But if this is the invariant of the different anger expressions, what is the invariant of the different anger feelings? Because there is no word in English—or, for that matter, in any other language—for such a putative invariant (*anger* itself being, as Ekman acknowledged, only a very rough approximation), the only way to capture this invariant (if there is one) is in the form of a hypothetical cognitive structure. In the absence of such a structure, the claim that there is a discrete emotion of anger and anger-like affective states seems to be lacking in clear content.

The Relationships Among Emotions, Sensations, and Feelings

In trying to elucidate the relationship among emotions, sensations, and feeling, it is useful to start with a description of a personal experience (Wierzbicka, contemporaneous record, July 26, 1991):

> Today, I was trying to resolve an important university matter, involving thousands of dollars. I came to the appointment with the university treasurer feeling, I would say, slightly shy, but otherwise calm. The interview was, as my colleague put it, "short and sweet," and the matter was resolved positively. The treasurer's manner was friendly and pleasant. Nonetheless I left the room with a pounding heart and with an intense (burning?) sensation in my chest, for which I tried, but couldn't, find a label. To begin with, I couldn't say whether the feeling was physical or psychological: it seemed to be both, but it was unitary, and in fact the question whether it was "physical" or "psychological" didn't seem applicable. Introspectively, I knew how I felt, in the sense that I was aware of an intense internal "disturbance" (and, metaphorically speaking, I could stare this disturbance in the face, observe it and scrutinize it with full attention), but I couldn't find any words to describe it to myself. I couldn't even tell whether I was feeling something "good" or something "bad."

Experiences of this kind suggest a number of ideas on the nature and conceptualization of subjective experience.

To begin with, they suggest that the gulf between emotion and sensation assumed by many scholars may be artificial and may be due to an unconscious absolutization of the Anglo folk dichotomy opposing body to mind (cf. Wierzbicka, 1989). For example, Coulter (1986) wrote that

> in one form or another, the basic categories of emotion (e.g., anger, fear, grief, shame, happiness, guilt, disgust, regret, envy, pride, wonder, remorse, sadness, jealousy, embarrassment) will admit of combination with the concept of feeling; thus, we get "feels angry," "feels grief-stricken," "feels ashamed," "feels proud," and so on. Because we can also combine the notion of feels with a wide range of sensation concepts, as in "I feel tired," "she feels toothache," "he feels hungry," "she felt thirsty," "I feel pain," the stage is set for the misassimilation of emotions to sensations (i.e., in the formal mode, the treatment of the categories of affects as if they functioned identically in our talk to the categories of sensation). This has been a pervasive mistake in the history of philosophical and psychological reflection on the subject. Hume (1739/1978) remarked: "When I am angry, I am actually possessed with the passion, and in that emotion have no more reference to any other object, than when I am thirsty, or sick, or more than five feet high."
>
> Clearly, this misses the point that we cannot even begin to *identify* the emotion we are dealing with unless we take into account how a person is appraising an object or situation. (p. 121)

Thus, Coulter assumed that emotions and sensations are essentially different phenomena (as body and mind are different entities), and that whoever fails to distinguish them sharply one from the other commits a serious error (misassimilation of emotions to sensations).

Yet, in natural languages, emotions are rarely distinguished from sensations, the two being usually subsumed under one category of feelings. In English, the verb *feel* applies to both bodily and mental phenomena. Scholars committed to the emotion–sensation distinction may deplore this vagueness of the verb *feel* or may even regard this verb as polysemous, but linguistic evidence does not support this view. The question, "How do you feel now?" or the statement, "I feel very well" can apply equally well to physical and mental feelings (or to an inextricable mixture of both), and there is no evidence of ambiguity here. The fact that one can say, "I feel cold and miserable," conjoining a physical and a mental predicate nominal with the same copula verb *feel* argues against any polysemy of this verb (one can't say, *"I know John and the answer to this question"). In other languages, which do not distinguish lexically between body and mind or between sensations and emotions, there is even less reason to suspect that the equivalent of the verb feel is polysemous.

This is not to say that the distinction between emotions and sensations is not a useful one. But it seems to be one of those distinctions that originate in the English language and in the ethnopsychology embodied in it and that have been taken over by the language of scholarship as one of its basic concepts, defining a domain of research, used repeatedly in the titles of academic books and journals, in the names of scholarly associations or institutions, and so on.

There is nothing wrong with such an elevation in status of an ordinary English concept. But it should be remembered that from a universal, language-independent point of view, it is the undifferentiated feel that is a truly fundamental human concept, not the more elaborated, more culture-dependent, and theory-laden emotion.

The concept of emotion involves a combination of feeling, thinking, and an unspecified internal process. In the language of universal semantic primitives, this may be represented as follows:

Emotion
Person X thought something.
Because of this, X felt something.
Because of this, something happened to (in) X.

One could say that the English concept of emotion picks out one type of feeling (cognitively based feelings) as an important category, distinct from other types of feelings, and that it links it with a vague reference to something that happens to or in a person as a result of the feeling in question. The English concept of sensation is probably built, by negation, on the concept of a cognitively based feeling:

Sensation
Person X felt something,
not because X thought something.

(The temptation to define emotion via mind and sensation via body must be resisted because the very notions of mind and body are culture-specific, and the tendency to view human beings in terms of a sharp dichotomy between mind and body is no doubt related to the tendency to distinguish sharply between emotions and sensations; cf. Wierzbicka, 1993b).

In his classic article, "What is an emotion?" James (1884) advanced the view that, as Solomon (1984) put it, "An emotion is the perception of a visceral disturbance brought about by a traumatic perception, for example, seeing a bear leap out in front of you or coming across a bucket filled with blood" (p. 238). James's theory would suggest the following semantic formula:

Person X thought something (e.g., "A bear!").
Because of this, X felt something.
Because of this, something happened to X (a visceral disturbance).

But the folk model of human experience reflected in the English language offers a different picture, with the bodily events being triggered by the feeling rather than causing the feeling. Linguistic evidence suggests that a blush is normally seen as triggered by the feeling of shame or embarrassment rather than being a trigger itself, that tears are normally interpreted as an expression of sadness rather than as its cause, and that our hidden visceral disturbances are seen as caused by, rather than causing, the feelings of fear, anger, or disappointment. The order of components proposed here reflects the folk model.

However, in real life, it is often difficult to understand the causes of one's feelings and to see clearly whether they are or are not due directly to certain thoughts. In the situation described at the beginning of this section, causal links between my feelings and my thoughts were by no means clear to me; and it was not clear whether any thoughts, and if so, which ones, were responsible for the burning feeling in my chest.

The existence in English of the lexical category of emotion (distinct from sensation) encourages speakers of English to interpret their experience in terms of the model suggested by this category. But there is no reason to think that people universally distinguish their mental feelings from their sensations, or expect to be able to do so (or that they view the former as a potential source of disruption, danger, or vulnerability). Languages that have a limited vocabulary for cognitively based feelings and that rely instead on body images do not encourage any sharp dichotomy between feelings based on thoughts and feelings not based on thoughts. For example, in the Austronesian language Mangap-Mbula of New Guinea, images involving *liver* are used for talking about all kinds of feelings (or states linked with feelings; Bugenhagen, 1990, p. 205). For example,

Expression	Gloss
kete- (i)malmal	angry (liver fight)
kete- (i)bayou	very angry (liver hot)
kete- (i)beleu	uncontrollably angry (liver swirl)
kete- pitpit	get excited too quickly (liver jumps)
kete- ikam ken	startled (liver does snapping)
kete- biibi	too slow (liver is big)
kete- kutkut	anxious (liver beats)
kete- iluumu	at peace (liver cool)
kete- imaraaza	painfully hungry (liver is torn)
kete- pas	out of breath or lose one's temper (liver removes)
kete- patnana	calm, unmoved, long-suffering (liver is rock-like)
kete- ise	aroused (liver goes up)
kete- isu	take a rest (liver goes down)
kete- pakpak	very angry (liver is sour).

It seems most unlikely that native speakers of a language like Mangap-Mbula would conceptualize their experience in terms of a dichotomy between emotions and other feelings; or that a Mangap-Mbula scholar would declare as confidently as Coulter (1986) did, that "emotions and sensations are different sorts of phenomena" (p. 122).

If words such as *emotion* or *sensation* are taken for granted and if their English-based character is not kept in mind, they can reify (for English speakers and English writers) phenomena that are inherently fluid and that can be conceptualized and categorized in different ways. Phrases such as "psychology of emotion," or "psychobiological theory of emotion," or "operational definition of emotion (such as galvanic skin response)" create the impression that emotion is an objectively existing category delimited from other categories by nature itself, and that the concept of emotion carves nature at its joints. We do not have to turn to exotic languages and cultures such as Mangap-Mbula to find evidence of different ways of conceptualizing and categorizing human experience.

In ordinary German, there is no word for emotion at all, and the word used as the translation equivalent of the English *emotion*, that is, *Gefühl* (from *fühlen*, to feel) makes no distinction between mental and physical feelings (although contemporary scientific German uses increasingly the word *emotion*, no doubt borrowed from scientific English; whereas in older academic German, the compound *Gemütsbewegung*, literally movement of the mind, was often used in a similar sense). At the same time, the plural form of this word, *Gefühle*, is restricted to cognitively based feelings, although—unlike the English *emotion*—it does not imply any bodily disturbances or processes of any kind. This can be represented as follows:

Gefühl (singular)
Person X felt something.
Gefühle (plural)
Person X thought something.
Because of this, X felt something.

In Polish, too, there is just one noun, *uczucie*, corresponding to both emotion and feeling, and again, the plural of this noun—*uczucia*—is restricted to cognitively based feelings. The same is true of Russian, where the noun *čuvstvo* (from *čuvstvovat'*, to feel) corresponds to both feeling and emotion, and where the plural form *čuvstva* suggests cognitively based feelings. In English, the plural "feelings" suggest cognitively based states and, unlike the singular "feeling," can hardly refer to a purely somatic experience:

I have a strange feeling in my stomach/throat/knee.
*I have strange feelings in my stomach/throat/knee/legs.

This contrast between singular and plural may be explained as follows. Plural tends to imply countability; countability implies discreteness; and in the realm of subjective experience, it is thoughts (cognitive structures) that provide discrete interpretive schemes, the raw experience being essentially nondiscrete.

To take one more example of a different categorization of subjective experience, we will note that French has no noun corresponding to an undifferentiated feeling (although it has the verb *sentir* corresponding to the English feel), and that it has instead the noun *sentiment*, which (in contemporary French) stands exclusively for a cognitively based feeling. French also has the word *émotion*, which differs in meaning from the English *emotion*, referring only to internal events that are intense and difficult to control. For example, *tristesse* (sadness) or *dépression*, *déprimé* (depression, depressed) are not considered by my French informants as *des émotions*, whereas in English, sadness and depression rate highly on the list of prototypical emotions (cf. Fehr & Russell, 1984, p. 472). The French *émotion* appears to be overwhelming as well as involuntary. This may be represented as follows:

Émotion
Person X thought something.
Because of this, X felt something.
Because of this, something happened to X.
X did not want to feel this.
X could not feel this.

(Again, in French scholarly literature the word *émotion* is used in a sense modeled on that of the English *emotion* and borrowed from English scientific publications.)

I will note in passing that the Italian word *emozione* and the Spanish word *emoción* are not equivalent to the English *emotion* either and are, in fact, closer to the French *émotion*, although by no means identical to it. (The *Collins Gem Italian Dictionary*, 1982, glosses *emozione* as emotion, excitement, and the *Collins Spanish Dictionary*, 1988, glosses *emoción* as "(a) emotion, feeling; (b) excitement, thrill, tension, suspense.") On the other hand, both Italian and Spanish have words corresponding to the French *sentiment* (*sentimento* in Italian and *sentimiento* in Spanish) and referring to cognitively based feelings. The basic meaning of these words may be represented as follows:

> Sentiment, Sentimento, Sentimiento
> Person X thought something.
> Because of this, X felt something.

This meaning differs in an interesting way from that of the rather marginal and not entirely "serious" English word *sentiment*, which *Webster's Dictionary* (1965) defines perceptively as "thought prompted by ... feeling":

> Sentiment
> Person X felt something.
> Because of this, X thought something.

Linguistic evidence suggests, then, that the English concept of emotion is highly language specific. It is also culture specific, insofar as it links the idea of cognitively based feelings with the idea of something like a bodily disturbance. Concepts such as *sentiment, sentimento, sentimiento, Gefühle, uczucia,* or *čuvstva* do not do that.

Fehr and Russell (1984) quoted the following characteristic sentence from an English-language introductory psychology textbook:

> A state of emotion is recognized by its holder as a departure from his or her normal state of composure; at the same time there are physical changes that can be detected objectively. (p. 473)

Sentences of this kind, seemingly objective and scientific, are loaded with unconscious cultural assumptions and are saturated with values of Anglo-American culture. The basic assumption is that a person's normal state is a state of composure, and that an emotion constitutes a departure from a normal state.

There is ample evidence showing that, from the point of view of Russian culture, emotions (states such as joy, worry, sadness, sorrow, grief, delight, and so on) constitute most people's normal state, and that an absence of emotions indicates a deadening of a person's *duša* (heart or soul). The cultural ideal of composure as a person's normal state is totally alien to that culture (cf. Wierzbicka, 1989, 1990a, 1992c).

Similarly, Ekman's (1992, p. 11) suggestion that "emotions are typically a matter of seconds, not minutes or hours" (based on the distinction between emotions and moods) reflects a highly culture-specific point of view and reifies distinctions drawn by the English lexicon (even French does not have a word for mood nor, we have seen, an exact equivalent for emotion). Anglo males, trained to control and suppress their feelings, may only experience excitement, anxiety, anguish, fear, sadness, or grief for a matter of seconds rather than minutes or hours; but this cannot be applied to all human beings.

In French or German culture, emotions do not occupy as central a place as they do in Russian culture, but here, too, the idea that *les sentiments* or *Gefühle* should be viewed as a departure from the normal state of composure would strike most people as bizarre, as would also the notion that they (*les sentiments* or *Gefühle*) tend to be dangerous and that they should be controlled. Let me quote a few more characteristic English sentences with the word *emotion*, adduced by Fehr and Russell (1984):

> When sufficiently intense, emotion can seriously impair the processes that control organized behavior.
> Sometimes emotion is hard to control.
> Emotion accompanies motivated behavior; the effect can be facilitating or interfering. (p. 473)

It is interesting to compare the characteristic Anglo attitude to emotions reflected in these sentences with that reflected in Goethe's reference to "the wonderful feelings which gave us life":

> *Die uns das Leben gaben, herrliche Gefühle*
> *Erstarren in dem irdischen Gewühle.*
> The fine emotions whence our lives we mold
> Lie in the earthly tumult dumb and cold.
> (Faust, Pt.i, sc.1, 1.286, quoted in Stevenson, 1958, p. 661)

From the point of view of German culture, *herrliche Gefühle* (literally, glorious feelings) are not something that must be controlled or something that threatens to impair or interfere with organized behavior, rather, they are positive forces that "give us life."

I am suggesting that whereas the concept of feeling is universal and can be used safely in the investigation of human experience and human nature, the concept of emotion is culture bound and cannot be similarly relied on.

Scholars who debate the nature of emotions are interested in something other than just feelings. The notion that emotions must not be reduced to feelings is one of the few ideas on which advocates of different approaches to emotion (biological, cognitive, and sociocultural) generally strongly agree (cf. Lutz, 1986, p. 295; Schachter & Singer, 1962; Solomon, 1984, p. 248). Because it is the universal concept of feel (rather than the Anglo concept of emotion) that provides a handle on the phenomena in question, we would do well to define the area under consideration with reference to feeling. We could ask, When people feel something, what happens to them (or in them)? What do they do? What do they think? What do they say? Do they think they know what they feel? Can they identify their feelings for themselves and for others? Does their interpretation of what they feel appear to depend on what they think they should feel or on what they think people around them think they should feel? How are people's reported or presumed feelings related to what is thought of, in a given society, as good or bad? How are they related to human interaction? And so on.

Ellsworth (chapter 2, this volume) states that

> even within English, ... the term "feel" was not generally used to refer to emotional states ("feel sad," "feel ashamed") until the nineteenth century; before that one simply *was* sad or ashamed, and "to feel something" typically meant to touch it (Miller, in press). Thus, the phrase that Wierzbicka commonly uses in her prototypical scenarios—"X feels something"—was not emotionally meaningful in English until quite recently. (chapter 2, this volume, p. 43)

Whereas it is true that until recently phrases such as "X was sad/ashamed" were more common than "X felt sad/ashamed," the verb feel has for centuries been used in English with reference to internal (in particular, emotional) states, and not only in reference to touching as the following quotes from the *Oxford English Dictionary* (1933) clearly demonstrate:

> Grete feblesse he fielde (1290).
> In myn herte I feele yet the fire ... that made me to ryse
> (Chaucer, 1385).
> I have not at all felt the emotion I shewed (1634).
> He best can paint 'em [woes] who shall feel 'em most
> (Pope, 1717).
> Feelest thou thy selfe well (1583)?
> He felt in his heart ... a ... conceit or feeling of feare (1632).
> I ... have ingenious feeling of my huge sorrowes
> (Shakespeare, 1604).

Cross-linguistic investigations suggest that, in most languages, one commonly uses phrases such as "X was sad/ashamed" rather than "X felt sad/ashamed," so premodern English is no exception in this regard. The rise and expansion of the two feel patterns in modern English ("X felt sad/ashamed," "X felt sadness/shame") reflects a heightened cultural attention to feelings as such, regardless of their cognitive, behavioral, social, and moral ramifications. But concepts such as sad or ashamed depend on the existence of a basic concept of feel and the presence of such a concept is attested to in all the languages that have been thoroughly investigated from this point of view (including Old and Middle English).

This concept is realized in a limited range of collocations, such as "I feel bad" and "I feel good" (or "I stomach/belly/insides [are] good," "I stomach/belly/insides [are] bad"), but it is demonstrably there. In addition, this concept is lexically embodied in a more complex concept, such as sad or ashamed, where it is combined with other components (cognitive, social, moral, or behavioral). As pointed out by Russell (1991), it is an illusion to think that one can speak about emotions without a reference to internal states (feelings) because the concept of emotion is built upon the concept of feeling. Whereas in many cultures, one seldom speaks about feelings as such and usually refers to feelings only as embedded in a social, moral, and behavioral context, evidence suggests that the concept of feeling is nonetheless universal; and being universal, it offers a firm point of reference in attempts to describe and compare cultures. Without using this concept, we could not say that, in many cultures, people seldom speak about feelings as such and that they usually combine references to how one feels with references to what one does and what one thinks, what other people do and think and to what is regarded as a good or a bad thing to do, and so on. Lutz (1982) wrote:

> Internal feeling states have commonly been assumed to be the primary referents of emotion words in Western thought, both social–scientific and lay.... Examination of the use of emotion words among several Oceanic peoples ... reveals an alternative view of emotion. In these societies, emotion words are seen as statements about the relationship between a person and an event (particularly those involving another person), rather than as statements about introspection on one's internal states. (p. 113)

Russell (1991) commented on this passage as follows:

> I take this assertion to mean, for example, that the Ifalukian word *song*, commonly translated as *anger*, refers not to the angry person's internal state, but to something external. There is first the question of whether Lutz's claim is consistent with her own ethnographic evidence. Lutz (1980) had earlier indicated that *song* refers to *niferash*, which she translated as "our insides." Second, there is the conceptual issue of how a word in any language that does not refer to an internal state could be said to be an emotion word. (p. 445)

I think that Russell is right: A word that does not refer to an internal state cannot be said to be an emotion word; Ifaluk words such as *song* do refer (on Lutz's evidence) to *niferash*, and *niferash* (again on Lutz's evidence) means (a) our insides and (b) feel. Lutz is right, too, in stressing the importance of the social and moral aspects of concepts such as *song*; but this is compatible with recognizing that feel (rather than emotion) constitutes a universal human concept, and that people all over the world (including the Ifaluk atoll) in their language-and-culture systems link feelings with notions of what people do and say and of what they regard as good or bad.

I am not suggesting that the term *emotion* should be banned, that journals such as *Cognition and Emotion* should change their names, or that the International Society for Research on Emotions should disband. *Emotion is* an important English word. There is no reason why it should be abandoned in English discourse, including academic discourse; and I have no qualms about using this word myself, in this chapter and elsewhere. However, it is important to realize the complex and culture-specific character of this concept and not to absolutize it, bearing always in mind its dependence on the concept of feel and on other conceptual primitives.

Panksepp (1982) wrote, "The semantic controversies that routinely arise in the discussion of emotion have long hindered the progress of research in this area" (p. 449; quoted in Fehr & Russell, 1984, p. 483), and "it is unlikely that we can resolve disagreements concerning the meanings of terms such as *emotions* and *feelings*" (p. 453).

I disagree. Given a coherent semantic theory and a well-developed semantic methodology, the meaning of words such as *feelings* and *emotions can* be stated in a nonarbitrary way open to intersubjective assessment; and it is the absence of serious investigation of the semantics of emotions, rather than its exaggerated pursuit, that has long hindered the progress of research in this area.

Cultural Scripts: Examples From Anglo and Polish Culture

Different cultures take different attitudes toward emotions, and these attitudes influence the way in which people speak. They influence human conceptualization of emotions reflected in lexical terms such as *happy* or *angry* in English, in grammatical patterns such as the various *experiencer constructions* (described by Ameka [1990] for the West African language Ewe, and by Bugenhagen [1990] for the Austronesian language Mangap-Mbula of Papua New Guinea) or in emotive interjections (cf. Wierzbicka, 1992d; and the other articles in Ameka, 1992).

However, different cultural attitudes toward emotions exert a profound influence on the dynamics of everyday discourse; they shape and color innumerable aspects of what Hymes (1962) has called the "ethnography of speaking."

Scholars and casual observers alike have often tried to describe differences of this kind by means of contrasting labels such as emotional and antiemotional, or expressive and nonexpressive. But labels of this kind are unsatisfactory. For example, cultures can be said to be emotional (e.g., the Russian, Polish, Jewish, or Black American cultures), but the word would stand for different attitudes and norms in each of these cases. Similarly, whereas both mainstream Anglo and Japanese cultures could be said to be nonemotional (e.g., from a Slavic perspective), applying the same word to both these cultures would probably be more misleading than useful. Many Japanese scholars see attitudes toward emotions as one of the key differences between the Japanese and Anglo cultures and would strongly object to attempts to lump the two together under a single label, such as nonemotional (cf. Doi, 1974; Honna & Hoffer, 1989; Lebra, 1974; Nakane, 1974; Suzuki, 1986). Even within the Anglo (White) culture, there are considerable differences in this regard, and global labels (e.g., emotional or nonemotional) would be of no use in trying to portray them.

To portray different cultural attitudes toward emotion in a revealing manner, we do not need global labels or schematic dichotomies, but individualized *culture scripts* written in lexical universals (or near-universals). In what follows, I will illustrate and substantiate this point by comparing Polish and Anglo cultures (drawing also some distinctions between Anglo-American culture and Anglo-Australian culture).[2] As my point of departure, I will take selected observations from the cultural autobiography of Eva Hoffman (1989), an American writer whose Polish–Jewish family emigrated from Poland to North America when the author was a teenager. Hoffman's book not only captured "the very essence of exile experience" (to quote the Czech writer Josef Skvorecky[3]) but also provided penetrating insights into Polish and Anglo cultural attitudes and norms that have clashed in the author's personal experience. Hoffman's

---

[2]For discussion of Anglo-Australian culture (as reflected in the Australian English language and ethnography of speaking), see Wierzbicka (1986, 1992c).
[3]I repeat here Skvorecky's words quoted on the jacket of Hoffman's book.

book provided excellent material for the study of Polish and Anglo cultural scripts concerning emotions. I will also draw, to an extent, on my own experience as a Polish–English bilingual who has lived for 20 years in Australia. To highlight some of the points that I want to make, I will also make fleeting references to a few other cultures, notably the Japanese, Jewish, and Balinese.

Expressing Good Feelings Toward the Addressee

> My mother says I'm becoming "English." This hurts me, because I know she means I'm becoming cold. I'm no colder than I've ever been, but I'm learning to be less demonstrative. I learn this from a teacher who, after contemplating the gesticulations with which I help myself describe the digestive system of a frog, tells me to "sit on my hands and then try talking." I learn my new reserve from people who take a step back when we talk, because I'm standing too close, crowding them. Cultural distances are different, I later learn in a sociology class, but I know it already. I learn restraint from Penny, who looks offended when I shake her by the arm in excitement, as if my gesture had been one of aggression instead of friendliness. I learn it from a girl who pulls away when I hook my arm through hers as we walk down the street—this movement of friendly intimacy is an embarrassment to her.
>
> Perhaps my mother is right, after all; perhaps I'm becoming colder. After a while, emotion follows action, response grows warmer or cooler according to gesture. I'm more careful about what I say, how loud I laugh, whether I give vent to grief. The storminess of emotion prevailing in our family is in excess of the normal here, and the unwritten rules for the normal have their osmotic effect. (Hoffman, 1989, pp. 146–147)

To be perceived as cold means to be perceived as someone who does not feel. In Polish culture, behavior that shows feeling is seen as the norm, not as a departure from the norm (the latter point of view is reflected in the English word *emotional*, which has no equivalent in Polish and which implies mild disapproval). This central place of feelings (spontaneously shown feelings) in Polish culture manifests itself in many ways. For reasons of space, only one or two can be touched upon here.

To begin with, speaking of any kind (including everyday conversation, abstract discussions, evaluation, even exchange of information) is normally expected to be accompanied by some degree of emotion. In Anglo culture, "cold speech" is associated with ideals such as self-control (discussed later) and the ability to be dispassionate. But if the word *dispassionate* has positive connotations in English, its closest counterpart in Polish, the adverb *beznamiętnie* (literally, without passion) has slightly negative connotations. It suggests indifference, lifelessness, apathy, coldness. On the other hand, the adjective *gorący* (hot) and the adverb *goraco* have very positive connotations in Polish (when applied to speech); whereas in English, the word *heated* (as in heated discussion) has slightly pejorative connotations. Similarly, the word *cool* has positive connotations in English (to keep cool); whereas the corresponding Polish temperature word (*chlodny*) when applied to talk, implies an unpleasant, hostile attitude. Safe speech genres (e.g., small talk) are not valued in Polish culture either (and there is no expression in Polish corresponding to small talk) because both animation and controversy are valued and expected. (One wants to talk about those things that one feels about; and if a subject [e.g., the digestive system of a frog] is worth talking about at all, it is only to the extent to which it can be invested with some emotion—interest, amusement, disgust.) The normal Polish attitude, then, may be represented as follows:

When I say what I think, I feel something.
I want people to know this.

Perhaps no feeling is more valued and more expected in Polish discourse than a good feeling directed at the addressee. The contrast between Polish warmth and Anglo coldness is particularly noticeable to all who have direct experience with both cultures (like Hoffman and her family). This interpersonal warmth may be linked to the following cultural script, reflected in Polish verbal and nonverbal communication:

I feel something very good toward you.
Because of this, when I say something to you,
I want to do something good to you at the same time.

The "doing something good to another person" may take the form of kisses, hugs, embraces, and so on, and it may take the form of covering another person with verbal endearments. The greater role of affectionate touching in Polish culture (and in Slavic culture in general) compared with Anglo culture is difficult to document by reference to rigorous studies but will be seen as an indubitable fact by anybody who has had any direct experience with the two cultures.

By contrast, verbal affection may be documented extensively with linguistic evidence. Terms of address always provide revealing clues to the style of social interaction prevailing in a given society; and expressive forms of people's names are as important in this regard as various polite or honorific pronouns, titles, or kinship terms.

Thus, Polish names like *Maria* and *Katarzyna* (Mary and Catherine) have entire families of derivative forms, each with its peculiar emotional attitude and emotional mood (cf. Wierzbicka, 1992c):

> *Maria*: Marysia, Marysieńka, Marychna, Marysiulka, Marysik, Mary-
> siątko, Maryśka, Marysieczka
> *Katarzyna*: Kasia, Kasieńka, Kachna, Kasiulka, Kasik, Kasiątko,
> Kaśka, Kasieńka, Kasiunia.

The very fact that in English only one or two expressive derivates are usually possible (e.g., Pamela → Pam → Pammy; Susan → Sue → Susie), and that for some names virtually no expressive derivates are readily available (e.g. Mary → ?, Beryl → ?, Justine → ?) makes interaction conducted via English seem extremely cold and unemotional to a native speaker of Polish.

It is true that some Polish expressive forms are used mainly in adult–child interaction, but others can be used generally. For example, a married couple called *Maria* and *Jan* (Mary and John) would be very likely to address one another frequently by affectionate forms such as *Marysieńko* and *Jasieńku* (both vocatives), whereas an Anglo couple called Mary and John have virtually no derivatives to draw on (Johnny being perceived as more suitable for a little boy than for a grown man).

The Polish cultural value of expressing good feelings toward the addressee is also reflected in its rich store of terms of endearment, especially metaphorical endearments (usually used in the vocative case), such as *ptaszku!* (bird-DIM), *słoneczko!* (sun-DIM), *kotku!* (kitten-DIM), *robaczku!* (worm-DIM), *żabko!* (frog-DIM), *skarbie!* (treasure), or *złotko!* (gold-DIM). Words of this kind may be used not only as parenthetical terms of address (like *honey* or *sugar* in American English), but also as exclamative utterances in their own right (like *darling!* or *sweetheart!* in English). Frequently, terms of this kind are used with the possessive pronoun *mój* (my), which underscores the personal character of the relationship, *moje złoto* (my gold), *mój skarbie* (my treasure), or *moje słoneczko* (my dear-little-sun; cf. English **My darling!* vs. **My honey!*). Metaphorical endearments are particularly common in addressing children, but are not restricted to adult–child interaction.

It is interesting to compare terms of this kind, many of them animal metaphor terms, with Australian English animal metaphor terms of address, such as chicken, chook, or possum. The Australian terms, too, imply something like affection (good feelings) to the addressee, but they cannot be used as exclamations (*Chicken! *Chook! *Possum!) and neither may they be used (as terms of address) with a possessive pronoun (*my chicken, *my chook, *my possum). Unlike the Polish endearments, which imply positive characteristics, either by virtue of their inherent semantics (e.g., gold, treasure) or by virtue of the diminutive suffix, the Australian terms in question do not imply any particular positive characteristics, and they have an antisentimental and lightly humorous aura about them (thus reflecting the characteristic Australian attitude toward emotions; cf. Wierzbicka, 1986, 1992c). They sound off-hand and slightly patronizing (though affectionate). They do not have the open, un-self-conscious tenderness of the Polish terms. The two attitudes (Polish and Australian English) may be represented as follows:

Polish: (a) I feel something very good toward you

(b) I want you to know this

(c) because of this, I want to say something very good to you

(d) I would not say something like this to other people

Australian English: (a) I feel something good toward you

(b) I don't want to say: "Something very good"

(c) because of this, I want to say something good to you, not something very good

(d) I would not say something like this to someone like me

The contrast between "very good" (Polish) and "good, not very good" (Australian) reflects the Polish love of overstatement and the Australian preference for understatement,[4] as well as the Polish need to express warmth openly and the Australian need to avoid any trace of sentimentality. Component (d) of the Polish script highlights the personal character of the affection expressed in the endearments in question, whereas the last component of the Australian script reflects the mildly patronizing and not-quite-serious character of the affection expressed in the Australian terms.

The antisentimental Australian script for endearments tallies well with the general cultural norm proscribing uninhibited expression of good feelings toward anybody or anything, which can be illustrated with the opening sentence of Alan Seymour's play *The One Day of the Year:* "I'm a bloody Australian and I'll always stand up for bloody Australia!" or in the following public statement made in the debate about the Australian flag and reported in the Australian daily newspaper, *The Australian:* "It's a bloody good flag, it's a bloody beautiful flag" (C. Stewart, 1992). The general norm reflected in such sentences, which combine an expression of good feelings with an element of defiance and toughness, may be represented as follows:

I don't want to say something like this of anyone or anything: "I feel something very good toward this person or thing"

if I feel something very good toward someone or something,

I can say something bad

(where saying something bad refers to violating a verbal taboo; cf. Wierzbicka, 1992a). Because the same rule applies in the case of very good

---

[4]The Australian penchant for (a certain kind of) understatement is reflected in the ubiquitous presence of the expression "a bit" in Australian conversation. Compare, also, the following characteristic sentence from a television advertisement for insurance: "The day our house burned down was fairly traumatic." In Polish, only adverbs like terribly (not fairly) would possibly be used in this kind of context.

feelings toward the addressee (e.g., the well-known Australian greeting: "G'day, you old bastard!"), the Australian norm for handling one's good feelings may be seen as almost an opposite of the Polish norm:

Polish
it is good to say something like this to someone:
"I feel something very good toward you"

Australian English
it is not good to say something like this to someone:
"I feel something very good toward you"
if I feel something very good toward someone (or something),
I can say something bad

The difference is not as extreme as it seems because devices for expressing good feelings are present in both these cultures. But the specific scripts for doing so are indeed very different.

My Feelings Versus Someone Else's Feelings

The Polish cultural emphasis on warmth or affection must be distinguished from the Anglo emphasis on consideration and tact and, more generally, from an attitude that may be represented as follows:

it is good to think often something like this of other people:
"I do not want this person to feel something bad
because of this, I will not say something"

Polish culture encourages the showing of good feelings toward the addressee rather than attempts not to hurt or offend the other person. For example, as pointed out by Hoffman (1989), in Polish culture, the speaker is not discouraged from saying bad things about the addressee and thus hurting the addressee's feelings:

I learn also that certain kinds of truth are impolite. One shouldn't criticize the person one is with, at least not directly. You shouldn't say, "You are wrong about that"—though you may say, "On the other hand, there is that to consider." You shouldn't say, "This doesn't look good on you," though you may say, "I like you better in that other outfit." I learn to tone down my sharpness, to do a more careful conversational minuet. (p. 146)

Of course this does not mean that Polish culture has a cultural script enjoining people to offend and hurt others along the lines of,

I want to say bad things about you
I want you to feel something bad

Rather, it has the cultural injunction to say what one thinks without the Anglo restrictions on saying what one thinks (personal remarks) about the addressee and the Anglo rules about the addressee's feelings:

Polish
it is always good to say what I think
if I think something bad about someone,
I can say this to this person

Anglo
it is not always good to say what I think
if I think something bad about someone,
it is not good to say this to this person
if I said this to someone, this person could feel something bad
I do not want this

This is not to say that Anglo culture discourages people from expressing their opinions and enjoins them not to say what they think. As has often been pointed out in various works comparing Anglo culture with Japanese culture (for references, see Wierzbicka, 1991a, 1991b), it is Japanese culture that discourages people from saying what they think and urges them always to pay attention to other people's feelings. In the case of Anglo culture, the restrictions on saying what one thinks about the addressee constitute a kind of filter on the more general assertive rule that says that everyone may say what he or she thinks:

Everyone can say: "I think this, I don't think this"

a rule that is not only different from, but virtually diametrically opposed to, the Japanese cultural norm:

I cannot say: "I think this, I do not think this"
someone could feel something bad if I said this

The consideration for other people's feelings is shared, to some extent, by both the Japanese and Anglo cultures. Within the Japanese culture, it is much more central; whereas in the Anglo culture, it is subordinated to key values (such as freedom) to express one's opinions and one's desires. Although in Anglo culture, consideration for other people's feelings is seen as subordinated to other values, nonetheless, it plays a very important role in the Anglo ethnography of speaking. In Polish culture, the emphasis is elsewhere.

In this connection, it is interesting to note the English concept of frankness (as distinct from sincerity), which has no exact equivalent in Polish. The concept of frankness acknowledges the value of saying what one thinks in spite of the fact that by doing so, one may cause someone to feel something bad (a consequence that is seen as clearly undesirable), and thus it celebrates two values at once: saying what one thinks and paying attention to other people's feelings. Polish, however, makes no lexical distinction between sincerity and frankness, and in its concept of *szczerość* (roughly, sincerity), it celebrates the value of saying what one thinks (especially with regard to personal relations).

As a further example, consider the common Anglo conversational routine of saying, "Thank you," in response to a range of positive remarks about the addressee and about anyone and anything associated with the addressee. For example,

A [owner of a country inn to a visitor]: Lovely day, isn't it?
B [visitor]: Yes, isn't it? Lovely place, too.
A: Thank you.

By saying, "Thank you," A attributes to B the following conversational attitude:

I want to say something good about this [place]
because I want you to feel something good

Having interpreted B's utterance in this way, A acknowledges it as a kind of personal gift and responds with a token repayment, in the form of professed good feelings:

I think you say this because you want me to feel something good.
because of this, I say:
"you did something good for me (by saying this)
because of this, I feel something good toward you"

In Polish, an exchange of this kind would not be possible, because A's interpretation of B's utterance would be potentially offensive to B. Because in Polish culture emotional spontaneity is valued more highly than a desire to make someone else feel good, it would be natural for the inn owner to assume that in saying, "Lovely place!", the visitor was spontaneously expressing delight. By attributing to the visitor an arrière pensée in the form of a desire to please someone (his interlocutor), the innkeeper would be questioning, by implication, the spontaneity (and, therefore, the value) of the visitor's exclamation.

A culturally encouraged desire to make one's interlocutor feel good is reflected in the important place that speech acts (such as compliments) play in Anglo culture, particularly in American culture. As Wolfson (1981, p. 123) pointed out, "in American English compliments occur in a very wide variety of situations" and "the frequency of compliments in American English is often remarked by foreigners." Wolfson suggested that compliments, as used in American English, "serve to produce or to reinforce a feeling of solidarity between speakers." But solidarity between speakers could be achieved and reinforced in many other ways (cf. Katriel's [1986] study of Israeli Hebrew or my own studies [Wierzbicka, 1986, 1991a, 1992c] of Australian English). What is characteristic of American discourse is the attitude that may be portrayed more precisely in the form of a script:

> I want to say something good about something (X)
> because I want you to feel something good

In Polish culture, the emphasis is on one's own feelings rather than on those of the addressee. The person who wants to please his or her interlocutor has to indicate that the proffered praise is spontaneous and motivated by the speaker's own feeling rather than by a desire to make the addressee feel good:

> I think something good about something (X)
> when I think about it, I feel something good
> I want to say what I feel

This is not to say that compliments have no place in Polish culture, but they are certainly more marginal than they are in American culture or even Anglo culture in general. The closest Polish equivalent of *compliment*, namely *komplement*, suggests a trivial, superficial, and insincere social game. In Polish, one can dismiss praise by calling it a *komplement* (rather like in English one can dismiss praise by calling it flattery); and common collocations involving this word include *puste komplementy* (empty compliments), *czcze komplementy* (worthless compliments), *zdawkowe komplementy* (meaningless compliments), and *sypać komplementami* (to shower someone with [empty] compliments). The English word *compliment* has no similar connotations and has a much wider range of use. All this shows that Polish culture values spontaneous expressions of feelings and not utterances motivated by anticipating the good or bad feelings of the addressee.

Spontaneity and Self-Control

In many languages, the emphasis on spontaneous self-expression is linked in a special way with the expression of bad feelings of different kinds. Australian English is particularly rich in (and makes free use of) swearing resources, reflecting a cultural norm that can be represented as follows:

when I feel something very bad,
I want to say something bad

Another language that is particularly rich in resources for expressing bad feelings is Yiddish (cf. Matisoff, 1979; Wierzbicka, 1992f). However, in Yiddish, unlike in Australian English, the cultural emphasis is clearly on impotent bad feelings ("I can't do anything" rather than "I want to do something"), and the highly developed system of lamentations and curses in Yiddish, in contrast to the highly developed system of swearing devices in Australian English, reflects this difference in cultural attitudes.[5] To quote a few examples (from Matisoff, 1979):

May a fiery pain meet her, the way she talks!
My wife—must she live?—gave it away to him for nothing.

[5]The great emphasis placed by Jewish culture on the expression of bad feelings, particularly bad feelings associated with misfortune, is highlighted by Matisoff (1979):

The Japanese, like the British, are trained from childhood to control or suppress linguistic and paralinguistic cues to their actual psychic states. It is good manners in Japan to smile when telling somebody about a death in one's own family, or indeed when conveying bad news of any kind. In Jewish culture the only way to make sense of such behavior would be to assume that the bereaved but smiling person had gone temporarily mad from grief. (The "normal" person would be weeping and uttering auto-malo-recognitive laments, vivo-bono-petitives, mortuo-bono-petitives, auto- and allo-malo-fugitives, and generally giving as much linguistic expression to his complex and turbulent emotions as he could.) (p. 90)

Salt into your eyes and pepper into your nose!
A lament to you, are you crazy or just feeble-minded?

The Yiddish norm may be represented as follows:

when I feel something bad, I want someone to know it
I can say because of this: "I want something bad to happen to some-
    one."
I cannot do anything else

Polish culture places no special emphasis on free expression of bad feelings, but it does encourage uninhibited expression of emotions in general
(in addition to good emotions directed at the addressee). As Hoffman
(1989) put it, the "storminess of emotions" in a Polish family (like her
own) is in excess of what is normal in an Anglo country; and the word
storminess refers here to both intensity and spontaneity of emotional
expression.

This spontaneous emotional expression has a communicative aspect
that can be represented as follows:

when I feel something very bad (very good),
I want someone to know it

But it cannot be reduced to the communicative aspect because when
people are alone, they are still likely to give full expression to their intense
feelings and to do so instinctively and unreflectively:

when I feel something very bad (very good),
I want to do something at the same time
I don't want to think: "I can do this, I can not do this"

The two scripts may be combined as follows:

when I feel something very bad (very good),
I want to do something at the same time
when I do it, people can know how I feel
I do not want to think: "I can do this, I can not do this"

In Wierzbicka (1991a), I represented the uninhibited emotional
expression characteristic of Polish culture in terms of the formula "I want
to say what I feel." But this may require slight modification because Polish

culture encourages people to *show* emotions (verbally or nonverbally) rather than to *speak* about them.[6] Polish culture does not have a tradition of elaborate verbalization of emotions (characteristic of French culture) or of highly developed analysis of one's own emotions (characteristic of modern American culture). Polish culture encourages spontaneity, not introspection. To quote Hoffman (1989) again:

> Between the two stories and two vocabularies, there's a vast alteration in the diagram of the psyche and the relationship to inner life. When I say to myself, "I'm anxious," I draw on different faculties than when I say, "I'm afraid." "I'm anxious because I have problems with separation," I tell myself very rationally when a boyfriend leaves for a long trip, and in that quick movement of self-analysis and explanation the trajectory of feeling is re-routed. I no longer follow it from impulse to expression; now that I understand what the problem is, I won't cry at the airport. By this ploy, I mute the force of the original fear; I gain some control. . . . I've become a more self-controlled person over the years—more "English," as my mother told me years ago. I don't allow myself to be blown about this way and that helplessly; I've learned how to use the mechanisms of my will, how to look for symptom and root cause before sadness or happiness overwhelm me. I've gained some control, and control is something I need more than my mother did. I have more of a public life, in which it's important to appear strong. I live in an individualistic society, in which people blend less easily with each other, in which "That's your problem" is a phrase of daily combat and self-defense. (pp. 269–270)

This time, Hoffman interprets her mother's epithet "English" not in terms of interpersonal warmth but in terms of control over one's emotions, control that is based on self-analysis.[7] Hoffman's comments based on

---

[6]One can say things (speak) manually as well as orally (e.g., by using American Sign Language or other sign languages); but communicative–expressive acts such as smiling, crying, or kissing must be distinguished from speaking by means other than the use of voice (Kendon, 1990; Wierzbicka, in press-b).

[7]The sociologist Arlie Hochschild (1983), who did a study of American students' ways of talking about their emotions (on the basis of questionnaires given to 261 students at the University of California, Berkeley), reports that her respondents "often spoke of acts *upon* feelings: of *trying* to fall in love or *putting a damper* on love, of *trying to feel* grateful, of *trying not* to feel depressed, of *checking* their anger, of *letting* themselves feel sad" (p. 13).

personal experience echo those of social commentators who have often pointed out the paramount importance of constant scanning of one's feelings in American culture. Bellah, Sullivan, Swidler, and Tipton (1985) linked this cultural preoccupation with the place of psychotherapy in American society and with the role of psychotherapy as a model of human relationships. They pointed out that "practitioners [of psychotherapy] stress the primary importance of 'knowing how you're feeling'" (p. 128). The culturally endorsed attitudes in question can be represented as follows:

> I want to know how I feel at this time
> I want to know why I feel like this
> I want to think about this
> if I know why I feel like this, I can do something

This constant attention to one's feelings and the inclination to analyze and verbalize them is clearly reflected in American popular literature where the authors seem to be constantly at pains to describe exactly just how they or their heroes were feeling at any given time. For example, in Elizabeth Glaser's (1991) moving autobiography, there are references to feelings on almost every page and often several times on one page:

> I felt so alienated from the normal world (p. 109).
> I still felt . . . nonstop nervousness when we were in public (p. 170).
> [I] feel lucky that I get to call her a friend (p. 171).
> I felt devoid of almost any optimism (p. 171).
> I began to think that I would feel dead until I died (p. 171).
> I knew I would feel cold and black inside (p. 171).
> . . . just how wretched I felt inside (p. 172).
> It was wonderful to feel momentarily alive (p. 175).
> I felt so devastated (p. 175).
> We felt like detectives (p. 176).
> I felt bleak and overwhelmed (p. 185).
> I felt scared (p. 183).
> I feel so frightened and helpless (p. 185).
> Paul and I felt awful (p. 184).
> I could feel my head reverberate (p. 189).

I hadn't felt that drenching sadness (p. 188).

I feel free, fast, and powerful (p. 190).

I feel almost normal (p. 190).

My knees felt weak (p. 190).

I could feel myself coming alive again (p. 190).

I felt invigorated and slightly reborn (p. 191).

Self-analysis and self-control are particularly encouraged in the case of negative feelings. To quote Hoffman (1989) again:

> In the project of gaining control, I've been aided by the vocabulary of self-analysis, and by the prevailing assumption that it's good to be in charge. "I've got to get some control," my friends say when something troubles them or goes wrong. It is shameful to admit that sometimes things can go very wrong; it's shameful to confess that sometimes we have no control. (p. 270)

The cultural attitude referred to in this passage can be represented as follows:

when I feel something bad, I want to think about it
when I think about it, I cannot feel like this (anymore)

The ability to analyze one's feelings rationally is important in Anglo culture because self-analysis enables people to gain some distance from their emotions, and this distance is a prerequisite of emotional self-control, in the double sense of controlling emotional expression ("I will not cry at the airport") and of changing one's feelings (shaping them and decreasing their intensity).

Culture plays a role at every level of this process: (a) One identifies one's feelings in terms of concepts provided by a language-and-culture system (e.g., anxious or afraid); (b) the element of thinking about one's feelings and of looking for their causes reflects the general emphasis of Anglo culture on rational analysis and on explanations; (c) the idea of controlling one's feelings is part of the general Anglo emphasis on control, on shaping events in accordance with one's will; and (d) the suppression of involuntary expressive behavior (such as crying) reflects the general abhorrence of the involuntary and the irrational.

Hoffman's personal testimony that, in gaining control, she was aided by the vocabulary of self-analysis, tallies with the general cultural norms reflected in American English and the American ethnography of speaking. In particular, crucial conceptual categories such as stress, depression, or relaxation (and the corresponding adjectives stressed out, depressed, relaxed) witness the enormous influence of psychotherapeutic language on everyday emotion talk. A comparison of the English and the Polish lexicon in this regard is revealing because Polish does not have common everyday words for any of these concepts. The recent emergence in Polish of English load words such as *stres* and *relaks* highlights the absence of concepts of this kind in Polish folk psychology. The Polish word *przygnębiony* could be said to be not too different from *depressed*, but it has no clinical connotations, and apart from the fact that it is used much more rarely than *depressed*, it is rarely used to describe purely internal states:

I feel depressed.

? Czuję się przygnębiony.

Przygnębiony is closer in its use to English words and expressions such as *downcast, dejected*, or *in low spirits*, which are most naturally used about other people, rather than about oneself and which are not entirely natural in the "I feel" frame:

He was downcast/dejected/in low spirits.

? I feel downcast/dejected/in low spirits.

The most common Polish emotion terms used about one's own current state appear to be *zdenerwowany(a), zły(a), wściekły*, and *zmartwiony*, all of which imply a lack of control over one's emotional state. *Zdenerwowany* is an extremely common word, with no equivalent or even near-equivalent in English, which implies a state of abnormal inner agitation and readiness to explode (a kind of opposite of calm). *Zły* (literally, bad) implies a kind of crude anger that one has no wish to control. *Wściekły* comes close to furious or mad, but it is much more readily used in self-reports referring to the speaker's current state:

Wściekła jestem!

? I am mad (furious)!

Finally, *zmartwiony*, which could be glossed roughly as worried, does not have the active (though uncontrolled) character of *zdenerwowany*, *zły*, or *wściekły*, but it does imply a passive kind of out-of-controlness not unlike that implied by the English word *upset*.

It is particularly interesting to note that none of these four common words for negative emotions corresponds to any of the supposedly universal basic emotions. None of them corresponds exactly to the English word *angry* or *anger*. As mentioned earlier, the closest Polish equivalent of anger, namely *gniew*, is not nearly so common and intuitively basic as anger is in English. It implies a level of awareness, discernment, and control that makes it inapplicable to children, and it is undoubtedly less common and intuitively basic than *złość* (literally, badness), which implies neither discernment nor control and which is, nonetheless, not pejorative like the English word *tantrum*.

In Polish culture, then, the normal attitude toward emotions is different from that of American culture. Instead of seeking to know "what I feel" and "why I feel like this," one wants *others* to know "what I feel" (or rather "how I feel"). In this cultural universe, there is no need for me to know what I feel or to think about what I feel, or why I feel it. Rather, there is a need to *express* my feeling and to express it *now* without thinking about it and without trying to analyze it, shape it, or suppress it:

> Once, when my mother was very miserable, I told her, full of my newly acquired American wisdom, that she should try to control her feelings. "What do you mean?" she asked, as if this was an idea proffered by a member of a computer species. "How can I do that? They are my feelings."
>
> My mother cannot imagine tampering with her feelings, which are the most authentic part of her, which are her. She suffers her emotions as if they were forces of nature, winds and storms and volcanic eruptions. She is racked by the movements of passion—*passio*, whose meaning is suffering. (Hoffman, 1989, p. 269)

The American folk philosophy stressing the need for control over one's emotions is reflected revealingly in the interviews on emotion conducted with 15 American men and women by Lutz (1988a). As Lutz observed,

> One theme that frequently arises in the interviews is what can be called "the rhetoric of control" (R. Rosaldo, 1978). When people are asked to talk about emotions, one of the most common set [*sic*] of metaphors used are those in which someone or something controls, handles, copes, deals, disciplines or manages either or both their emotions or the situation seen as creating the emotion. (p. 4)

To illustrate, one of Lutz's female respondents spoke as follows of a friend grieving over her son's death two years earlier: "You've got to pick up and go on. You've got to try and get those feelings under control (p. 74)."

The Polish cultural emphasis on the involuntary character of feelings is reflected in Polish grammar, which has a productive pattern for talking about involuntary emotions. For example,

A. *Jaś*   *był*   *smutny.*
    Johnny-NOM   was   sad-ADJ.
    Johnny was sad.

B. *Jasiowi*   *było*   *smutno.*
    Johnny-DAT   was-IMP   sad-ADV.

In the A pattern, the experiencer is in the nominative, the copula agrees with the subject in gender (masculine), and the predicate word is an adjective; in the B pattern, the experiencer is in the dative, the copula has an impersonal (neuter) form, and the predicate word is an adverb. Semantically, Pattern A corresponds to the English gloss (Johnny was sad); Pattern B, however, has no exact English equivalent (the closet being probably "sadness came over Johnny").

Pattern B, which plays a very important role in the Polish conceptualization of emotions, does not always have a Pattern A counterpart at all when it is based on a predicate that, in its adjectival form, does not designate an emotion. For example,

Jasiowi   *było*   *przykro.*
Johnny-DAT   was-IMP   unpleasant-ADV.
Johnny was hurt.

Because this grammatical pattern focuses entirely on the experiencer's subjective feeling, it occurs most often and most naturally in the first person:

Było   *mi*   *gorzko/nieprzyjemnie/przyjemnie.*
Was-IMP   me-DAT   bitter/unpleasant/pleasant-ADV.
I was in a better/unpleasant/pleasant state.

Było   *mi*   *ciężko/leko na sercu.*
(It)was-IMP   me-DAT   heavy/light-ADV on heart-LOC.
I was in a heavy (oppressive)/light state.

Admittedly, Polish has also a voluntary pattern for talking about emotions, but this voluntary pattern does not indicate that the feelings are controlled, but rather, that the experiencer is giving in to a feeling. For example, verbs such as *smucić się* (from *smutny*, sad) or *złościć się* (from *zły*, angry/cross/bad-tempered) imply a kind of voluntary (unchecked) wallowing in a feeling, and therefore can hardly be linked with emotional self-control. The fact that Polish is very rich in verbs of this kind (many of them without any corresponding adjectives) highlights the salience of this attitude in Polish culture. Some examples:

cieszyć się	rejoice
martwić się	worry
denerwować się	(cf. *nerwy*, nerves)
wstydzić się	(cf. *wstyd*, shame)
gniewać się	(cf. *gniew*, anger)
niepokoić się	(cf. *niepokój*, anxiety)
złościć się	(cf. *zły*, bad or angry/mad).

Far from suggesting any control over one's emotions, verbs of this kind suggest that the experiencer is acting out an involuntary impulse, amplifying it, and giving it full vent. They imply nothing of that "rerouting of the trajectory of feeling" (from impulse to expression) that Hoffman (1989) linked with "the quick movement of self-analysis and explanation" encouraged by Anglo culture (p. 269). On the contrary, they imply both a voluntary attitude of giving in to the impulse and an immediate expression of the feeling.

There is a clear difference in this respect between the adverbial–dative pattern and the verbal pattern. For example, the sentence

Wstyd   *mi.*
Shame-ADV   me-DAT.
I was in a state of shame.

means, roughly speaking, that I am ashamed and that I cannot do anything about it and refers to a passive inner state inaccessible to external observers; whereas the corresponding verbal construction

Wstydzę   *się.*
shame-VERB-1stSg   REFL

implies not only an active inner attitude (as if it were intentionally amplifying the involuntary feeling) but also some sort of external expression. The passive versus active contrast is reflected in the differential use of the imperative construction:

A. *Nie wstydź się!*
   Don't shame yourself!
B. *? Niech ci nie będzie wstyd!*
   Let you not experience shame!

The difference with regard to external expression is reflected in the fact that an external observer can report someone else's emotion in the verbal pattern, but not in the adverbial–dative construction:

A. *Zauważyłem, że Jaś zawstydził się.*
   I noticed that Johnny got ashamed (verb).
B. *? Zauważyłem, że Jasiowi zrobiło się wstyd.*
   ? I noticed that Johnny became (inwardly) ashamed (adverb).

Thus, both the involuntary pattern of talking about emotions and the voluntary one suggest a view of emotions different from that embodied in the Anglo folk philosophy with its stress on self-control. The fact that emotion verbs in English are not only rare but also tend to develop pejorative connotations provides further linguistic evidence for this folk philosophy. For example, verbs such as *sulk* or *fume* suggest the same combination of voluntariness and external expression as the Polish verbs of emotion discussed earlier, but they also reflect the culture's negative attitude to this kind of uncontrolled emotional reactions.

Again, linguistic evidence parallels in this respect "participant observations" on nonverbal behavior, such as Hoffman's comment about her friend Penny, who "looks offended when I shake her by the arm in excitement, as if my gesture had been one of aggression instead of friendliness." From an Anglo point of view, behavior such as Hoffman's is lacking in the necessary restraint and reserve: the emotion itself (excitement) should have been restrained and harnessed; and whatever the emotion, it should not be allowed to express itself in uncontrolled physical behavior (shaking someone's arm).

From an Anglo point of view, the idea of shaking another person is particularly unacceptable because this action combines uncontrolled emotional expression with violation of another person's bodily autonomy (as well as of their personal space). But even if this kind of assault on another person's territory and bodily integrity is absent, the unchecked flow of emotion translating itself into action is discouraged in the Anglo cultural world while treated as normal and natural in Polish culture:

Polish
when I feel something, I want to do something
because of this, at the same time
    when I do it, people can know how I feel

Anglo
when I do something, I want to be able to think:
"I do this because I want to do it
not because I feel something"

This Polish script reflects a tendency to spontaneous emotional expression, whereas the Anglo script reflects the cultural emphasis on self-control. One might be tempted to propose for Anglo culture a script more directly opposite to the Polish one (especially as far as negative feelings are concerned), along the following lines:

when I feel something bad,
I don't want people to know this

This latter script corresponds better to Javanese culture than to Anglo culture (cf. Geertz, 1976, p. 241; see also Wierzbicka, 1991a, pp. 128–129). The apparent Anglo tendency to suppress spontaneous expression of feelings is in fact a by-product of a different norm: the norm encouraging controlled behavior. Control over expression of emotions is not the same thing as suppression of emotional expression. To quote one of Lutz's (1988a) American informants:

> Let me explain control. It's not that you sit there and you take it [some kind of abuse] and, you know, I think controlling them [emotions] is letting them out in the proper time, in the proper place. (p. 9)

In practice, "letting emotions out in the proper time, in the proper place" often means *talking* about one's emotions rather than *showing* them: "I want to say what I feel."

It is interesting to note that in spite of some superficial similarities, the Anglo rule formulated here is different from the Javanese emotional suppression rule, which can be formulated as follows:

> sometimes when a person feels something,
> this person does something because of this at the same time
> because of this, other people can know how this person feels
> it is bad to do this
> other people can feel something bad because of this

(cf. Honna & Hoffer, 1989, pp. 88–90; Wierzbicka, 1991a, pp. 126–128.)

Good Feelings in American Culture

In contrasting "talking about emotions" with "showing emotions" and in saying that Polish culture places greater emphasis on the latter, I do not mean to suggest that emotional expression ("I want to show what I feel") plays no role in American culture. Social commentators agree that, far from suppressing all expression of emotion, Anglo culture fosters certain kinds of (carefully monitored) emotional expression. In particular, American culture fosters and encourages "cheerfulness." To quote Eva Hoffman (1989) once again:

> If all neurosis is a form of repression, then surely, the denial of suffering, and of helplessness, is also a form of neurosis. Surely, all our attempts to escape sorrow twist themselves into the specific, acrid pain of self-suppres-

sion. And if that is so, then a culture that insists on cheerfulness and staying in control is a culture that—in one of those ironies that prevails in the unruly realm of the inner life—propagates its own kind of pain. (p. 271)

Assessments of the psychological costs of obligatory cheerfulness may or may not be correct, but few commentators would disagree with the basic idea that something like cheerfulness is encouraged by American culture. More precisely, the norm in question can be represented as follows:

it is good if people think that I feel something good all the time
I want people to think this

What can I do to comply with the above norm? I can, of course, smile—and American culture is one of those cultures that value and encourage the "social smile" (cf. Wanning, 1991, p. 10; for the concept of social smile, see Ekman, 1989).

Again, the American social smile must be distinguished from the Japanese social smile, which may be used as a cover for bad and painful feelings:

when I feel something bad,
I don't want people to know it
I want people to think that I feel something good

The American social smile has a different function: It projects a positive image, causing people to think something good about the smiler, and it expresses the experiencer's conscious or semiconscious effort to get rid of bad feelings (in particular, to analyze them away) and to generate in oneself genuine good feelings:

1. I want people to think that I feel something good
   because of this, I want to do *this* (smile)
2. I want to feel something good
   because of this, I want to do *this* (smile)

As these scripts show, the American social smile is also different from the obligatory Balinese smile, as analyzed by Wikan (1989). The most striking difference between the two has to do with different attitudes toward self-analysis. In Balinese culture (according to Wikan), people are constantly enjoined to forget their troubles, *to not think*, and to become cheerful and smiling as a result of this strategy. By contrast, in American culture (with its tradition of psychotherapy and self-analysis), one is enjoined to achieve a similar result by taking the opposite route. For example, American flight attendants are trained to deal with their negative feelings caused by obnoxious passengers by trying to think something good or charitable about them (e.g., "This woman is like my sister," or "This man is only doing this because he is scared"; Hochschild, 1983). Roughly:

Balinese route: if I feel something bad,
it is good not to think about it
if I don't think about it,
I will not feel like this
I can then feel something good

Anglo route: if I feel something bad,
it is good to think about it
if I think about it,
I will not feel like this
I can then feel something good

The extraordinary importance of controlled smiles in American culture is epitomized in the training in smiling to which American flight attendants are widely subjected. A vignette from Hochschild's (1983) account of her visit to the Delta Airlines Stewardess Training Center illustrates this emphasis on smiling particularly well:

> The young trainee sitting next to me wrote on her notepad, "Important to smile. Don't forget smile." The admonition came from the speaker in the front of the room, a crewcut pilot in his early fifties, speaking in a Southern drawl: "Now girls, I want you to go out there and really *smile.* Your smile is your biggest asset. I want you to go out there and use it. Smile. *Really* smile. Really *lay it on.*" (p. 4)

As Hochschild emphasized, the smiles that the air hostesses are expected to have on their faces must be spontaneous and sincere:

> As the Pacific Southwest Airlines jingle says, "Our smiles are not just painted on." Our flight attendants' smile, the company emphasizes, will be more human than the phony smiles you're resigned to seeing on people who are paid to smile. There is a smile-like strip of paint on the nose of each PSA

plane. Indeed, the plane and the flight attendant advertise one another.... Now that advertisements, training, notions of professionalism, and dollar bills have intervened between the smiler and the smiled upon, it takes an extra effort to imagine that spontaneous warmth can exist in uniform—because companies now advertise spontaneous warmth, too. (p. 5)

Because passengers "are quick to detect strained or forced smiles," what flight attendants are required to do is not just smile and smile well (i.e., adroitly, skillfully), but to manufacture within themselves feelings that match the smile. Thus, a stewardess is required to "really work on her smiles" and is expected to "manage her heart" in such a way as to trigger a smile that will both seem and be "spontaneous and sincere" (Hochschild, 1983, p. 105). The company lays claim not simply to her physical motions—how she handles food trays—but to her emotional actions as well and to the way these show in the ease of the smile (p. 7). American society at large values not just "painted smiles," but smiles reflecting genuine cheerfulness, genuine enthusiasm, a genuine state of feeling happy.

The cultural strategies that are probably most relevant from the point of view of stewardess training may be represented as follows:

1. I want people to think that I feel something good
   because of this, I want to do *this* (smile)
   if people think that I feel something good,
   they will think something good about me

2. I want people to think that I feel something good toward them
   because of this, I want to do *this* (smile)
   if people think that I feel something good toward them,
   they will feel something good
   because of this, they will think something good about me

3. I want people to think that I feel something good toward them
   because of this, I want to do *this* (smile)
   if people think I feel something good toward them,
   they will feel something good toward me

4. if I feel something bad, I want to think something good
   if I think something good, I can feel something good

Script 1 reflects the idea that a person who evidently feels something good inspires confidence and commands respect (in American culture);

one can assume that such a person is competent and successful and has things under control (in other words, people tend to think something good about such a person).

Script 2 reflects the idea that a person exuding good feelings toward other people will make those other people feel good (by satisfying their need to be liked). In the case of airplane passengers, a smiling stewardess can make them feel relaxed and comfortable and can help them to enjoy the flight. As a result, the passengers may think something good about the airline that the flight attendants represent.

Script 3 reflects the need to be liked and the expectation that by showing good feelings toward other people, we may trigger in them a similar attitude toward us (i.e., that they will feel something good toward us).

Script 4 reflects the cultural injunction to positive thinking as a means to good feeling (an important part of stewardess training and of American popular wisdom).

All these attitudes reflect important American norms of social interaction, with great emphasis being placed on being liked and approved of, on being perceived as friendly and cheerful, and as someone who is competent and in control of oneself and of the surrounding world.[8]

The importance of being liked and approved of in American culture is given special emphasis in E. C. Stewart's (1972) book *American Cultural Patterns* in which he wrote:

> The characteristic of using others as responses is reflected in the emphasis on communication in interaction and in the great value placed on being

[8]The Anglo cultural emphasis on "staying in control" is illustrated clearly in the following American revision of a Spanish tautology:
Que será, será
  is a lovely song,
  but a lousy philosophy.
Nothing worthwhile
  was ever accomplished
  by anybody who met life
  with a shrug.
Instead your motto should be:
Que quiero será
  what I will, will be.
  (Edwin C. Bliss)

liked.... Whenever the American is deliberately denied expressions of friendship or popularity, his reactions are confused, since he is denied one of the requirements for personal assurance.... Americans tend to judge their personal and social success by popularity—almost literally by the number of people who like them.... Popularity or friendship are both matters of social success and not the conditions for establishing warm, personal relationships. (p. 58)

The attitude described here may be portrayed as follows:

I want this:
people will feel something good toward me

Or perhaps even more strongly:

I want this:
everyone will feel something good toward me

The words *popular* and *popularity* used by E. C. Stewart (1972) are again especially revealing, and the fact that these words have no equivalents in other European languages underscores the validity of Stewart's remarks.[9]

Renwick's (1980) comments on the differences between American and Australian cultural attitudes are relevant here:

Americans need to be liked.... Australians are less concerned than Americans about what others think of them; they are not as interested in whether someone likes them or not. Therefore, they do not try as hard as Americans to influence other people's opinion of them.... When asked what they find most difficult to understand about Americans, Australians sometimes reply, "Their obsession with making a 'good' impression." (p. 23)

The cultural importance of positive feelings in American society is reflected in linguistic routines such as the common greeting routine, with an expected positive reply:[10]

How are you?
I'm fine/very well, thank you/etc.

---

[9]Polish does have a rough translation equivalent of the word *popular*, namely the loan word *popularny*. But in Polish, this word is used only with regard to articles of public consumption, such as a popular song or a popular actress.

[10]A positive feeling is also encoded in the cheerful and enthusiastic American greeting *Hi!* The Australian greeting *G'day!* is not similarly exuberant.

The fact that in Australian culture the prevailing greeting routine is less positive (in expression, if not in the intended message) highlights the difference in cultural attitudes to emotion in these two different traditions:[11]

How are you?
Not bad/not too bad/can't complain/etc.

The central importance of positive feelings in American culture is also reflected in the key role that the adjective *happy* plays in American discourse, an adjective that is widely used as a yardstick for measuring people's psychological well-being as well as their social adjustment. The crucial role of this adjective in American life has often been commented on by newcomers. For example, Stanisław Barańczak (1990), professor of Polish literature at Harvard University, wrote,

> Take the word "happy," perhaps one of the most frequently used words in Basic American. It's easy to open an English–Polish or English–Russian dictionary and find an equivalent adjective. In fact, however, it will not be equivalent. The Polish word for "happy" (and I believe this also holds for other Slavic languages) has a much more restricted meaning; it is generally reserved for rare states of profound bliss, or total satisfaction with serious things such as love, family, the meaning of life, and so on. Accordingly, it is not used as often as "happy" is in American common parlance.... Incidentally, it is also interesting that Slavic languages don't have an exact equivalent for the verb "to enjoy." I don't mean to say that Americans are a nation of superficial, backslapping enjoyers and happy-makers, as opposed to our suffering Slavic souls. What I'm trying to point out is only one example of the semantic incompatibilities which are so firmly ingrained in languages and cultures that they sometimes make mutual communication impossible. (pp. 12–13)

[11]The importance of positive expressives such as *Hi!* or *great* in American culture, and of positive conversational routines, is well illustrated by the following beginning of a conversation, offered in an American bestseller as a model of successful human interaction (Smith, 1975, p. 93):

Pete: Hi, Jean.
Jean: Hi, Pete, how are you?
Pete: I'm fine, how are you?
Jean: I feel like having a good time.
Pete: Great. So do I.

The pressure on people to be happy can only be compared with the pressure to smile: By being happy, one projects a positive image of oneself (as a good person). The fact that some American psychologists have elevated the state of being happy to the status of a basic human emotion is revealing in this respect: From a cross-cultural perspective, the word *joy* (with equivalents such as *Freude, joie, gioia, radost'*, etc. in other European languages) would have seemed a much better candidate for the status of a basic human emotion. But in American culture, the concept of happy is indeed much more central than the concept of joy. It is easy to understand how the centrality of this concept in American culture may have influenced the researchers' perspective on human emotions in general.

To be happy is to feel something good for personal reasons—an ideal quite consistent with the general orientation of "a culture dominated by expressive and utilitarian individualism" (Bellah et al., 1985, p. 115). The fact that *happy* is an adjective, whereas its closest counterparts in other European languages are verbs (e.g., *sich freuen* in German, *se rejouir* in French, or *cieszyć się* in Polish) is also significant because these verbs indicate a temporary occurrence (as the archaic verb *rejoice* does in English), whereas the adjective *happy* is compatible with a long-term state (the expected norm). As Barańczak (1990) pointed out, people can be expected to be happy most of the time, but they could not be expected to rejoice most of the time (cf. Kitayama & Markus, 1992, pp. 23–25; for a fuller discussion of the concept of happy, see Wierzbicka, 1992e).

The concept of enjoyment mentioned by Barańczak is also culturally significant as it links good feelings with the idea of an activity: In contrast to pleasure, which can be entirely passive, one can only enjoy something that one is *doing* (e.g., talking, swimming, dancing, sitting in the sun, and so on). The fact that other European (or non-European) languages do not have a word corresponding to the English *enjoy* highlights the characteristically Anglo nexus of feeling and control and of actively achieving a desired emotional state:

X is enjoying Y =
when X does Y,   X feels something good
because of this,   X wants to do Y

Equally revealing is the key Anglo (and, especially, Anglo-American) concept of fun, which also links the idea of doing something with that of feeling something good (and adds to it a further component of the speaker's own good feelings at the idea of doing something for pleasure).

Another core American value, which is also associated with a smile, is the value of friendliness—not the value of friendship, associated with an exclusive personal bond between two people, but the value of being friendly toward people in general (like a flight attendant, who is expected not to form exclusive personal bonds with individual passengers but to be friendly toward passengers in general). Speaking of the rise of the value of friendliness in American life, Bellah et al. (1985, p. 111) quoted Toqueville's comment that "Democracy does not create strong attachments between man and man, but it does put their ordinary relations on an easier footing"; and they commented that

> in the mobile and egalitarian society of the United States, people could meet more easily and their intercourse was more open, but the ties between them were more likely to be casual and transient.... In the new, mobile middle-class world, one autonomous individual had to deal with other autonomous individuals in situations where one's self-esteem and prospects depended on one's ability to impress and negotiate. "Friendliness" became almost compulsory as a means of assuaging the difficulties of these interactions, while friendship in the classical sense became more and more difficult. (pp. 117–118)

As pointed out by Wanning (1991) the American "friendliness" is often a source of culture shock for newcomers to the country:

> There's often a disappointment waiting for the newcomer who takes American friendliness at face value. Americans are indiscriminate with their smiles and their chatter. Foreigners . . . on arrival may . . . imagine they have instantaneously acquired a slew of fine friends. "But it doesn't mean anything," says an Indian woman. (p. 139)

The cultural norm of friendliness encourages displays of an attitude that can be represented as follows:

> I feel something good toward everyone
> (not toward you, but toward everyone).

One linguistic routine that reflects this attitude is the characteristic American ditto, often displayed on badges, shop windows, and so forth, and having currency in service encounters: "Have a nice (great) day" or "Have a nice weekend." Words such as *popular*, *enjoy*, *happy*, or *friendly* are, of course, widely used outside American English, but they do appear to have special importance in American discourse.

In addition to cheerfulness, happiness, and friendliness, another emotional attitude highly valued in American society is enthusiasm.[12] For example, Sommers's (1984) cultural study of attitudes toward emotions showed that Americans place an exceptional emphasis on enthusiasm and value it far above the other cultural groups with which they were compared (Greeks, West Indians, Chinese). In a similar vein, Renwick (1980) contrasted the "Australian art of deadpan understatement" with the American penchant for "exaggeration and overstatement" and observed that "Australians also add a dash of cynicism to their conversation, especially when they want to counterpoint an American colleague's overenthusiasm" (p. 28).

One linguistic reflection of this attitude is the ubiquitous presence of the word *great* in American discourse (cf. Wolfson, 1983, p. 93) both as a modifier (especially of the verb *to look*) and as a "response particle":

You look great!
Your X (hair, garden, apartment, etc.) looks great!
It's great! That's great! Great!

It is particularly interesting to note the link between evaluation and social response reflected in the use of *great*: Not only can it be used both as an evaluative modifier and a response particle (like an enthusiastic version of *OK*), but even when used as a modifier, it appears to express a reaction to the addressee's explicit or implicit question (whispering to oneself, one would be more likely to whisper "beautiful ..." or "wonderful ..." than "great ... great ...").

---

[12]It is interesting to note that American airlines' recruitment literature refers continuously to "enthusiasm" as well as to "friendliness" and "cheerfulness" (cf. Hochschild, 1983, pp. 96–97, 104, 108).

The basic meaning of the "great" conversational routine may be represented as follows:

1. I think this is very good
2. I think this is not like other things
3. because of this, when I think about it, I feel something very good
4. I want you to know this

Component 1 spells out the positive evaluation; Component 2 accounts for the links between *great* as an expression of enthusiasm and *great* as a description of size; Component 3 accounts for the emotive character of this adjective (cf. *Objectively speaking, that was a great meal*); and Component 4 accounts for the tendency of *great* to be used as a response particle.

In Australian English, *great* is not used nearly as much as it is in American English because of the Australian preference for understatement and negative expression (cf. Renwick, 1980). Its cultural counterpart in Australian English is *not bad at all* (or, if something is regarded as exceptionally wonderful, *a bloody beauty*). But at least, the word *great* (in the relevant meaning) is there and is used in a range of situations. In Polish, there is simply no similar device with a similarly general enthusiastic meaning. There are Polish adjectives and adverbs similar to *wonderful*, *marvelous*, and *splendid* (*wspaniale, cudownie, świetnie, znakomicie*), but their range of use is much narrower than that of *great* or even *wonderful*. If something is said to look *wspaniale*, this would imply grand and impressive as well as wonderful. For happy events, *wspaniale* can be used a little more broadly, but not as broadly as *wonderful* or *great*. For example, if a child receives a very good mark at school, responses such as "That's wonderful!" or "That's great!" are quite in order, but "*To wspaniale!*" would not sound appropriate (it would be just too "grand"). Polish simply does not have a general, universally usable word of enthusiastic response, comparable to the English word *great*. This is another illustration of the links between the structure of the lexicon and the prevailing attitudes to emotions characteristic of a given culture and society.

The importance of good feelings (such as cheerfulness, friendliness, enthusiasm, and fun) in American culture and the absence of similar norms in Polish culture are illustrated particularly well in Eva Hoffman's (1989) reminiscences of different farewell rituals as she experienced them in Poland and in America:

> But as the time of our departure approaches, Basia ... makes me promise that I won't forget her. Of course I won't! She passes a journal with a pretty, embroidered cloth cover to my fellow classmates, in which they are to write appropriate words of good-bye. Most of them choose melancholy verses in which life is figured as a vale of tears or a river of suffering, or a journey of pain on which we are embarking. This tone of sadness is something we all enjoy. It makes us feel the gravity of life, and it is gratifying to have a truly tragic event—a parting forever—to give vent to such romantic feelings.
>
> It's only two years later that I go on a month-long bus trip across Canada and the United States with a group of teenagers, who at parting inscribe sentences in each other's notebooks to be remembered by. "It was great fun knowing you!" they exclaim in the pages of my little notebook. "Don't ever lose your friendly personality!" "Keep cheerful, and nothing can harm you!" they enjoin, and as I compare my two sets of mementos, I know that, even though they're so close to each other in time, I've indeed come to another country. (p. 78)

These contrasting attitudes can be formulated as follows:

Polish
it is good to think sometimes that bad things happen to people
it is good to feel something bad because of this
it is good if people think that I sometimes feel something bad because
    of this
American
It is good to think often that good things can happen to people
It is good to feel something good because of this
It is good if people think that I always feel something good

Conclusion

All cultures evolve different attitudes toward feelings, different communication strategies associated with feelings, and different norms governing the handling of feelings (one's own and other people's). These norms, which are shared by a given speech community on an unconscious level, may be made explicit in the form of cultural scripts formulated exclusively in terms of conceptual and lexical universals.

Anglo-American culture offers scripts that encourage people to feel something good all the time, to be aware of what they feel at any given moment, to be able to analyze and verbalize their feelings, to control their feelings and thus to prevent themselves from feeling something very bad for a long time, to think before saying something to someone when the thing one wants to say could cause the addressee to feel something bad, to separate the expression of one's opinions from any expression of feelings, to behave as though one felt something good toward everyone and as though one felt something good all the time (or most of the time), and so on.

Polish culture does not offer these particular scripts. It offers scripts that encourage people to express their feelings freely; to act upon their feelings; to be guided in their actions by their feelings; to express their thoughts and the feelings caused by these thoughts at the same time; to feel and to express very good feelings toward individual people and to do so spontaneously, on the spur of the moment; to express both good and bad feelings spontaneously and fully without inhibitions, delays, and self-censorship; and so on.

Different cultural norms reflected in such scripts shape different ways of behaving, different styles of interaction, different modes of communication, and different personality structures.

In every culture, local cultural scripts involving emotions can be discovered partly on the basis of linguistic evidence (both lexical and grammatical); and the reality of proposed scripts can also be tested against such evidence. Key words such as *happy, enjoy, fun, popular, hi!*, or *great* in American English, or the extensive system of expressive derivation, and the grammatical distinctions between voluntary and involuntary emotion in Polish can be regarded as linguistic evidence for cultural attitudes toward emotion. Similarly, Russian cultural attitudes toward emotions are reflected in the use of the key word *duša* (roughly, soul/heart; cf. Wierzbicka, 1989, 1992c), whereas Australian attitudes toward emotion are epitomized, inter alia, in the key word *bloody* (the so-called "great Australian adjective") or in the Australian English forms of address such as

Shaz or *Shazza* for *Sharon*, *Kez* or *Kezza* for *Kevin*, and so on (cf. Wierzbicka, 1992a, 1992c).

Next to lexical and grammatical data, conversational routines and culture-specific speech acts also provide important evidence for cultural norms. The "thank you" response to praise and compliments in American English, the speech act of "chayacking" in Australian English (cf. Wierzbicka, 1991a), or the common combination of the bare imperative with affectionate diminutives in Polish requests (cf. Wierzbicka, 1991a) offer important clues for the interpretation of the links between emotion and culture (for further discussion and illustrations, see Wierzbicka, in press-b).

Emotion and culture are inextricably intertwined. To study the role of emotion in cultural patterns and the role of culture in the shaping and conceptualization of emotions, we need to pay close attention to language, in all its aspects—lexical, grammatical, and pragmatic.

References

Ameka, F. (1990). The grammatical packaging of experiences in Ewe: A study in the semantics of syntax. *Australian Journal of Linguistics 10*, 139–182.

Ameka, F. (Ed.). (1992). Interjections [Special issue]. *Journal of Pragmatics, 18*(5).

Barańczak, S. (1990). *Breathing underwater and other East European essays*. Cambridge, MA: Harvard University Press.

Bellah, R. N., Sullivan, W. M., Swidler, A., & Tipton, S. M. (1985). *Habits of the heart*. Berkeley: University of California Press.

Bugenhagen, R. D. (1990). Experiential constructions in Mangap-Mbula. *Australian Journal of Linguistics, 10*, 183–216.

Collins Gem Italian dictionary: Italian–English, English–Italian. (1982). London: Collins & Milan: Mondadori.

Collins Spanish–English English–Spanish dictionary. (1988). (2nd ed.). London: Collins.

Coulter, J. (1986). Affect and social context: Emotion definition as a social task. In R. Harré (Ed.), *The social construction of emotions* (pp. 20–134). Oxford, England: Basil Blackwell.

Doi, T. (1974). Amae: A key concept for understanding Japanese personality structure. In T. S. Lebra & W. P. Lebra (Eds.), *Japanese culture and behavior: Selected readings* (pp. 45–154). Honolulu: University of Hawaii Press.

Ekman, P. (1975, September). The universal smile: Face muscles talk every language. *Psychology Today*, pp. 35–39.

Ekman, P. (1980). *The face of man: Expressions of universal emotions in a New Guinea village.* New York: Garland STPM.

Ekman, P. (1989). The argument and evidence about universals in facial expressions of emotion. In H. Wagner & A. Manstead (Eds.), *Handbook of social psychophysiology* (pp. 43–164). New York: Wiley.

Ekman, P. (1992). An argument for basic emotions. *Cognition and Emotion, 6,* 169–200.

Fehr, B., & Russell, J. A. (1984). Concept of emotion viewed from a prototype perspective. *Journal of Experimental Psychology: General, 13,* 464–486.

Geertz, C. (1976). *The religion of Java.* Chicago: University of Chicago Press.

Geertz, C. (1984). "From the native's point of view": On the nature of anthropological understanding. In R. A. Schweder & R. A. LeVine (Eds.), *Culture theory: Essays on mind, self, and emotion* (pp. 23–136). Cambridge, England: Cambridge University Press.

Glaser, E. (1991). *Absence of angels.* New York: Berkley Books.

Goddard, C. (1990). The lexical semantics of "good feelings" in Yankunytjatjara. *Australian Journal of Linguistics, 10,* 257–292.

Goddard, C. (1991). Anger in the Western Desert: Semantics, culture and emotion. *Man, 26,* 602–619.

Goddard, C. (1993). Testing the translatability of semantic primitives into an Australian Aboriginal language. *Anthropological Linguistics, 33,* 31–56.

Goddard, C., & Wierzbicka, A. (Eds.). (in press). *Semantic and lexical universals.* Amsterdam: John Benjamins.

Hall, E. (1983). *The dance of life.* New York: Doubleday.

Harkins, J. (1990). Shame and shyness in the Aboriginal classroom: A case for "practical semantics." *Australian Journal of Linguistics, 10,* 293–306.

Harré, R. (1986). An outline of the social constructionist viewpoint. In R. Harré (Ed.), *The social construction of emotions* (pp. 2–14). Oxford, England: Basil Blackwell.

Hochschild, A. R. (1983). *The managed heart: Commercialization of human feeling.* Berkeley: University of California Press.

Hoffman, E. (1989). *Lost in translation.* New York: Dutton.

Honna, N., & Hoffer, B. (Eds.). (1989). *An English dictionary of Japanese ways of thinking.* N.p.: Yuhikaku.

Howell, S. (1981). Rules not words. In P. Heelas & A. Lock (Eds.), *Indigenous psychologies: The anthropology of the self* (pp. 33–143). San Diego, CA: Academic Press.

Hume, D. (1978). *Treatise of human nature.* Oxford, England: Clarendon Press. (Original work published in 1739)

Hymes, D. H. (1962). The ethnography of speaking. In T. Gladwin & W. Sturtevant (Eds.), *Anthropology and human behavior* (pp. 5–53). Washington, DC: Anthropological Society of Washington.

Izard, C. (1969). *The face of emotion.* New York: Appleton-Century-Crofts.

Izard, C. (1977). *Human emotion.* New York: Plenum Press.

James, W. (1884). What is an emotion? *Mind, 9,* 188–205.

James, W. (1890). *The principles of psychology.* New York: Holt.

Johnson-Laird, P. N., & Oatley, K. (1989). The language of emotions: An analysis of a semantic field. *Cognition and Emotion, 3,* 81–123.

Katriel, T. (1986). *Talking straight: Dugri speech in Israeli Sabra culture.* Cambridge, England: Cambridge University Press.

Kendon, A. (1990). Gesticulation, quotable gestures, and signs. In M. Moerman & M. Nomura (Eds.), *Culture embodied* (pp. 53–77). Osaka: National Museum of Ethnology. (Senri Ethnological Studies 27.)

Kitayama, S., & Markus, H. R. (1992, May). *Construal of the self as a cultural frame: Implications for internationalizing psychology.* Paper presented at the Internationalization and Higher Education Symposium, University of Michigan.

Lebra, T. S. (1974). Reciprocity and the asymmetric principle: An analytical reappraisal of the Japanese concept of On. In T. S. Lebra & W. P. Lebra (Eds.), *Japanese culture and behavior: Selected readings* (pp. 92–207). Honolulu: University of Hawaii Press. (Reprinted from *Psychologia,* 1969, pp. 29–138)

Lloyd, S. M. (Ed.). (1984). *Roget's thesaurus of English words and phrases* (rev. ed.). Harmondworth, Middlesex, England: Penguin Books.

Lutz, C. (1980). *Emotion words and emotional development on Ifaluk Atoll.* Unpublished doctoral dissertation, Harvard University.

Lutz, C. (1982). The domain of emotion words on Ifaluk. *American Ethnologist, 9,* 113–128.

Lutz, C. (1985). Ethnopsychology compared to what? Explaining behavior and consciousness among the Ifaluk. In G. M. White & J. Kirkpatrick (Eds.), *Person, self, and experience: Exploring Pacific ethnopsychologies* (pp. 35–79). Berkeley: University of California Press.

Lutz, C. (1986). Emotion, thought and estrangement: Emotion as a cultural category. *Cultural Anthropology, 1,* 287–309.

Lutz, C. (1987). Goals, events and understanding in Ifaluk emotion theory. In D. Holland & N. Quinn (Eds.), *Cultural models in language and thought* (pp. 290–312). Cambridge, England: Cambridge University Press.

Lutz, C. (1988a, March). Engendered emotion: Gender, power and the rhetoric of emotional control in American discourse. Paper presented at the Accounts of Human Nature Workshop, Windsor, England. To appear in revised form, in C. Lutz & L. Abu-Lughod (Eds.), *Affecting discourse: Language and the politics of emotion.* Cambridge, England: Cambridge University Press.)

Lutz, C. (1988b). *Unnatural emotions: Everyday sentiments on a Micronesian atoll and their challenge to Western theory.* Chicago: University of Chicago Press.

Matisoff, J. A. (1979). *Blessings, curses, hopes, and fears: Psycho-ostensive expressions in Yiddish.* Philadelphia: Institute for the Study of Human Issues.

Miller, W. I. (in press). *Humiliation.* Ithaca, NY: Cornell University Press.

Nakane, C. (1974). The social system reflected in interpersonal communication. In J. C. Condon & M. Saito (Eds.), *Intercultural encounters with Japan: Communication—contrast and conflict* (pp. 24–131). Tokyo: Simul Press.

Oxford English dictionary (2 vols.). (1933). Oxford, England: Clarendon Press.

Panksepp, J. (1982). Toward a general psychobiological theory of emotions. *Behavioral and Brain Sciences, 5*, 407–467.

Renwick, G. W. (1980). *InterAct: Guidelines for Australians and North Americans.* Yarmouth, ME: Intercultural Press.

Rosaldo, M. Z. (1980). *Knowledge and passion: Ilongot notions of self and social life.* Cambridge, England: Cambridge University Press.

Rosaldo, R. (1978). The rhetoric of control: Ilongots viewed as natural bandits and wild Indians. In B. Babcock (Ed.), *The reversible world: Symbolic inversion in art and society* (pp. 240–257). Ithaca, NY: Cornell University Press.

Rosch, E. (1973). On the internal structure of perceptual and semantic categories. In T. E. Moore (Ed.), *Cognitive development and the acquisition of language* (pp. 111–144). San Diego, CA: Academic Press.

Russell, J. A. (1991). Culture and the categorization of emotions. *Psychological Bulletin, 10*, 426–450.

Schachter, S., & Singer, J. E. (1962). Cognitive, social, and physiological determinants of emotional state. *Psychological Review, 69*, 379–399.

Smith, M. J. (1975). *When I say no, I feel guilty: How to cope—using the skills of systematic assertive therapy.* New York: Bantam Books.

Solomon, R. C. (1984). Getting angry: The Jamesian theory of emotion in anthropology. In R. A. Schweder & R. A. LeVine (Eds.), *Culture theory: Essays on mind, self, and emotion* (pp. 238–255). Cambridge, England: Cambridge University Press.

Sommers, S. (1984). Adults evaluating their emotions: A cross-cultural perspective. In C. Z. Malatesta & C. E. Izard (Eds.), *Emotion in adult development* (pp. 319–338). Beverly Hills, CA: Sage.

Stevenson, B. (1958). *Stevenson's book of proverbs, maxims and familiar phrases.* London: Routledge & Kegan Paul.

Stewart, C. (1992, April). Designer's son defends the flag. *The Australian*, p. 1.

Stewart, E. C. (1972). *American cultural patterns: A cross-cultural perspective.* Yarmouth, ME: Intercultural Press.

Suzuki, T. (1986). Language and behavior in Japan: The conceptualization of personal relations. In T. S. Lebra & W. P. Lebra (Eds.), *Japanese culture and behavior: Selected readings* (rev. ed., pp. 42–157). Honolulu: University of Hawaii Press. (Reprinted from *Japan Quarterly*, 1976, *23*, 255–266).

Wanning, E. (1991). *Culture shock! USA.* Singapore: Time Books International.

Webster's new school and office dictionary. (1965). New York: The World & Crest.

Wierzbicka, A. (1986). Does language reflect culture? Evidence from Australian English. *Language in Society, 5,* 349–374.

Wierzbicka, A. (1989). Soul and mind: Linguistic evidence for ethnopsychology and cultural history. *American Anthropologist, 91,* 41–58.

Wierzbicka, A. (1990a). *Duša* (≈ soul), *toska* (≈ yearning), *sud'ba* (≈ fate): Three key concepts in Russian language and Russian culture. In Z. Saloni (Ed.), *Melody formalne w opisie jezyków slowiańskich* (pp. 13–36). Bialystok, Poland: Bialystok University Press.

Wierzbicka, A. (1990b). The semantics of emotions: *Fear* and its relatives in English. *Australian Journal of Linguistics, 10,* 359–375.

Wierzbicka, A. (1991a). *Cross-cultural pragmatics: The semantics of human interaction.* Berlin: Mouton de Gruyter.

Wierzbicka, A. (1991b). Japanese key words and core cultural values. *Language in Society, 20,* 333–385.

Wierzbicka, A. (1991c). Lexical universals and universals of grammar. In M. Kefer & J. van der Auwera (Eds.), *Meaning and grammar* (pp. 383–415). Berlin: Mouton de Gruyter.

Wierzbicka, A. (1992a). Australian b-words (*bloody, bastard, bugger, bullshit*): An expression of Australian culture and national character. In A. Clas (Ed.), *Le mot, les mots, les bons mots/Word, words, witty words* (pp. 21–38). Montreal: Les Presses de l'Université de Montréal.

Wierzbicka, A. (1992b). Defining emotion concepts. *Cognitive Science, 6,* 539–581.

Wierzbicka, A. (1992c). *Semantics, culture, and cognition: Universal human concepts in culture-specific configurations.* New York: Oxford University Press.

Wierzbicka, A. (1992d). The semantics of interjection. *Journal of Pragmatics, 8,* 159–192.

Wierzbicka, A. (1992e). Talking about emotions: Semantics, culture and cognition. *Cognition and Emotion, 6,* 285–319.

Wierzbicka, A. (1992f). Wschodnio-Europejska kultura żydowska w świetle żydowskiej "etnografii mowy" [East European Jewish culture in the light of the Jewish "ethnography of speaking]. *Teksty Drugie, 17,* 5–26.

Wierzbicka, A. (1993a). Reading human faces: Emotion components and universal semantics. *Pragmatics and Cognition, 1,* 1–23.

Wierzbicka, A. (1993b). A conceptual basis for cultural psychology. *Ethos, 21,* 205–231.

Wierzbicka, A. (in press-a). Kisses, handshakes, bows: The semantics of nonverbal communication. *Semiotica.*

Wierzbicka, A. (in press-b). "Cultural scripts": A new approach to the study of cross-cultural communication. In M. Pütz (Ed.), *Intercultural communication: Proceedings of International Symposium in Duisburg.* Amsterdam: John Benjamins.

Wierzbicka, A. (in press-c). Cognitive domains and the structure of the lexicon: The case of emotions. In S. Gelman & L. Hirschfield (Eds.), *Mapping the mind: Doman specificity in cognition and culture.* Cambridge, England: Cambridge University Press.

Wikan, U. (1989). Managing the heart to brighten face and soul: Emotions in Balinese morality and health care. *American Ethnologist, 6,* 294–312.

Wolfson, N. (1981). Compliments in cross-cultural perspective. *TESOL Quarterly, 5,* 117–124.

Wolfson, N. (1983). An empirically based analysis of complimenting in American English. In N. Wolfson & E. Judd (Eds.), *Sociolinguistics and language acquisition* (pp. 82–95). Rowley: Newbury House.

CHAPTER 6

Cognitive Science's Contributions to Culture and Emotion

Michael I. Posner, Mary K. Rothbart, and Catherine Harman

This chapter is in three sections. The first section examines views attempting to incorporate emotion into cognitive theory and methodological contributions applying cognitive techniques to the analysis of emotion. The second section considers cognitive science in relation to culture and an analogy between appraisal theories of emotion and the role of semantic categories in perception. The third section continues the analogy between perception and emotion, considering these in terms of new developments in cognitive neuroscience.

Cognitive Views of Affect

The classical approach to cognitive science is based on the symbol processing theory of artificial intelligence identified with the work of Simon

This research was supported by National Institute of Mental Health Grant 43361, Office of Naval Research Contract N0014-89-J3013, and by the Center for the Cognitive Neuroscience of Attention supported by the Pew Memorial Trusts and the James S. McDonnell Foundation.

(1967) and Newell (1990). According to this view, cognition is the study of artificial and natural intelligence and is seen in both cases as the search of a constrained, limited-capacity processor through a problem space, with the problem space being set by a complex environment. In this view, culture operates primarily through setting different contexts or environments in which human intelligence operates. In its early form, the symbol processing approach viewed the human as a simple organism with little internal structure. The complex environments in which people found themselves provided the apparent complexity in human problem solving. Cultures, like other environments, provided the problem spaces through which humans search.

The symbol processing approach to cognition had little interest in emotion per se. However, an emotion-like process called *satisficing* was the basis for terminating the search for problem solution. Simon (1967) argued that searches end not with an optimal but with a satisfactory solution. Emotions were also thought to interrupt ongoing problem-solving behavior when the person was confronted with high-priority internal or external events. Emotions then are regulators of cognitive activity. By providing a high-priority interrupt, they prevent an internally motivated stored hierarchy of goals from completely dominating behavior during the search process involved in problem solving. Unlike most computer programs, humans could be interrupted by physical or emotional needs.

This view of emotion had an empirical rationale as well as a theoretical one. The empirical rationale came from psychological studies supporting the idea that emotions consisted largely of generalized arousal coupled with an interpretive cognitive process (Schachter & Singer, 1962). One part of the process, *arousal*, was similar for all emotions. The *interpretation* of the arousal would be specific to given situations and could certainly be influenced by cultural differences. This viewpoint, much like the early Newell (1990) and Simon (1967) approach, considered the main aspects of human problem solving to be directed by a single serial processor. Only very simple processing such as that leading to an overall change in arousal could occur outside of this processor.

Whereas some of these basic assumptions continue to influence the cognitive approach to emotion (see Simon, 1982), research on semantic networks in the 1970s and 1980s (Anderson & Bower, 1973; Posner, 1978) expanded the range of activity seen to be driven by input, even when the subject was not conscious of it. Cognitive science views began to stress the automatic nature of activation of semantic networks. In studies of memory, complex semantic information could be activated without attention, although attention could also be used to access ideas and to alter their content. Problem-solving studies focused on puzzles stressing simple heuristics, and little stored knowledge (information-lean problem solving) gave way to studies involving information-rich domains in which search was structured by large amounts of stored knowledge (information-rich problem solving; Von Lehn, 1989).

Bower and Cohen (1982) analyzed the proposition "Mary kissed me" in terms of a network containing a subject (Mary) and a predicate. The predicate consists of a relationship (kissed) and an object (me). To incorporate the emotion, one simply introduces an additional relationship (feel) that connects the emotion (joy) to the object. In this view, emotions are parts of a relational cognitive network in which emotions may play a special role. The emotion may serve to amplify cognitive activity involved in recognizing situations and thus act as a kind of selective filter that leads to concentration on some things and reduced awareness of others. When in a joyful mood, concepts of pleasure may be processed selectively from the environment and would have more ready access to retrieval from memory.

In commenting on the work of Bower and Cohen (1982), Simon (1982) distinguished between affect, evaluation, emotion, and mood. Affect is a generic term that can apply to all of the more specific terms. An evaluation may be automatically represented by a node in semantic memory. However, an emotion always interrupts and becomes attended. Thus, only affects that become conscious will be called emotions by Simon. Moods establish contexts that can guide cognitive activity. A mood is an enduring affect that interacts with cognitive activity over time. Simon's definitions reflect the gradual acceptance, within cognitive science, of the thinking of the 1970s and 1980s that processes occurring outside the focal awareness of the subject were both lawful and complex. The structure of human memory carried as much importance for the organism as the conscious search process.

According to the Schachter and Singer (1962) view, stimuli could produce arousal depending on their properties, but emotions were always provided by a cognitive process of conscious appraisal relating to one's feelings. Once cognitive science views had accepted the existence of complex semantic networks, however, it was no longer possible to consider affect as only conscious appraisals. Instead, affects could be structured like other complex propositions by the semantic memory system. In the latter views, the classification of a stimulus as emotional, like other semantic-level classificatory processes, occurred automatically outside of the central processor (consciousness) and the output of the classification could influence later cognition (Uleman & Bargh, 1989). Although it was widely recognized within cognitive science that classifications of stimuli were automatic processes, subject to the laws of spreading activation that serve as background from which consciousness was constructed, the significance of this was not well appreciated outside of the discipline.

In the 1980s, a controversy arose outside of cognitive science about the relationship between cognition and emotion (Lazarus, 1982; Zajonc, 1980). Zajonc correctly pointed out that emotional classifications could arise prior to our awareness of the emotion. If this view allows specific emotion and not just general arousal to occur outside of consciousness, it clearly opposes the Schachter and Singer ideas, but other cognitive science approaches to emotion had already taken the view that semantic classifications could occur even when subjects were not consciously attending to them. If specific emotions were nodes within the semantic network, they would also be subject to automatic activation. From this perspective, the Zajonc argument was similar to the conclusions of many other papers showing that activation of semantic nodes could be made without active attention (Posner, 1978) and at duration thresholds well below those for conscious report of the stimulus contents (Marcel, 1983).

A current issue within cognition is how emotions may serve to guide ongoing cognitive activity. Viewing emotion as an interruption of the central processor is not a sufficient basis for most of the important roles for emotion described in this volume. Moreover, the idea that there are many different cognitive processors dealing with differing aspects of stimuli suggests that emotions might serve to coordinate the activity of these processors. Oatley and Johnson-Laird (1987) proposed that emotions serve as rapid nonpropositional means for tuning cognitive processes to common underlying states. A state of fear tunes many processors (e.g., enhancing the selection of particular ideas and plans related to flight, etc.). Oatley and Johnson-Laird recognized five basic emotions that can alter the operations of the cognitive system and outlined the effects of each on cognitive processes. This work represents two important trends within cognitive science. One is to consider emotion as a basic topic that may have principles of its own and not be represented as merely a special part of a semantic network. The other is to return more seriously to the physical basis of emotion. The latter point is part of the general development of what we consider in this chapter under the topic of cognitive neuroscience.

Methods of Study

Although it is arguable whether cognitive theories of affect have been extremely useful in its study, there is little doubt that the methods of cognitive science have been helpful in exploring the structure of normal and pathological emotions. The dominant methods for the study of emotional processes have measured the speed and accuracy of responding to emotional events or to memory judgments based on previous emotional events. These methods have been well reviewed in the cognitive literature (Bower & Clapper, 1989) and have been applied in detail by social psychologists to many issues of affect (Uleman & Bargh, 1989). They have also been used in studies of pathological states. For example, studies of anxiety (McLeod & Matthews, 1988) have used cognitive methods to study attention to emotional stimuli (Broadbent, 1958; Posner, 1978). Similarly, studies of depression have centered on the probability of recalling negatively charged stimuli in comparison with positive ones. The idea of mood-congruent memory and the methods for assessing it are taken over from the more general study of context effects that have been popular in studies of human memory (Bower & Clapper, 1989). A basic theme of cognitive psychology during the last two decades is that judgments of probability and preference are subject to a wide range of heuristics or biases (Tversky & Kahneman, 1974). Such judgments have been used to assess depression, which appears to induce biases against the belief in self-control and in favor of the likelihood of negative events. We believe that the methods of cognitive science will make lasting contributions to the study of affect.

Ellsworth (chapter 2, this volume) comments on the importance of subdividing the emotional reaction to a stimulus into reactions that are affected by the cultural context and those that are not. Cognitive science provides methods for doing this. Consider our comprehension of the sentence, "She slept beneath the palm." Our conscious reaction is to think about a woman lying in the shade of a tree. However, measures of reaction time show that, for a brief period, both the selected association of palm (e.g., tree) and its noncontextual meanings (e.g., hand) are activated by the word. Thus, we might imagine that, in one culture, the critical remark of an elder activates systems related to anger, but that a cultural context involving respect for elders serves to inhibit its expression. Methods from cognitive science exist for exploring these kinds of issues in detail (Bower & Clapper, 1989; Posner & Rothbart, 1989).

How Culture Influences Cognition

Having examined theories and methods of cognitive science related to the study of emotion, we now turn to issues of cognition and culture. Cognitive approaches to culture have probably been even more restricted than the approaches to emotion that we have discussed. From a cognitive science perspective, persons store propositions induced by their culture in a way similar to the storage of any other semantic information. Thus, culture-like, domain-specific knowledge of any type may be seen as information present within memory that can aid in determining the search processes of people during problem solving. The main topic under which the influence of high levels of domain-specific knowledge is studied is the field of *expertise* (Chi, Glaser, & Farr, 1988). Although the domains of expertise outlined include typewriting, reading, chess, table waiting, programming, and medical diagnosis, the principles could be applied as well to experts in American, Hindu, or Zulu culture or experts in the female and male domains of action, thought, and feeling within each of these cultures.

An example of the application of cognitive science to emotion is found in *Foundations of Cognitive Science*, in which D'Andrade (1989) begins his study of culture and emotion by saying that

> the cross cultural study of emotion is like the cross cultural study of color in that it also involves problems concerning universals of experience and the cognitive aspects of different lexically coded systems of categorization. (p. 814)

The study of how color labels influence our perceptions is probably the most successful story of the application of cognitive science methods and theory to culture (Brown, 1976; D'Andrade, 1989). The lessons learned from the study of color categories can also help us to understand the relationship between emotion and culture. In the 1950s under the influence of the Whorfian hypothesis, studies were conducted to see whether our perceptions of visual color chips were influenced by their codability into words. Such studies involved three of the most powerful cognitive methods. In some studies, subjects were required to make speeded same–different judgments to pairs of chips either within or between a linguistic boundary (mental chronometry). Other experiments required subjects to remember and pick out a previously perceived color chip from a new array (recognition memory) or to describe in words the selected chip to another person.

Brown (1976) summarized the results of a generation of research in this area in what is one of the most beautiful articles ever written about research in the field of cognition. Brown briefly reviewed how the neurology of the brain's color perception system provides a basis for understanding the way in which the color domain is coded by lexical items in the world's languages. Each culture develops its own set of lexical items, but the structure of the items chosen is constrained by the organization imposed on the visible light spectrum by a universal neurology. Brown concluded with a quote from his student, Eleanor Rosch:

> In short, far from being a domain well suited to the study of the effect of language on thought, the color space would seem to be a prime example of the influence of underlying perceptual–cognitive factors on the information and reference of linguistic categories. (p. 20)

This story has relevance to issues of culture and emotion. Just as the words for colors differ in different cultures, so do the words for emotion. But we might expect that when we look deeper than the words themselves, we will find an underlying order based upon universals of emotion that are expressed by the face (Ekman, 1992), encoded in potential universals of communication (Wiersbecka, chapter 5, this volume), and measured in self-report scales (Mauro, Sato, & Tucker, 1992).

One should not forget another, often neglected side of the color perception story. When a person is asked to communicate about a color to another person or has to store information about the color for a brief period and then pick it out of an array, the particular way in which the culture chooses to name the color exerts an important influence on performance. The internal communication that we call memory, even when it involves brief intervals, depends on the surface linguistic structure. If this principle also carries over to emotion, we will find that the use of emotional ideas to account for our own behavior, to recall our own experiences, and to think about the causes of our pain will differ in important ways among members of different cultural and linguistic communities. Thus, the study of the domain of color suggests that we will find cross-cultural commonalities and nontrivial differences in the influence of culture on our emotional life. As White points out (this volume) the degree to which color perception serves as an analogy for emotion and culture can be disputed. We need to look deeper than the subjective perception of color and emotion to understand the full force of their relation. This requires us to look at the neural systems involved in color and in emotion.

Cognitive–Neuroscience Approach

The crux of the issue of cognitive theories of emotion appears to be how they relate to ongoing cognitive activity. How do emotions summon attention and how does attention regulate emotion? Once again, we can return to the study of color perception to obtain an idea of how attention may be involved in the perception of a cognitive category. The perception of color appears to rest on the operation of a pathway of small neural cells that arise in the retina and conduct information to the lateral geniculate and to the primary visual cortex. Cells responsive to color have a strong representation in prestriate areas of monkeys labeled V4 (Zeki, 1992).

Recently, it has been possible to study areas of the human brain that are differentially responsive to stimuli that differ only in hue. A study conducted by the London Positron Emission Tomography (PET) Center (Zeki et al., 1991) showed activation in a prestriate area when stimuli are shown differing only in hue. A very different way of activating this area is to ask a person to attend to color information. In this study, the control condition was one in which subjects reported as targets stimulus pairs that differed in color, shape, or motion. In the focal condition, they reported only changes in color (Corbetta, Meizin, Dobmeyer, Shulman, & Petersen, 1991). When blood flow in the control condition was subtracted from blood flow in the focal condition, prestriate areas were found to be increased in activation by the instruction to attend specifically to color. In other words, attention serves to amplify particular areas of the visual system, and one of these areas is identical to the prestriate region active during pure hue perception. Attention apparently can activate the same prestriate areas involved in color perception, but there is no evidence of activation on the retinal or primary visual cortex. Attention serves to boost the activation of the visual stimulus in the cortical area corresponding to the dimension that defines the target. These findings suggest the general principle that attention boosts the activation of the visual stimulus in the cortical areas corresponding to the dimension that defines the target (Posner, 1992). In this example, we dealt with perceptual features of the object; the same principle applies to semantic information about the meaning of an object. If we take the view of cognitive science that emotions also involve the extraction of information (in this case concerning its affective value), we should also expect amplification of the relevant emotional computations when people attended to them.

Which brain networks are involved in processing emotional information?

We do not have all the information needed to answer this question, but just as particular areas of the brain are involved in identifying and locating visual information, there also seem to be particular areas of the brain that code the emotional significance of stimuli (LeDoux, 1987). Most of our knowledge of this circuitry emerges from animal research and implicates the amygdaloid complex, working in conjunction with other structures.

Lesions of the amygdala lead to a condition of *affective blindness* (the Kluver–Bucy syndrome) in which the animal is not able to be guided by the emotional significance of the stimulus. Each of the sensory processing areas of cortex projects to the amygdala, and when one of these connections is severed, modality-specific symptoms are found (e.g., fearfulness to visually presented stimuli, but not to those stimuli when heard or touched). The thalamo–amygdala connections allow for early affective processing of sensory stimuli with the possibility of the amygdala influencing further processing of stimuli by the cortex. Thus, stimuli may be processed at a simple sensory level and at levels in which object information in an environmental context is related to representations stored in memory.

As affect is linked to sensory stimulation, there is further activation of autonomic, behavioral, and endocrine circuits. For the fear stimulus, Davis, Hitchcock, and Rosen (1987) identified separate peripheral connections leading to each of the following: arrest of ongoing behavior, changes in heart rate and blood pressure related to cardiovascular conditioning, changes in respiration, increased reflex excitability potentiating startle, mouth and jaw movements, and increases in dopamine and norepinephrine related to increased vigilance and motor preparation. Feedback from peripheral effects activates ascending circuits projecting to the areas that initially activated the amygdala, allowing for further emotional processing and amplification of emotional experience (LeDoux, 1989).

How does the emotional network interact with attention? There have been no detailed studies designed to observe how attention and emotional networks interact in adults. However, if we consider pain perception as being related to the emotion of distress, two anatomical areas provide a possible basis for attention and emotion interactions. One part of the brain involved in attention is the *superior colliculus*. The superior colliculus is a structure of the midbrain known to exert control over eye movements in response to visual targets. Recently, this structure has also been shown to be involved in the control of attentional orienting, even when no eye movements are involved (see Posner, 1992, for a review). The deeper layers of the superior colliculus also contain cells that respond to pain and that are in intimate contact with the multimodal cells involved in orienting (McHaffie, Kao, Chank-Quing, & Stein, 1989). The close relationship between pain and attention may reflect the importance of opposed approach and avoidance systems in the control of behavior and could relate to the attentional control of distress.

A second system in which distress and attention appear to be represented in very close physical proximity lies in the anterior cingulate gyrus. This is a frontal midline structure that receives input from networks related to emotion, but that plays a central role in selective attention (Posner, 1992). A PET study by the Montreal group (Talbot et al., 1991) attempted to determine the areas of the brain activated when a small amount of heat was delivered to the finger that moved the subject from the sensation of warmth to that of pain. When the heat was sufficient to produce pain, there was strong activation of the anterior cingulate. The coordinates make this area appear to be close to those active during attentional conditions. Pain has an intrusive character, and this could be related to its close physical proximity to the anterior attention network. These two findings suggest anatomy that could underlie a close interaction between attention and distress.

Orienting and Distress in Infants

In adults, whatever role the emotional and attentional networks play in self-regulation may be obscured by years of exercising the controls required by life in a particular environment. In early infancy, the facial expressions and vocalizations that accompany distress are frequent and easily elicited by even mild environmental events. For this reason, we have turned to studies of human infants to provide a basis for observing the interaction between attention and distress and for examining the role of the caregiver as a socializing agent who introduces cultural influences that could shape the form of the interaction.

Caregivers provide a hint of how attention is used to regulate the infant's state. For earlier than 3 months of age, caregivers usually report themselves as using holding and rocking as the main means of quieting their infants. However, by 3–6 months of age, caregivers, particularly those in Western cultures, attempt to distract their infant by bringing their attention to other stimuli. As infants attend, they are often quieted and their distress appears to diminish (Harman & Rothbart, 1992). A systematic study suggests that the loss of overt signs of stress is not always accompanied by a genuine loss of distress. Harman and Rothbart coded from videotape the level of distress in infants prior to the presentation of a new toy and following its removal. Although infants quieted as they oriented to the toy, as soon as it was removed, the initial level of distress returned. Control conditions indicated that infants did not soothe when the distractors were not presented and that the distress was not caused by a toy removal, but instead reflected the level prior to the toy's presentation. Some internal system thus appears to hold the initial level of distress when the infant's orientation to the novel event is lost.

There is also evidence that different cultures may direct the developing infant's attention in different ways. In a comparison of maternal care in Japanese, Japanese–American, and American infants, American caregivers induced soothing by orienting to external events more frequently and spent much more time stimulating their infants into positive expressions of emotion. Japanese parents used rocking and soothing by contact more frequently, thus perhaps directing attention more to internal events. Japanese–American caregivers were intermediate between these two groups in their soothing procedures (Caudill & Frost, 1972).

We may think about the early experience of infants in soothing as setting the stage for the later importance of others in achieving relief from pain. Observations of parent behavior in northern Europe suggest that infants who are especially distress prone will have mothers who are likely to ignore them (van den Boom, 1989) or to encourage them to manage for themselves in an independent fashion (Grossman, Grossman, Spangler, Suess, & Unzner, 1985). By the age of one year, in an attachment setting where infants may turn their attention to the mother for comforting, infants in these cultures observed earlier as being highly susceptible to distress show a tendency to ignore their mothers (Van Ijzendoorn & Kroonenberg, 1988). In the same setting, more distress-prone Japanese infants show a strong tendency to direct their emotions of distress toward caregivers (Miyake, Chen, & Campos, 1985).

The role of orienting in the control of distress in infants appears to be a very important early model for the study of the interaction between biology and culture. The biological basis of the attention-orienting network that develops heavily between the ages of 3 and 6 months has been outlined in detail (Posner, 1992). In the future, we hope to understand how socialization by the caregiver influences the structures involved.

There is a possibly related phenomenon in the adult. American adults who report themselves as having good ability to focus and shift attention also report less susceptibility to negative affect (Derryberry & Rothbart, 1988). Attention may serve to control levels of distress in adults in a manner somewhat similar to that found early in infancy. Indeed, many of the ideas of modern cognitive therapy are based on links between attention and negative ideation. Increased anatomical knowledge and the clear evidence for the development of attention in early infancy may serve to illuminate these therapeutic efforts.

Voluntary Attention in Infancy

In our infant experiments, there is a marked change in the behavior of infants participating in the same experiment at 6 months and at 12 months of age. The change is not so evident in the results of the experiments as in the infants' approach to them. At 4–6 months, it is possible to capture the infants' gaze by visual stimuli, getting them to look back and forth almost in a robotlike manner. Often, saliva dripping from the mouth is a sign of the intensity of this concentration. Four to 6-month-old infants appear to be little looking machines, as if designed to be fully absorbed by visual change. On the other hand, by 12 months of age, the infants could be characterized as having an agenda of their own, which may or may not correspond to the experimenter's protocol.

It seems likely that the development of the infant's agenda is related to the specific maturation of frontal brain systems, including the more anterior attention system involved in higher levels of attentional control (Posner, 1992). There is as yet no clear marker of the development of this system. Because of the diverse nature of the computations performed by this system, perhaps no single course of development is likely. Rather, we might expect to come to understand how different aspects of anterior control systems develop over time.

One important transition appears to occur between 9 and 12 months of age. When adults attempt to deal with words, they activate an area of the midfrontal lobe that appears to be closely related to attention (Posner, 1992). At approximately 9 to 12 months of age, infants begin to use single words. The PET data suggest that the semantic association among words involves a left lateral frontal area. The earliest use of words is closely related to gestures toward objects by the infant. Indeed, the initial use of words is hardly language at all, but may be seen as a substitute for the object to which the word refers. Gesturing is also frequently used to aid in the development of word use by language-delayed children. Frontal brain areas are involved with the control of motor movements. The close connection between initial word use and gesturing may explain why a frontal area would be intimately related to the process of looking up the meaning of isolated words.

Approximately eight months later, 18–20-month-old infants begin to use words in combination to express more complex ideas. The use of words as part of language involves two new aspects. First, the combination of words begins to require a grammar or a set of organizational rules. Second, it begins to draw upon the short-term memory system. It is known that damage to frontal areas posterior to the semantic area on the lateral aspect of the left hemisphere (Broca's area) is somehow related to aspects of grammatical processing; damage to areas in the midtemporal region of the left side leads to deficits in verbal short-term memory. Given the idea of the maturation of specific pathways underlying the coordination of specific codes, we might hypothesize that the frontal area begins to become related to more posterior regions in the process of the formulation of linguistic strings. The rapid onset of spoken language at about 18 months of age has led investigators to postulate that the maturation of language brain areas must underlie the explosive development of child language. Our proposal is in this spirit, but is more detailed in specifying the pathways involved because they would have to connect the left lateral frontal area with the posterior parietal–temporal area.

We believe that the more anterior attention system is undergoing very active development during the period when infants are beginning to acquire language. It is important that the development of language, as we describe it, occurs in close relation to the development of joint attention between the infant and the caregiver. During early combinations of gesture and word, the caregiver and the child share a joint focus that is usually driven by the child's needs and desires. By the age of 18 months, however, the infant is not only attending more strongly to an object when it is marked by the adult with a label, but the infant is also looking to see where the adult is looking when giving the name for an object (Baldwin, 1991). With language acquisition, the caregiver and later the teacher will be actively guiding the child's focus of attention.

Luria (1975) described the importance of the interaction between voluntary attention and the social life of the infant as follows:

> This identification of the social roots of the higher forms of voluntary attention, which Vygotsky first recognized, is of decisive importance; it bridged the gap between the elementary forms of involuntary activity and the higher forms of voluntary attention. (p. 259)

Although Luria (1975), following Vygotsky, regarded the origin of voluntary attention as entirely social, we think that it is actually more in keeping with his general orientation to view the joint influences of the biological and social in the development of all attentional systems.

Culture and Self-Regulation

By the time children reach middle childhood, one might expect that differences would be found across cultures varying in their evaluation of the positive and the negative emotions and the related response tendencies of approach and inhibition. We have investigated temperamental characteristics of 6–7-year-old children in the People's Republic of China (P.R.C.) and in the United States, using a parent-report instrument, the Children's Behavior Questionnaire, and defining temperament as individual differences in emotional, motor, and attentional reactivity and self-regulation (Ahadi, Rothbart, & Ye, 1993). Over 600 parents completed the questionnaire, and principal axis factor analysis on data from the two cultures analyzed separately indicated that there was considerable similarity of factor structure from one culture to the other. Factors identified were those of Approach/Positive Affect, Negative Affect, and attentional Effortful Control.

We also found differences across cultures, with Approach and Effortful Control scores being relatively higher than Negative Affect in children from the United States, and Negative Affect scores being relatively higher than Approach and Effortful Control in children from the P.R.C. Interestingly, we found different patterns of relationships between the attentional self-regulation factor (Effortful Control) and the affective factors across cultures. Scores on Effortful Control in the P.R.C. were negatively correlated with Approach; whereas for the United States sample, Effortful Control was negatively correlated with Negative Affect, and uncorrelated with Approach. These findings are congruent with the interpretation that approach is discouraged in the P.R.C. and negative affect discouraged in the United States. Self-regulation might then be seen as taking the direction indicated by the value of a characteristic within a culture. There is much more to learn about the ways in which particular affective expressions and response tendencies are received in these and other cultures, but attentional self-regulation can serve to influence the expression of the emotions and related motivation tendencies in culturally approved directions.

Conclusion

In this chapter, we have discussed the contributions of cognitive science defined as the study of intelligent systems to the study of culture and emotion. It is clear from work in artificial intelligence that intelligent systems can be designed that do not include emotions and that this probably accounts for the slight contribution that cognitive science theory has made to the study of emotion. However, the human being is an organism whose evolution includes both intelligence and emotionality. The part of cognitive science most likely to help future empirical studies of affect and to advance the study of affect at a theoretical level seems to be cognitive neuroscience. Cognitive neuroscience studies how the human brain constrains the experience of the human mind. Cognitive neuroscience draws upon cognitive science for the abstract study of the component operations that constitute the domains of investigation. However, it seeks to relate these operations to the underlying brain systems that support them.

In this chapter, we have referred chiefly to the relation of attention to the emotions of pain, fear, and distress. We have seen that the brain's attention system can be viewed in terms of specific anatomical networks carrying out such functions as orienting and detecting. These physical systems can in turn be related to the systems that carry out emotional computations. Based on our analogy with the color perception system, we should not view cognitive processes as subject merely to the output of the emotional computations. Whereas color perception has a rich anatomy that is automatically activated by input, attention can also activate many of the same anatomical structures and thus regulate aspects of the input likely to influence behavior. Even relatively early parts of the color pathways can be penetrated by attention.

We believe that similar results will emerge from the next generation of studies on the voluntary control of emotion. We are aware that students given instructions to imagine a sad situation in their real life can shed real tears. We assume that in doing so, they activate substantial portions of the pathways involved in computing sadness. Just as expertise in any domain can be trained, we expect that actors may acquire the skills to contact emotional systems over a wider range of domains and with more effectiveness than those of us not so trained. It seems entirely likely that different genders or cultures may provide differential training in these skills.

We believe that the study of the early development of attentional systems in relation to the developing infant and the child's emotional life will be fruitful in furthering our understanding of the interaction between attentional and emotional networks in development. Here, too, we are influenced by cognitive science findings in the color domain. The underlying biology of color perception appears to be universal. Biology structures the way in which cultures use color terms and forces a certain universality to color concepts and artistic use. Thus, we would expect a universal underlying structure of emotion. That having been said, important differences exist between the use of color in diverse cultures. So, too, we expect nontrivial differences to exist in the communication, awareness of others, and even self-awareness of emotion among different cultures. These cultural differences are likely to be trained in early and important ways, leading to the exciting diversity of emotion that is the principal subject of this volume.

References

Ahadi, S. H., Rothbart, M. K., & Ye, R. (1993). Child temperament in the U.S. and China: Similarities and differences. *European Journal of Personality, 7,* 359–377.

Anderson, J. R., & Bower, G. H. (1973). *Human associative memory.* New York: Wiley.

Baldwin, D. A. (1991). Infants' contribution to the achievement of joint reference. *Child Development, 62,* 875–890.

Bower, G. H., & Clapper, J. P. (1989). Experimental methods in cognitive science. In M. I. Posner (Ed.), *Foundations of cognitive science* (pp. 245–300). Cambridge, MA: Bradford Books, MIT Press.

Bower, G. H., & Cohen, P. R. (1982). Emotional influences in memory and thinking: Data and theory. In M. S. Clark & S. T. Fiske (Eds.), *Affect and cognition* (pp. 291–331). Hillsdale, NJ: Erlbaum.

Broadbent, D. E. (1958). *Perception and communication.* Elmsford, NY: Pergamon Press.

Brown, R. (1976). In memorial tribute to Eric Lenneberg. *Cognition 4,* 125–153.

Caudill, W., & Frost, L. (1972). A comparison of maternal care and infant behavior in Japanese–American, American and Japanese families. In U. Bronfenbrenner (Ed.), *Influences on human development* (pp. 329–342). Hinsdale, IL: Dryden Press.

Chi, M. T. H., Glaser, R., & Farr, M. J. (1988). *The nature of expertise.* Hillsdale, NJ: Erlbaum.

Corbetta, M., Meizin, F. M., Dobmeyer, S., Shulman, G. L., & Petersen, S. E. (1991). Selective and divided attention during visual discrimination of shape, color and speed: Functional anatomy by positron emission tomography. *Journal of Neuroscience, 11,* 2382–2402.

D'Andrade, R. (1989). Cultural cognition. In M. I. Posner (Ed.), *Foundations of cognitive science* (pp. 795–830). Cambridge, MA: Bradford Books, MIT Press.

Davis, M., Hitchcock, J. M., & Rosen, J. B. (1987). Anxiety and the amygdala: Pharmacological and anatomical analysis of the fear-potentiated startle paradigm. *The Psychology of Learning and Information, 21,* New York: Academic Press.

Derryberry, D., & Rothbart, M. K. (1988). Arousal, affect, and attention as components of temperament. *Journal of Personality and Social Psychology, 55,* 953–966.

Ekman, P. (1992). Facial expressions of emotion: New findings, new questions. *Psychological Science, 3,* 34–38.

Grossman, K., Grossman, K. E., Spangler, G., Suess, G., & Unzner, L. (1985). Maternal sensitivity and newborn orientation responses as related to quality of attachment in Northern Germany. In I. Bretherton & E. Waters (Eds.), *Growing points of attachment theory and research: Monographs of the Society for Research in Child Development, 50,* 233–256.

Harman, C., & Rothbart, M. K. (1992, May). *Orienting and the soothing of distress.* Paper presented at the meeting of the Western Psychological Association, Portland, OR.

Lazarus, R. S. (1982). Thoughts on the relations of emotion and cognition. *American Psychologist, 37,* 1019–1024.

LeDoux, J. E. (1987). Emotion. In F. Plum (Ed.), *Handbook of physiology: Section I. The nervous system: Vol. 5. Higher function of the brain* (pp. 419–460). Bethesda, MD: American Physiological Society.

LeDoux, J. (1989). Cognitive–emotional interactions in the brain. *Cognition and Emotion, 3,* 267–289.

Luria, A. R. (1975). *The working brain.* New York: Basic Books.

Marcel, A. J. (1983). Conscious and unconscious perception: Experiments on masking and word recognition. *Cognitive Psychology, 15,* 197–237.

Mauro, R., Sato, K., & Tucker, J. (1992). The role of appraisal in human emotions: A cross-cultural study. *Journal of Personality and Social Psychology, 62,* 301–317.

McHaffie, J. G., Kao, C.-Q., & Stein, B. E. (1989). Nociceptive neurons in rat superior colliculus: Response properties, topography and functional implications. *Journal of Neurophysiology, 62,* 510–523.

McLeod, C., & Matthews, A. (1988). Anxiety and the allocation of attention to threat. *Quarterly Journal of Experimental Psychology, 38,* 659–670.

Miyake, K., Chen, S., & Campos, J. J. (1985). Infant temperament, mother's mode of interaction, and attachment in Japan: An interim report. *Monographs of the Society for Research in Child Development, 50,* 276–297.

Newell, A. (1990). *Unified theories of emotion.* Cambridge, MA: Harvard University Press.

Oatley, K., & Johnson-Laird, P. N. (1987). Toward a cognitive theory of emotion. *Cognition and Emotion, 1,* 29–50.

Posner, M. I. (1978). *Chronometric explorations of mind.* Hillsdale, NJ: Erlbaum.

Posner, M. I. (1992). Attention as a cognitive and neural system. *Current Directions in Psychological Science, 1*, 11–14.

Posner, M. I., & Rothbart, M. K. (1989). Intentional chapters on unintended thoughts. In J. S. Uleman & J. A. Bargh (Eds.), *Unintended thought: The limits of awareness, intention and control* (pp. 450–469). New York: Guilford Press.

Schachter, S., & Singer, J. E. (1962). Cognitive social and physiological determinants of emotional state. *Psychological Review, 69*, 379–399.

Simon, H. A. (1967). Motivational and emotional controls of cognition. *Psychological Review, 74*, 29–39.

Simon, H. A. (1982). Comments. In M. S. Clark & S. T. Fiske (Eds.), *Affect and cognition* (pp. 333–342). Hillsdale, NJ: Erlbaum.

Talbot, J. D., Marrett, A., Evans, A. C., Meyer, E., Bushnell, M. C., & Duncan, G. H. (1991). Multiple representation of pain in human cerebral cortex. *Science, 251*, 1355–1357.

Tversky, A., & Kahneman, D. (1974). Judgment under uncertainty: Heuristics and biases. *Science, 185*, 1124–1131.

Uleman, J. S., & Bargh, J. A. (1989). *Unintended thought.* New York: Guilford Press.

van den Boom, D. (1989). Neonatal irritability and the development of attachment. In G. Kohnstamm, J. Bates, & M. K. Rothbart (Eds.), *Temperament in childhood.* New York: Wiley.

Van Ijzendoorn, M. H., & Kroonenberg, P. M. (1988). Cross-cultural patterns of attachment: A meta-analysis of the strange situation. *Child Development, 59*, 147–156.

Von Lehn, K. (1989). Problem solving and cognitive skill acquisition. In M. I. Posner (Ed.), *Foundations of cognitive science* (pp. 527–580). Cambridge, MA: MIT Press.

Zajonc, R. B. (1980). Feeling and thinking: Preferences need no inferences. *American Psychologist, 35*, 151–175.

Zeki, S. (1993). *A vision of the brain.* London: Brackwell.

Zeki, S., Watson, J. D. G., Lueck, C. J., Friston, K. J., Kennard, C., & Fracowiak, R. S. J. (1991). A direct demonstration of the functional specialization of the human cortex. *Journal of Neuroscience, 11*, 641–649.

PART THREE

Emotion as Moral Category and Phenomenon

CHAPTER 7

Affecting Culture: Emotion and Morality in Everyday Life

Geoffrey M. White

T he topic of emotion and morality conjoins two often opposed terms: one (emotions) lodged in a naturalized realm of the body and feeling, the other (morality) associated with a cultural realm of socially constructed norms and conventions. Indeed, the tension between these two spheres, between the natural dispositions of the individual and the cultural constraints of the collectivity, has been a central problem for much of Western theorizing about the self and society.

In this chapter, I discuss the interrelation of these opposed terms—emotion and morality—in a way that subverts the dichotomous separation of the natural–emotional and the cultural–moral and leads to a reconceptualization of emotion generally. Whereas standard definitions of emotion usually locate emotion in the body first and then add on cognitive and social–interactive processes as secondary factors, I argue that the social and the conceptual need to be incorporated as *primary* determinants of emotion rather than as secondary or surface phenomena.

Similar arguments have been put forward by a number of writers working in the interstices of anthropology, linguistics, and psychology (e.g., Gergen, 1990; Lutz, 1988; Markus & Kitayama, 1991; Rosaldo, 1984; Wierzbicka, 1992). Researchers working this borderland region (sometimes known as *cultural psychology*—see Bruner, 1990; Howard, 1985; Shweder, 1990) have begun to take seriously the charge that an adequate theory of emotion will have to take account of the specific meanings and uses of emotion in people's everyday lives, that is, of the interpreted significance of emotion in individual subjectivity and in social interaction. It is in these contexts that emotional processes obtain meaning and force as part of personal and social reality.

Just in the background of these problems lies a series of dichotomies that have long burdened emotion theory (and culture theory): mind/body, individual/society, affect/cognition, innate/acquired, universal/relative, material/ideational, and so on (see Lutz & White, 1986). These polarities consistently force theoretical positions into oppositional alignments. My intention is not to promote a constructivist or interpretivist theory of emotion to the exclusion of physiological or psychobiological processes, but to suggest that emotions are, if nothing else, *semiotic mediators* linking the body, the subject, and the social. Rather than simply invert or reproduce old dichotomies, we might work toward a theory in which biological, cultural, and social processes interrelate in dynamic and contingent ways. This sort of theory building will require cultural–interpretive tools capable of identifying emotions as meaningful (and forceful) elements of everyday life.

Of course, emotion theories have for some time articulated a place for cognitive and cultural factors (usually as surface variables) noting points of linkage between primary inner affect and secondary external expression (White, 1993). But in isolating real emotion in a realm of physiologically based affect, research on the causes of emotion is directed away from the cognitive, semiotic, and social factors that constitute emotional meaning in social reality. Even clinical and psychodynamic research, dealing with subjective experience, focuses on the masking or distortion of basic affects rather than on the significance of emotions within socially constituted worlds of meaning.

To a large extent, it has been the comparative study of emotion in non-Western languages and cultures that has brought issues of interpretation and translation onto the spotlight. Converging with social constructionist theories (e.g., Harré, 1986), comparative studies have drawn attention to the culturally constituted character of much of emotional experience and to the need to unpack the extensive cultural baggage bundled up in terms such as the English words anger or fear (e.g., Lakoff & Kövecses, 1987; Wierzbicka, 1992).

At the core of most emotion words are social and moral entailments capable of creating social realities and of directing social behavior. Sociolinguistic studies in particular have produced clear evidence that the meanings of emotion language are contingent upon the contexts of practical action in which emotions are expressed, talked about, and negotiated in interaction (Besnier, 1990; Lutz & Abu-Lughod, 1990). I use the phrase *emotional meaning*, useful for its ambiguity, to make the point that the meanings of emotion and the emotions of meaning are not so easily separated, and that realms of cognition and emotion exist in mutual, contingent interaction. All emotions entail some element of interpretation or appraisal (however rapid or unconscious), just as all language in use is emotionally valenced (Ochs, 1986).

Considering issues of interpretation, representation, and translation (issues often raised only in cross-cultural research) is one way of opening up questions of the social and moral meanings of emotion. The section that follows discusses problems of translation and representation as a way of examining the significance of emotion within broader cultural models of the person, action, and social life. This discussion lays the groundwork for an argument that human emotions are *prototypically* social and moral, and that a comprehensive theory of emotion will be one that incorporates social and communicative processes as central elements. One of the implications of this argument is that culturally variant conceptions of self, particularly the varieties of interpersonal self described for a range of non-Western societies, can be seen to have significant effects upon the conceptualization and experience of emotion (see Kitayama & Markus, chapter 1, this volume).

Morality and the Representation of Emotional Meaning

Much of the enthusiasm for a universalizable, scientific theory of emotion based on common biologically based features of emotion has come from comparative research on facial expressions. In a series of pathbreaking studies, Ekman and his colleagues found cross-cultural convergences in the recognition and labeling of facial expressions associated with a set of six to eight basic English emotion terms (e.g., Ekman, 1984). They (and others) interpreted these findings as evidence for the claim that humans are programmed for at least six universal core affects (e.g., anger, fear, disgust, happy, sad, and surprise).

It is testimony to the importance of this work that nearly all subsequent comparative research on emotion has addressed or cited the Ekman findings and their relevance for interpreting culturally variable emotions. Cognizant of the fact that people who live in societies as different as those of America and Papua New Guinea will have different ways of expressing and talking about emotion, Ekman posited "display rules" or secondary filters that modulate the social–interpretive aspects of emotion. At base, however, emotions are seen as rooted in neural programs of and for basic affects that may be universally read in facial expressions. Although these data say something interesting about human capacities for recognizing facial expressions labeled with emotion words, what do they tell us about emotion as an element of mind or action? Not only do we not have the answers to these wider issues, we have hardly begun to formulate the questions—for reasons discussed later in this chapter.

So long as emotion research essentializes the definition of emotion as grounded in or determined by invariant physiological structures, problems of interpretation will not even be posed in a serious way. In work on facial expressions, the meanings of basic emotion words, such as anger, surprise, fear, and the like, are taken for granted. This is so largely because of an underlying referential theory of language that presumes that words function essentially as labels for objects or processes, providing a convenient way to discriminate or categorize a preexisting reality: in this case, facial expressions or corresponding feeling states. Using the analogy of color, it has been suggested that emotion words label discrete feelings and expressions in much the same way in which color terms denote a portion of the spectrum of visible wavelengths. In each case, a small set of basic terms is seen as labeling or discriminating among objects or states, forming an organized set of categories. By extending this analogy, some have suggested that the notion of prototypic categories, which has been applied with considerable success to color terminology, may also be an effective way of approaching the analysis of emotion terms (e.g., D'Andrade, 1987; Gerber, 1985; Heider, 1991; Posner, Rothbart, & Harman, chapter 6, this volume).[1]

The difficulty with this approach, as I have argued elsewhere (White, 1993), is that emotions are not colors. When emotions are actually expressed or talked about in ordinary language, they are socially significant processes that have immediate interpersonal meaning and effect. Emotion talk is highly generative of inferences about social events and relations that may readily adjust or transform both the emotions and the social realities that surround them. The greatest claims for the universality of a small set of core affects have come from studies that have done the greatest amount of decontextualizing, of removing emotion from its social conditions and effects, and of stripping away antecedents and consequents only to add them back in, problematically, as cultural rules of variation (cf. Crapanzano, 1989).

The problems in representing emotion concepts reflect the evolution of anthropological approaches to linguistic meaning over the past few decades. Put briefly, early successes in developing models of meaning for terminologies such as kinship terms or color terms proved to be ill-suited to more complex domains such as terms for illness or personality (White, 1992). Lexical methods used to represent meaning in terms of similarities and contrasts among a set of terms proved insufficient on both semantic and pragmatic grounds. These methods were incapable of tapping the

---

[1]The success of prototype models of color categorization is related to the availability of a universal or etic grid representing the color spectrum that may be used for the elicitation and comparison of color denotation in any language or culture.

more complicated knowledge structures that underlie much of ordinary language, and the approach was entirely ideational and missed the pragmatic force of language used in social context. As a result, techniques such as cluster analysis or multidimensional scaling that represent meaning in terms of a map of word-to-word similarities have only heuristic value, at best, for analyzing conceptual schemas.

Several studies have used lexical techniques to represent the meanings of emotion terms in different languages (Gerber, 1985; Heider, 1991; Lutz, 1982). These studies show that scaling emotion words in a dimensional space consistently produces a few broad connotational dimensions that can be accounted for largely in terms of the semantic differential dimensions of evaluation (pleasure, social desirability), potency (power, dominance), and activity (arousal; Lutz, 1982; Russell, 1991).

Let me illustrate briefly with an example from my own research on emotion words in an Oceanic language: the A'ara language of Santa Isabel in the Solomon Islands. Consider the picture that emerges from analysis of a set of representative A'ara emotion words. Figure 1 shows the results of scaling judgments of similarity among 15 commonly used emotion words made by a small sample of A'ara speakers.[2] The pattern represented fits well the dimensional structure described above, particularly the dimensions of solidarity and power found in many studies of interpersonal vocabulary (White, 1980), with the first (horizontal) dimension separating evaluatively positive and negative terms, and the second (vertical) axis contrasting emotions along a dimension of power (often labeled dominance/submission).

The emergence of a strong evaluative dimension in emotion lexicons reflects the fact that emotion words carry moral weight. They are not simply neutral descriptions of states of affairs; rather, they say something about the subject's perception of what is good or bad, right or wrong,

---

[2]These data were obtained from a small sample of 11 men between the ages of 32 and 50 years. Each informant was asked to review words written, one apiece, on 3 × 5 index cards and to sort them into any number of piles according to which words were judged to be "similar in meaning" (*kaisei gaogatho di*, literally, have the same thought [behind them]). Similarity measures were adjusted for size and number of piles formed by each informant (Burton, 1975) and then scaled into two, three, and four dimensions (Kruskal, Young, & Seery, 1977), with the two-dimensional solution showing the best fit.

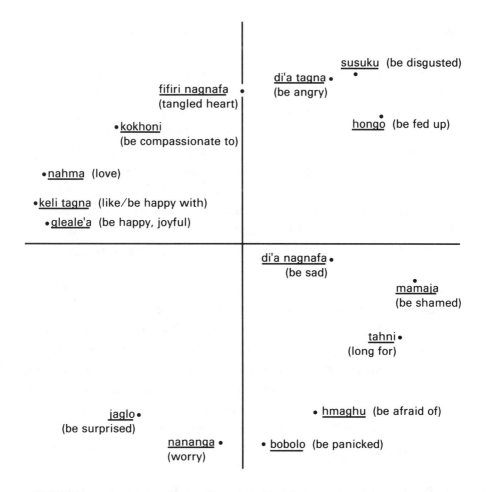

FIGURE 1.   Two-dimensional scaling of 15 A'ara (Solomon Islands) emotion words.

desirable or undesirable. Even when taken out of context, as they were in the sorting task, these connotations significantly shape judgments of meaning. In line with the view that emotion terms are essentially labels for internal feeling states, the evaluative dimension of emotion terms has often been labeled "pleasure/displeasure"—giving it an essentially physiological interpretation rather than a social or moral one. Although both aspects of evaluative meaning may be operative, the consistent foregrounding of feeling tone and the marginalization of the social–moral exemplifies the process by which emotions have been psychologized in scientific representations.

Not only are emotion words always evaluative in meaning, but emotion lexicons inevitably contain a preponderance of negative terms designating undesirable or unpleasant emotions (e.g., Lutz, 1982).[3] I take this bias toward the negative to be a reflection of the moral work that emotion words and expressions perform in ordinary discourse. Specifically, to express or describe emotion in natural language is to make a commentary about some state of affairs and about one's intentions vis-à-vis that state of affairs. As others have noted, emotion words are always valenced (Ortony, Clore, & Collins, 1988), signifying an evaluation of events and a desire to maintain or adjust some state of affairs. Whereas positive emotions express an acceptance or willingness to maintain a situation, negative emotions often function as signs of moral discontent, signifying a desire to change the situation, the self, or both.[4]

In considering what would be required to translate the emotion words in Figure 1, and what is left out of this sort of dimensional representation, plotting single words in this fashion implies that they function mainly as labels for discrete objects or states. This format tends to nominalize the meaning of emotion words (translated as nouns, such as *anger*, *surprise*, etc.) even though, in this case, the vernacular terms in Figure 1 are mostly verbs. Most of these words are stative verbs (roughly, *be angry*, *be surprised*, etc.) that function something like adjectives, but that entail a temporal process with a past, present, and future: A process in which the person experiencing the emotion is linked, through the emotional response, to both antecedent events and possible consequents.[5] Indeed, it is difficult for A'ara speakers to even talk about emotions

---

[3]Figure 1 is misleading in this regard, insofar as the ratio of positive to negative terms is out of line with the much greater number of negative emotion words that make up the lexicon as a whole.

[4]We might speculate that, because much of human effort and action is devoted to bringing social realities in line with ideal models, negative emotions are more finely conceptualized and lexicalized. In this way, human languages produce a wider array of symbolic resources that may be used to pursue goals and otherwise affect the social environment.

[5]This verbal aspect of A'ara emotion language also captures the sense that emotional process is something that *happens to* the subject, such that the person experiencing the emotion is conceived of as having been caused to feel or think the emotion in question.

as abstract or discrete states of mind independent of these contextual linkages.

When informants were asked to judge similarities among words for emotion, they did so by invoking commonsense knowledge about the types of situations to which they are typically applied: to knowledge that can be represented in the form of scripts, scenarios, or event schemas. One way to interpret Figure 1 is to see the similarity distances as a measure of the degree to which conceptual schemas associated with each word overlap. Thus, for example, the terms "be angry," "be disgusted," and "be fed up" cluster together in the diagram because they all entail appraisals of a prior action or event as an offense against the self: a violation of expectations for desired or desirable behavior. They differ in intensity and, more important, in implied response, such that being angry involves a desire for harm or retribution, being disgusted implies rejection or avoidance, and being fed up implies impatience and reprimand.

Dimensional models such as Figure 1 (or cluster diagrams, see Gerber, 1985; Heider, 1991) obviously do not capture the kinds of specific or detailed knowledge associated with such contexts. However, recent work in schema theory suggests ways in which this type of knowledge may be represented, at least in simplified or prototypic outline, as a set of interrelated propositions and inferences.[6] Studies in linguistics (Lakoff & Kövecses, 1987; Wierzbicka, chapter 5, this volume), anthropology (Lutz, 1987; White, 1990b), and psychology (Ortony et al., 1988) have all proposed models that use some kind of event schema to represent emotion concepts. By asking what talk of emotions "says," at least implicitly, about persons, events, and interactions, it is possible to probe the kinds of commonsense reasoning that constitute the social meanings of emotion.

A growing number of studies of emotion language cross-culturally are finding that cultural knowledge of emotion (or, more broadly, cultural psychologies of the self or person) are organized in terms of interpersonal schemas that link action or event sequences through personal or affective

---

[6]It is likely that the multiple channels characteristic of emotional perception and comprehension will also prove a suitable subject for parallel distributed processing (PDP) models now being developed in cognitive science. However, transforming schema-type models to PDP models would affect the form but not, in principle, the substance of the argument about emotional meaning developed here.

response. Although important differences remain, a simplified outline of the form of these models (cf. Lakoff & Kövecses, 1987; Lutz, 1987; White, 1990a, 1990b; Wierzbicka, 1992) may be represented as follows:

EVENT → EMOTION (AFFECT) → ACTION RESPONSE.

Although highly condensed, this general schema, organized in the form of a sequence of propositional inferences, indicates one of the ways in which emotions and talk of emotions acquire directive (moral) force within wider systems of thought: Emotion concepts occupy a strategic, mediating position in reasoning chains that link social events with goals, desires, and actions (cf. D'Andrade & Strauss, 1992). To feel in a certain way is to subscribe to a specific kind of appraisal of prior events and a specific type of culturally constituted response. In other words, emotions are a moral rhetoric that implicates both descriptions of the world and recommendations for acting upon it.

Definitions and examples offered by A'ara informants asked to characterize the meaning of emotion terms usually include at least one of the inferences represented in the above chain of reasoning. More significantly, analysis of naturally occurring talk of emotions indicates that emotion attributions consistently occupy this kind of mediating "slot" in longer sequences of cultural reasoning about social events (White, 1990b). Indeed, the formulaic quality of this kind of reasoning about emotion is such that talk of emotions can be used as an idiom or rhetorical code for indirectly characterizing actions and events (White, 1990a). For example, if "moral transgression against the self" is a type of event that typically evokes anger, then to say that one is angry about an event is to invite the "backward inference" that it constitutes a moral transgression.

The findings of comparative research that emotion concepts frequently take the form of a processual schema such as that shown here provide a kind of particularistic, "bottom-up" view of the ways in which emotion is conceptualized cross culturally. Studies in numerous languages show emotions to be thought of as a personal response that mediates the episodic scenes and events of everyday life. Interestingly, this processual structure of folk models of emotion resembles closely the form of more "top-down" scientific theories that have proposed representing emotions as a process connecting antecedent events, subjective perceptions, feelings, and subsequent responses. Thus, something like the following sequence was put forward during the 1992 APA conference on which this volume is based:

EVENT → EVENT CODING → APPRAISAL → ACTION TENDENCY, SOMATIC EXPERIENCE → MANAGEMENT.

This type of theoretical schema is isomorphic with the episodic structure of commonsense models, represented previously as a sequence of antecedent event, emotion, action response. The convergence of these definitions of emotion, seen from both the bottom-up perspective of ordinary language and the top-down perspective of psychological theory, suggests that this is a robust conceptualization, rooted in widely shared structures of language and experience.

Although many processual models of emotion have been proposed over the years, approaches differ markedly in the degree to which they regard any one component as primary or necessary and others as secondary or derivative. Thus, by privileging the somatic component (sometimes called *affect*), psychobiological approaches have made a science out of studying emotions strictly as feeling states and as facial expressions. In the following section, I argue that essentializing the definition of emotion in this way eliminates social and semiotic (communicative) processes that are in fact basic, constitutive elements of emotion. A more powerful theory of emotion would be capable of representing the full range of determinants of emotional experience and, hence, of articulating relations between emotion and a wider range of thought and behavior.

Culture, Emotions, and the Interpersonal Self

The events and scenes that A'ara speakers mention when explaining the meanings of emotion words are not typically occurrences such as "didn't catch any fish" or "sudden rainstorm." Rather, they are activities that involve other people. When I asked informants to explicate the meanings of the terms in Figure 1 with examples, nearly all of the examples offered took the form of action scenarios involving other people. The degree to which this is so varies from one term to another. For example, being shamed *always* involves other people (usually in some violation of food etiquette), whereas fear could involve people (fear of sorcerers or of powerful chiefs) or not (fear of snakes). But where many emotion theories have ignored this distinction, the interpersonal motifs in A'ara talk of emotion emerge as central or prototypic to the meaning of the domain. I have outlined elsewhere (White, 1990b) an analysis of several of the words represented in Figure 1 (particularly the words glossed as "be angry," "be sad," and "be shamed") showing that A'ara emotion language in general and these words in particular constitute a moral rhetoric commonly used to negotiate the social realities of everyday life. When put to use, emotion words in Santa Isabel, like emotion words everywhere, are embedded in more general understandings of the person and of the social–psychological process. In Santa Isabel society, this kind of commonsense reasoning places interpersonal relations in the foreground. Socially and culturally, the most pertinent personal concerns are those that implicate relations with others.

Citing numerous cases from Oceania, Lutz (1988) generalized this point, arguing that, for many non-Western societies, concepts of emotion and person are oriented toward external, social relations. She contrasted the more interpersonal or relational conceptions of emotional process with American concepts of internal, individualized affects:

> Internal feeling states have commonly been assumed to be the primary referents of emotion words in Western thought, both social-scientific and lay. In these views, the function of the emotion word is to label an internal state and perhaps communicate that state to others. Examination of the use of emotion words among several Oceanic peoples ... reveals an alternative view of emotion. In these societies, emotion words are seen as statements about the relationship between a person and an event (particularly [an event] involving another person), rather than as statements about introspection on one's internal states. (Lutz, 1982, p. 113)

Interestingly, this passage was cited in two recent review articles by psychologists challenging Lutz's claim for radical cultural difference (Russell, 1991, p. 445; Shaver, Wu, & Schwartz, 1991, p. 201). These critics argued that her assertion that emotions in some non-Western societies are conceptualized as outside the person in relations and events rather than in the body is not supported either by her own data or by comparative research (cf. Wierzbicka, chapter 5, this volume).

What can be made of these conflicting interpretations? The psychological critics of Lutz's interpretation cite her own criterion for eliciting emotion words on Ifaluk: They are words that, the Ifaluk say, are "about our insides (*niferash*)." For example, Russell (1991) wondered whether a word could even count as an emotion word if it did not refer to an internal state: "If song [Ifaluk, "justified anger"] were a member of a class of words that, like *marriage* or *kinship*, referred to a relationship, then the reason for calling *song* an emotion word is unclear" (p. 445). Whereas Russell suggested that Ifaluk emotion words are about internal states, Shaver et al. (1991) took the opposite position and argued that, in fact, American emotion concepts are, like the Ifaluk, also more about social relations than internal states: "U.S. accounts are concerned with the same general issue that Oceanic people's emotion accounts: the relationship between a person (with desires, goals, and values) and an event, usually an event involving at least one other person" (p. 201).

The answer to this interpretive wrangle ought now to be obvious. Emotions and the ways in which people think about them are fundamentally relational. Emotions are neither entirely inside nor outside the body. They are mediators (both social and semiotic) and are conceptualized as such in most folk models of emotion (see White, 1993). Note that Lutz (1982) herself did not say that Ifaluk emotion words have nothing to do with internal states, but that they are "statements about the relationship between a person and an event" (p. 113). In this regard, the findings of Shaver et al. (1991) that American understandings of emotion also focus on interpersonal scenarios provided added evidence that folk models of emotion are prototypically social. Although Shaver et al. used their findings to argue that the cultural differences cited by Lutz are overdone, their results argued for a theory that predicts far more variability in emotion schemas based on the complex, culturally specific ways in which social environments are organized.

To attempt to identify or measure emotions in isolation from their social contexts decouples affect from relations that are otherwise necessary features of emotional meaning. At issue here is nothing less than the definition of the domain of emotion as an object of study. Although there is still some argument about what kinds of words and concepts count as emotion, there is general agreement about which words represent English-language concepts of emotion: Most exclude strictly bodily states such as *hungry* or *tired*; whereas most would include *angry* and *sad*, and words such as *interested* or even *guilty* remain borderline cases (Ortony, 1986). Although all of the candidate terms refer to some kind of cognitive–affective state of mind, the words regarded as the best exemplars of emotion are those that are also *social* and *moral*. By social, I mean embedded in a field of interpersonal relations and actions; and by moral, I mean possessing evaluative entailments and behavioral valence. In other words, the social and moral aspects of emotion are primary and not simply programmed responses that are given social and moral meaning as a kind of cultural overlay.

One of the reasons for the confusion in interpreting and assessing Ifaluk emotion concepts in relation to American concepts is the absence of sufficiently detailed models of ordinary thinking and talking about emotion (in either society). Lutz and others working in non-Western societies have argued that basic ideas about human agency, causality, and the forces that shape social life may differ markedly from comparable American or Western notions (Geertz, 1984; Miller & Bersoff, 1992; Shweder & Bourne, 1982). To assess the nature of emotion concepts in any given society, we need to know something of the broader ethnopsychology, of culturally organized ways of thinking about the self (including concepts of mind, thought, and emotion) and the social environment.

The dominant theme in comparative literature on the self is that the Western self marks perhaps an extreme case of the ideology of individualism, that is, of the enshrining of the autonomous individual in social and cultural institutions (everything from ideas about marriage to educational and legal norms; e.g., Lutz, 1988; Rosaldo, 1984; Shweder & Bourne, 1982). Together with concepts of personality, popular understandings of emotion are one of the primary means through which individualistic concepts of the self or person are articulated in popular (and academic) culture (White, 1992). But what could be meant by a nonindividualistic psychology of emotion? In what ways do relational concepts of self influence the ways in which people think and talk (and feel) about emotion? I take up these questions in a brief discussion of the emotion of shame in Santa Isabel (represented as *mamaja* in Figure 1).

As argued at the beginning of this chapter, psychology's focus on bodily states or on facial expressions has worked to individuate the problem of emotion. It is symptomatic of the consistent skewing of emotion theory toward the individuated features of emotion that relatively little attention has been given to emotions of shame within psychology. Shame is mentioned in the Ekman (1984) studies of facial expression, but perhaps because it received among the lowest reliability scores, it is usually left off lists of the basic or core affects. Given the *strong* cultural salience of emotions of shame in many societies around the world, this marginalization suggests the operation of a Eurocentric model that amplifies the importance of somatic and affective elements and minimizes the social–moral. Although shame in many cultures may have little somatic phenomenology, it is inevitably an intensely moral concept used in complex ways in discourse about social relations and events (see Mesquita & Frijda, 1992, for a review of several examples).

The A'ara word for shame, *mamaja*, is polysemous: used to signify both the feeling of shame and to refer to genitalia. There is clearly some connection between these senses of the term, because public exposure of one's genitals is an immediate cause of shame. Yet, interpreting the A'ara notion of *mamaja* on the basis of this sort of scenario would miss the most important or culturally salient meanings of the term. Rather than signifying an internal feeling of discomfort evoked by an exposure of the self or by a violation of societal standards of comportment, *mamaja* is fundamentally about social relations. Fleshing out a bit what is meant by "fundamentally about social relations" provides an example of the type of cultural model of emotions associated with interpersonal selves.

Mamaja is typically evoked in situations in which a person behaves in a way that breaches or upsets an important or valued social relation. In such situations, *both* parties are likely to report feeling shame (or, more correctly, being shamed). The prototypic context for eliciting or experiencing shame is the violation of expectations surrounding the sharing or nonsharing of food. Food is a symbol of social relationships. To give or exchange food is to affirm the value of enduring relations. To move about with ease and share food is to *not* feel shame, to feel constricted and observant of the proper distance or respect associated with a relationship *is* to feel shame.

The close proximity of *mamaja* (be shamed) and *di'a nagnafa* (be sad, literally, bad heart) in Figure 1 reflects the similarity of the event schemas that underlie their meaning. To oversimplify, both are associated with moral transgressions between the self and another person with whom the self is in an important, valued relation. Unlike "be angry" (*di'a tagna*), which is ideally not expressed between closely related people and which implies some form of rupture or break in the relationship, both *mamaja* and *di'a nagnafa* pertain to close relations in need of repair. In the logic of emotional meaning for these terms, it is the state of the *relation* between two persons that is the object of prediction, not the individual and not two individuals. Talk of *mamaja* constitutes a kind of relational calculus that works to calibrate or mark intersubjective distance and boundaries in social relations.

I have discussed the logic of A'ara shame or *mamaja* at more length elsewhere (White, 1990b). However, brief mention of the type of schema that may be derived from ordinary talk about shame will illustrate the kind of conceptualization associated with such an emphatically moral emotion:

$$\text{TRANSGRESSION (Self, Other)}$$
$$+$$
$$\text{CLOSE (Self, Other)}$$
$$\Downarrow$$

mamaja (be shamed).

This condensed schema represents the eliciting situation for a larger scenario that would include inferences about the appropriate response(s) as well—in this case, some form of withdrawal or avoidance. As in the case of implied antecedents, the responses implicated by any particular emotion are likely to have powerful interpersonal implications for the state of relationships between self and other(s). It is these implications that constitute the social meanings of A'ara emotion; in other words, that make emotions about relationships between persons and persons (or persons and events). If, for the sake of convenience, we combine these antecedents of A'ara shame as a proposition about the violation of relational expectations (such as not giving enough food or failing to show respect), the larger scenario of event, emotion, response, can be summarized as follows:

RELATIONAL VIOLATION
⇓
mamaja (shamed)
⇓
WITHDRAWAL/AVOIDANCE.

This sketchy example indicates that claims about the more intensive interpersonal or relational qualities of the self in many non-Western societies can be articulated in terms of specific features of cognition, emotion, and moral reasoning. However, it is important to note that these differences do not imply some kind of radical otherness or incommensurability of culturally relative forms. So, for example, when an old Solomon Islands woman sitting outside a chief's house notices some unruly children playing on the veranda and yells out "We're shamed!" (*Mamaja noda!*) to chastise the children and get them to move away, she is invoking her relationship to the children to add force to her injunction. This does not imply that the woman is unaware of her individuality so much as it underscores the fact that the culture provides a set of conventions for thinking and talking in relational terms that express collective forms of thought and feeling more readily, and with more consequence, than in many Western languages. To ignore these differences in social cognition and practical action is to leave emotion theory suspended in the realm of conjecture about abstract universals.

Conclusion

Research in a wide range of languages and cultures indicates that when people talk about emotion, they are not talking primarily about states inside the individual, nor are they talking about responses or events outside the person. Rather, they are talking about processes that *mediate* or link persons, actions, and events. The strong version of this argument is that emotions are everywhere prototypically social; that their core meanings and pragmatic consequences pertain to interpersonal relations and interactions. But this is a claim about the workings of emotional process (affective/cognitive/social), not about the official or normative conceptions of emotion, which vary widely in the degree to which they emphasize or externalize the social.

Given the increasingly sophisticated literature on ethnopsychology across cultures, it is becoming possible to query the manner in which official, culturally constituted models of emotion produce particular types of emotional dilemma or methods for solving them. Thus, the tendency of many Western cultures to individuate emotions may produce discrepancies, gaps, and tensions between the social nature of emotion and its more internalized, psychological representation in popular culture. Thus, most of the culturally sanctioned institutions for identifying and transforming emotional distress in the West tend to strip away the social–moral–political contexts of emotion and focus on internal, psychological states of the individual. To some extent, interest in group therapies, family therapies, community psychology, and the like represent attempts to attend to social determinants of emotion that are otherwise obscured or marginalized in normative models. In contrast, many small-scale or traditional cultures, characterized by a more intensely interpersonal self, evince coordinated, collective means for ameliorating or transforming socioemotional conflict (e.g., Watson-Gegeo & White, 1990).

Contrary to the common Western view of emotions as inchoate and hidden in the unknowable recesses of the mind, emotions and emotion concepts play a strategic role in cultural reasoning about the social realities that link the self and others. In this chapter, I have tried to draw a link between the forms of reasoning about interpersonal relations associated with emotions and the social–moral work that emotions do in everyday life. Thus, the shared models of emotion that lead people to make inferences jointly and interactively about the antecedents of emotion make it possible for people engaged in conversation to use emotional expressions (linguistic and nonlinguistic) to appropriate or transform the meaning of social situations.[7] In this manner, emotions are used, both consciously and unconsciously, to mediate actively social relations in much the same way in which any set of cultural signs or symbols may be used to structure interaction or manage impressions (e.g., Bailey, 1983).

Far from residing out of view, centered in some kind of unarticulated primary process, emotions arise in contexts of transaction, marking boundaries between inside and outside, and defining relations between me and you, or we and you-plural, that are probably always in flux and subject to the moment-by-moment negotiations of social interaction. As such, emotions are well suited to the moral work of (re)shaping the course of events and (re)defining the nature of social relations. Foucault put this nicely when he said, simply, "you can say, in general, that in our society the main field of morality, the part of ourselves which is most relevant for morality, is our feelings" (Foucault, 1983, p. 238, cited in Lutz, 1988, p. 77).

References

Bailey, F. G. (1983). *The tactical uses of passion*. Ithaca, NY: Cornell University Press.

Besnier, N. (1990). Language and affect. *Annual Review of Anthropology, 19*, 419–451.

Bruner, J. (1990). *Acts of meaning*. Cambridge, MA: Harvard University Press.

Burton, M. (1975). Dissimilarity measures for unconstrained sorting data. *Multivariate Behavioral Research, 10*, 409–423.

Crapanzano, V. (1989). Preliminary notes on the glossing of emotions. *Kroeber Anthropological Society Papers*, Nos. 69–70, 78–85.

D'Andrade, R. G. (1987). A folk model of the mind. In D. Holland & N. Quinn (Eds.), *Cultural models in language and thought* (pp. 112–148). Cambridge, England: Cambridge University Press.

D'Andrade, R. G., & Strauss, C. (Eds.). (1992). *Human motives and cultural models*. Cambridge, England: Cambridge University Press.

Ekman, P. (1984). Expression and the nature of emotion. In K. Scherer & P. Ekman (Eds.), *Approaches to emotion* (pp. 319–340). Hillsdale, NJ: Erlbaum.

Foucault, M. (1983). On the genealogy of ethics: An overview of work in progress. In H. Dreyfus & P. Rabinow (Eds.), *Michel Foucault: Beyond structuralism and hermeneutics* (2nd ed., pp. 229–252). Chicago: University of Chicago Press.

---

[7] I am grateful to Shinobu Kitayama for this point and for his perceptive reading of this chapter.

Geertz, C. (1984). From the native's point of view. In R. A. Shweder & R. A. LeVine (Eds.), *Culture theory: Essays on mind, self, and emotion* (pp. 123–136). Cambridge, England: Cambridge University Press.

Gerber, E. (1985). Rage and obligation: Samoan emotions in conflict. In G. White & J. Kirkpatrick (Eds.), *Person, self and experience: Exploring Pacific ethnopsychologies* (pp. 121–167). Berkeley: University of California Press.

Gergen, K. (1990). Social understanding and the inscription of self. In J. Stigler, R. Shweder, & G. Herdt (Eds.), *Cultural psychology: Essays on comparative human development* (pp. 569–606). Cambridge, England: Cambridge University Press.

Harré, R. (Ed.). (1986). *The social construction of emotions.* Oxford, England: Basil Blackwell.

Heider, K. G. (1991). *Landscapes of emotion: Mapping three cultures in Indonesia.* Cambridge, England: Cambridge University Press.

Howard, A. (1985). Ethnopsychology and the prospects for a cultural psychology. In G. White & J. Kirkpatrick (Eds.), *Person, self and experience: Exploring Pacific ethnopsychologies* (pp. 401–420). Berkeley: University of California Press.

Kruskal, J., Young, F., & Seery, J. (1977). *How to use KYST-2, a very flexible program to do multidimensional scaling and unfolding.* Murray Hill, NJ: Bell Laboratories.

Lakoff, G., & Kövecses, Z. (1987). The cognitive model of anger inherent in American English. In D. Holland & N. Quinn (Eds.), *Cultural models in language and thought* (pp. 195–221). Cambridge, England: Cambridge University Press.

Lutz, C. (1982). The domain of emotion words on Ifaluk. *American Ethnologist, 9,* 113–128.

Lutz, C. (1987). Goals, events and understanding in Ifaluk emotion theory. In D. Holland & N. Quinn (Eds.), *Cultural models in language and thought* (pp. 290–312). Cambridge, England: Cambridge University Press.

Lutz, C. (1988). *Unnatural emotions: Everyday sentiments on a Micronesian atoll and their challenge to Western theory.* Chicago: University of Chicago Press.

Lutz, C. A., & Abu-Lughod, L. (Eds.). (1990). *Language and the politics of emotion.* Cambridge, England: Cambridge University Press.

Lutz, C. A., & White, G. M. (1986). The anthropology of emotions. *Annual Review of Anthropology, 15,* 405–436.

Markus, H. R., & Kitayama, S. (1991). Culture and the self: Implications for cognition, emotion, and motivation. *Psychological Review, 98,* 224–253.

Mesquita, B., & Frijda, N. H. (1992). Cultural variations in emotions: A review. *Psychological Bulletin, 112,* 179–204.

Miller, J. G., & Bersoff D. M. (1992). Culture and moral judgment: How are conflicts between justice and interpersonal responsibilities resolved? *Journal of Personality and Social Psychology, 62,* 541–554.

Ochs, E. (1986). From feelings to grammar: A Samoan case study. In B. Schieffelin & E.

Ochs (Eds.), *Language socialization across cultures* (pp. 251–272). Cambridge, England: Cambridge University Press.

Ortony, A. (1986). Is guilt an emotion? *Cognition and Emotion, 1*, 283–298.

Ortony, A., Clore, G. L., & Collins, A. (1988). *The cognitive structure of emotions.* Cambridge, England: Cambridge University Press.

Rosaldo, M. Z. (1984). Toward an anthropology of self and feeling. In R. A. Shweder & R. A. LeVine (Eds.), *Culture theory: Essays on mind, self, and emotion* (pp. 137–157). Cambridge, England: Cambridge University Press.

Russell, J. A. (1991). Culture and the categorization of emotions. *Psychological Bulletin, 110*, 426–450.

Shaver, P. R., Wu, S., & Schwartz, J. C. (1991). Cross-cultural similarities and differences in emotion and its representation. *Review of Personality and Social Psychology, 13*, 175–212.

Shweder, R. A. (1990). Cultural psychology: What is it? In J. Stigler, R. A. Shweder, & G. Herdt (Eds.), *Cultural psychology: Essays on comparative human development* (pp. 1–43). Cambridge, England: Cambridge University Press.

Shweder, R. A. & Bourne, E. (1982). Does the concept of the person vary cross-culturally? In A. Marsella & C. White (Eds.), *Cultural conceptions of mental health and therapy* (pp. 97–137). Boston: D. Reidel.

Watson-Gegeo, K., & White, G. (Eds.). (1990). *Disentangling: Conflict discourse in Pacific societies.* Stanford, CA: Stanford University Press.

White, G. M. (1980). Conceptual universals in interpersonal language. *American Anthropologist, 82*, 759–781.

White, G. M. (1990a). Moral discourse and the rhetoric of emotion. In C. Lutz & L. Abu-Lughod (Eds.), *Language and the politics of emotion* (pp. 46–68). Cambridge, England: Cambridge University Press.

White, G. M. (1990b). Emotion talk and social inference: Disentangling in a Solomon Islands society. In K. Watson-Gegeo & G. White (Eds.), *Disentangling: Conflict discourse in Pacific societies* (pp. 53–121). Stanford, CA: Stanford University Press.

White, G. M. (1992). Ethnopsychology. In T. Schwartz, G. White, & C. Lutz (Eds.), *New directions in psychological anthropology* (pp. 21–46). Cambridge, England: Cambridge University Press.

White, G. M. (1993). Emotions inside out: The anthropology of affect. In M. Lewis & J. M. Haviland (Eds.), *Handbook of emotions* (pp. 29–39). New York: Guilford Press.

Wierzbicka, A. (1992). *Semantics, culture and cognition.* New York: Oxford University Press.

CHAPTER 8

Kali's Tongue: Cultural Psychology and the Power of Shame in Orissa, India

Usha Menon and Richard A. Shweder

This chapter is about an Oriya Hindu facial expression (biting the tongue) and the Oriya emotion that it conveys (*lajya or lajja*), and about the narrated meanings of a core Oriya cultural symbol, a particular iconic representation of the Great Mother Goddess of Hinduism (see Figure 1). The Great Goddess, who is variously referred to in local South Asian discourse as Devi, Ma, Parvati, Durga, Kali, Chandi, and numerous other appellations, is depicted in this icon in her manifestation as Kali,

The narrative materials analyzed in this essay were collected in connection with research by the MacArthur Foundation Research Network on Successful Midlife Development on ethnic and cross-cultural variations in images of female social roles across the life cycle. An earlier analysis by Usha Menon was submitted, in fulfillment of her trial research requirements, to the Committee on Human Development of the University of Chicago. We are very grateful to Manamohan Mahapatra and Sarat Kumar Mahapatra for their field assistance and advice; to Bert Brim, Roy D'Andrade, Wendy Doniger, Raymond Fogelson, Jon Haidt, Lene Jensen, Stanley Kurtz, McKim Marriott, A. K. Ramanujan, A. Kimball Romney, Paul Rozin, and Thomas Weisner for their helpful comments on a draft of the manuscript; and to the Health Program of the MacArthur Foundation for its research support.

with eyes bulging and tongue out, fully equipped with weapons in ten arms, garlanded with skulls, wearing a girdle of severed arms and heads, grasping a bloody decapitated head, and poised with her right foot on the chest of her husband, the god Siva, who is lying supine on the ground beneath her (Siva is the reigning deity of the temple town of Bhubaneswar where our research in Orissa [India] was conducted).

The icon is a normative collective representation or core cultural symbol that is all about *lajya* and the meaning of the emotionally expressive act of biting the tongue. For the moment, we hazardously and inadequately translate *lajya* as shame (for a detailed discussion of the difficulties in translating *lajya* with any single term, such as *shame, embarrassment, modesty,* or *shyness,* from the English emotion lexicon, see Shweder, 1992; see also Parish, 1991). In the Oriya language, the linguistic expression "to bite your tongue" is an idiom signifying *lajya.* In towns and villages in India where Oriya is spoken, it is a good and powerful thing for a woman to be full of "shame" (*lajya*). The icon of the Great Goddess, in her manifestation as Kali, is the key to understanding why.

Shame, happiness, and *anger* are three words for emotions in the English language. Were one to ask bilingual (Oriya–English) speakers for equivalent words in the Oriya language, they would most likely generate *lajya* (for shame), *sukha* (for happiness), and *raga* (for anger). When Anglo-American college students are asked to evaluate similarities and differences among shame, happiness, and anger using a triads test format (Which of the three emotions is most different from the other two?), they typically respond in one of two ways. A majority say that happiness is most different. Many say that shame is most different. Almost no one says that anger is most different.

Those who say that happiness is most different have in mind some kind of hedonic component of comparison. They judge that it feels pleasant to be happy, but unpleasant to feel either shame or anger. Those who say that shame is most different have in mind that to experience happiness or anger is to feel expansive and full of one's self, whereas to experience shame is to experience a diminishment of the ego.

On the other hand, Oriyas frequently say that anger (*raga*) is most different from the other two. They say that anger is destructive of social relationships and of everything of value. They say that shame (*lajya*) and happiness (*sukha*) are the glue of social relationships. Armed with an appreciation of the cultural psychology of Kali's tongue in Oriya culture, it is to be hoped that the reader will understand why Oriyas typically judge the emotion of anger (and not happiness or shame) to be the most different from the other two, and why Oriyas in the temple town of Bhubaneswar believe that shame (*lajya*) is a feminine virtue that is both powerful and good.

The Cultural Psychology of Emotions

The aim of this chapter is to increase our knowledge of emotional functioning in a different cultural tradition by examining the stories told about a core cultural symbol. In recent years, a new interdisciplinary field of research known as *cultural psychology* has emerged on the interface of anthropology, psychology, linguistics, and philosophy, promoting theory and research on domains of psychological functioning, including the cultural psychology of the self, the cultural psychology of cognition, the cultural psychology of emotions, and so forth (see Bruner, 1990; Cole, 1990; D'Andrade, 1990; Jahoda, 1992; Markus & Kitayama, 1991, 1992; Miller, Potts, Fung, Hoogstra, & Mintz, 1990; Much, 1992; Shweder, 1990, 1992; Shweder & Sullivan, 1990, 1993; Stigler, Shweder & Herdt, 1990; Wertsch, 1992). Cultural psychology is the study of how culture and psyche make each other up (see Wiggins, 1991, for a philosophical discussion of psychological states and their objects as equal and reciprocal partners and of the necessity of softening received distinctions between inside and outside points of view). The aim of cultural psychology is to document and explain divergences in the way in which the psyche functions across different ethnic and cultural groups. Among the many questions definitive of the research agenda of the cultural psychology of emotions, we focus on the following: What particular emotional meanings (e.g., Oriya *lajya*) are constructed or brought "on-line" in different ethnic groups and in different temporal–spatial regions of the world? How are these emotional meanings brought "on-line," socialized, or otherwise acquired? More specifically, what is the role of core cultural symbols (e.g., the icon of the Great Goddess and the storytelling norms associated with its interpretation) in the activation of emotional meanings (see Bruner, 1990; Garvey, 1992; Lutz, 1988; Miller, Mintz, (Hoogstra, Fung, & Potts, 1992; Miller, Potts, et al., 1990; Miller & Sperry, 1987; Shweder, 1992; Wierzbicka, 1992)? And perhaps more important, what evidence is there that the various meanings (psychological, metaphysical, social) narrated about a core cultural symbol such as the icon of Kali are *normative* meanings?

Narratives, Numbers, and Norms

We address the issues of narratives, numbers, and norms by examining the extent to which the various narrated meanings associated with the icon of the Great Goddess (see Figure 1) are organized into culturally sanctioned and enforced norms of correct meanings definitive of cultural competence or expertise in storytelling.

In this study, we infer the existence of a culturally sanctioned and enforced norm for generating correct meanings by relying on the logic of metric scaling, in particular Guttman scaling (Ghiselli, Campbell, & Zedeck, 1981; Gordon, 1977; Weller & Romney, 1990). If a local norm for generating culturally correct meanings exists, it is to be expected that it will exercise an influence not only on the likelihood of certain meanings being activated at all (e.g., that a protruding tongue bitten between the lips means "I am ashamed") but also on the distribution and pattern of sharing of those meanings across members of a single cultural community. We discovered that the distribution of meanings associated with the icon of Kali suggests the existence of a unidimensional scale or a cumulative hierarchy of normative meanings, which constrains the telling of a culturally correct story about the Goddess, organizes the order in which meanings unfold, and establishes a standard for differentiating levels of local cultural competence or expertise. Clearly, the very existence of such hierarchical levels of competence presupposes the reality and existence of a cultural norm that members of a community share in common even though they have mastered it to different degrees.

The Canonical Story of Kali's Tongue

The following is the canonical story about Kali's tongue as told in the temple town of Bhubaneswar. The expert narrator here is a 74-year-old

FIGURE 1. Icon of the Goddess Kali used in the study.

Brahman man, the father of three sons and two daughters. A retired hotelkeeper, he spends his time these days keeping an eye on his grandchildren and going regularly to the Lingaraj Temple.

Q. Do you recognize this picture?

A. Kali.

Q. Can you describe the incident that is portrayed in this picture?

A. This is about the time when Mahisasura became so powerful that he tortured everyone on earth and heaven.... He had obtained a boon from the gods according to which no male could kill him. All the gods then went to Narayana and they pondered on ways to destroy Mahisasura ... each contributed the strength and energy of his consciousness—his *bindu*—and from that Durga was created. But when Durga was told that she had to kill Mahisasura, she said that she needed weapons to do so and so all the gods gave her their weapons. Armed thus, Durga went into battle. She fought bravely, but she found it impossible to kill the demon ... he was too strong and clever. You see, the gods had forgotten to tell her that the boon Mahisasura had obtained from Brahma was that he would only die at the hands of a naked woman. Durga finally became desperate and she appealed to Mangala to suggest some way to kill Mahisasura. Mangala told her that the only way was to take off her clothes, that the demon would only lose strength when confronted by a naked woman. So Durga did as she was advised to; she stripped, and within seconds of seeing her, Mahisasura's strength waned and he died under her sword. After killing him, a terrible rage entered Durga's mind, and she asked herself, "What kinds of gods are these that give to demons such boons, and apart from that, what kind of gods are these that they do not have the honesty to tell me the truth before sending me into battle?" She decided that such a world with such gods did not deserve to survive, so she took on the form of Kali and went on a mad rampage, devouring every living creature that came in her way. Now, the gods were in a terrible quandary. They had given her all their weapons. They were helpless without any weapons, while she had a weapon in each of her 10 arms. How could Kali be checked and who would check her in her mad dance of destruction? Again, the gods all gathered and Narayana decided that only Mahadev (Siva) could check Kali, and so he advised the gods to appeal to him. Now, Siva is an ascetic, a yogi who has no interest in what happens in this world; but when all the gods begged him to intervene, he agreed to do his best. He went and lay in her path. Kali, absorbed in her dance of destruction, was unaware that Siva lay in her path, so she stepped on him all unknowing. . . . When she put her foot on Siva's chest, she bit her tongue, saying, "Oh! My husband!" There is in Mahadev a *tejas*, a special quality of his body that penetrated hers, that made her look down, that made her see reason . . . she had been so angry that she had gone beyond reason, but once she recognized him, she became still and calm. This is the story about that time.

Q. How would you describe the expression on her face?

A. She had been extremely angry, but when her foot fell on Mahadev's chest—after all, he is her own husband—she bit her tongue and became still; gradually, her anger went down.

Q. So is there still any anger in her expression?

A. Oh yes, in her eyes you can still see the light of anger shining.

Q. And her tongue? What is she feeling when she bites it?

A. What else but shame (*lajya*)? Shame . . . because she did something unforgivable, she is feeling shame (*lajya*).

What follows is our analysis of this story of Kali's tongue: a Guttman scaling of the distribution of narrated meanings across 92 informants and a discussion of the normative meaning of shame in Orissa, India.

The Icon of Kali: The Study

The study was conducted in the Old Town section of Bhubaneswar, Orissa, India in the neighborhood surrounding the Lingaraj Temple. Lingaraj is one of the many names of the Hindu god Siva (also spelled Shiva). The temple dates back to at least the 11th–12th century. It is an important pilgrimage site for Hindu wanderers (for a more detailed description of the community, see Mahapatra, 1981; Seymour, 1983; Shweder, 1991; Shweder, Mahapatra, & Miller, 1990; Shweder, Much, Mahapatra, & Park, in press).

The Narrators

A total of 92 informants participated in the study: Seventy-three were Brahmans, and the remaining 19 were members of what are referred to locally as clean castes. Women outnumbered men: There were 66 women to 26 men in the sample interviewed. The narrators spanned an age range from 18 to 86 years: The average age of the male narrators was 58.8 years, and that for the female narrators was 42.1 years. Except for the two oldest men, who were widowers, and the two youngest, who were bachelors, all the men were married. Of the 66 women, 53 were married, 6 were still unmarried, 5 were widows, and 2 were separated from their husbands and had chosen to return to their fathers' homes. The mean length of education for the men was 9.6 years, whereas it was 6.5 for the women. Fifteen women had no schooling at all, although no woman was completely illiterate. With one exception, all the men in the sample were literate: 15 had more than 10 years of schooling and 5 were particularly learned in Sanskrit. With the exception of the unmarried and separated women, all of the women maintained traditional female roles in their households or joint families as wife, daughter-in-law, mother-in-law, or widowed matriarch. Most of the men were civil servants, schoolteachers, shopkeepers, hotel owners, and small-time politicians. In spite of this involvement in nontraditional activities, their status in the community continued to be defined by their roles or by that of a family member's in the ritual activities of the temple.

The Storytelling Task

All interviews were conducted in Oriya by Usha Menon, coauthor of this chapter, at the homes of the narrators during the months of June through September, 1991. The interviews began with the interviewer showing to the informant the icon of the Great Goddess in her manifestation as Kali (see Figure 1) and consisted of a short series of probes.

The probes for the study had been designed so as to encourage every narrator to spontaneously generate his or her story about the icon. The first two probes were as follows: "Do you recognize this picture" and "Can you tell me the story that is associated with this picture."

After the narrator had told his or her story, there were additional follow-up probes, such as, "In this picture, how would you describe Kali's feelings?" "Have you seen this expression in everyday life?" If yes, "Who and under what circumstances?" "Is Kali merely stepping on Siva or is she dancing on him?" "Why do you think Siva is on the ground?" "Do you think that Siva is on the ground to subdue Kali?" "Whom do you see as dominant in this picture: Kali or Siva?" Additional probes or paraphrased variations of the probes were occasionally introduced in an effort to determine what the narrator knew about the icon, and whether the narrator had anything further to say.

The pragmatic context in which the narrators told their stories to Usha Menon is one in which we wanted to learn what they knew about their own cultural symbols, but the task was not constructed or presented as a test of knowledge. We imagine that the experience is much like asking a Christian to explain, to a seriously interested and persistent visitor, the meaning of the iconography of the Crucifixion scene. We do not know whether or in what ways the stories told by our narrators would be different if told within a different context or to a different interviewer.

We also cannot be certain about the cognitive status of absent meanings. Absent meanings are meanings that a particular narrator failed to produce in our interview context and in our follow-up probes. We do not know whether our informants would have incorporated those absent meanings into their narratives had we primed those meanings by making them readily available in the form of a true/false or recognition task.

Later in the chapter, we briefly survey several types of interpretations of the cognitive status of those meanings that a narrator does not mention while telling the story of the Great Goddess. Given the evidence at hand, we cannot know for certain whether an absent meaning is an indication of a lack of sufficient knowledge of normative meanings to support the verbal production of a story, or an indication of the repression of certain normative meanings (perhaps because they are too emotionally "hot" to handle consciously), or perhaps even an indication of a deliberate unwillingness to narrate particular normative meanings in the context of our storytelling task. For reasons that we shall discuss later in the chapter, we favor the lack of knowledge interpretation of the cognitive status of absent meanings, although further research is needed to settle this important issue and to sort out possible interpretations of the psychological significance of absent meanings.

What we do know with some confidence from our study is that the meanings that are narrated (or left out) in any particular narration are narrated (or left out) in a very systematic way, which is suggestive of the existence of a cultural norm for ascribing meanings to the icon of the Goddess in her manifestation as Kali.

Within the pragmatic context of our storytelling task, some of the older married women, though eager to chat and entertain, exhibited a certain reluctance to be interviewed. They would disclaim having any knowledge about the icon and would suggest that their husbands would make better informants. There is certainly a cultural aspect to this behavior pattern, in that women in the community are encouraged to be modest and self-effacing in such contexts, and such self-effacing behavior may even be an aspect of *lajya*. As we shall see, it is also possible that the task was especially problematic for some of those older married women because of their relatively limited mastery of available storytelling norms.

The interviews rarely lasted longer than half an hour. All were tape-recorded and later transcribed and translated into English. What follows is an interview with one of the more expert of our narrators. As can be seen, she adheres closely to the canonical story as it is told in the Old Town. This narrator (Narrator 78) was a married Brahman woman of 50, the mother of a grown-up son and daughter, who, although she had had no formal education, could read and write Oriya fluently. Two sections from her extensive narrative are given here.

Q. Do you recognize this picture?

A. Yes, of course. This is Kali.

Q. Can you tell me what is happening in this picture?

A. She has put her foot on Siva.

Q. Why has she done that? Has she done it deliberately?

A. No, Ma hasn't done it deliberately. When she came after killing Mahisasura, she was in a terrible rage, filled with the desire to destroy, and she was powerful—every god and goddess having given her their particular strengths, their particular weapons. Then, she took on the form of Ugra Chandi, the most destructive of Ma's forms and it is like this that she stepped on Siva. She didn't know what she was doing, and when she did, she asked herself, "What have I done? Have I stepped on my husband?" And she bit her tongue. When we have made mistakes and realize that we have made them, don't we too bite our tongues? Don't we ask ourselves, "Eh, Ma, what have I done?" It is the same kind of *ma shakti* (mother power). Here, she is shown destructive and wild, but she has a peaceful form too, which she shows to the true believer. What we should do is close our eyes and pray to her without any fear or anxiety. She will then appear not as she is in this picture but otherwise. If I focus on you and pray to Ma, I will see her in you and if you focus on me and pray to Ma, you will see her in me. But we will neither of us see her as she is in this picture, fierce and bloodthirsty. What does this picture teach us? That none of us is free of her. She devours each one of us so that she can create more. Also, by standing with her foot on her husband, she shows that she doesn't pay heed to anyone. She is supreme. No one can question her.

Q. How would you describe Kali's expression here?

A. Kali here is frightening. She strikes terror. She is killing demons and so naturally she would look fierce. But once she recognized her husband lying under her foot, she bit her tongue and felt shame. She became calm and her anger began to go down.

Q. So there is both shame and anger in her face?

A. There is shame in her face. But can you look at her face alone? You can't. You look at everything else, the weapons she is carrying, the garland of skulls, her girdle of heads and arms, the way she is standing. And when you look at all that she doesn't look as though she is feeling shame. That is all part of her Ugra Chandi form.

Q. And her eyes? What do they show?

A. They too show how angry she has been.

Q. Is there a name or a way of describing this expression?

A. This is the way Kali is worshipped. She is a warning to all sinners. In this *kali yuga* (the fourth and final stage in the cycle of time)—I call it *korla yuga* (the age in which one has to work), one has to struggle to do one's *dharma* (duties of station). In other *yugas*, doing one's *dharma* came easily, but not in this *yuga*. And this way of portraying Kali is useful since it shows us which way we should not go.

Q. Have you ever seen this expression in everyday life?

A. I've told you already. All women, Ma included, bite their tongues when they feel they have not behaved properly. So to that extent, there is some similarity. But that is all. Kali is the mother of the world, and we may resemble her a little, but we are only weak shadows. Ma can take our forms, look like us if she wishes to because she likes to play with us, but we can never look like her.

Q. Who do you see as more dominant in this picture, Ma or Siva?

A. Here? Ma's strength is definitely greater. Why? Listen to me. What do the gods do? They give boons. They give boons to demons, but when it is necessary to destroy the demons they pray to Ma. And what sort of boons do they give these demons? That only when they see a naked *yoni* (female genitals) will they die. Like Ravana, he only became vulnerable to death because he desired Sita [the reference is to the Hindu epic, Ramayana]; and the Kauravas, would they have died but for the fact that they tried to strip Draupadi in public [the reference is to events in the Hindu epic, Mahabharata]? They are all instances of Ma Shakti (the power of the mother goddess). Similarly, here Ma took the form of Durga so as to kill Mahisasura, but her humiliation at the hands of the demon lead to the death of many more. All this can be found in the Chandi Purana.

The Analysis of Normative Meaning

Initially, the interviews were analyzed into 60 elements of meaning (e.g., "This is Kali," "There was a demon named Mahisasura," "Mahisasura was given a boon by the gods that he could only be killed by a naked woman") that were mentioned at least once by any one of the 92 narrators. Of those 60 elements of meaning, 25 were mentioned by fewer (typically far fewer) than 15 narrators and were not included in our subsequent analyses (e.g., that "it was a voice from the sky who advised Kali that she had to strip," that "Kali was full of remorse"). We also decided to eliminate from the analysis all elements of meaning that were not narrations about the story of the icon per se but were propositions about side topics or the broader context of social life and morality in Orissa. Thus, some of the elements of meaning elicited by the probes ("Have you seen this expression in everyday life?" "Who and under what circumstances?") were not included in the Guttman scaling analyses (e.g., "that when a person is ashamed, he or she looks like Kali"; "that women rather than men feel shame"; "that a woman feels shame when she uncovers her face in front of an elder"; "that only those who are conscious of their duties—*dharma*—experience shame"). Such elements of meaning are, of course, relevant to any characterization of the nature of Oriya *lajya*, and we make use of them in the interpretation of our results.

We ultimately settled on 25 elements of meaning that were thematically relevant to telling stories about the icon per se and were mentioned by at least 15 of the narrators. These 25 elements of meaning are listed in Table 1, where they are presented as three packages or modules of meanings.

The first module (Kali's *lajya* as the antidote to her anger) involves 11 elements of meaning in which the narrator talks about Kali and Siva, their marital relationship, and the received hierarchy of domestic status relationships in which the husband is the social superior of the wife, while mentioning that Kali felt angry and accidentally stepped on Siva, but then experienced acute shame (*lajya*) at having been so outrageously inmodest and disrespectful, thereby restraining herself and cooling out her anger.

The second module (the destructive nature of female anger) involves nine elements of meaning in which the narrator elaborates on the magnitude and destructive nature of the Goddess's anger, mentions that the Goddess is a tremendously powerful force created by the male gods to kill demons, in particular a demon named Mahisasura (buffalo demon), but that after her battle with the demon, she was so enraged that she turned into Kali and lost awareness of her surroundings and her ability to discriminate right from wrong, which had disastrous implications for the very survival of the world. This required the male gods to enlist Siva to hatch a plan to bring the Great Mother Goddess back to her normal protective and nurturing sensibilities, which Siva carried out by deliberately positioning himself in Kali's path so that she might step on his chest and experience *lajya*.

The third module (men humiliate women and are the cause of their anger) involves five elements of meaning in which the narrator explains the source of Kali's anger. These elements of meaning link Kali's rage to a boon given by the male gods to the demon Mahisasura and to the

TABLE 1
25 Elements of Meaning (Listed as Three Modules)

Module 1. Kali's *lajya* (shame) as the antidote to her anger.

1. This is the Goddess Kali.
2. All goddesses are incarnations of the Great Goddess.
3. That is the God Siva.
4. Siva is Kali's husband.
5. Kali stepped on Siva accidentally.
6. Males are superior to women in social status.
7. Kali is more dominant and powerful than Siva.
8. Kali's expression is one of anger.
9. Kali's expression is one of shame.
10. Kali exercises self-control/self-restraint.
11. To "bite the tongue" is an expression of Kali's shame.

Module 2. The destructive nature of female anger.

12. There once was a demon, called Mahisasura.
13. Durga was created by the male gods to help them fight the demon.
14. In her rage, the Great Goddess transformed herself into Kali.
15. Rage is a loss in the capacity to discriminate, a loss of awareness of one's surroundings.
16. As Kali, the Great Goddess threatened the survival of the world.
17. Kali destroys the world with her dance.
18. Siva lay in Kali's path at the request of the male gods or of mortal men.
19. Siva lay in Kali's path deliberately.
20. When she stepped on Siva, Kali became calm/still/statuesque.

Module 3. Men humiliate women and are the cause of their anger.

21. A boon was given by the male gods to the demon that he could never be killed except by a naked woman.
22. When the male gods were challenged by the demon, they were helpless to defend themselves.
23. Durga was helpless against the demon until she stripped naked.
24. Durga was humiliated at having to strip naked.
25. Durga's humiliation was followed by uncontrollable rage.

ultimate humiliation experienced by the Goddess when she had to take off her clothes and stand naked before the demon to rescue the male gods from the demonic powers that they themselves had bestowed on him.

Captured in these three modules of meanings is a certain narrative logic for generating stories about the icon of the Great Goddess. The various meanings in Module 3 (the explanation of the Goddess's destructive rage and rampage by reference to the nakedness of the Goddess and the humiliating boon given to a demon by the male gods) seem to presuppose and build upon the various meanings in Module 2 (the elaboration of the nature and destructive implications of Kali's anger), just as the various meanings in Module 2 seem to presuppose and build upon the various meanings in Module 1 (the reality of Kali and Siva as divine characters, their social relationship, and Kali's basic moral and emotional attitudes).

As we shall see, the 25 elements of meanings in Table 1, analyzed either as 25 individual elements of meaning or as three modules or metameanings, form a transitive hierarchy of meanings suggestive of a unidimensional Guttman Scale. The stories told by different narrators unfold their meanings in a relatively fixed order so that the particular meanings narrated can be predicted by the number of meanings narrated, and the least frequently mentioned or distinctive meanings are narrated by precisely those informants who seem to know the most about how to ascribe meaning to the icon of Kali. The Guttman Scale seems to measure the degree to which a narrator exhibits competence or expertise in the norms for telling culturally correct stories about the Great Goddess.

In Table 2, the 25-item scale was also used to order the 92 informants in terms of their relative expertise or competence in producing a culturally correct narration about the meaning of the icon of the Great Goddess. A Guttman Scale score (ranging from 0 to 25) for each of the narrators is listed in Table 2. Based on their pattern of narrated meanings, this scale score is the best estimation of where each narrator would be located along a perfect cumulative 25-item unidimensional scale.

The 25 elements of meaning in Table 2 can also be aggregated into three modules of meaning. Module 1 consists of the 11 elements of mean-

TABLE 2

Distribution of 25 Elements of Meaning Across 92 Narrators

				Stage 1	Stage 2	Stage 3		
Elements of meaning				0 0 0 0 0 0 1 1 0 0 0 / 2 1 6 3 4 5 1 0 7 9 8	1 1 1 1 1 2 1 1 1 / 6 8 5 3 9 2 2 4 7	2 2 2 2 2 / 4 5 1 3 0		
Narr ID no.	Sex	Age	EL	Module 1	Module 2	Module 3	GSS1	GSS2
88	F	44	00	1 1 1 1 1 1 1 1	1 1 1 1 1 1 1	1 1 1 1	25	3
19	M	75	12	1 1 1 1 1 1 1 1	1 1 1 1 1 1 1 1	1 1 1 1 1	25	3
50	M	74	16	1 1 1 1 1 1 1 1 1	1 1 1 1 1 1 1 1 1	1 1 1 1 1	25	3
73	F	22	14	1 1 1 1 1 1 1 1 1	1 1 1 1 1 1 1	1 1 1 1 1	25	3
78	F	50	00	1 1 1 1 1 1 1 1 1 1	1 1 1 1 1 1 1	1 1 1 1 1	25	3
87	F	25	00	1 1 1 1 1 1 1 1 1	1 1 1 1 1 1 1	1 1 1 1 1	25	3
11	F	53	00	1 1 1 1 1 1 1	1 1 1 1 1 1 1 1	1 1 1 1 1	25	3
60	M	82	16	1 1 1 1 1 1 1 1 1 1 1	1 1 1 1.1 1	1 1 1 1 1	25	3
30	F	36	12	1 1 1 1 1 1 1 1 1	1 1 1 1 1 1 1 1 1	1 1 1 1 1	25	3
36	M	44	12	1 1 1 1 1 1 1 1 1	1 1 1 1 1 1	1 1 1 1 1	25	3
17	M	26	16	1 1 1 1 1 1 1 1 1 1	1 1 1 1 1 1 1 1	1 1 1 1 1	25	3
77	M	36	12	1 1 1 1 1 1 1 1 1 1	1 1 1 1 1 1 1	1 1 1 1 1	25	3
90	F	29	12	1 1 1 1 1 1 1 1 1 1	1 1 1 1 1 1 1 1	1 1 1 1	25	3
38	F	31	08	1 1 1 1 1 1 1 1 1	1 1 1 1 1 1	1 1 1 1	24	3
07	M	60	03	1 1 1 1 1 1 1 1 1	1 1 1 1 1 1 1	1 1 1 1	24	3
32	F	24	06	1 1 1 1 1 1 1	1 1 1 1 1 1	1 1 1 1	24	3
34	F	58	00	1 1 1 1 1 1 1	1 1 1 1 1 1 1	1 1 1 1	24	3
57	M	71	08	1 1 1 1 1 1 1 1 1	1 1 1 1 1 1 1 1	1 1 1	24	3
81	F	70	00	1 1 1 1 1 1 1 1 1	1 1 1 1 1 1 1 1 1	1 1 1	22	3
79	M	48	12	1 1 1 1 1 1 1 1 1	1 1 1 1 1 1 1	1 1 1	22	3
12	M	62	12	1 1 1 1 1 1 1	1 1 1 1 1 1 1	1 1 1	21	3
47	F	34	12	1 1 1 1 1 1 1 1 1	1 1 1 1 1 1 1		19	2
06	F	31	10	1 1 1 1 1 1	1 1 1 1 1		19	2
02	M	25	16	1 1 1 1 1 1 1 1	1 1 1 1 1		18	2
59	F	38	04	1 1 1 1 1 1 1 1 1 1	1 1 1 1 1 1 1 1	1	18	2
56	M	55	02	1 1 1 1 1 1 1 1 1	1 1 1 1 1 1 1 1		18	2
89	F	32	08	1 1 1 1 1 1 1 1	1 1 1 1 1 1		17	2
80	F	30	04	1 1 1 1 1 1 1 1 1	1 1 1 1 1		16	2
27	F	55	00	1 1 1 1 1 1 1 1 1	1 1 1 1 1 1		15	2
29	M	65	16	1 1 1 1 1 1 1 1	1 1 1 1 1 1		15	2
16	M	62	16	1 1 1 1 1 1 1 1	1 1 1 1 1 1		15	2
68	F	24	14	1 1 1 1 1 1 1 1	1 1 1 1 1		15	1
03	F	42	08	1 1 1 1 1 1 1 1 1 1	1 1 1		15	1
70	M	48	07	1 1 1 1 1 1 1 1 1	1 1		14	1
83	M	78	08	1 1 1 1 1 1 1 1 1	1 1		14	1
51	F	38	12	1 1 1 1 1 1 1 1	1 1 1		14	1
24	F	78	00	1 1 1 1 1 1 1 1	1 1		13	1
13	F	54	12	1 1 1 1 1 1 1 1	1 1		13	1
65	F	25	00	1 1 1 1 1 1 1 1	1 1 1		13	1
54	M	50	02	1 1 1 1 1 1 1 1	1 1 1		13	1
84	F	68	00	1 1 1 1 1 1 1 1 1 1	1 1		13	1
82	F	32	07	1 1 1 1 1 1 1 1 1	1 1 1		13	1
25	M	86	08	1 1 1 1 1 1 1 1	1 1 1 1 1		12	2
01	F	18	14	1 1 1 1 1 1 1 1 1 1	1 1		12	1
58	F	60	00	1 1 1 1 1 1 1 1 1	1 1		12	1
41	F	37	12	1 1 1 1 1 1 1 1			11	1
52	F	52	00	1 1 1 1 1 1 1 1 1			11	1
85	F	52	06	1 1 1 1 1 1 1 1	1 1		11	1
44	M	65	05	1 1 1 1 1 1 1 1	1		11	1
10	F	29	16	1 1 1 1 1 1 1 1 1 1	1		11	1
67	F	70	00	1 1 1 1 1 1			11	1
45	F	58	00	1 1 1 1 1 1 1 1 1	1 1		11	1
86	F	30	07	1 1 1 1 1 1 1 1			10	1
15	F	30	06	1 1 1 1 1 1 1 1			10	1
04	F	23	16	1 1 1 1 1 1 1 1 1			10	1
74	M	42	07	1 1 1 1 1 1 1 1	1		10	1
09	F	21	16	1 1 1 1 1 1			10	0
21	M	70	10	1 1 1 1 1	1		10	0
66	F	35	02	1 1 1 1 1 1 1			10	1
22	F	65	00	1 1 1 1 1 1 1 1	1		09	1
75	F	26	05	1 1 1 1 1 1 1 1	1		09	1
48	F	29	16	1 1 1 1 1 1 1	1 1		09	1
76	F	28	09	1 1 1 1 1 1 1 1 1	1		09	1
91	F	67	00	1 1 1 1 1 1 1 1	1 1		09	1
08	F	55	03	1 1 1 1 1 1 1			09	1
18	F	26	12	1 1 1 1 1 1	1		09	1
23	F	52	16	1 1 1 1 1 1 1 1	1 1		08	1
64	M	32	00	1 1 1 1 1 1 1 1	1		07	1
69	F	38	00	1 1 1 1 1			07	0
63	F	21	16	1 1 1 1 1			07	0
35	F	33	14	1 1 1 1 1 1			07	0

(continues)

TABLE 2 (continued)
Distribution of 25 Elements of Meaning Across 92 Narrators

				Stage 1 — 0 0 0 0 0 0 1 1 0 0 0 / 2 1 6 3 4 5 1 0 7 9 8	Stage 2 — 1 1 1 1 1 2 1 1 1 / 6 8 5 3 9 2 2 4 7	Stage 3 — 2 2 2 2 2 / 4 5 1 3 0		
Elements of meaning				Module 1	Module 2	Module 3	GSS1	GSS2
Narr ID no.	Sex	Age	EL					
05	F	33	08	1 1 1 1			06	0
26	M	64	16	1 1 1 1 1			06	0
31	F	22	12	1 1 1 1 1			06	0
72	F	33	07	1 1 1 1 1 1			06	0
20	F	50	14	1 1 1 1 1 1			06	0
92	F	77	00	1 1 1 1 1	1		06	0
28	F	40	06	1 1 1 1 1	1		06	0
14	F	25	12	1 1 1 1 1 1 1			05	1
43	F	35	06	1 1 1 1 1			05	0
40	M	70	02	1 1 1 1 1 1			05	0
37	F	35	14	1 1 1 1 1 1 1			05	1
42	F	65	00	1 1 1 1 1			03	0
46	F	41	04	1 1 1 1	1		03	0
61	M	75	12	1 1 1 1 1			03	0
39	F	63	00	1 1			02	0
33	F	78	00	1 1 1 1			02	0
49	F	25	12	1 1	1 1		02	0
53	M	65	03	1 1 1	1		02	0
71	F	70	00	1			00	0
55	F	43	04	1			00	0
62	F	63	00	1			00	0

Note. 1 = Presence of meaning; EL = education level (years);
GSS1 = Guttman Scale Score 1; GSS2 = Guttman Scale Score 2.

ing focusing on *lajya* as a divinely sanctioned antidote to female anger. Module 2 consists of the 9 elements of meaning elaborating on the destructive implications of female anger. Module 3 consists of the 5 elements of meanings explaining how men humiliate women and are the cause of their anger.

There are two types of justification that may be offered for aggregating the 25 meanings into three distinct modules of meaning. The first justification appeals to narrative coherence; the second appeals to empirical coherence.

We have already discussed the narrative coherence of the three modules and have presented evidence that the 11 meanings in Module 1 have less extreme Guttman Scale positions than the 9 meanings in Module 2, which in turn have less extreme positions than the 5 meanings in Module 3. Narrators who tended to know the meanings in Module 3 tended to know the meanings in Module 2 and Module 1. Narrators who tended to know the meanings in Module 2 tended to know the meanings in Module 1, but not vice versa.

Convergent evidence can be provided by analyzing the three modules of meanings (Module 1 = the proposition that *lajya* is a divinely sanctioned antidote to female anger; Module 2 = the elaboration on the destructive nature and on the implications of female anger; Module 3 = the explanation of how men humiliate women and are the cause of their anger) as three meta-meanings definitive of four stages of expertise in the narrative forms of the community. From that perspective, the most expert narrators in the temple town community might be designated Stage 3 narrators. Stage 3 narrators told stories about the Goddess by using meanings from Module 1 + Module 2 + Module 3. Stage 2 narrators used meanings from Module 1 + Module 2. Stage 1 narrators used meanings from Module 1. In contrast, Stage 0 narrators lacked even a minimum level of competence for attributing culturally correct meanings to this core cultural symbol of their community.

In our sample of 92 narrators, there was not a single narrator whose story violates the four-stage pattern (Stage 0 = precompetent; Stage 1 = competent in meanings from Module 1; Stage 2 = competent in meanings from Module 1 + Module 2; Stage 3 = competent in meanings from Module 1 + Module 2 + Module 3). There was no narrator in the sample who mentioned 50% of the elements of meaning in Module 3 but not 50% of the elements in Module 2, or who mentioned 50% of the elements of meaning in Module 2 but not 50% of the elements of meaning in Module 1. A second Guttman Scale score (ranging from 0 to 3) for each narrator is listed in Table 2. Based on the pattern of narrated meanings, this score is the best estimation of where each narrator would be located along a perfect cumulative three-module unidimensional scale.

Table 2 displays the Guttman Scale ordering of the 25 elements of meaning (which, as seen, may be also interpreted as three transitively ordered clusters or modules of meanings). The table also lists two sets of Guttman Scale scores (one ranging from 25 to 0; the other, from 3 to 0) for the 92 narrators and visually designates (the bold lines) subsets of narrators in terms of their approximate stage of competence.

The 92 narrators arrange themselves in a descending order or cline that reflects the degree of their narrative involvement with the 25 elements of meaning, viewed as a transitive unidimensional scale. The first 21 narrators (23%), those in the top rows, told their stories using elements of meaning from Modules 1, 2, and 3 (Stage 3). Moving down the rows, we come to 12 narrators (13%) who told their stories using elements of meaning from Modules 1 and 2 (Stage 2). Farther down are 38 narrators (40%) who used elements of meaning from Module 1 only (Stage 1). Finally, at the bottom of Table 2 are 21 narrators (23%) who might be characterized as cultural "duds." They adduced very few of the meanings available in the local culture for telling "culturally correct" stories about the Great Goddess. Their stories did not convey even the most basic meta-meaning of the icon for members of the temple town community. In some instances, they explicitly professed ignorance of what the icon is all about. However, no narrator knew absolutely nothing about the icon. The alternative ordering of narrators based on their scale scores (3–0) from the second Guttman Scale analysis reveals the following distribution of competence: Stage 3 (23%), Stage 2 (13%), Stage 1 (43%), Stage 0 (20%).

There is one final empirical justification for arranging and designating the 25 elements of meaning in Table 2 as three meta-meanings or modules of meanings. The elements in each module tended to be narrated as packages of meanings. If they were mentioned at all, there was a tendency for them to be told together as clusters of meanings. This may be seen in Table 3, which presents the results of a hierarchical cluster analysis of the 25 elements of meaning and indicates the degree of correlation of each pair of meanings as they were narrated across all 92 informants. The measure of relationship used in the cluster analysis and presented in Table 3 is G, recognized as a form of the correlation coefficient (r; Driver & Kroeber, 1932, p. 219; Kelley, 1923, p. 190).[1]

G is the geometric mean of two proportion scores, the first being the number of narrators (c) who mentioned *both* elements of meaning divided by the number of narrators (a) who mentioned only the *first* element of meaning, and the second being the number of narrators (c) who mentioned *both* elements of meaning divided by the number of narrators (b) who mentioned the *second* element of meaning. G may be computed as $c \div \sqrt{a \times b}$.

[1]We are grateful to Roy D'Andrade for drawing our attention to this measure.

TABLE 3

Hierarchical Cluster Analysis (Maximum Distance Method) Ordering of Columns and Rows, and Correlations (G) among 25 Elements of Meaning

| | Cluster 1 | | | | | | | | | | | Cluster 2 | | | | | | | | | | | | |
| | Module 1 | | | | | | | | | | | Module 2 | | | | | | | | | Module 3 | | | | |
	08	07	02	10	06	01	03	04	05	09	11	19	18	17	15	20	14	16	12	13	22	23	21	25	24
08		97	90	88	82	86	77	76	73	78	82	55	63	49	64	69	48	66	60	43	45	58	45	48	49
07	97		90	88	79	87	76	73	71	78	82	56	65	50	65	70	49	67	57	44	46	57	46	49	50
02	90	90		85	78	83	79	74	63	79	81	61	69	55	72	75	53	74	62	48	51	60	51	53	55
10	88	88	85		69	91	79	66	56	78	88	52	61	45	64	75	51	66	57	39	40	52	40	43	45
06	82	79	78	69		69	58	62	58	67	63	51	61	44	58	62	48	63	59	47	44	56	44	48	49
01	86	87	83	91	69		80	67	48	69	82	55	61	45	65	74	49	67	59	42	46	52	46	46	48
03	77	76	79	79	58	80		70	54	67	80	58	64	52	68	64	47	64	47	45	50	60	50	53	52
04	76	73	74	66	62	67	70		54	64	67	61	67	56	66	60	57	60	64	49	50	58	50	54	56
05	73	71	63	56	58	48	54	54		62	50	31	36	28	45	31	19	44	39	28	33	41	33	32	31
09	78	78	79	78	67	69	67	64	62		75	54	63	48	64	58	40	69	57	41	45	52	45	46	48
11	82	82	81	88	63	82	80	67	50	75		56	64	45	69	77	55	72	63	49	52	56	52	52	54
19	55	56	61	52	51	55	58	61	31	54	56		83	64	69	61	57	64	75	74	83	81	79	83	86
18	63	65	69	61	61	61	64	67	36	63	64	83		70	79	74	72	69	71	68	68	73	68	72	74
17	49	50	55	45	44	45	52	56	28	48	45	64	70		65	62	59	60	46	60	46	51	51	63	62
15	64	65	72	64	58	65	68	66	45	64	69	69	79	65		62	63	78	67	63	63	63	63	67	69
20	69	70	75	75	62	74	64	60	31	58	77	61	74	62	62		70	68	57	47	48	53	48	49	51
14	48	49	53	51	48	49	47	57	19	40	55	57	72	59	63	70		54	47	45	42	48	42	45	49
16	66	67	74	66	63	67	64	60	44	69	72	64	69	60	78	68	54		65	57	57	55	57	62	64
12	60	57	62	57	59	59	47	64	39	57	63	75	71	46	67	57	47	65		65	74	84	74	74	76
13	43	44	48	39	47	42	45	49	28	41	49	74	68	60	63	47	45	57	65		71	67	77	89	87
22	45	46	51	40	44	46	50	50	33	45	52	83	68	46	63	48	42	57	74	71		76	94	84	87
23	58	57	60	52	56	52	60	58	41	52	56	81	73	51	63	53	48	55	84	67	76		76	76	78
21	45	46	51	40	44	46	50	50	33	45	52	79	68	51	63	48	42	57	74	77	94	76		90	93
25	48	49	53	43	48	46	53	54	32	46	52	83	72	63	67	49	45	62	74	89	84	76	90		98
24	49	50	55	45	49	48	52	56	31	48	54	86	74	62	69	51	49	64	76	87	87	78	93	98	

Note. Shown are two decimal digits.

One advantage of this type of correlational measure—the geometrical mean of the two proportion scores—is that it does not assume that the two proportion scores must be identical. A second advantage is that the degree of correlation between two elements of meaning is determined entirely by the narrators who actually mentioned one or the other or both of the relevant elements of meaning. In other words, in those instances in which a narrator mentioned neither of the elements of meaning (perhaps because of ignorance of the meaning of the icon) that failure to narrate either of those two absent meanings is not treated as an indication of the high degree of relationship between them. Two meanings are not considered interrelated merely because a narrator did not know either of them.

The coefficient of relationship G used in Table 3 helps to answer the following question: Considering all possible pairs of comparisons among the 25 meanings in Table 3, which pairs of meaning were more likely to be mentioned together, if one takes into account only those narrators who mentioned at least one of the meanings of the relevant pair? The hierarchical cluster analysis, using the maximum distance algorithm of the Anthropac 3.25 software program (Borgatti, 1990), revealed that the most fundamental partition of the 25 elements of meaning is between the first 11, Module 1 meanings and all the rest. The high level of intercorrelation G among these 11 elements can be seen in Table 3. A boundary has been drawn in Table 3 separating the first 11 elements of meaning from the rest.

We have also drawn a second boundary between the last 5 elements of meaning (Module 3 meanings) in Table 3 and the rest. On correlational ground alone, there is probably more than one way to divide reasonably the remaining 14 (non-Module 1) elements of meaning in Table 3 into two clusters. There are two reasons for drawing the second boundary as we did between the 9 elements of meaning in Module 2 and the 5 elements of meaning in Module 3.

The first reason is that this particular partitioning is not only consistent with the ordering of elements of meaning in the hierarchical cluster analysis but is also sensitive to the evidence in Table 3 of *extremely* high intercorrelations among the five elements of meaning in Module 3, all of which tended to be told together, if and when they were told at all. It also appears that this particular partitioning of the elements of meaning is sensitive to the special narrative character of the meanings in Module 3, all of which have to do with the cause and consequences of the nakedness and humiliation of the Goddess.

The Four Stages of Cultural Competence

On narrative and empirical grounds, we feel justified in characterizing the local normative meaning of the icon of Kali in terms of three modules of meaning and in characterizing local cultural competence in terms of four stages or levels of expertise.

The lowest level of expertise includes those who have not even progressed to the first stage of competence. The Old Town community of high caste narrators is a relatively well-defined community, yet even in our sample, approximately 21 narrators (23% of the sample) seemed to be either ignorant of the normative meanings associated with this core cultural symbol or else (in the case of two *Tantric* narrators, to be discussed later) narrated their stories under the influence of story telling standards that are not normative in the local Bhubaneswar community (see Appendix). Most of these 21 narrators may well be members of a subculture of (real or feigned) "ignorance": These narrators might be referred to as *cultural duds*. They are either unaware of or unwilling to reveal their knowledge of the storytelling norms of the community.

Correlates of Expertise

Diversity in the production of a culturally competent story about the meaning of the icon of Kali clearly exists in our sample. The question that arises is, Does this cognitive diversity relate in any obvious way to the dynamics of the cultural system?

One aspect of our sample of narrators is that, at first blush, variations in degrees of cultural competence appear to be patterned according to differences in gender, with men more likely to exhibit a higher level of narrative expertise. Thus, if we divide the 92 narrators into two groups, the 33 Stage 2 or Stage 3 narrators (Guttman Scale score of 15 or greater) versus the 59 Stage 0 or Stage 1 narrators (Guttman Scale score of less than 15), as in Table 2, gender is a significant correlate of expertise $\chi^2(1) = 5.06, p < .05$. However, upon closer examination, it turns out that this gender effect is significant when comparing relatively educated men (with 12 years of education or more) with relatively educated women, $\chi^2(1) = 12.45, p < .001$, yet, it disappears entirely when comparing less educated men (with less than 12 years of education) with less educated women. It is not gender per se that is a correlate of expertise in our sample, as we shall see.

A second aspect of our sample of narrators is that, for the men, cultural competence is patterned according to number of years of formal schooling. The educated men (with 12 years of education or more) were far more likely to be Stage 2 or Stage 3 narrators than their less educated male counterparts, $\chi^2(1) = 10.84, p < .001$. This was not the case for the women in the sample. The relatively more competent female narrators (Stage 2 or Stage 3, scale score of 15 or greater) were not more educated than the relatively less competent female narrators. In fact, the mean number of years of schooling among more competent female narrators was marginally lower than the mean number of years of schooling among the less competent women. The educated men may have been more competent than the less educated men in their ascriptions of culturally correct meanings to the icon, but this did not appear to be the case for the women.

Age seems to play no part in the distribution of cultural competence for either men or women. Those who were 50 years of age or older did not exhibit higher levels of cultural expertise (Stage 2 or 3) than those who were younger. There was no evidence of an age effect on narrative expertise.

In sum, neither age, nor education, nor gender per se was a correlate of cultural competence in ascribing meanings to the icon of the Great Goddess. However, there was an interaction effect between schooling and gender such that education was associated with the enhancement of the narrative expertise of men but not of women. Thus, although there were female experts, it was the educated men in Bhubaneswar for whom a high level of cultural competence in ascribing meaning to the icon of Kali was most commonplace. Indeed, 85% of the men with 12 years or more of formal education were Stage 2 or Stage 3 experts, whereas this was true of only 23% of women with 12 years or more of education. Less educated men had no such advantage over their female counterparts; 23% of the men with less than 12 years of formal schooling were Stage 2 or Stage 3 experts, whereas this was true of 32% of the less educated women. Nevertheless, the intuition of some female informants that they knew less than their men folk about the icon may be justified, especially if they were married to an educated narrator.

Given the high levels of narrative expertise among educated men but not among educated women, it appears likely that the intracultural variation in cultural competence observed in the sample reflects more than just individual variability in native intelligence, although precisely what it reflects remains to be documented.

At best, our findings are merely invitations to further research on the sources of cognitive diversity in the production of a culturally correct story about the Great Goddess. Differences in social contexts of learning and in social identities (Boster, 1986) may account for some of the cognitive diversity, but the range of plausible accounts is vast. We have favored the view that the diversity in our sample regarding the culturally competent ascription of meanings to Kali is an index of differential mastery of local narrative norms. We would expect mastery of those narrative norms to be related to differential *exposure effects* that, in turn, we would expect to be related to the pragmatic contexts of storytelling in everyday life (e.g., the importance of both education and knowledge of the Gods for the social standing and prestige of high caste Hindu men, the socially sanctioned narration of the story of Kali on public ritual occasions run by educated male religious specialists, and the differential use of the story of Kali in familial contexts as an exhortation about feminine virtues).

Yet, given the limited evidence available, other views cannot be ruled out totally. It is conceivable that in Bhubaneswar everyone is well-exposed to the narrative norms of the community and that the diversity in our sample is an index of differential (conscious or unconscious) resistance to certain of the meanings of the icon. Psychoanalytically inclined theorists will have little difficulty generating hypotheses of this kind, for example, by postulating male identification and oedipal fascination with a demon whose fate is to be decapitated at the hands of a naked, tongue-wagging Mother Goddess, or female defensiveness against the recognition of one's own rage and potential to do harm.

It is even conceivable, given a slight stretch of the imagination, that everyone in the community really is a Stage 3 expert in the local narrative norms, but that in the context of our storytelling task, only certain informants were motivated or willing to reveal all that they knew. Some of the educated men might have wanted to show off their knowledge to an educated female interviewer. Some of the females might have been so devoted to the Goddess and afraid to talk about her that they decided to feign ignorance. However, on the basis of our experience in the community and with the narrators, these hypotheses feel a bit ad hoc and somewhat contrived. Yet, personal testimony is no substitute for more systematic evidence on cognitive diversity in the ascription of meanings to the Goddess and, at the moment, we cannot rule out absolutely any of the hypotheses.

Our various analyses were designed only to determine whether the pattern of sharing of ascribed meanings across informants in the temple town suggests the influence of a culturally defined standard of correctness for telling stories about the icon of Kali. We believe that they do. But precisely how the local cultural norm exercises its influence (e.g., via selective flow of symbols, differential rates of face to face interaction, hegemonic control over or differential access to education institutions, defensive identification with authority figures, etc.), we are not in a position to access.

There are other limitations to the study. It is perhaps worth reiterating that our study relied on evidence from a story production task not from a story recognition task. The failure by an informant to narrate (produce) certain meanings associated with the icon of Kali is not an index of his or her failure to acknowledge those meanings as culturally correct. It seems likely that some of our Stage 0 and Stage 1 narrators would have recognized and endorsed many of the meanings in Modules 2 and 3 had those meanings been made cognitively available to them by means of a true/false test.

Because our sample of narrators oversampled the female population of the temple town, we can only guess what the distribution of narrative expertise would have looked like for a sample more evenly balanced by gender. It seems likely that the proportion of expert Stage 3 storytellers would have been higher than 23%. Nevertheless, it seems clear that whatever the sample selected for study in Bhubaneswar, the normative meanings associated with Module 1 are going to be the most widely distributed meanings across the community. In our study, those meanings were narrated by 80% of the members of our sample.

Perhaps the most relevant finding of the study for a discussion of the cultural psychology of the emotions was that the meaning of *lajya* as a divinely sanctioned antidote to destructive anger expressed by biting the tongue (Module 1) was widely distributed across the community. We feel confident about making the following claim: that in the temple town of Bhubaneswar, a conception of *lajya* (shame) as a highly valued mental state is the local cultural norm.

Is There a Canonical Scriptural Version of the Story?

When asked about the icon of the Great Goddess in her manifestation as Kali, members of the Bhubaneswar temple community produced stories that suggested that the icon was a representation of events or scenes that could be found in the traditional corpus of medieval scriptural narratives, the *Puranas*, in particular the *Devi Mahatmya* and the *Devi Bhagvata Purana*, two texts that reflect on the nature of the Great Goddess and try to establish that ultimate reality is feminine in nature. Thinking that it might be instructive to compare the local contemporary versions of the story to a canonical version in the scriptures, we turned to the scriptural literature to locate an original, or at least an early official version, of the key events (the boon to the demon Mahisasura that he could be killed only by a naked woman, the striptease by the Goddess, the foot on Siva's chest) leading up to the moment of Kali's shame (expressed by her protruding tongue) as portrayed in the icon as told by Oriya narrators.

To our surprise, the most popular meaning of the icon (that the Goddess is full of shame and that her protruding tongue expresses this shame) cannot be found in the traditional scriptural narratives, neither

Sanskritic nor Oriya. There are many classical Puranic variations of the stories about the Great Goddess, but none that matches precisely the version that is currently the local cultural norm for ascribed meanings to the icon of the Goddess in the temple town of Bhubaneswar. One can find variations in which the male gods beg the Goddess to become a celestial nymph and to seduce, weaken, and kill Mahisasura, although no boon is mentioned (O'Flaherty, 1975, p. 241). One can find variations in which the demon receives a boon that he will be released from all his sins by dying at the hands of the Goddess, although no mention is made of nakedness or shame (O'Flaherty, 1975, p. 242). One can find Puranic stories in which the Goddess behaves recklessly and indiscriminately and is overcome by shame, for example, when she curses her own son in a fit of anger (O'Flaherty, 1975, p. 260), but these do not occur in the context of a battle with demons or with a foot on Siva's chest.

In Tulsi Das's *Adhbhuta Ramayana*, Sita as Kali does step on Siva, but there is no boon, no stripping, no humiliation, and no rage. A fifteenth-century Oriya text, the *Chandi Purana*, is the only one that provides a story that comes tantalizingly close to the structure of meanings that is normative in the vicinity of the Lingaraj Temple in Orissa, India, but, in the end, it too fails because it makes no mention of the Goddess stepping on Siva or her sense of shame (*lajya*). We are now entertaining the alternative hypothesis that there is no single canonical scriptural version of the story of Kali's shame as told in the temple town, and that the events and psychological attitudes narrated by our informants are imaginative synthetic constructions of the local folk mind, which is well-deserving of note and comment.

Shards of Meaning Reworked by the Local Oriya Imagination

The Oriya story of the Goddess as Kali does not match any of the canonical stories in the *Devi Mahatmya* or the *Devi Bhagvata Purana*. If the icon of the Great Goddess, which is today a core symbol in the temple town of Bhubaneswar and in other locations in Eastern India, does not have its source in the orthodox Puranic scriptural literature, where does it come from? If it is not a Puranic image, could it have its source in the more heterodox Tantric way of depicting the Great Goddess?

In Eastern India (and in nearby Nepal; see Levy, 1990), Tantra has long been the subaltern, heterodox voice of Hinduism, existing on the edges of mainstream Brahmanical culture, an exotic cult of dark fortnight sacrificial rites and magical powers. Tantrics are ideologically committed to the inversion of traditional orthodox values and conceptions. In Tantric rituals, menstrual blood is not polluting, it is sanctifying; in Tantric metaphysics, the world is run by women, not men. Men are passive and inert; it is female power, especially the erotic power of naked young women, that makes the world go round.

One particular Tantric text, *The Mahanirvana Tantra* (4.34), describes the Great Goddess as black skinned because she encompasses everything in the universe, "just as all colors disappear in black, so all names and forms disappear in her"; as naked because she is beyond all illusions; as having a red, lolling tongue because that represents the passion and creativity of nature; and as standing on the lifeless corpse of Siva, awakening him, because she is the giver of life and its destroyer. In his monumental study of Hinduism and Tantra in the Newar city of Bhaktapur in nearby Nepal, Robert Levy (1990) noted that, in Tantric imagery, Siva is represented as a corpse, and he mentioned a Newar representation of the Great Goddess in her manifestation as Mahakali in which her vehicle or mount is not the lion described in the Puranic scriptures but "an anthropomorphic male form, at or under her foot" (pp. 212, 251).

Jeffrey Kripal (1993), in his work on the nineteenth century Bengali saint Ramakrishna, discussed the Tantric meanings attached to Kali's tongue and described it as a "consumer of blood sacrifice, a provoker of horror." He also saw it as indicating the "goddess's erotic arousal": Her tongue is extended in passion, as she stands on her husband, Siva, engaged in "aggressive intercourse" (p. 12).

Curiously enough, though Tantrism is a rather exotic cult of the night and of nighttime fantasy, peripheral to local Brahmanical culture in the temple town of Bhubaneswar, it would appear that it is a Tantric icon that has become a core symbolic representation in the local community. Most informants had no difficulty in recognizing the icon as Kali because, in Bhubaneswar, it is a typical way of depicting the Great Goddess. Although it is impossible to offer a definitive explanation for the popularity of Kali's image, some insight into the core of the symbol may be gained by juxtaposing this icon against its social context.

In the patriarchal social world of Oriya Hindus, hardly anyone questions the superior position of the male. And yet in Eastern India (in Bengal, Orissa, and the Eastern border districts of Madhya Pradesh), there is a strong tradition of goddess worship as well as of Tantric belief that the power and energy of the universe is female. This particular combination of beliefs and practices makes the maintenance of the patriarchal social order more problematic than it would have been if the superiority of the male had been unabashedly acknowledged and celebrated.

It is in this context of conflicting cultural beliefs about superior male social status and supreme female divine power that the icon of the Great Goddess gathers its significance because it symbolizes, for Oriya Hindus, the essentially unresolvable nature of male–female relationships. The local narrators of the story of the Great Goddess, especially those who are most expert in the storytelling norms of the community, articulate these ambiguous and often contradictory themes as they interpret the icon.

By and large, the local narrators ignore the pure Tantric view that consistently subordinates men to female power. Instead, they prefer to integrate certain highly edited incidents from the second story in the *Devi Bhagvata Purana* about a battle between a demon named Mahisasura and the Great Goddess (which contains no mention of the Goddess as Kali or of the Goddess's nakedness) with the provocative imagery of the *Chandi Purana* story and certain key elements that have social significance locally to create a new and compelling narrative. This synthesis has produced the canonical story of the icon as it is told in the temple town of Bhubaneswar.

Apparently, one of the more striking features that the narrators felt the need to explain is the Goddess's nakedness in the iconic representation. In their search for a plausible explanation, they went back to the *Chandi Purana*, a fifteenth-century Oriya extrapolation of classical Puranic literature, in which Sāralā Dāsa, the author, modifies the boon, making the conditions for the demon's death even more stringent than any condition to be found in the Puranas themselves. In his imagination, Mahisasura may be killed only by a naked woman. Thus, the Goddess's nakedness becomes part of the logic of the story and is used to make sense of the sequence of the narrated events.

It is fascinating that such an explanation tends to strengthen the Tantric view of the power of female sexuality. After all, none of the weapons provided by the male gods suffices to kill the demon. Ultimately, the only weapon that the demon cannot withstand is that which is intrinsically the Goddess's own: her gendered anatomy, her female genitals.

An equally plausible non-Tantric explanation for the demon's death could be that he is undone by his own uncontrolled lust. Such an explanation shifts the emphasis from Tantric notions regarding the power of women to the more common Puranic view that desire, in and of itself, is evil and can have only disastrous consequences.

The Oriya narrators do not explicitly articulate one or the other interpretation, leaving it to the listener to sift through the ambiguous meanings of the demon's death. Unlike the Tantrics who see in the Goddess's creativity and in her absolute destructiveness the ultimate meaning of life, the narrators with the broadest narrative reach (Stage 3) offer a moral justification for the devastation caused by her. They believe that having been, in a sense, set up by the gods in her battle with Mahisasura, she is not entirely unjustified or irrational when she goes berserk with rage. Finally, with great finesse and in clear contradiction to Tantric descriptions, the experts point to Kali's protruding tongue as the mark of her shame (lajya) at having stepped on her husband. They fashion an explanation that harmonizes perfectly with notions of male superiority inherent in the patriarchal social order.

Thus, it seems plausible to suggest that this contemporary way of telling the story of the Great Goddess in the temple town of Bhubaneswar represents a local Brahmanical synthesis of a Tantric icon with the moral requirements of a patriarchal social world. In trying to integrate the images of female power invoked by the Tantric icon with the idea that lajya (self-control, shyness, modesty, and a sense of shame) is an essential attribute of female virtue, the local folk imagination has invented a new and different story that has only the most tenuous associations with the canonical Puranic versions of the Goddess narratives.

We have no way to assess the creative historical role played by local experts in synthesizing or transforming local narrative norms. D'Andrade

(1990) has suggested that not only do cultural experts know a great deal about their own particular domains, but more important, that they are adept at integrating more esoteric knowledge with meanings and understandings that are shared more commonly. It is also possible that the social recognition of the "expertise" of experts gives them a special authority to introduce new elements of meaning into their narratives and generate fresh interpretations of cultural symbols, which then become normative. We do not know whether this is the historical process that produced a distinctive local Oriya version of the story of the Great Goddess. We do know that a reworked and reconstructed story that has no direct parallel in either the Puranic or the Tantric scriptures is today culturally correct in the wards of the old temple town of Bhubaneswar and lends definition to what it means to be an expert in that small, close-knit community of orthodox, Saivite (Siva worshipping) Brahmans.

Beyond the Narrative Norm: A Tantric Story

Given all these ambivalent and conflict-laden themes about male–female relationships and the attempt by Oriya narrators in the temple town to reconcile them within a single narrative framework, it is instructive to examine what happens to the two pure Tantric narrators in our analysis of local Oriya norms. They end up looking like the cultural duds. However, unlike the cultural duds who seem ignorant of any storytelling norms, the problem for the Tantric narrators in the sample is that they narrated the meanings of the icon under the influence of a canon that is not normative in the Bhubaneswar community. They possessed heterodox specialized knowledge that is so esoteric and counterhegemonic that it was not shared by most local informants. Thus, pure Tantric stories about the (admittedly Tantric) icon of Kali have so little in common with the stories that are generally shared in the temple town that Tantric informants are identified as ignorant and grouped with those who know nearly nothing about the icon. In the context of local cultural norms, their stories are exotic and from out of the underground, making no concessions to commonly held notions about traditional hierarchy and social relations.

In the example of the Tantric narration presented below, the narrator (No. 21) is a 70-year-old Brahman man, married with two sons and two daughters. All his adult life, he has been a priest at the Lingaraj Temple.

During the interview, he admitted having attended some Tantric ceremonies, although he claimed that he was not a true worshiper of the Goddess.

Q. Do you recognize this picture?

A. This is the Tantric depiction of Kali. Kali here is naked, she has thrown Siva to the ground and is standing on him. She displays here absolute, overwhelming strength. She is in a terrible rage, wearing her garland of skulls and in each arm a weapon of destruction. Look, in this hand, the trisul; in this, the *chakra* (the disc); in this, the sword; in this, the sickle; in this, the bow and arrow. This is how Kali is shown in Tantric *pujas* where the devotee is praying to the goddess for perfect knowledge and awareness. All this kind of worship goes on in the Ramakrishna Mission. The monks there are all Tantrics and they know all about it. Sri Ramakrishna and Swami Vivekananda, both great sages, knew about such *sakti* pujas and Tantric rites.

Q. Can you tell me the story that is associated with this picture?

A. In all these Tantric pujas, the goal is to acquire perfect knowledge and ultimate power. The naked devotee worships Mother on a dark, moonless night in a cremation ground. The offerings are meat and alcohol. Ordinary people cannot participate in such worship; if they were even to witness it, they would go mad. I have attended such worship once, but I am not a true worshiper, and I have no special knowledge of Tantric worship.

Q. How would you describe Kali's expression here?

A. She is the image of fury.

Q. You mean she is angry? She is in a rage?

A. Yes ... yes. You must understand that this is how she appears to her devotee. He has to have the strength of mind to withstand her fierceness. She is not mild or tender, but cruel and demanding and frightening.

Q. Do you think that she has put out her tongue in anger?

A. Yes, she has put out her tongue in anger. Kali is always angry, she is always creating and, at the same time, destroying life. Here you see her standing with her foot placed squarely on Siva's chest. When the time comes for the universe to be destroyed entirely, no one will be spared, not even the gods—whether Visnu or Siva—everyone will be destroyed.

Q. Some people say that she is feeling deeply ashamed at having stepped on her husband and that is why she has bitten her tongue. You don't agree?

A. People have different views. People believe whatever makes them feel comfortable and if they like to think that Kali is ashamed, then let them. What I have told you is what the special devotees of Kali believe. They believe that Mother is supreme. Even Brahma, Visnu, and Siva are her servants.

Q. Have you seen this expression, that is, Kali's here, in daily life?

A. No, if one was to see this expression on an ordinary human being's face, he would have to be mad, to have lost all his senses. Kali, in fact, is mad with rage, but her rage has nothing that is remotely human about it, it is a divine rage that only a human being who has completely lost his mind can duplicate.

Q. Can you tell me why Siva is lying on the ground?

A. Kali has thrown him to the ground and she puts her foot on him to make clear that she is supreme.

Q. So you don't think that he is lying on the ground to subdue Kali?

A. No, that is beyond Siva's capacity. If Kali becomes calm, it is because she wishes to, not because she is persuaded to be so. Even to her most faithful devotee, Kali's actions sometimes don't make sense, but life itself often doesn't make sense, so what can one say?

Q. Who would you say is dominant in this picture: Is it Kali or Siva?

A. Obviously, Kali. But it is also important to realize that while Sakti is absolutely necessary for the creation and evolution of the universe, by itself even Sakti cannot achieve anything. Sakti has to combine with consciousness for the process of creation to take place and so consciousness, as symbolized by Siva, has a unique position. Just as it is only through the union of a man and a woman that a child can be conceived, so too, only when Sakti and Cit (consciousness) come together does creation occur.

In many ways, this is an impressive informant, especially if one is not interested in the representation of local narrative norms. He is helpful and self-reflective and his narration is "juicy." His narration might even be informative for an investigation of Tantric meanings. Yet, he cannot be viewed as a local cultural expert, and it would have been a disaster for an anthropologist to rely on him as a key informant for the reconstruction of the meaning of this core cultural symbol in the temple town. From the perspective of the approach to the study of cultural norms developed in this essay, an expert or competent informant is not just a helpful member of another culture or even a helpful and highly self-reflective and imaginative member. An expert is a community member whose imaginative reflections are helpful in identifying locally sanctioned and culturally defined truths or canons of correctness. The Kali of Tantric lore is the antithesis of the model of domestic female restraint idealized in Bhubaneswar. The meanings of Tantra are in tension with the local narrative norm.

The Moral of the Story: The Two Castes of Orissa (Male and Female)

Interestingly, the Oriya norms for telling culturally correct stories about the icon of the Goddess explicitly affirm the view that all the goddesses, Kali, Durga, Parvati, and so forth, are but different manifestations of the Great Goddess Devi (see Kurtz, 1992, on the theme that all the goddesses are one). More than half the narrators insist that all the goddesses are lower embodied forms of the transcendental Goddess, merging, separating, and taking on different identities depending on the circumstances and on the particular action that has to be undertaken. They do not portray, as might Western psychoanalytic narrators, a splitting of the divine Mother, with Kali epitomizing the Bad Mother, whose identity is distinct from that of the Good Mother. Rather, for these indigenous storytellers, Kali is represented as one side or aspect of the Divine Mother who, just like any human mother, has her cruel as well as her tender aspects. As one of the women narrators said, "How can a mother be one and not the other? If she genuinely desires the best for her child now and in the future, she has to be both harsh and demanding as well as indulgent and forgiving; only then will her child come to know what the real world is like."

Also, unlike certain Western psychoanalytic narrators, our local Oriya narrators do not portray the female as an incomplete male. Tantric stories about the Great Goddess portray her as self-creating, autonomous, and capable of reproduction through her own emanations. She is parthenogenic. Even in those Puranic portrayals, where the Goddess is the creation of the male gods, she has the combined powers of the male gods and is greater than any one of them. In the stories of the local narrators, Devi's awesome potential for self-sufficiency is recognized even as she is called upon to renounce it and to acknowledge her cosmic interdependency with and social subordination to her husband for the sake of the social good. Unlike narrators in the West who are under the influence of psychoanalytic norms for storytelling, Oriyas do not construct a story about the female as a castrated male. The idea of the female as an incomplete male (a castrated male; an emanation from the rib of Adam) seems to be more characteristic of storytelling norms in the Judeo-Christian traditions, of which contemporary psychoanalytic storytelling may be a local variant.

Whereas the first Oriya module of meanings (Module 1) seems to be saying that the world is truly energized when women regulate, control, and rein in their power, the other two modules of meanings (Modules 2 and 3) offer somewhat ambivalent views regarding female power. At one level, there appears to be the notion that female power is, in and of itself, essentially dangerous because it is always in imminent danger of slipping out of control. At another level, there is the sense that men are often so treacherous, untrustworthy, and exploitative that women would be justified in destroying the world. Taken together, the different interpretations seem to reveal a deep set of ambivalences in the culture regarding the power and potency of the female.

One reason for the popularity of this particular iconic representation of the Great Goddess (as Kali with her tongue out and foot planted on a supine Siva) may well be because of the value that members of the community place on the meta-commentary that it provides on the problem of organizing and understanding a key existential issue or universal social existence theme: the issue of what is male and of what is female and the nature of male–female relations (Shweder, 1982, 1993). That the informants are aware of this interpretive function of the icon is made abundantly clear by the way in which they make pragmatic use of the icon and its narrative. When discussing the disastrous consequences of uncontrolled rage, or proper wifely conduct, or the kind of restraint and modesty valued in a daughter-in-law, the icon is used time and time again to prove points and support arguments. The story of Kali articulates the concerns of a patriarchal society that seeks to establish its own legitimacy.

At the same time, in a place like India where "the preferred medium of instruction and transmission of psychological, metaphysical and social thought continues to be the story" (Kakar, 1989, p. 1), the story of the Great Goddess does not merely reflect a preexisting sensibility but also creates and maintains such a sensibility in a positive manner. In most discussions about the icon, there is an effortless moving back and forth between the world of gods and that of humans, divine action being explained in terms of human needs and failings and standing as an ideal for mortal beings. Every time an informant discusses or interprets the icon, the story told generates and regenerates the very subjectivity that it seems to display.

The significance and popularity of this icon appears to lie in the way in which it crystallizes several themes important to the culture: female power and female shame, anger as socially disruptive and destructive, the disjunction between a male dominated hierarchical social order and the potential power of women, and self-control and self-discipline as the only effective means of regulating destructive power. The stories about the Great Goddess in her manifestation as Kali give order to these themes within an encompassing narrative structure and represent them in such a way as to throw into relief a particular view of their essential nature.

As one female narrator put it: There are only two castes in the world, male and female. All other caste barriers can be breached, but the one that divides men and women is so fundamental that it can never be transcended. Therefore, men and women are different and unequal, an inequality that is context sensitive (Ramanujan, 1989), moving in either way in favor of or against women depending on the circumstances. Thus, men, being more *sattvika* (pure), rank higher than women in ritual status, whereas women partake of the Great Goddess's power to create and destroy, and to nurture and deconstruct simply by virtue of being female and of having female bodies. As the Great Goddess creates and destroys the universe, so does every woman contain within herself the power to sustain or destroy her family.

Durga's ability to kill Mahisasura—the mere sight of her naked genitals (*yoni*) sufficing to destroy the demon—epitomizes the potency of female sexuality. Yet, as the icon displays so dramatically, uncontrolled power may have disastrous consequences. Kali's foot on Siva's chest symbolizes the most shocking reversal of traditional hierarchy. As the story goes, Kali's power, when unchecked, leads not only to death and devastation, but more important, to a complete collapse of family values. She forgets the respect that she owes her husband as his servant, she forgets her wifely duties, and she forgets her dharma.

In other words, the story articulates the fear that anger, when unchecked, could destroy the social order, and the belief that uncontrolled power is immoral. Therefore, power, although a natural consequence of being female, has to be controlled. Because the most effective and the most moral way to control one's power is through means that originate within oneself, Oriyas work to cultivate the emotion of *lajya*, imperfectly translated as shame, to achieve precisely such control.

Bite Your Tongue: The Meaning of *Lajya*

Everyday, Oriya Hindu morality requires self-regulation through sensitivity to the emotion of *lajya*. To have a sense of *lajya* is to be civilized; to know one's rightful place in society; to conduct oneself in a becoming manner; to be conscious of one's duties and responsibilities; to persevere in the performance of social role obligations; to be shy, modest, and deferential and not encroach on the prerogatives of others; and to remain silent or lower ones eyes in the presence of social superiors. *Lajya* is something that one shows or puts on display, just as one might show gratitude or loyalty through various forms of public presentation. Like gratitude or loyalty, *lajya*, which is a way of displaying one's continuing commitment to the maintenance of social harmony, is judged in Bhubaneswar to be a very good thing.

Because everyone concedes that women rather than men have natural power, it is primarily women who need to exercise control over it, and it is they who have to develop their capacity to experience shame.

Lajya is analogized to a gorgeous ornament worn by women. *Lajya* is the linguistic stem for a local plant (a touch-me-not) that is so coy that it closes its petals and withdraws into itself at the slightest contact. Every time a woman covers her face or ducks out of a room to avoid affiliation with an "avoidance relative" (e.g., her father-in-law or husband's elder brother), she is displaying *lajya*, giving evidence of her civility and intimating that she has within herself the power to do otherwise and to wreck the entire social show. In Orissa, there is not only virtue in *lajya*; there is also terrifying power in it as well.

It is noteworthy that when narrators comment on the manner in which Kali is recalled to a sense of her wifely duties, nearly two thirds of them insist that it happens by her reining in her own power and not through any external control that Siva might exercise. They point to Siva's passivity and argue that Kali could have, if she had wished, trampled on him and gone on. That she chose to recognize him is a measure of her self-control and of her sensitivity to *lajya*. (For more on *lajya*, see Parish, 1991; Shweder, 1992.)

The ultimate message of the icon is to display the cultural truth that it is women who uphold the social order. The more competent narrators, both men and women, articulated this view. They described wives and mothers as the centripetal forces that hold families together. They contrasted those roles with those of husbands and fathers who contribute only financially to the welfare of the family, a contribution that most informants did not view as terribly significant to the family's well-being. Curiously enough, this view of women coincides with the Tantric one that also sees women as the power that upholds the universe. The difference is that although the Tantric view sees women as achieving this position through the unchecked exercise of power, the narrators in the sample saw it as being attained through the moral self-control of such power.

Conclusion

Our analysis demonstrates that expert knowledge about the icon of Kali is hierarchically structured, consisting of four different levels or stages of competence. The Stage 0 level is one of apparent or real ignorance of local narrative norms. The Stage 1 level of normative knowledge adduces female shame as an antidote to female anger. The Stage 2 level of normative knowledge encompasses that first stage of understanding and elaborates on the destructive nature of female anger. The Stage 3 level of normative knowledge offers, in addition to everything else, an explanation for the anger, a critique of male authority, and an appeal to women to control their awesome powers for the sake of social reproduction.

The set of meanings that is most frequently narrated across the community (Module 1 meanings) appears to postulate the view that women keep the world going by reining in their power and by regulating it through sensitivity to the emotion *lajya*. This message is within the competence of anyone with at least a Stage 1 level of expertise. Perhaps it is the most important message that the icon conveys in the sense that the greatest number of people mention it. They accept Kali as the embodiment of power but see in her expression and in the biting of her tongue in particular, the mark of her shame at not controlling her damaging force.

For Oriyas, female *lajya* is an antidote to anger. The icon of the Great Goddess freezes and commemorates a particular divine moment in which the Goddess realized her potential for destructiveness and chose to recognize the necessity for reining herself in. By biting her tongue, she gave expression to her sense of deep shame at having forgotten herself in the first place. The facial expression has become a culturally standardized expression of shame, one that is lexicalized in the Oriya idiom "to bite your tongue," which forms part of everyday discourse.

At the beginning of this essay we asked which emotion was most different from the other two: *sukha* (happiness), *lajya* (shame), or *raga* (anger). Perhaps the reader will no longer be surprised that for residents of the temple town of Bhubaneswar, it is *lajya* (shame) and *sukha* (happiness) that go together and *raga* (anger) that is judged most different from the other two. In Orissa, India, *lajya* is both powerful and good, and the icon of the Great Goddess in her manifestation as Kali is the key to understanding why.

References

Borgatti, S. P. (1990). *Provisional Documentation, Anthropac 3.0*. University of South Carolina, Columbia.

Boster, J. S. (1986). Requiem for the omniscient informant: There's life in the old girl yet. In J. Dougherty (Ed.), *Directions in cognitive anthropology* (pp. 177–197). Urbana: University of Illinois Press.

Bruner, J. S. (1990). *Acts of meaning.* Cambridge, MA: Harvard University Press.

Cole, M. (1990). Cultural psychology: A once and future discipline? In J. J. Berman (Ed.), *Cross-cultural perspectives: Nebraska Symposium on Motivation (1989).* Lincoln: University of Nebraska Press.

D'Andrade, R. G. (1990). Some propositions about the relations between culture and human cognition. In J. Stigler, R. Shweder, & G. Herdt (Eds.), *Cultural psychology: Essays on comparative human development* (pp. 65–129). Cambridge, England: Cambridge University Press.

Driver, H. E., & Kroeber, A. L. (1932). Quantitative expression of cultural relationships. *University of California Publications in Archaeology and Ethnology, 31,* 211–256.

Garvey, C. (1992). Talk in the study of socialization and development. *Merrill–Palmer Quarterly, 38,* iii–viii.

Ghiselli, E. E., Campbell, J. P., & Zedeck, S. (1981). *Measurement theory for the behavioral sciences.* San Francisco: Freeman.

Gordon, R. L. (1977). *Unidimensional scaling of social variables.* New York: Free Press.

Jahoda, G. (1992). *Crossroads between culture and mind: Continuities and change in theories of human nature.* London: Harvester Wheatsheaf.

Kakar, S. (1989). *Intimate relations: Exploring Indian sexuality.* Chicago: University of Chicago Press.

Kelley, T. L. (1923). *Statistical method.* New York: Macmillan.

Kripal, J. (1993). *Kali's tongue: Shame and disgust in a Tantric world.* Unpublished manuscript.

Kurtz, S. N. (1992). *All the mothers are one: Hindu India and the cultural reshaping of psychoanalysis.* New York: Columbia University Press.

Levy, R. I. (1990). *Mesocosm: Hinduism and the organization of a traditional Newar city of Nepal.* Berkeley: University of California Press.

Lutz, C. (1988). *Unnatural emotions: Everyday sentiments on a Micronesian atoll and their challenge to western theory.* Chicago: University of Chicago Press.

Mahapatra, M. (1981). *Traditional structure and change in an Orissa temple.* Calcutta: Punthi Pustak.

Markus, H. R., & Kitayama, S. (1991). Culture and the self: Implications for cognition, emotion, and motivation. *Psychological Review, 98,* 224–253.

Markus, H. R., & Kitayama, S. (1992). The what, why and how of cultural psychology. *Psychological Inquiry, 3,* 357–364.

Miller, P., Mintz, J., Hoogstra, L., Fung, H., & Potts, R. (1992). The narrated self: Young children's construction of self in relation to others in conversational stories of personal experience. *Merrill–Palmer Quarterly, 38,* 45–67.

Miller, P., Potts, R., Fung, H., Hoogstra, L., & Mintz, J. (1990). Narrative practices and the social construction of self in childhood. *American Ethnologist, 17*, 292–311.

Miller, P., & Sperry, L. (1987). Young children's verbal resources for communicating anger. *Merrill–Palmer Quarterly, 33*, 1–32.

Much, N. C. (1992). Analysis of discourse as methodology for a semiotic psychology. *American Behavioral Scientist, 36*, 52–72.

O'Flaherty, W. D. (1975). *Hindu myths.* New York: Penguin Books.

Parish, S. (1991). The sacred mind: Newar cultural representations of mental life and the production of moral consciousness. *Ethos, 19*, 313–351.

Ramanujan, A. K. (1989). Is there an Indian way of thinking? An informal essay. *Contributions to Indian Sociology, 23*, 41–58.

Seymour, S. (1983). Household structure and status and expressions of affect in India. *Ethos, 11*, 263–277.

Shweder, R. A. (1982). Beyond self-constructed knowledge: The study of culture and morality. *Merrill–Palmer Quarterly, 28*, 41–69.

Shweder, R. A. (1990). Cultural psychology: What is it? In J. Stigler, R. Shweder, & G. Herdt (Eds.), *Cultural psychology: Essays on comparative human development* (pp. 1–43). Cambridge, England: Cambridge University Press.

Shweder, R. A. (1991). *Thinking through cultures: Expeditions in cultural psychology.* Cambridge, MA: Harvard University Press.

Shweder, R. A. (1992). The cultural psychology of the emotions. In M. Lewis & J. Haviland (Eds.), *Handbook of emotions* (pp. 417–431). New York: Guilford Press.

Shweder, R. A. (1993, Winter). "Why do men barbecue?" and other postmodern ironies of growing up in the decade of ethnicity. *Daedalus, 122*, 281–310.

Shweder, R. A., Mahapatra, M., & Miller, J. G. (1990). Culture and moral development. In J. Stigler, R. Shweder, & G. Herdt (Eds.), *Cultural psychology: Essays on comparative human development* (pp. 130–204). Cambridge, England: Cambridge University Press.

Shweder, R. A., Much, N. C., Mahapatra, M. M., & Park, L. (in press). The "Big Three" of morality (autonomy, community and divinity), and the "Big Three" explanations of suffering. In P. Rozin, S. A. Brandt (Eds.), *Morality and health.* Stanford, CA: Stanford University Press.

Shweder, R. A., & Sullivan, M. (1990). The semiotic subject of cultural psychology. In L. A. Pervin (Ed.), *Handbook of personality: Theory and research* (pp. 399–416). New York: Guilford Press.

Shweder, R. A., & Sullivan, M. (1993). Cultural psychology: Who needs it? *Annual Review of Psychology, 44*, 497–523.

Stigler, J., Shweder, R., & Herdt, G. (Eds.). (1990). *Cultural psychology: Essays on comparative human development.* Cambridge, England: Cambridge University Press.

Weller, S. C., & Romney, A. K. (1990). *Metric scaling.* Newbury Park, CA: Sage.

Wertsch, J. (1992). Keys to cultural psychology. *Culture, Medicine and Psychiatry, 16,* 273–280.

Wierzbicka, A. (1992). *Semantics, culture and cognition: Universal human concepts in culture-specific configurations.* New York: Oxford University Press.

Wiggins, D. (1991). Truth, invention and the meaning of life. In D. Wiggins (Ed.), *Needs, values, truth.* Oxford, England: Basil Blackwell.

Appendix: Interview With Cultural "Dud"

(Narrator is a 70-year-old Brahman widow.)

Q. Do you recognize this picture?

A. ... an image of Durga?

Q. Kali.

A. Yes, Kali of course.

Q. You do recognize her, don't you? ... Can you tell me who is lying on the ground?

A. ... I can't tell you....

Q. You can't tell me who is lying on the ground? ... Can you see clearly?

A. Oh, I can see all right ... but I can't tell you....

Q. You can't tell me who is lying on the ground? ... So, you don't know the story associated with this picture?

A. ...

Q. All right. Can you see Kali's face clearly? ... You can, can't you?

A. She is Kali.

Q. Yes. Can you describe her expression here?

A. I can't see properly.

Q. Tell me what you see in her face: Is she angry? Is she sad? Is she happy? Tell me what you see in her face.

A. I can't tell you these things.

Q. But surely you can say what she looks like here.

A. She is not angry here.

Q. She is not angry ... then, what is she?

A. She is peaceful here.

Q. What about her tongue? Why has she put that out?

A. Kali always puts out her tongue ... that is Kali ... she always has her tongue out.

Q. But she has not put out her tongue in anger?

A. Why should she be angry?

Q. When I ask others these questions, many people tell me that Kali has bitten her tongue in shame: She has stepped on her husband and when she realizes that, in shame, she bites her tongue. What do you think? Are they right in saying that?

A. ... I don't know all these things ... I can't tell you.

Q. Have you ever seen this expression—Kali's expression here—in everyday life?

A. . . . I don't know what you are asking . . . I don't go out anywhere, how will I see anything?

Q. Who do you see as dominant in this picture: Kali or Siva?

A. . . . I don't know all these things. . . .

Q. It's not a matter of knowing or not knowing . . . when you look at this picture, what do you think? Do you think Kali is stronger than Siva or that Siva is stronger?

A. Siva.

Q. Why do you think that?

A. Can a woman ever be stronger than a man? Is it possible? How can Kali be stronger than Siva?

Q. But Kali here has weapons in each of her 10 arms and Siva has nothing. She is also standing on his chest. You don't think that she is stronger than he in this picture?

A. After Siva, Kali is the most powerful . . . but you know best . . . maybe she is stronger; maybe the two are equally strong. . . . I don't know.

CHAPTER 9

Major Cultural Syndromes and Emotion

Harry C. Triandis

C ulture is to society what memory is to individuals (Kluckholn, 1954). As people struggle to survive in particular ecologies, some of their actions are effective and adaptive and are incorporated as standard operating procedures, transmitted as *customs* to new generations and widely shared among those who speak the same language and live in the same ecological niche within the same time period.

Cultures include more than customs. They develop characteristic ways of categorizing experience, linguistic terms that correspond to these categories, widely shared associations among the categories, beliefs about how the categories are linked to each other, beliefs about correct action in specific situations (norms), beliefs about actions that are appropriate for persons who hold specific positions in social structures (roles), and guiding principles that direct the lives of individuals (values). These en-

I thank D. Bhawuk, Sharon Goto, and Lois Kurowski for useful comments on an earlier version of this chapter.

tities constitute some of the elements of subjective culture (Triandis, 1972) that are widely shared and transmitted from generation to generation.

To facilitate transmission of the elements of subjective culture, people develop specialized vocabularies and learn to feel differently in different situations. The more important the domain of subjective culture, the more differentiated is the vocabulary used to transmit it, and correspondingly, the more complex are the emotions that are experienced. These emotions reflect the schedules of reinforcement that have been experienced in particular ecologies in the past and the current patterns of transmission of the elements of subjective culture.

When subjective culture is transmitted, emphasis will be placed on elements that functioned well in the past. However, some of those elements no longer generate reinforcements (i.e., are no longer functional). In spite of that lack of reinforcement, customs, stereotypes, and other elements of subjective culture persist. It may be that traditions provide a sense of cultural competence and of environmental control that is rewarding in itself, regardless of its correspondence with reality.

The emotions that are experienced reflect biological mechanisms inherited from our animal ancestors. However, the way in which these emotions are expressed reflect display rules that are compatible with culture (Ekman, 1972, 1992). The selection of display rules depends on how the perceiver appraises the situation (Ellsworth, chapter 2, this volume). Such appraisals can be identified in different cultures (Mauro, Sato, & Tucker, 1992) and are influenced by culture. Thus, to understand how emotions are expressed, one needs to know how the elements of culture are assembled in a particular time period. Both universal and culture-specific links are likely between cultures and the probabilities of various emotions (Matsumoto, Kudoh, Scherer, & Wallbot, 1988).

Cultures differ in a myriad of ways that cannot be explored in a short chapter. For that reason, I will discuss only one way, which I call *individualism–collectivism* and which appears to be the most important worldview that differentiates cultures. The chapter will define and describe this cultural syndrome, discuss its major antecedents and consequences, and identify the emotions that are likely to be expressed in individualistic and collectivist cultures.

Definition of Individualism and Collectivism

Gould and Kolb (1964), in their social science dictionary, defined individualism as the "belief that the individual is an end in himself, and as such ought to realize the 'self' and cultivate his own judgment, notwithstanding the weight of pervasive social pressures in the direction of conformity." Triandis (1988) took this definition as the basis for contrasting individualism and collectivism. The individualistic pattern stresses that

- the views, needs, and goals of the self are most important, whereas the collectivist emphasizes the views, needs, and goals of some collective;
- behavior can be explained by the pleasure principle and the computation of personal profits and losses, whereas the collectivist stresses that behavior is a function of norms and duties imposed by the collective;
- beliefs distinguish the individual from the in-group, allowing the individual to be an autonomous entity, whereas the collectivist pattern emphasizes shared beliefs, that is, what the individual and the collective have in common;
- social behavior is independent of and emotionally detached from the collective, whereas in the collectivist pattern, it is dependent, emotionally attached, and involved with the collective. Furthermore, social behavior in collectivist cultures is cooperative and even self-sacrificing toward in-group members, but indifferent, even hostile, toward out-group members.

The collective in these definitions may be the family, the work group, a political or religious group, a social class, or an ideological or national entity that is centrally important to the individual's self-definition. Experiments with "minimal groups" (Tajfel, 1982) suggest that the mere categorization of a person in a group has the effect of making that person favor his or her group more than the other group. When members of a group experience a common fate, it strengthens their bonds. Among a group of artists, even the admiration of the work of another artist can be the basis of the formation of an in-group or of a collective. Each culture has its own constellation of important in-groups; for example, the family and some other groups (such as in Africa, the tribe; in the U.S. one's own race; in the Middle East, religion; in Japan, the corporation). Collectivist cultures seem to be more common in East Asia and among traditional populations around the world than in the West or in modern societies.

Description of Individualism and Collectivism

As I reviewed the literature (Triandis, 1990), I discovered a wide range of labels describing societies and cultures that had strong parallels to the constructs just defined. Specifically, Durkheim's (1949) mechanical solidarity, with its emphasis on similarity among members of a society, suggested collectivism; whereas his discussion of organic solidarity, with its emphasis on interdependence resulting from division of labor (because I do not grow tomatoes, I depend on others to grow them, then I buy them) suggested individualism. Similarly, Toennies's (1957) *Gemeinschaft* and *Gesellschaft*, Parson and Shils's (1951) collectivity versus self-emphasis, Bakan's (1966) community versus agency, Witkin and Berry's (1975) dependent versus independent cognitive style, and Weber's (1947) and Inkeles and Smith's (1974) traditionalism versus modernity had much in common with collectivism versus individualism. More recently, Hofstede's (1980) collectivism versus individualism, Fiske's (1990) community sharing versus market pricing, and Markus and Kitayama's (1991) interdependent versus independent self reflected similar contrasts.

Triandis (1994) assembled 64 attributes that were hypothesized to contrast collectivists and individualists. Some of these contrasts have already been mentioned, as part of the definition, but many more seem to be related to the cultural pattern. Empirical research reviewed in Triandis (1990, 1994) supports the presence of these elements.

It is important to discuss how the reader should understand the contrast between individualist and collectivist elements. In considering the attribute of goal subordination, in collectivist cultures, when there is conflict between personal goals and an in-group's goals, people subordinate their personal goals to the in-group's goals; and in individualist cultures, people subordinate their in-groups's goals to their personal goals. This does *not* mean that, in collectivist cultures, people never subordinate their in-group goals to their personal goals, or that, in individualist cultures, people never subordinate their personal goals to their in-group goals. Rather, these are central tendencies, that is, one is more probable than the other.

For example, Benedict (1946) wrote 40 years ago that the Japanese are a "shame culture." She was severely criticized by social scientists who found instances in which "guilt" was used by Japanese samples. Clearly, this is not what Benedict meant. A review of 40 years of this controversy by Creighton (1990) found considerable utility in Benedict's position, but this position must be understood probabilistically, not as an all-or-none argument.

In visualizing 64 contrasting elements, one must think that each has some probability of being sampled to construct social situations. Collectivism simply means that the probabilities of sampling the collective side of each contrast are higher than the probabilities of sampling the individualist side of each contrast.

It is also important to remember that there is enormous variability within cultures so that, in both collectivist and individualistic cultures, there are individuals who are countercultural. It is convenient to have terms to refer to personality differences that correspond to the cultural differences. Thus, Triandis, Leung, Villareal, and Clack (1985) used the terms *allocentric* and *idiocentric* to designate those whose personalities correspond to collectivists and individualists, respectively. There are idiocentrics in collectivist cultures and allocentrics in individualistic cultures, and there is evidence that allocentrics receive more social support, whereas idiocentrics are more likely to be lonely in both types of cultures (Triandis, Bontempo, Villareal, Asai, & Lucca, 1988).

Description of Some of the Contrasting Elements

Collectivists are more likely to categorize experience by using groups rather than individuals. For example, in Indonesia, *teknonyms* are used more frequently than personal names. Teknonyms connote, for example, "the second son of the Brown family." When people use such names, it clearly suggests that social reality is cut up into families rather than into individuals.

Collectivists believe that behavior can best be explained by group influences (attributes of groups, norms, and the like) as opposed to psychological processes (attitudes or beliefs). For example, Kashima, Siegel, Tanaka, and Kashima (1992) found that the collectivist Japanese do not think that attitudes are the causes of behavior as much as do the more individualistic Australians.

Differences in attributions between these two types of cultures were reviewed by Miller (1984) and Markus and Kitayama (1991). In general, collectivists use more context to understand the causes of behavior than do individualists.

Differences in self-definitions may be seen in content analyses of the responses of people who completed 20 sentences beginning with the words "I am." The responses were content analyzed by using a simple instruction: If the response suggests common fate, score it S (social); otherwise, it is not S. Interrater reliabilities were in the high .90 range with these instructions. For example, "I am a son" is an S response because it suggests family, and members of a family have a common fate. "I am a member of the communist party" is an S response. "I am a resident of X" is also an S response because it suggests a common fate (same earthquakes, etc.) On the other hand, "I am kind" does not suggest common fate. In fact, most personality attributes do not suggest common fate. We then took the percentage of all responses given by the subject who was coded S and called this the $\%S$ score (Triandis, McCusker, & Hui, 1990).

Typically, collectivists use more self-definitions that reflect the incorporation of collectives in their thinking about themselves than do individualists. Collectivists average a large $\%S$ score; individualists have a small average score. In fact, modal University of Illinois students gave *no* responses that suggested the presence of a collective when they performed this task, in contrast to a modal response of $\%S = 52\%$ in China (Triandis et al., 1990). Table 1 shows the $\%S$ average scores obtained from several different samples. All 20 of the responses of about 10% of the students in the People's Republic of China suggested a collective (e.g., I am a member of the communist party; I am a member of my work unit; I am a son; etc.). This method has by now been used by others as well,

TABLE 1

Average Percentage of Subjects Giving Social Responses in Several Samples

Student Sample	N	M	Range of Social Responses
University of Illinois	509	19	0–60%
University of Athens	118	15	0–56%
University of Hawaii Mainland background	28	21	10–62%
University of Hawaii Chinese background	19	29	10–71%
University of Hawaii Japanese background	37	28	10–65%
University of Hong Kong	118	20	10–68%
People's Republic of China	34	52	28–100%

and the general finding is that, in traditional cultures, the %S is larger than 30%; and in modern–industrial cultures, it usually averages less than 15%.

In one study (Trafimow, Triandis, & Goto, 1991), we manipulated the cognitions of the subjects by asking a random half of them to think for two minutes about "what you have in common with your family and friends," whereas the other half was asked to think about "what makes you different from your family and friends." Table 2 shows the results.

When asked to think of what they had in common with their in-group, Illinois students with English names had a %S score of 23% and Illinois students with Chinese names had a %S score of 52%. When asked

TABLE 2

Percentage of Subjects with Chinese or English Names Giving Social Responses after Priming with Collectivist or Individualist Themes

Subjects	n	Social Response Percentages
What subjects have in common with family and friends		
With English names	24	23
With Chinese names	18	52
What makes subjects different from family and friends		
With English names	24	7
With Chinese names	18	30

to think of what made them different from their family and friends, the students with English names averaged 7%, and those with Chinese names averaged 30%. In another experiment in which students with English names were exposed to a collectivist story (a king of Sumeria sent his brother to help another king) versus an individualist story (a king of Sumeria sent his most able general to help another king) and the %S scores were 20% and 9%, respectively. In short, it is possible to prime people so that their self becomes collectivist or individualist, at least for a short time and on this one measure. From these studies, it was concluded that individualist and collectivist cognitive elements are somehow inter-related in the cognitive systems of individuals so that it is possible to prime one of these elements and increase the probability of the emission of other elements of *that* type.

The attitudes and values of collectivists reflect support for inter-dependence and family integrity (e.g., agreement with "Old parents should live at home with their children until they die") and emphasis on the values of security, obedience, duty, in-group harmony, in-group hierarchy, and personalized relationships; the attitudes and values of individualists favor pleasure, personal achievement, competition, freedom, autonomy, and fair exchange (Schwartz, 1992, in press; Triandis et al., 1986, 1988, 1990). The importance of in-group harmony emphasized by collectivists and the lesser concern for in-group harmony among individualists has been widely reported in literature contrasting Japanese and American samples, reviewed in Triandis (1990).

There is also a strong contrast between Hispanics and non-Hispanics in the United States reflected in the *simpatia* script described in Triandis, Marin, Lisansky, and Betancourt (1984). Hispanics in this study were U.S. Navy recruits who had Hispanic names and were self-identified as His-panics. They were both of African and European backgrounds. The non-Hispanics were Navy recruits who were randomly drawn from the same incoming class. The *simpatia* script indicates that Hispanics expect other people to be more positive and less negative in their interactions with them than is the case for non-Hispanics. In short, they expect the other person to be *simpatico*.

The social behavior of collectivists is very different when the other person is an in-group as opposed to an out-group member. This difference is not as sharp in the case of individualists. For example, in a study by Chan (1992), students randomly assigned to two conditions thought that they were negotiating with (a) a friend or (b) a stranger. In fact, they were negotiating with a computer program. The data were collected in Illinois and Hong Kong. When interacting with a friend, they made more concessions during the negotiations than when interacting with a stranger. This difference was greater among the subjects in Hong Kong than among those in Illinois (significant Culture × Condition interaction).

Collectivists interact mostly with in-group members and relatively little with strangers or in formal situations. The result is that they value intimacy and feel uneasy about superficial relationships. By contrast, individualists enter and leave groups of strangers with considerable ease (the cocktail party is an individualist invention) and have excellent skills for meeting strangers, but not for developing close relationships (Wheeler, Reis, & Bond, 1989).

During communication, collectivists focus on paralinguistic cues more than do individualists (Gudykunst, 1991). Thus, they communicate indirectly, paying attention to how something is said rather than to what is said; they focus on the other person during the communication, especially on evidence concerning that person's emotions. Because maintaining relationships is very important to them, they prefer to suppress negative communications and tell others what they want to hear, rather than tell the truth and create bad feelings. Thus, collectivists are more likely to lie and less likely to say "no" than are individualists. Individualists, by contrast, have no difficulties in "telling it like it is."

Because collectivists know much about the other person to whom they are speaking, they do not have to be as explicit in their communication. Thus, the quantity of communication is lower and "silence is golden." By contrast, individualists feel uneasy with silence (Iwao, 1993). Much of the social behavior of collectivists occurs together with others (e.g., skiing in groups rather than alone; Brandt, 1974) and in groups of more than two. Individualists spend much time alone and value their privacy.

In the case of collectivists, social behavior is best explained as action governed by the proper norms, customs, and traditions and, in the case of individualists, as action governed by computations of profits and losses and by implicit contracts. Bontempo and Rivero (1992) found that when models that predict behavioral intentions from attitudes and norms were used in different cultures, the beta weight for attitudes less the beta weight for norms correlated .73 with the individualism index published by Hofstede (1980) for that culture.

Antecedents

I use an ecological functionalist perspective to understand the emergence of culture, that is, in some environments, particular behavioral patterns are rewarded and become institutionalized. Elements of subjective culture consistent with those reinforced behaviors are transmitted from generation to generation and become widely shared by members of the culture. For example, low population density can be an antecedent of low aggression. In an environment with low population density, the presence of others is generally helpful, fostering the development of norms of suppressing anger and hostile emotions consistent with the low levels of aggression observed in such environments (e.g., the Utku Eskimos condemn the expression of anger; Briggs, 1970). However, when the population density is also extremely high, norms that will permit the group to "get along" must develop. Japan is a good example. Thus, a curvilinear relationship may exist between population density and the expression of aggression. In environments of intermediate density (which are the majority of environments), one may observe the most aggression. Use of this type of reasoning suggests some probable antecedents of collectivism and individualism.

The more homogeneous the culture, the more collectivist it can be. Clearly, if in-group norms are to be the main determinants of social behavior, it is necessary for the in-group to agree about norms and have clear norms, and such norms require cultural homogeneity. The more heterogeneous the culture, the more individuals need to decide for themselves whose norms to follow, and so the more individualistic is the culture.

The interdependence that is typical of collectivists is long-term. There is little keeping of track of who has contributed how much to a relationship. The interdependence that is typical of individualists is short-term, and people do keep track of how much each has contributed to the relationship.

The more interdependence is required in productive activities (e.g., agriculturists must cooperate in building irrigation systems, storage facilities, food distribution systems, and so on), the more collectivist is the culture. The more activities can be independent (e.g., food gathering, hunting, fishing, writing a book), the more individualistic the culture.

The more complex the division of labor and functional specialization, the more people will use money to buy the services of others, and the more "market pricing" (Fiske, 1990) is likely to be used. This is an individualistic pattern. On the other hand, the simpler the division of labor, with every person doing all the available jobs, the more similar the activities of all the people, and hence, the concept of homogeneity takes over and the society is more collectivist.

The more stratification there is in a society, the more people at the top can "do their own thing" and be individualistic (Daab, 1991). The more affluent the society, the more people can decide for themselves how to act, and therefore, the more people are individualistic. For example, people who have much money can buy companionship, whereas people with less money must earn it by acting interdependently. If one is affluent, one can buy services, and such economic transactions are typical of individualistic cultures; whereas among the poor, there is more interdependence. For example, in hunting societies, a hunter is likely to kill something every three or four days (Holmberg, 1969). Because there is no refrigeration and eating an entire antelope is impossible, much of the food would be spoiled if it were not for the custom of sharing it. This custom is obviously functional because it allows most of the members of the in-group to eat. If there are enough hunters in an in-group, there will be some food coming in every day. Similarly, if the in-group has several wage earners, there is a greater chance of some income coming in during periods of economic crisis. These ideas result in Figure 1, which represents how various samples might be located on the individualism–collectivism axis.

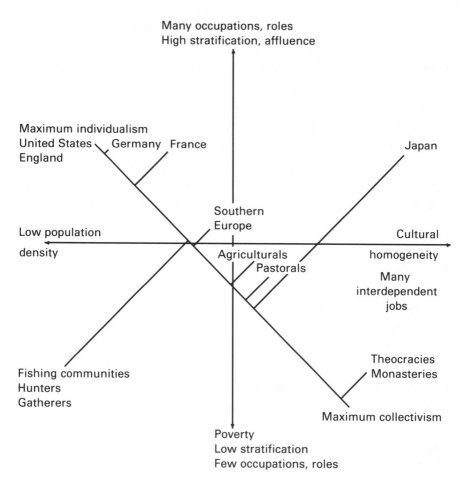

FIGURE 1. Correlates of tightness (horizontal axis) and cultural complexity (vertical axis) as determinants of individualism and collectivism.

The horizontal axis of Figure 1 contrasts cultures that are homogeneous (with many interdependent jobs) with cultures that have low population densities (e.g., the open frontier of the American West). The homogeneous–interdependent cultures are tight, in the sense that they impose sanctions on those who do not conform with in-group norms even if the deviation is minor. The left hand of this axis represents cultures that are loose, in the sense that norms do not exist for many behaviors/ situations, and when they do exist, they are imposed loosely (i.e., members of the culture tolerate large deviations and impose sanctions only when an individual has deviated from the norms in a very important way).

The vertical axis contrasts societies that are complex, with many occupations (a quarter of a million in the *Dictionary of Occupational Titles*), roles, and much stratification (usually, these are also more affluent, industrial, or information societies) with societies that are relatively poor, simple, with little stratification and few occupations and roles.

The hypothesis is that individualism will be maximal in societies in which there is both complexity and looseness; collectivism will be maximal in societies in which there is both simplicity and tightness. Thus, the United States is on the most individualistic end of the diagonal line (as found by Hofstede, 1980). Next to it are England, Germany, France, and so on. The most collectivist cultures can be found in theocracies, Western monasteries, and the like in which there is little occupational differentiation, few roles, and generally low affluence. The most extreme form of collectivism can be found in cults (e.g., in which members may commit mass suicide under the control of a charismatic leader).

Nonliterate cultures that depend on fishing, hunting, and gathering are relatively individualistic because they exist in loose environments. Agricultural and pastoral cultures are relatively collectivist because they exist in tight environments. Japan is both tight and complex and hence on the collectivist side of the dimension but not extremely collectivist.

Emotions in Collectivism and Individualism

This last section is speculative, in the sense that I will not review studies that explicitly measured collectivism and individualism and emotions. The argument follows from the description of the cultural syndromes suggesting that collectivists and individualists will experience emotions under different circumstances.

Cultural differences are likely to emerge along the dimensions of appraisal of emotions (see Ellsworth, chapter 2, this volume, Table 1). Exactly which dimensions are to be used is still unclear. Historically, dimensions such as pleasant versus unpleasant, attention (focusing on the stimulus) versus rejection (rejecting the stimulus as for instance in disgust), and level of arousal ranging from sleep to extreme arousal (e.g., Schlosberg, 1954) have been proposed and supported by cross-cultural empirical studies (e.g., Triandis & Lambert, 1958). The generality of evaluation, potency, and activity in Osgood's cross-cultural work (Osgood, Miron, & May, 1975) that does correspond to Schlosberg's dimensions would suggest that these may be the appropriate dimensions for cross-cultural work. However, Ellsworth's principal dimensions provide a richer domain for comparisons and have much in common with the three dimensions used by earlier psychologists. Attention/novelty appears to be related to arousal, pleasantness/valence is clearly the evaluation dimension, and certainty may be related to potency. Thus, it may be fruitful to examine how collectivism and individualism will influence emotions using Ellsworth's appraisal dimensions.

Attention/Novelty

In all cultures, people notice those aspects of the environment for which they have categories and that occur with unexpected frequencies and are useful to notice. Thus, collectivists are more likely to notice group memberships than personality traits or attitudes, group-linked success more than individual success, other-focused (e.g., empathy) rather than self-focused emotions (e.g., anger), the context of what was said more than the content of what was said, the possibility of ostracism more than the possibility of dependence on others, and vertical rather than horizontal relationships.

Some emotional terms will reveal what is important in a culture. For example, the Japanese have an emotional term, *oime*, which indicates the unpleasant realization that one is heavily indebted to another. This idea exists in the West also (e.g., we are not pleased when someone gives us a large gift when we expected nothing). However, there is no monoleximic term for this emotion in Western languages. This indicates that the Japanese are more likely to pay attention to this emotion than are people in Western cultures. It is known (Brown & Lenneberg, 1954) that when a monoleximic term is available, the codability of experience is higher and that makes communication easier and more accurate. In all cultures, the presence of monoleximes indicates that the concept is worth paying attention to. Thus, the Japanese are likely to find it easier to talk about *oime* than we are to talk about the corresponding emotion.

We know that cultures differ in what values are emphasized, and that individualistic cultures emphasize *pleasure* more than collectivist cultures. From this observation, one might anticipate that individualistic cultures would be more accurate in identifying *happiness* than collectivist cultures. This was found by Matsumoto (1989) by correlating Hofstede's (1980) individualism index with his own measure of accuracy in the perception of emotions ($r = .51$, $N = 15$ cultures). Matsumoto (1989) also found a correlation of $-.50$ when correlating the Hofstede individualism index and the accuracy of the perception of sadness. However, this relationship apparently was not replicated by Matsumoto (1992) when he compared a presumably individualistic sample from the United States with a presumably collectivist sample from Japan. In that case, the Americans were more accurate than the Japanese in their perception of anger, disgust, fear, and sadness. It is important to note that Matsumoto's cultural effects are relatively small, so that some instability might be expected when measurements are not perfectly accurate. Obviously, more research is needed to confirm these types of findings.

Conversely, individualists will notice, more reliably, traits, individual success, self-focused emotions, the content rather than the context of communications, and the possibility of becoming dependent on others.

Valence/Pleasantness

We hypothesize that the most positive emotions will be found among collectivists when in-group cultural expectations are realized. In in-group settings, when people feel interdependent or when the collective achieves important goals, collectivists should experience more positive emotions than individualists. When there is in-group cooperation, when there is nurturance within the in-group, when there is order and self-control, collectivists should experience positive emotions. When in-group goals are reached, when people conform to in-group expectations, when all participants save face, and when behaviors are personal, collectivists should feel more positive than individualists. When groups are homogeneous, harmonious, and orderly, and hierarchy is unchallenged, collectivists should feel especially positive emotions. Collectivists who express or view modesty will feel more positive emotions than individualists, whereas individualists will feel most positive when they are distinguished and stand above the crowd.

Among collectivists, negative emotions will be associated with being alone (Briggs, 1970), with a failure of the collective, and will be most intense when dealing with the out-group and when aggressing toward out-groups. Collectivists will feel negative emotions more strongly than individualists when in-group goals are not met, when a member of the group must be ostracized, when social behavior is inappropriate (e.g., resulting in shame), and when one must work with unfriendly people.

For example, in a study by Alexander and Barrett (1982), 4,532 managers from 20 countries indicated how much extra pay should be received by a person who works under unfavorable conditions. One of these conditions was having to work with unfriendly co-workers. Managers from collectivist countries indicated that it was appropriate to compensate much more a person who has to work under these conditions than did managers from individualistic countries.

One can easily reverse the direction of the relationships just outlined to hypothesize how individuals from individualistic countries will feel in the circumstances that were just outlined. For example, privacy and being alone will be valued by individualists more than by collectivists. Mesquita and Frijda (1992) reviewed several studies supportive of these points.

Considering also that collectivism is associated with cultural homogeneity, we hypothesize that in collectivist cultures people will feel more positive in culturally homogeneous than heterogeneous groups and will feel less negative about high population density than will people in individualistic cultures.

Finally, we hypothesize that individualists will feel more positive than collectivists about situations in which there is much division of labor, stratification, and affluence and about occupations in which only one person is needed.

Uncertainty

Cultures differ in *uncertainty avoidance* (Hofstede, 1980), with homogeneous cultures (like Japan and Greece) especially high in this attribute and heterogeneous, cosmopolitan cultures (such as Austria and the Scandinavian countries) especially low on this attribute. Those that are high in uncertainty avoidance dislike surprises and behaviors that are unexpected and nonconforming to norms. Thus, we hypothesize that they will become strongly emotionally aroused when they observe deviant behavior. For example, in Nara, Japan, Adamopoulos (personal communication, July 10, 1990) crossed against a red light after checking that no traffic was coming and aroused the anger of a Japanese passerby who chased him, shouting at him for two long blocks.

Agency/Control

Collectivists are more likely to attribute positive events to help from others and negative occurrences to their personal failure. Ellsworth (chapter 2, this volume) gives an excellent example in which a person who wins a prize may experience pride if from an individualist culture and may experience gratitude for the help received from others if from a collectivist culture. Several relevant empirical studies were reviewed by Mesquita and Frijda (1992).

The collectivist emphasis on in-group harmony increases the chances that the in-group will not be under stress. Individualists are more likely to attribute events to the actions of individuals and collectivists to the actions of groups or of outside agencies (gods, fate). Shame is a more common emotion among collectivists, whereas guilt is somewhat more common among individualists (Creighton, 1990).

The collectivist concern with the possible disruption of in-group harmony will press individuals to avoid the expression of negative emotions and to avoid assigning responsibility for negative events to others. Individualists, on the other hand, are more likely than collectivists to engage in actions that may cause anger in others. The differences in communication patterns between Japan and the United States (see Triandis, in press, for a review), in which the Japanese favor "indirect sugges-tions" and avoid saying "no," whereas Americans favor unambiguous statements, are examples of such tendencies. Most cultures (about 85% of known cultures according to Murdock, 1971) also specify that some role relationships (e.g., mother-in-law/son-in-law, father-in-law/daughter-in-law) must be marked by avoidance-respect-formality, which has the effect of avoiding disruptions of the in-group.

Norm/Self-Concept Compatibility

In collectivist cultures, as we have seen, norms are very powerful regulators of behavior. Kidder (1992) has described the difficulties of Japanese individuals who return to Japan after spending some time abroad. They are frequently criticized, teased, and bullied by their peers, and even by authorities such as teachers, for "non-Japanese behaviors" such as having a sun tan or a permanent-wave hairstyle or for eating Western food. Thus, negative emotions will occur in collectivist cultures when *minor* norms are violated to a greater degree than in individualistic cultures. The threat of ostracism is an especially powerful source of fear in collectivist cultures. Acting impolitely seems an ever present danger among the Japanese (Iwao, 1993), whereas Americans rarely worry about that.

Conclusion

The cultural pattern described above has specific antecedents and consequences. One of the domains of these consequences is the type of emotions that is most likely to occur in collectivist than in individualistic societies. We have argued that emotions will be more elaborated in those domains that are most important in the particular culture. Also, positive and negative emotions will have different distributions, depending on how they are linked to events that have high or low probabilities in those cultures. The use of Ellsworth's (chapter 2, this volume) dimensions of appraisal of emotions appears useful in identifying contrasts in emotional behavior between collectivists and individualists.

However, we must keep in mind that within-culture variations are present in these tendencies. In collectivist cultures, there are idiocentrics who behave as people do in individualistic cultures; and in individualist cultures, there are allocentrics who behave as people do in collectivist cultures. For example, Americans who join communes, gangs, and devote much time to secret societies, cults, movements, and so on behave as collectivists, and their emotional life probably resembles that of people in collectivist societies. Evidence reported in the press supports this point. Just as the Japanese criticize the "un-Japanese" behavior of those who return from abroad, so the Branch Davidian religious cult in Texas criticized the authorities for giving ice cream to their children when they came out of the compound and allowing these children to jump on the sofa. Strict obedience to the norms of the in-group occurs anywhere where collectivism is to be found. Anger when norms are broken is common in such societies to a greater extent than in individualistic cultures.

In short, the cultural syndrome that can be identified in a particular geographic region and during a particular historical period has important implications for the kinds of emotions that are most likely to be experienced and expressed in those times and places.

References

Alexander, R. A., & Barrett, G. V. (1982). Equitable salary increase judgments based upon merit and non-merit considerations: A cross-cultural comparison. *International Review of Applied Psychology, 31*, 443–454.

Bakan, D. (1966). *The duality of human existence.* Chicago: Rand McNally.

Benedict, R. (1946) *The chrysanthemum and the sword: Patterns of Japanese culture.* Boston: Houghton Mifflin.

Bontempo, R., & Rivero, J. C. (1992, August). *Cultural variation in cognition: The role of self-concept in the attitude–behavior link.* Paper presented at the meeting of the American Academy of Management, Las Vegas, NV.

Brandt, V. S. (1974). Skiing cross-culturally. *Current Anthropology, 15*, 64–66.

Briggs, J. L. (1970). *Never in anger: Portrait of an Eskimo family.* Cambridge, MA: Harvard University Press.

Brown, R., & Lenneberg, E. H. (1954). A study of language and cognition. *Journal of Abnormal and Social Psychology, 49*, 454–462.

Chan, D. K. S. (1992). *Effects of concession pattern, relationship between negotiators, and culture on negotiation.* Unpublished master's thesis, University of Illinois, Urbana–Champaign.

Creighton, M. R. (1990). Revisiting shame and guilt cultures: A forty-year pilgrimage. *Ethos, 18*, 279–307.

Daab, W. Z. (1991, July). *Changing perspectives on individualism.* Paper presented at the meeting of the International Society for Political Psychology, University of Helsinki, Finland.

Durkheim, E. (1949). *The division of labor in society.* Glencoe, IL: Free Press.

Ekman, P. (1972). Universals and cultural differences in facial expressions of emotions. *Nebraska Symposium on Motivation* (Vol. 19, pp. 207–283). Lincoln: University of Nebraska Press.

Ekman, P. (1992). Facial expression of emotion: New findings, new questions. *Psychological Science, 3,* 34–38.

Fiske, A. (1990). *Structures of social life.* New York: Free Press.

Gould, J., & Kolb, W. V. (1964). *A dictionary of the social sciences.* Glencoe, IL: Free Press.

Gudykunst, W. B. (1991). *Bridging differences.* Newbury Park, CA: Sage.

Hofstede, G. (1980). *Culture's consequences.* Beverly Hills, CA: Sage.

Holmberg, A. (1969). *Nomads of the long bow: The Siriono of Eastern Bolivia.* Garden City, NY: Natural History Press.

Inkeles, A., & Smith, D. H. (1974). *Becoming modern.* Cambridge, MA: Harvard University Press.

Iwao, S. (1993). *The Japanese woman: Traditional image and changing reality.* New York: Free Press.

Kashima, Y., Siegel, M., Tanaka, K., & Kashima, E. S. (1992). Do people believe that attitudes cause behaviors? Toward a cultural psychology of attribution processes. *British Journal of Social Psychology, 31,* 111–124.

Kidder, L. H. (1992). Requirements for being "Japanese": Stories of returnees. *International Journal of Intercultural Relations, 16,* 383–394.

Kluckhohn, C. (1954). Culture and behavior. In G. Lindzey (Ed.), *Handbook of social psychology* (Vol. 2, pp. 921–976). Reading, MA: Addision–Wesley.

Markus, H. R., & Kitayama, S. (1991). Culture and self: Implications for cognition, emotion, and motivation. *Psychological Review, 98,* 224–253.

Matsumoto, D. (1989). Cultural influences on the perception of emotion. *Journal of Cross-Cultural Psychology, 20,* 92–105.

Matsumoto, D. (1992). American–Japanese cultural differences in the recognition of universal facial expressions. *Journal of Cross-Cultural Psychology, 23,* 72–84.

Matsumoto, D., Kudoh, T., Scherer, K., & Wallbot, H. G. (1988). Emotion antecedents and reactions in the U.S. and Japan. *Journal of Cross-Cultural Psychology, 19,* 267–286.

Mauro, R., Sato, K., & Tucker, J. (1992). The role of appraisal in human emotions: A cross-cultural study. *Journal of Personality and Social Psychology, 62,* 301–317.

Mesquita, B., & Frijda, N. H. (1992). Cultural variations in emotions: A review. *Psychological Bulletin, 112,* 179–204.

Miller, J. G. (1984). Culture and the development of everyday social explanation. *Journal of Personality and Social Psychology, 46,* 961–978.

Murdock, G. P. (1971). Cross-sex patterns of kin behavior. *Ethnology, 10,* 359–368.

Osgood, C. E., Miron, M., & May, W. (1975). *Cross-cultural universals of affective meaning.* Urbana: University of Illinois Press.

Parson, T., & Shils, E. A. (1951). *Toward a general theory of action.* Cambridge, MA: Harvard University Press.

Schlosberg, H. (1954). Three dimensions of emotion. *Psychological Review, 61,* 81–88.

Schwartz, S. H. (1992). Universals in the content and structure of values: Theoretical advances and empirical tests in 20 countries. In M. Zanna (Ed.), *Advances in experimental social psychology* (Vol. 25, pp. 1–65). San Diego, CA: Academic Press.

Schwartz, S. H. (in press). Cultural dimensions of values: Toward an understanding of national differences. In U. Kim, H. C. Triandis, S. Choi, C. Kagitcibasi, & G. Yoon (Eds.), *Individualism and collectivism: Theory method, and applications.* Newbury Park, CA: Sage.

Tajfel, H. (1982). *Social identity and intergroup relations.* Cambridge, England: Cambridge University Press.

Toennies, F. (1957). *Community and society.* East Lansing: Michigan State University Press.

Trafimow, D., Triandis, H. C., & Goto, S. G. (1991). Some tests of the distinction between the private and the collective self. *Journal of Personality and Social Psychology, 60,* 649–655.

Triandis, H. C. (1972). *The analysis of subjective culture.* New York: Wiley.

Triandis, H. C. (1988). Collectivism and individualism: A reconceptualization of a basic concept in cross-cultural social psychology. In G. K. Verma & C. Bagley (Eds.), *Personality, attitudes, and cognitions* (pp. 60–95). London: Macmillan.

Triandis, H. C. (1990). Cross-cultural studies of individualism and collectivism. In J. Berman (Ed.), *Nebraska Symposium on Motivation, 1989* (pp. 41–133). Lincoln: University of Nebraska Press.

Triandis, H. C. (1994). *Culture and social behavior.* New York: McGraw-Hill.

Triandis, H. C., Bontempo, R., Betancourt, H., Bond, M., Leung, K., Brenes, A., Georgas, J., Hui, C. H., Marin, G., Setiadi, B., Sinha, J. P. B., Verma, J., Spangenberg, J., Touzard, H., & de Montmollin, G. (1986). The measurement of etic aspects of individualism and collectivism. *Australian Journal of Psychology, 38,* 257–267.

Triandis, H. C., Bontempo, R., Villareal, M. J., Asai, M., & Lucca, N. (1988). Individualism and collectivism: Cross-cultural perspectives on self-ingroup relationships. *Journal of Personality and Social Psychology, 54,* 323–338.

Triandis, H. C., & Lambert, W. W. (1958). A restatement and test of Schlosberg's theory of emotion with two kinds of subjects from Greece. *Journal of Abnormal and Social Psychology, 56,* 321–328.

Triandis, H. C., Leung, K., Villareal, M., & Clack, F. L. (1985). Allocentric vs idiocentric tendencies: Convergent and discriminant validity. *Journal of Research in Personality, 19,* 395–415.

Triandis, H. C., Marin, G., Lisansky, J., & Betancourt, H. (1984). Simpatia as a cultural script of Hispanics. *Journal of Personality and Social Psychology, 47,* 1364–1375.

Triandis, H. C., McCusker, C., & Hui, C. H. (1990). Multimethod probes of individualism and collectivism. *Journal of Personality and Social Psychology, 59,* 1006–1020.

Weber, M. (1947). *The theory of social and economic organization.* Glencoe, IL: Free Press.

Wheeler, L., Reis, H. T., & Bond, M. H. (1989). Collectivism–individualism in everyday social life: The Middle Kingdom and the melting pot. *Journal of Personality and Social Psychology, 57,* 79–86.

Witkin, H., & Berry, J. (1975). Psychological differentiation in cross-cultural perspective. *Journal of Cross-Cultural Psychology, 6,* 4–87.

CHAPTER 10

Culture, Emotion, and Psychopathology

Janis H. Jenkins

This chapter contributes an anthropological examination of the nexus among culture, emotion, and psychopathology. The first section is a brief introduction to current approaches to the topic. The second section is a critical appraisal of two conceptual issues underlying these approaches, namely the distinctions between normal and pathological emotion and between feeling and emotion. The validity of these distinctions is called into question through presentation of an ethnographic case. The third section is a brief review of issues surrounding studies of emotion and particular major mental disorders (schizophrenia and depression). Finally, I suggest new directions for studies of emotion based on intersubjective dimensions of culture and experience, as a step beyond cognitive–linguistic and ethnopsychological studies of emotion.

I begin by providing an orientation to the constructs of culture, emotion, and psychopathology. For culture, I draw on a recent definition by Jenkins and Karno (1992):

> Culture can be defined as a generalized, coherent context of shared symbols and meanings that persons dynamically create and recreate for themselves in the process of social interaction. In everyday life, culture is something people come to take for granted—their way of feeling, thinking and being in the world—the unselfconscious medium of experience, interpretation, and action. Culture is thus the most generalized baseline from which individuals may deviate,[1] and hence invaluable for comparative studies of psychopathology. (p. 10)

Culture is therefore not a variable that can be operationalized for use in research protocols; culture is a complex context through which all human experience and action—including emotions—is interpreted (Geertz, 1973). In addition, culture is best conceived as a dynamic process that may be contested by diverse cultural members. In this emergent and processual sense, culture is neither static nor monolithic. As recently argued by White and Lutz (1992), the notion of culture as neither contested nor historically grounded is of limited use.

Although emotion is by no means absent in classic ethnographies (Bateson, 1958; Benedict, 1934; Hallowell, 1955; Mead, 1935), explicit interest in this topic has occurred as the result of a paradigm shift in conceptualizations of emotion. Rather than presuming emotion as a psychobiological universal, emerging anthropological theories of emotion have instead posited emotion as inherently cultural (Geertz, 1973; Lutz, 1982, 1988; Rosaldo, 1980, 1984). Consider Rosaldo's anthropological conceptualization of emotion as

> self-concerning, partly physical responses that are at the same time aspects of moral or ideological attitudes; emotions are both feelings and cognitive constructions, linking person, action, and sociological milieu. Stated otherwise, new views of culture cast the emotions as themselves aspects of cultural systems, of strategic importance to analysts concerned with the

---

[1] For a theoretical discussion of culture and deviance (including psychopathology), see Edgerton (1985). For a review of a controversial thesis concerning the notion that widespread or institutionalized forms of deviance (including psychopathology) may constitute a "sick society," see Edgerton (1992).

ordering of action and the ways that people shape and are shaped by their world. (Levy, 1983, p. 128)

Identification of the specifically cultural nature of emotion has led to a proliferation of anthropological studies (Abu-Lughod, 1986; Abu-Lughod & Lutz, 1990; Desjarlais, 1992; Gaines & Farmer, 1986; B. Good & Good, 1988; Hollan, 1988; Jenkins, 1991b; Kitayama & Markus, chapter 1, this volume; Kleinman & Good, 1985; Lutz, 1985, 1988; Lutz & Abu-Lughod, 1990; Lutz & White, 1986; Mathews, 1992; Myers, 1979; Ochs & Schieffelin, 1987; Rosaldo, 1980; Roseman, 1990; Scheper-Hughes & Lock, 1987; Schieffelin, 1983; Shweder & LeVine, 1984; Wellenkamp, 1988; Wikan, 1990). These studies have provided extensive ethnographic evidence that emotional experience and expression differ cross culturally. In addition, these ethnopsychological studies of emotion examine factors such as notions of the self, indigenous definitions and categories of emotion, salience of particular emotions within sociocultural settings, interrelations among diverse emotions, contextual identification of those situations in which emotions are thought to occur, and ethnophysiological accounts of the bodily experience of emotion (Jenkins, Kleinman, & Good, 1991).

Because the ethnographic record provides compelling evidence that emotional expression differs cross culturally, it follows that we can expect emotional disorders to be manifest in culturally distinctive ways as well. Thus, the cross-cultural validity of diagnostic categories of psychopathology is the subject of controversy (Kleinman, 1988a; Kleinman & Good, 1985; Manson, Shore, & Bloom, 1985). At issue is the extent to which symptoms and syndromes described in the revised third edition of the American Psychiatric Association's (1987) *Diagnostic and Statistical Manual of Mental Disorders (DSM–III–R)* are appropriately used in clinical and research assessments of groups other than those for whom it was empirically derived (i.e., Euro-American populations). It is possible that the form, content, and constituent components of a given syndrome may vary across cultural groups. Indeed, Kleinman (1987) cautioned that failure to analyze *DSM* categories critically in cross-cultural research may result in a *category fallacy.* "A category fallacy is the reification of a nosological category developed for a particular cultural group that is then applied to members of another culture for whom it lacks coherence and whose validity has not been established" (Kleinman, 1987, p. 452). While acknowledging the widespread agreement among psychiatric anthropologists that the *DSM* categories are grounded in cultural conventions, B. Good (1992a) advanced a compelling argument for the productive use of specific *DSM* categories—rather than generalized distress—as a starting point for comparative research. By submitting the *DSM* categories to cross-cultural analysis, the cultural conventions on which they are based—including indigenous definitions of normal (and abnormal) behavior, variations in the experience and expression of emotion and self, and culturally informed assessments of what constitutes distressing life circumstances[2]—are brought to light. In addition, diagnostic criteria on the basis of thresholds for symptom severity and duration should also be cross culturally scrutinized.

Current Anthropological Approaches

Current approaches to culture, emotion, and psychopathology can be summarized within the following interrelated domains of inquiry: (a) studies from psychological anthropology of the cultural constitution of emotion and self; (b) studies from medical anthropology of dysphoric affects and affective disorders; (c) phenomenological accounts of the body as a generative source of culture; (d) sociopolitical analyses of emotion; and (e) experiential accounts of dysphoria and suffering. I will briefly summarize selected relevant works from each of these areas.

Emotion topics studied by psychological anthropologists include cross-cultural variations in the experience and expression of emotion (Briggs, 1970; Edgerton, 1971; Levy, 1973; Myers, 1979; Roseman, 1990; Schieffelin, 1983; Shweder & LeVine, 1984; Wikan, 1990); the cultural constitution of the self (Csordas, 1993; Hallowell, 1955; Marsella, DeVos, & Hsu, 1985; Shweder & Bourne, 1984; Stigler, Shweder, & Herdt, 1990; White & Kirkpatrick, 1985); the socialization of emotion (Clancy, 1986; LeVine, 1990; Ochs & Schieffelin, 1987; Weisner, 1983); linguistic studies of emotion (Beeman, 1985; Lutz, 1988; Ochs & Schieffelin, 1987); cognitive studies

---

[2]For further discussion on this point, see Karno and Jenkins (in press) and Jenkins and Kinzie (in press).

of emotion (D'Andrade, 1987; Holland, 1992; Lakoff & Kovecses, 1987; Lutz, 1982; Mathews, 1992; Solomon, 1984; White & Kirkpatrick, 1985); and theoretical analyses of the emotion construct in Western scientific discourse (Lutz, 1988; Lutz & Abu-Lughod, 1990; Rosaldo, 1984).

Medical and psychiatric anthropologists have provided cultural analyses of dysphoric affects and affective disorders. Studies in this area have been advanced in recent years with the advent of "the new cross-cultural psychiatry" by Kleinman (1977) and "meaning-centered medical anthropology" by Byron Good and Mary-Jo DelVecchio Good and colleagues (1982). Prior to Kleinman's introduction of a revised approach to cross-cultural psychiatric research, the guiding paradigm of universalism and culture as important to the content but not the form or process of psychopathology held sway. This produced a rather static state of academic affairs until the new cross-cultural psychiatry revolutionized the field. Several new anthropological questions have been advanced: (a) To what extent does the course and outcome of psychiatric disorders differ cross culturally? (b) Is there a tacit model in cross-cultural psychiatric research that exaggerates the biological dimensions of disease and deemphasizes the cultural dimensions of illness? (c) What place does translation have in cross-cultural research? (d) Does the standard approach to cross-cultural research in psychiatry commit a category fallacy? (Kleinman, 1987, pp. 448–452). Meaning-centered medical anthropology, introduced by B. Good and Good (1982), has also led the field through an interpretive approach to questions of cultural meaning that invariably constitute illness experience. With regard to the question of cultural translation, for example, B. Good and Good (1988) observed that

> the referents of symbols—i.e., their meaning—are aspects of a culture or a life world, not objects outside of language through which language obtains meaning. "Heart distress" for Iranians is not the equivalent of "heart palpitations" for Americans; it does not *mean* the same thing (cf. B. Good, 1977). It is a symbol which condenses a distinctive set of meanings, a culture-specific semantic network. (p. 14)

Topics in the area of the new cross-cultural psychiatry and meaning-centered medical anthropology are by now vast and include cultural meanings and indigenous definitions of distress and disorder (Gaines & Farmer,

1986; B. Good, 1993; B. Good & Good, 1982; Guarnaccia, Good, & Kleinman, 1990; Jenkins, 1988a, 1988b; Kirmayer, 1989; Low, 1985; Lutz, 1985; Tousignant, 1984); culture-bound "syndromes" (Carr & Vitaliano, 1985; Simons & Hughes, 1985); the cultural validity of *DSM–III–R* categories cross culturally (Gaines, 1992; B. Good, 1992a; B. Good, Good, & Moradi, 1985; Hopper, 1991; Kleinman, 1980, 1986, 1988a; Manson et al., 1985); affective styles and the course of mental disorder (Corin, 1990; Jenkins, 1991a; Jenkins & Karno, 1992; Karno et al., 1987); the epidemiology of affective disorders cross culturally (Beiser, 1985; Guarnaccia et al., 1990; Manson et al., 1985); and critiques of medicalized representations of distress and suffering in Western scientific discourse (Fabrega, 1989; Kleinman, 1988b; Kleinman & Good, 1985; Scheper-Hughes & Lock, 1987).

Another current approach to the study of culture, emotion, and psychopathology is rooted in phenomenological accounts of embodiment (Csordas, 1990, 1993; Frank, 1986; B. Good, 1992b; Kleinman, 1986; Ots, 1990; Scarry, 1985). One aspect of this approach is conceptualization of the body as a generative source of culture (Csordas, 1993). Such approaches move beyond mentalistic and representational studies of culture as located "from the neck up."[3] Often the body is relegated to the role of an object upon which cultural meaning is imposed or "inscribed." Recognizing that meaning presupposes embodiment also means more than that the body is a source domain for image schemas and other mental representations (Lakoff & Kovecses, 1987). It means shifting the conceptualization of culture away from emphasis on symbol, structure, propositions, or schema to emphasis on sense, orientation, gesture, and habit. Foregrounding embodiment in cultural analysis brings out the immediacy of emotion (Scheper-Hughes & Lock, 1987) and problematizes the distinction between subject and object (Csordas, 1990, 1993; Ots, 1990). Another contribution of this literature is to highlight (a) the distinction between body as representation and as being in the world (Csordas, 1990), and (b) the existential ambiguity or indeterminacy underlying categories

---

[3]I owe the characterization of the restricted relevance of culture as primarily "from the neck up" to Csordas (1990, 1993) from his work on culture and embodiment in medical and psychological anthropology.

like intuition, imagination, perception, and sensation in relation to emotion (Csordas, 1993).

A fourth area is the sociopolitical analysis of emotion. Theorizing by B. Good and Good (1988) on culture and emotion has taken a new direction in attempting to account for the force exerted by the nation-state in producing emotional tones, sentiments, and actions within a society. They urge examination of "the role of the state and other political, religious, and economic institutions in legitimizing, organizing, and promoting particular discourses on emotions" (p. 4). Lutz and Abu-Lughod's (1990) analysis of the interplay of emotion talk and the politics of everyday social life has also redirected scholarly attention away from largely privatized and culturalized representations of emotion to examination of emotion discourse in the contexts of sociability and power relations. Kleinman's (1986) case studies from China convincingly demonstrated the social and political production of affective disorders in China. However, analysis of the mental health sequelae of the profound sociopolitical change has scarcely begun (Farias, 1991; Jenkins, 1991b; Mollica, Wyshak, & Lavelle, 1987; Suarez-Orozco, 1989; Swartz, 1991; Westermeyer, 1989).

Emphases on sociopolitical aspects of affectivity expands the parameters of emotion theory beyond those previously conceived as primarily biological, psychological, or cultural. Much of this current thinking is explicitly or implicitly embedded in feminist theory that has long been concerned with power relations and inequities in social worlds, both personal and public (Rosaldo & Lamphere, 1974). Feminist analyses also question the limits of cultural relativism through grounded locational perspectives on human experience and the human condition (Haraway, 1991). The emerging agenda for studies of emotional processes and experience must therefore take political dimensions into account of intentional worlds large and small.

A final area for advancing emotion theory centers around the concept of experience (Hallowell, 1955; Kleinman & Kleinman, 1991; White & Kirkpatrick, 1985; Wikan, 1990). According to Kleinman and Kleinman (1991), experience can be defined as

> an intersubjective medium of social transactions in local moral worlds. It is the outcome of cultural categories and social structures interacting with

psychophysiological processes such that a mediating world is constituted. Experience is the felt flow of that intersubjective medium ... in practical terms, that mediating world is defined by what is vitally at stake for groups and individuals. (p. 277)

The need to focus attention on experiential dimensions of emotion is critical because an understanding of ethnopsychological categories, though important, is insufficient. Kleinman and Kleinman (1991) argued that, in the absence of experientially based accounts of emotion generally, and suffering in particular, social scientific categories (not unlike those from medicine) do not adequately represent (and indeed may seriously distort) human worlds of suffering. This critique can apply to any of an array of prevailing social science concepts that homogenize or romanticize some of the more complex and subtle dimensions of psychocultural worlds. For example, Kleinman and Kleinman critiqued ethnographic characterizations of the self as sociocentric in many non-Western societies as being not fully adequate.[4]

Whereas previous anthropological theory may have been quick to endorse the assumption of the fundamental universality of emotional life in each of the above five areas of inquiry, contemporary approaches are more likely to be concerned with cultural specificity and situatedness. The new emphasis calls into question essentialist[5] claims of basic, universally shared emotions that are based upon innate, uniform, biological processes. Such notions of stratigraphic levels, where "brute, precultural fact" is bedrock have been critiqued by cultural anthropologists (Geertz, 1973). These presumably more fundamental and somehow "pure" biologic realities have long been awarded analytic primacy by many psychologists

---

[4]See Kleinman and Kleinman (1985, 1991) and Kleinman (1986) for illustrative case examples from China following the Cultural Revolution. For individual variability of emotion within cultural contexts, see Edgerton (1971) and Shostak (1983).

[5]Essentialist approaches seek to confirm notions regarding essential, pan-human, underlying human characteristics and processes. A principal problem of essentialist approaches is an empirically unexamined readiness to assume the similarity, regularity, and homogeneity of human phenomena. As such, the appreciation of another order of "inherent" qualities such as diversity, irregularity, and heterogeneity may be sacrificed. Essentialist approaches have been critiqued as reductionistic and overinclusive, imposing order where nonuniform and unpatterned "characterizations" might better suit. Lutz and Abu-Lughod (1990) and Kirmayer (1992) provided excellent discussions of the problems generated by essentialist presumptions.

who endorse natural science paradigms for the study of emotion (Rosaldo, 1984). The psychological research of Plutchik (1980) exemplifies this approach:

> Although there is nothing like a consensus as yet on definitions, psychology may well come up with some system of describing the basic elements of personality—the emotions—that will be the equivalent in impact on behavioral science as Mendeleyev's period table in physics or Linnaeus' system of classifications in biology. (p. 78)

As indicated above, current anthropological views of emotion are not inclined toward natural science models as the most productive means for conceptualizing or investigating the key research questions.

Conceptual Distinctions in Anthropological Studies of Emotion and Psychopathology

We turn our attention now to consideration of two conceptual issues surrounding the distinctions between (a) normal and pathological emotion, and (b) emotion and feeling. These distinctions and their inherent problems are fundamental to current studies of culture, emotion, and psychopathology.

First is the distinction between *normal* and *pathological* emotion: If we consider normal emotions to be those commonly shared within a given community, are abnormal emotions those outside the range of normal human experience within that setting? Are concepts of the normal and the pathological better conceived as discontinuous categories or as poles on a continuum? Are there distinct qualitative differences between a normal emotion and a pathological state? Could a qualitative continuum between happiness and sadness, for instance, be contrasted with clinical mania and depression at the pathological extremes of the continuum? Is abnormality to be defined in quantitative terms as simply "more" of what otherwise might fall within the parameters of normal experience? In the case of the *DSM–III–R* (American Psychiatric Association, 1987), specific symptoms are organized quantitatively according to severity, duration, and co-occurrence with one or more other symptoms that comprise a particular syndrome. According to psychiatric diagnostic procedure, emotions are abnormal if they are severe, are prolonged, and co-occur with other behavioral or cognitive symptoms.

The second conceptual distinction concerns the relationship between feeling and emotion. Thus, although there is a developing consensus among psychologists that even the subjective component of emotion is constructed (Ellsworth, chapter 2, this volume; Frijda & Mesquita, chapter 3, this volume), it is still common to assume that there is some basic and irreducible aspect of emotion. One way in which this problem is manifest is in the distinction between (biologically sensation-based) feeling and (culturally interpreted) emotion. Frijda (1987) has identified what makes physical feelings particularly affective:

> "Elementary feelings" differentiate affective from nonaffective experience in that they presuppose some object the feeling is about. That is, they have the property of subjectivity: They are experienced as one's own subjective response, rather than ascertain a property of the object. They are evaluative: They imply acceptance or nonacceptance of the stimulus or of the experience itself.... They cannot be localized in space; they cannot be objectified, that is, referred to stimulus properties.... They are evanescent when attention is directed upon them. (p. 179)

Thus, both feelings and emotions can be placed under the broad class of affect. The issue here, much contested at the turn of the century by introspectionists, concerns whether feeling should or should not be considered to be a distinct class of experience (Frijda, 1987, pp. 179–180). According to Wundt (1903) and Titchener (1908), feelings are a basic, irreducible kind of mental element that cannot be analyzed in terms of other kinds of mental elements, sensory sensations, and images (and thoughts). If for them feelings were distinct as mental acts, the contemporary distinction tends to construe their nature more as physical in contrast to the mental nature of emotion. The consequences are two: (a) Feelings are understood to be biological, whereas emotions are understood to be cultural; and (b) because they are biological, feelings are understood to be universal and immutable, whereas emotions are understood to be cross-culturally variable. Because they are immutable, feelings are no longer problematic, and attention is devoted to emotion defined as cultural, cognitive, and interpretive. This biologization, universalization, and ultimately exclusion of feeling thus has remained problematic. It may prove to be more productive to collapse this distinction at the outset and to define emotion as necessarily both a physical response *and* a cognitive construction (Rosaldo, 1984).

Cultural Realms of Pangs, Vapors, and Twinges: An Ethnographic Account of *El Calor* (the Heat) Among Salvadorans

I am not convinced that feelings and emotions are neatly separable; nor am I convinced that as a basically irreducible emotion element, feelings are primarily biologically based. Dichotomous presumptions of the cultural as mental and the bodily as biological have deemed the sensate realm of pangs, vapors, and twinges as unimportant to culture theory, considering them instead as largely unelaborated by cultural–linguistic symbols. Recent conceptualizations of the body as a wellspring of culture, experience, and engagement in the world may counterbalance more cognitive approaches to culture that emphasize the study of mental representations (e.g., knowledge, schemes, and discourse) as the centerpiece of culture. When both feelings and emotions are recognized as cultural, their relationship, indeed the very distinction between them, becomes problematic.

Here, we introduce what we found to be an illuminating example from ethnographic–clinical work with Salvadoran women refugees seeking help at an outpatient psychiatric hospital in Cambridge, Massachusetts.[6] The women offer three principal reasons for their flight from El Salvador: escape from large-scale political violence, escape from domestic violence,[7] and escape from impoverished economic conditions (Jenkins, 1991b). At the time of entry into the study, nearly all the women reported symptoms of affective and posttraumatic stress disorders (PTSD). Among a diverse set of culturally specific bodily phenomena reported by the

---

[6]This research was conducted collaboratively with colleague Martha E. Valiente, a clinical psychologist specializing in the treatment of this population. For a fuller description of *el calor* than can be provided here, see Jenkins and Valiente (in press).

[7]Regular, so-termed *domestic* violence and abuse are the bodily experience of many of the Salvadoran women refugees in the study. Indeed, some of them cited escape from abusive husbands and fathers as a principal reason for migrating from El Salvador.

women, *el calor* (the heat) stood out as a particularly salient form of bodily experience. Accounts of personal experience with *el calor* were offered either spontaneously during the course of the interviews or in response to direct queries.[8] Although "heat" has been reported as central to depressive experience in some cultural settings (Ifabumuyi, 1981), heat is not represented in the *DSM* symptom profiles of depression or of PTSD.

El calor is the experience of intense heat that may rapidly spread throughout the entire body. It sometimes emanates from the head (e.g., face, ears, nose, and mouth, including taste and breath), neck, back, leg, stomach, chest, and hands. Such body sites are often described as a focal point of *el calor*. Although *el calor* occurs within one's body, it invades from without. It may be brief (momentary) or prolonged (continuous for days). Although some women narrated experiences of *el calor* as both infrequent and largely insignificant, others' more frequent bouts with it were often described as insufferable. *El calor* was observed among women aged 25–56 years (Jenkins & Valiente, 1994).

What are the relevant criteria for defining the emotions surrounding *el calor* as normal or abnormal? In our view, the wide array of symptomatic distress commonly observed among refugees is arguably a normal human response to abnormal (i.e., pathological) human conditions. This is so because sustained exposure to sociopolitical turmoil in the context of war-related violence or terror is likely to produce such emotional distress in nearly anyone. Such distress is culturally patterned and sociopolitically produced in ways that may have relatively little to do with individually based patterns of response or adaptation (Jenkins & Kinzie, in press).

Emotion words associated with strong experiences of *el calor* include *miedo, temor, susto,* and *preocupaciónes* (fear, dread, fright, and worry); *desesperación* (despair/desperation); *agonía* and *muerte* (agony, death), and *coraje, enojo, enfado* (anger).[9] Tropes for *calor* include similes

---

[8]Thanks to Jeff Jacobson and Maria-Jesus Vega for research assistance in the transcription and data analyses of the interview materials.

[9]Emotion terms in Spanish here are not readily translated into English. The English-language terms with which the Spanish emotion words are juxtaposed can only be considered general glosses, but by no means precise equivalents. As for *song* among the Ifaluk, an emotion that includes both anger and sadness (Lutz, 1988), *calor* is unrecognizable as a primary Euro-American ethnopsychological domain because it incorporates an unfamiliar range of both anger and fear.

and metaphors such as *vapor* (vapor), *corrientes* (electrical currents/ surges), *fuego* (fire), or *llama* (flame). For instance, *un vapor* (a vapor) is a sort of steam heat that may begin in the feet and quickly rise up to the head. Although intense, *el calor* may also have an insubstantial, momentary quality that soon dissipates from the body. Therefore, *un vapor* is a representation of a type of incarnate substance.

Although it is true that *el calor* is a cultural experience for Salvadorans, it is only a partially objectified one. This indeterminacy is evident in the linguistic ambiguity over how best to refer to *el calor*. For example, some women used the term readily, whereas a few claimed no familiarity with it. Nevertheless, those women who did not directly use the term *el calor* typically went on to narrate experiences that are not readily distinguishable from those women who made common mention of it. Some women preferred relatively straightforward descriptions of *el calor*; others shifted freely between metaphor and simile to convey a strong, yet apparently elusive, bodily experience (Jenkins & Valiente, 1994).

Common situations in which *el calor* is experienced include threats to one's physical integrity, such as ongoing civil warfare, impending domestic violence, family conflict, or life-threatening illness. However, aside from these more serious situations, *el calor* also occurs in everyday, mundane circumstances in which no conflict or immediate threat is apparent. Some contexts that evoke this response may be culturally specific (as in situations in which one interprets a particular action as a grave challenge to one's status or security). In other contexts, one might hypothesize that there are cross-culturally similar shared features that evoke the primordial fight or flight response.

How then is *el calor* better conceptualized: as a feeling or as an emotion? We wonder whether this very distinction is predicated on the traditional dualist idea that *the closer we come to the body, the farther away we must be from culture*. With *el calor*, however, we do not have the simple situation of an inchoate feeling that is culturally made over into an emotion by being framed, interpreted, elaborated, and objectified. Rather, we have what might appear to be an intermediate phenomenon, one that is sometimes identified and labeled, but as a feeling rather than as an emotion. Does this mean that it is not yet an emotion? Or does it mean that our distinction between feeling and emotion is overdrawn? Cross-cultural studies of emotion categories frequently demonstrate that the emotional world is carved up differently, with observations of the sort that different emotion concepts do not map directly onto our own. *El calor* is a category of a different order. It is not correct merely to say that it does not directly map onto English-language distinctions between anger and fear. It incorporates these as a bodily metaphor, sometimes blending both, sometimes inarticulate, and sometimes evoking the response "of course I was angry/afraid." From the standpoint of the lexicon of emotion words, the important observation is not that *el calor* fails to distinguish between anger and fear and therefore must be considered to be subemotional. Instead, one can as easily conceive of *el calor* as *meta-emotional*, a concept that merges the physicality of the socially informed body and the mentality of a culturally constituted self, the evanescence of feeling and the communicability of emotion, the intimate relation between anger and fear, and the primordial "fight or flight" response. It is less correct to say that a person felt *el calor* and had the emotion of fear than it is to say that *el calor* is an emotion—a bodily one, yet no less cultural than any other.

To make a general conclusion, I point out the consequence of distinguishing between biological feeling and cultural emotion in the domain of psychopathology. Here, the distinction is nothing less than the condition of possibility for the concept of somatization of emotion. If feelings are somatized emotions or if emotions are psychologized feelings, a conceptual problem exists. But in the debate about psychopathology, it is typically implied that emotions are somehow more pure, and somatized emotions are distorted or masked forms of this pure experience. The distortion or masking connotes pathology in itself—thus feelings are implicitly pathological by nature.

Thus, the conceptual and methodological separation of feeling, emotion, mood, and disorder remains problematic. There can be no neat boundaries among these diverse emotion realms (Kleinman & Good, 1985). Moreover, the problematic nature of distinctions between emotion and illness extends beyond scientific to popular contexts as well. Popular ethnotheories place emotion on a continuum between lesser amounts that are proper, healthy, or normal, and greater degrees of emotion understood as socially or spiritually dangerous and potentially illness-engendering. In Latin American ethnopsychologies, for example, the personal experience of anger or fear, whether caused by intimate or unknown sources,[10] often poses serious dangers to one's health (Jenkins, 1988b, 1991b).

Studies of Emotion and Major Mental Disorder: Schizophrenia and Depression

Both schizophrenia and depression incorporate a wide range of cognitive, behavioral, and affective symptoms. Thus, it seems somewhat arbitrary that schizophrenia is often conceived as a thought disorder and depression as an affective or mood disorder. Both disorders are affectively mediated with regard to culture and to (a) symptomatic expression and (b) the course and outcome of an illness. This section briefly reviews these issues in light of longitudinal evidence from the World Health Organization's (WHO; 1979) International Pilot Study of Schizophrenia (IPSS): Ibadan (Nigeria), Cali (Colombia), Agra (India), Aahras (Denmark), Washington, DC (United States), London (England), Moscow (Russia), Prague (Czechoslovakia), and Taipei (China). Studies of family expressed emotion (Brown, Birley, & Wing, 1972) are also summarized.

Schizophrenia, regarded by contemporary psychiatry as the most biogenetic of disorders, is noteworthy for its considerable heterogeneity of manifestation. Although some of this variation may be biologically produced, the patterned variation in symptoms such as hallucinations, delusions, social withdrawal, and *flat affect* provide powerful cross-cultural evidence of an important role for culture in mediating symptomatic expression. Although any of the symptoms might arguably be considered affective, flat affect is of special interest here. Flat or blunted affect, often thought of as pathognomonic of schizophrenia, has been defined as "a disturbance of affect manifested by dullness of feeling tone" (Freedman, Kaplan, & Sadock, 1976, p. 1280). For example, a common situation in

---

[10]Each of these (intimate or unknown sources) may be perpetrated by means of witchcraft.

which flat affect might be manifest is the failure to express appropriate emotion upon hearing the news of the death of a beloved family member. The clinical belief is that a person with schizophrenia may either fail to register any emotional response or may respond inappropriately (e.g., with laughter).

The WHO IPSS symptom profiles reveal that patients from the more industrialized research sites (Moscow, Aarhus, Taipei, and Prague) were more likely to have been rated positively for flat affect. In addition, a wide range of flat affect was found for the IPSS sample: 8% in Ibadan as compared with 50% in Moscow (WHO, 1979).[11] On the other hand, the average percentage of flat affect across all research centers was only 24%, a figure that might be considered low for a symptom often touted as pathognomonic for schizophrenia (Bleuler, 1950).

In light of the above general review on the relationship between culture and emotion, it is to be expected that what constitutes flat or inappropriate affect in Society A cannot be considered directly equivalent to that observed in Society B or C. Given this observation, it is troubling that the IPSS investigators neglected to report on the cross-cultural validity of their comparative assessments.[12] This problem is made all the more salient in light of the overall low frequency of flat affect and the concomitant finding that it was the second most common symptom observed at follow-up.[13]

---

[11]The differences between the nonindustrialized and the more industrialized countries are not uniform, however; only 9% of London patients and 11% of Washington patients displayed flat affect at follow-up.

[12]Apart from the cultural issues surrounding the display of affect across different settings, a different point concerns the fact that surface displays of flat or inappropriate affect may belie an underlying and everyday "sustained terror" commonly reported by persons who experience schizophrenic states (Glass, 1989).

[13]The rating of "lack of insight" as the most common symptom may represent a clash between professional psychiatric formulations of the problem (in cultural categories that feature psychiatric, nervous, or mental problems) and popular illness categories that may conceptualize the problem more broadly to include spiritual or supernatural, socioeconomic, or nonindividualized understandings. Another major difference is a tendency among persons of little formal education not to "psychologize" illness but rather to experience and express their illness in culturally elaborated bodily terms (e.g., physical sensations, total body experience). In this regard, the IPSS failure to appreciate these cross-cultural differences anthropologically in what Kleinman (1980) termed "explanatory models" has likely resulted in an ethnocentric representation of the most frequently reported symptom in the IPSS follow-up data.

An issue that has yet to receive adequate attention concerns the contribution of individual symptoms to course and outcome. According to the IPSS (WHO, 1979), different symptoms predict different outcomes across the various research centers. These findings appear to provide strong evidence for the contextual specificity of particular sociocultural and clinical features that mediate the course of schizophrenia cross culturally. The Western prognostic expectation is that affective symptoms are associated with a good outcome and flatness of affect with a poor outcome. This general expectation is not uniformly endorsed by the IPSS findings: only in Agra, Ibadan, and Moscow was flat affect among the five best predictor variables. This leaves much of the sample outside the reach of standard clinical expectation concerning the prognostic associations for flat affect.

Two-year follow-up data from the WHO IPSS on 1,202 patients from nine nations provide the basis for the well-known conclusion that "on virtually all course and outcome measures, a greater proportion of schizophrenic patients in Agra (India), Cali (Colombia), and Ibadan (Nigeria) had favorable, nondisabling courses and outcomes than was the case in Aarhus, London, Moscow, Prague, and Washington" (Sartorius, Japlensky, & Shapiro, 1978, p. 106). The better outcome for schizophrenia in developing countries relative to the more industrialized nations led the IPSS to conclude that "one could consider the social or cultural environment as the possible key to understanding the observed differences in course and outcome between developing and developed countries" (Sartorius et al., 1978, p. 111). In particular, the IPSS investigators hypothesized that family and community response to the illness may provide a central link among culture, emotion, and the course of schizophrenia.

Emotions expressed by family members toward an ill relative have been found to be significant to the course and outcome of schizophrenia. Indeed, substantial evidence from the *expressed emotion* psychiatric research paradigm has established that the course of schizophrenia varies in relation to kin affective response (Brown et al., 1972; Karno & Jenkins, in press; Karno et al., 1987; Vaughn & Leff, 1976; Vaughn, Snyder, Jones, Freeman, & Falloon, 1984). Hypotheses for why this is so have generally focused on a pronounced sensitivity (or extra-sensitivity) and responsiveness to the social–affective environment (Vaughn & Leff, 1976). Although both positive (e.g., warmth) and negative (e.g., hostility) emotions have been investigated, several studies have been replicated that identify three affective responses with a poor course of illness: anger and hostility (expressed though criticism) and emotional overinvolvement (expressed in unusually self-sacrificing, overprotective, or intrusive behaviors on the part of close relatives).[14]

Theoretical issues surrounding the expressed emotion research require further attention. These include questions on the nature and meaning of the construct and its cultural validity for use in comparative research. A cross-culturally informed review of expressed emotion studies was provided by Jenkins (1991a) and Jenkins and Karno (1992). As Jenkins and Karno (1992) argued, the fact that the expressed emotion factors are substantially cultural in nature has yet to be fully appreciated. Although these authors have provided an outline of diverse cultural, psychobiological, and social–ecological features of expressed emotion, they argue that the expressed emotion construct is tapping primarily into cross-culturally variable features of family response to an ill relative. Specifically, the cross-cultural variance occurs in relation to differences in those features tapped by the expressed emotion index: (a) cultural interpretations of the nature of the problem (i.e., relatives' interpretations of the problem with regard to its cause, nature, and course, such as laziness caused by illicit drug use if the patient called upon personal reserves of willpower); (b) cultural meanings of kin relations (culturally prescribed definitions of family life and kin ties); (c) identification of cultural rule violations; (d) vocabularies of emotion (culturally salient emotions); (e) relatives' personality traits or dispositions; (f) degrees and kinds of patients' psychopathology; (g) family interaction dynamics; (h) attempts to socially control a deviant relative; (i) availability and quality of social supports; and (j) historical and political economic factors (Jenkins & Karno, 1992, p. 17).

---

[14]Although affects of warmth and praise are undoubtedly important to many qualitative dimensions of family life, these have yet to be significantly predictive of recovery from major mental disorder. The relationship among criticism, hostility, and emotional overinvolvement has also been found for depressive illness, at even lower thresholds than for schizophrenia (Hooley, Orley, & Teasedale, 1986; Vaughn & Leff, 1976).

Several summary points can be made on the relationship between culture and emotional response to schizophrenic illness: (a) there is considerable cross-cultural variability in social response (e.g., tolerance, support, hostility); (b) variations in emotional response partially account for differential illness outcomes cross culturally; and (c) cultural conceptions of the problem (construed, for example, as witchcraft, *nervios* [nerves], laziness, or schizophrenia) mediate the nature of relatives' emotional response (Jenkins, 1988a, 1988b, 1991a). For example, some conceptions confer a culturally legitimate status that may preclude high levels of personally directed criticism or emotional overinvolvement. Among Mexican-descent families in the United States, the concept of *nervios* serves as a cultural category for schizophrenic illness among the majority of relatives. Because severe cases of *nervios* are not believed to be within a person's control, the afflicted person is deserving of sympathy and tolerance:

> The complex of cultural notions including sadness, *nervios*, and tolerance provides the cultural logic in terms of which Mexican–American families adapt to the illness through sympathetic inclusion . . . the families in this study did not adopt the much more severely stigmatizing label for "craziness," *loco*. As a *loco*, the individual is considered to be completely out of control, with virtually no chance of recovery. (Jenkins, 1988b, pp. 321–322)

Thus, emotion can mediate conceptions of illness that may, in turn, be important to the course of schizophrenic disorders.

The most comprehensive anthropological source on depressive disorders is an edited collection by Kleinman and Good (1985), *Culture and Depression: Studies in the Anthropology and Cross-Cultural Psychiatry of Affect and Disorder*. This volume addresses fundamental issues concerning the cultural mediation of affect and affective disorders, depressive cognition and communication, and epidemiological approaches in psychiatric anthropology. This interdisciplinary treatment has contributed to the task of refining the key theoretical issues and empirical study of culture and depression.

When viewed in world perspective, depression is more often symptomatically expressed in somatic than in psychological terms (Kleinman,

1986, 1988a). This observation is highly significant in several regards. First, the fact that depression is often experienced and expressed through an array of bodily complaints (e.g., "my back aches") rather than psychological complaints (e.g., "I feel blue") calls into question the cross-cultural validity of depressed mood or loss of pleasure as universal criterial symptoms of the disorder. Cultural tendencies toward psychologization versus somatization have been more fully reviewed elsewhere (Kirmayer, 1984, 1989; Kleinman, 1986; Kleinman & Kleinman, 1985; Ots, 1990). As summarized by the leading theorist in this area, Kleinman (1986) explained that

> individuals experience serious personal and social problems but interpret and articulate them, and indeed come to experience and respond to them, through the medium of the body. . . . High rates of somatization in depressive disorder, for example, have been found [in numerous cross-cultural studies]. . . . The research literature indicates that depression and most other mental illnesses, especially in non-Western societies and among rural, ethnic, and lower-class groups in the West, are associated preponderantly with physical complaints. (pp. 51–52)

This cross-cultural view of somatic versus psychological symptomatic expression of depression provides the basis for a critical appraisal of dichotomous mind–body approaches to psychological and somatic manifestations of depression. The current *DSM–III–R* defines depression as necessarily a mood disorder with associated somatic symptoms and therefore presupposed a dichotomous mind–body approach to psychological and somatic manifestations of depression. Jenkins et al., (1991) have argued that "insofar as this dichotomous approach distinguishes psyche and soma, it reproduces assumptions of Western thought and culture, [but] must from the outset be suspended in formulating a valid comparative stance. (p. 67)" Thus, an important cross-cultural question is whether the psychiatric construct of depression can validly include both somatic and psychologized forms of depressive suffering or whether these are really distinct kinds of illnesses.

Somatized versus psychologized expressions of dysphoric or depressive affect more generally suggest differences in cultural styles of sadness, demoralization, suffering, and so forth (Kleinman & Kleinman, 1991). Cultural styles of dysphoria are best understood as elements of indigenous or ethnopsychological models of affect (Lutz, 1988; White & Kirkpatrick, 1985). An understanding of ethnopsychological models of depressive-related affects is essential to cultural studies of depression (Kleinman & Good, 1985). Cultural knowledge of ethnopsychological models is important to specification of the normative bounds of everyday depressive affects, on the one hand, and more serious, extraordinary states that might ethnopsychologically be considered constitutive of a type of depressive illness, on the other.

Several other sets of sociocultural factors must also be taken into account in cross-cultural studies of depression. Jenkins et al., (1991) have provided a critical review of the varying roles of diverse sociocultural factors in the production of and recovery from depressive illness. Principal among these are socially inculcated gender differences in susceptibility to depression, documented in an overwhelming number of Western and non-Western studies. Lower socioeconomic status has commonly been found to be associated with symptoms of depression, and a growing body of research suggests that adverse life events and conditions may partially underlie the broad-based conclusions regarding social class and vulnerability to depression (Brown & Harris, 1978). Migrant status (immigrant or refugee) and social change have also commonly been found to be associated with major depressive illness (Farias, 1991; Jenkins, 1991b; Kinzie, Frederickson, Rath, Fleck, & Karls, 1984; Mollica et al., 1987; Westermeyer, 1988, 1989). Also relevant are cultural variations in family factors such as composition and organization, socialization practices, family histories of depression, marital discord, and expressed emotion (reviewed above for schizophrenia; see also Hooley et al., 1986; Vaughn & Leff, 1976). Review of these foregoing factors leads to the conclusion that "culture is of profound importance to the experience of depression, the construction of meaning and social response to depressive illness within families and communities, the course and outcome of the disorder, and thus to the very constitution of depressive illness" (Jenkins et al., 1991, p. 68).

Conclusion

I have summarized current anthropological approaches to culture, emotion, and psychopathology as falling within five interrelated domains of study. These include psychological anthropological studies of emotion and self, medical anthropological studies of dysphoric affects and affective disorders, phenomenological accounts of the body as a generative source of culture, sociopolitical analyses of emotion, and experiential accounts of dysphoria and suffering. All of these areas are critical fields of study from which arise key questions concerning the relations among culture, emotion, and psychopathology. There is a short supply of emotion studies based on intersubjective dimensions of culture and experience as a complement to studies of emotion based on lexicon, discourse, ethnopsychological category, and expression. In addition, the anthropological and psychological literature has typically failed to integrate experiential, sociocultural, and political dimensions of sentiment. A methodological limitation of emotion studies has been the disproportionate reliance on verbal (and nonverbal) communication.

Cultural approaches to the study of emotion and psychopathology have proliferated in recent years. Nevertheless, we have yet to see the full development of what could be considered affective anthropology or affective psychology. Along with Western traditional views of the superiority of mind over body, there is currently a strong bias toward cognitive science. Although cognitive anthropology has made a powerful scientific contribution to the anthropological endeavor, relatively little psychological and anthropological attention has been directed toward the full range of emotion phenomena and can productively be addressed in future studies.

References

Abu-Lughod, L. (1986). *Veiled sentiments: Honor and poetry in a Bedouin society.* Berkeley and Los Angeles: University of California Press.

Abu-Lughod, L., & Lutz, C. (1990). Introduction: Emotion, discourse, and the politics of everyday life. In L. Abu-Lughod & C. Lutz (Eds.), *Language and the politics of emotion* (pp. 1–23). Cambridge, England: Cambridge University Press.

American Psychiatric Association. (1987). *Diagnostic and statistical manual of mental disorders* (3rd ed., rev.). Washington, DC: Author.

Bateson, G. (1958). *Naven.* Stanford, CA: Stanford University Press.

Beeman, W. O. (1985). Dimensions of dysphoria: The view from linguistic anthropology. In A. Kleinman & B. Good (Eds.), *Culture and depression: Studies in the anthropology and cross-cultural psychiatry of affect and disorder* (pp. 216–243). Berkeley: University of California Press.

Beiser, M. (1985). A study of depression among traditional Africans, urban North Americans, and Southeast Asian refugees. In A. Kleinman & B. Good (Eds.), *Culture and depression: Studies in the anthropology and cross-cultural psychiatry of affect and disorder* (pp. 272–298). Berkeley: University of California Press.

Benedict, R. (1934). *Patterns of culture.* New York: Penguin Books.

Bleuler, E. (1950). *Dementia praecox or the group of schizophrenias* (J. Zinkin, Trans.). Madison, CT: International Universities Press.

Briggs, J. (1970). *Never in anger: Portrait of an Eskimo family.* Cambridge, MA: Harvard University Press.

Brown, G., Birley, J. L. T., & Wing, J. (1972). Influence of family life on the course of schizophrenic disorders: A replication. *British Journal of Psychiatry, 121,* 241–258.

Brown, G., & Harris, T. (1978). *Social origins of depression: A study of psychiatric disorder in women.* London: Tavistock.

Carr, J. E., & Vitaliano, P. P. (1985). The theoretical implications of converging research on depression and the culture-bound syndromes. In A. Kleinman & B. Good (Eds.), *Culture and depression: Studies in the anthropology and cross-cultural psychiatry of affect and disorder* (pp. 244–266). Berkeley: University of California Press.

Clancy, P. (1986). The acquisition of communicative style in Japanese. In E. Ochs & B. Schieffelin (Eds.), *Language socialization across cultures* (pp. 213–250). Cambridge, England: Cambridge University Press.

Corin, E. (1990). Facts and meaning in psychiatry: An anthropological approach to the lifeworld of schizophrenics. *Culture, Medicine, and Psychiatry, 14,* 153–188.

Csordas, T. J. (1990). The 1988 Stirling Award Essay: Embodiment as a paradigm for anthropology. *Ethos, 18,* 5–47.

Csordas, T. J. (1993). *The sacred self: Cultural phenomenology of a charismatic world.* Berkeley: University of California Press.

D'Andrade, R. (1987). A folk model of the mind. In D. Holland & N. Quinn (Eds.), *Cultural models in language and thought* (pp. 112–150). Cambridge, England: Cambridge University Press.

Desjarlais, R. (1992). *Body and emotion: The aesthetics of illness and healing in the Nepal Himalayas.* Philadelphia: University of Pennsylvania Press.

Edgerton, R. B. (1971). *The individual in cultural adaptation: A study of four East African peoples.* Berkeley: University of California Press.

Edgerton, R. B. (1985). *Rules, exceptions, and social order*. Berkeley: University of California Press.

Edgerton, R. B. (1992). *Sick societies: Challenging the myth of primitive harmony*. New York: Free Press.

Fabrega, H. (1989). Cultural relativism and psychiatric illness. *Journal of Nervous and Mental Disease, 177*, 415–430.

Farias, P. (1991). The socio-political dimensions of trauma in Salvadoran refugees: Analysis of a clinical sample. *Culture, Medicine, and Psychiatry, 15*, 167–192.

Frank, G. (1986). On embodiment: A case study of congenital limb deficiency in American culture. *Culture, Medicine, and Psychiatry, 10*, 189–219.

Freedman, A., Kaplan, H., & Sadock, B. (1976). *Modern synopsis of comprehensive psychiatry* (Vol. 2). Baltimore, MD: Waverly Press.

Frijda, N. (1987). *The emotions*. Cambridge, England: Cambridge University Press.

Gaines, A. (1992). From DSM–I to II–R: Voices of self, mastery and the other: A cultural constructivist reading of a U.S. psychiatric classification. *Social Science and Medicine, 35*(1), 3–24.

Gaines, A., & Farmer, P. (1986). Visible saints: Social cynosures and dysphoria in the Mediterranean tradition. *Culture, Medicine, and Psychiatry, 10*, 295–330.

Geertz, C. (1973). *The interpretations of cultures*. New York: Basic Books.

Glass, J. (1989). *Private terror, public life: Psychosis and the politics of community*. Ithaca, NY: Cornell University Press.

Good, B. (1977). The heart of what's the matter: The semantics of illness in Iran. *Culture, Medicine, and Psychiatry, 1*, 25–58.

Good, B. (1992a). Culture and psychopathology: Directions for psychiatric anthropology. In T. Schwartz, G. White, & C. Lutz (Eds.), *New directions for psychological anthropology* (pp. 181–205). Cambridge, England: Cambridge University Press.

Good, B. (1992b). A body in pain: The making of a world of chronic pain. In M.-J. DelVecchio Good, P. Brodwin, B. Good, & A. Kleinman (Eds.), *Pain as human experience: An anthropological perspective* (pp. 1–28). Berkeley: University of California Press.

Good, B. (1993). *Medicine, rationality, and experience: An anthropological perspective*. Cambridge, England: Cambridge University Press.

Good, B., & Good, M-J. DelVecchio. (1982). Toward a meaning-centered analysis of popular illness categories: "Fright illness" and "heart distress" in Iran. In A. J. Marsella & G. White (Eds.), *Cultural conceptions of mental health and therapy* (pp. 141–166). Boston: D. Reidel.

Good, B., & Good, M.-J. DelVecchio, (1988). Ritual, the state and the transformation of emotional discourse in Iranian society. *Culture, Medicine, and Psychiatry, 12*, 43–63.

Good, B., Good, M.-J. DelVecchio, & Moradi, R. (1985). The interpretation of Iranian depressive illness and dysphoric affect. In A. Kleinman & B. Good (Eds.), *Culture and depression: Studies in the anthropology and cross-cultural psychiatry of affect and disorder* (pp. 369–428). Berkeley: University of California Press.

Guarnaccia, P., Good, B., & Kleinman, A. (1990). A critical review of epidemiological studies of Puerto Rican mental health. *American Journal of Psychiatry, 147,* 1449-1456.

Hallowell, A. I. (1955). The self in its behavioral environment. In A. I. Hallowell (Ed.), *Culture and experience* (pp. 75–111). Philadelphia: University of Pennsylvania Press.

Haraway, D. (1991). *Simians, cyborgs, and women: The reinvention of nature.* New York: Routledge, Chapman, & Hall.

Hollan, D. (1988). Staying "cool" in Toraja: Informal strategies of the management of anger and hostility in a nonviolent society. *Ethos, 16,* 52–72.

Holland, D. (1992). How cultural systems become desire: A case study of American romance. In R. D'Andrade & C. Strauss (Eds.), *Human motives and cultural models* (pp. 61–89). Cambridge, England: Cambridge University Press.

Hooley, J., Orley, J., & Teasedale, J. D. (1986). Levels of expressed emotion and relapse in depressed patients. *British Journal of Psychiatry, 148,* 642–647.

Hopper, K. (1991). Some old questions for the new cross-cultural psychiatry. *Medical Anthropology Quarterly, 5,* 299–330.

Ifabumuyi, O. I. (1981). The dynamics of central heat in depression. *Psychopathologie Africaine, 17,* 127–133.

Jenkins, J. H. (1988a). Conceptions of schizophrenic illness as a problem of nerves: A comparative analysis of Mexican–Americans and Anglo–Americans. *Social Science and Medicine, 26,* 1233–1243.

Jenkins, J. H. (1988b). Ethnopsychiatric interpretations of schizophrenic illness: The problem of *nervios* within Mexican–American families. *Culture, Medicine, and Psychiatry, 12,* 303–331.

Jenkins, J. H. (1991a). The 1990 Stirling Award Essay: Anthropology, expressed emotion, and schizophrenia. *Ethos, 19,* 387–431.

Jenkins, J. H. (1991b). The state construction of affect: Political ethos and mental health among Salvadoran refugees. *Culture, Medicine, and Psychiatry, 15,* 139–165.

Jenkins, J. H., & Karno, M. (1992). The meaning of "expressed emotion": Theoretical issues raised by cross-cultural research. *American Journal of Psychiatry, 149,* 9–21.

Jenkins, J. H., & Kinzie, D. (in press). Adjustment disorders. In J. E. Mezzich, A. Kleinman, H. Fabrega, B. Good, G. Johnson-Powell, Keh-Ming sin, & S. Marson (Eds.), *Cultural considerations for DSM-IV: A sourcebook.* NIMH-Sponsored Task Force on Cultural Considerations for *Diagnostic and Statistical Manual–IV.* Washington, DC: American Psychiatric Association.

Jenkins, J. H., Kleinman, A., & Good, B. J. (1991). Cross-cultural aspects of depression. In J. Becker & A. Kleinman (Eds.), *Advances in affective disorders: Theory and research: Vol. 1. Psychosocial aspects* (pp. 67–100). Hillsdale, NJ: Erlbaum.

Jenkins, J. H., & Valiente, M. (1994). Bodily transactions of the passions: *El calor* among Salvadoran women refugees. In T. J. Csordas (Ed.), *Embodiement and experience.* Cambridge, England: Cambridge University Press.

Karno, M., & Jenkins, J. H. (in press). Schizophrenia and related disorders. In J. E. Mezzich, A. Kleinman, H. Fabrega, B. Good, G. Johnson-Powell, Keh-Ming Sin, & S. Marson (Eds.), *Cultural considerations for DSM-IV: A sourcebook.* NIMH-Sponsored Task Force on Cultural Considerations for *Diagnostic and Statistical Manual–IV.* Washington, DC: American Psychiatric Association.

Karno, M., Jenkins, J. H., de la Selva, A., Santana, F., Telles, C., Lopez, S., & Mintz, J. (1987). Expressed emotion and schizophrenic outcome among Mexican–American families. *Journal of Nervous and Mental Disease, 175,* 143–151.

Kinzie, D., Frederickson, R., Rath, B., Fleck, J., & Karls, W. (1984). Posttraumatic stress disorder among survivors of Cambodian in concentration camps. *American Journal of Psychiatry, 141,* 645–650.

Kirmayer, L. (1984). Culture, affect and somatization (Parts 1 and 2). *Transcultural Psychiatric Research Review, 21,* 159–162.

Kirmayer, L. (1989). Cultural variations in the response to psychiatric disorders and emotional distress. *Social Science and Medicine, 29,* 327–339.

Kirmayer, L. (1992). The body's insistence on meaning. *Medical Anthropology Quarterly, 6,* 323–346.

Kleinman, A. (1977). Depression, somatization and the new cross-cultural psychiatry. *Social Science and Medicine, 11,* 3–10.

Kleinman, A. (1980). *Patients and healers in the context of culture: An exploration on the borderland between anthropology, medicine, and psychiatry.* Berkeley: University of California Press.

Kleinman, A. (1986). *Social origins of distress and disease. Depression, neurasthenia, and pain in modern China.* New Haven, CT: Yale University Press.

Kleinman, A. (1987). Anthropology and psychiatry: The role of culture in cross-cultural research on illness. *British Journal of Psychiatry, 151,* 447–454.

Kleinman, A. (1988a). *Rethinking psychiatry.* New York: Free Press.

Kleinman, A. (1988b). *The illness narratives: Suffering, healing and the human condition.* New York: Basic Books.

Kleinman, A., & Good, B. J. (Eds.). (1985). *Culture and depression: Studies in the anthropology and cross-cultural psychiatry of affect and disorder.* Berkeley: University of California Press.

Kleinman, A., & Kleinman, J. (1985). Somatization: The interconnections in Chinese society among culture, depressive experiences, and meanings of pain. In A. Kleinman & B. J. Good (Eds.), *Culture and depression: Studies in the anthropology and cross-cultural psychiatry of affect and disorder* (pp. 429–490). Berkeley: University of California Press.

Kleinman, A., & Kleinman, J. (1991). Suffering and its professional transformation: Toward an ethnography of interpersonal experience. *Culture, Medicine, and Psychiatry, 15*, 275–301.

Lakoff, G., & Kovecses, Z. (1987). The cognitive model of anger inherent in American English. In D. Holland & N. Quinn (Eds.), *Cultural models in language and thought* (pp. 195–221). Cambridge, England: Cambridge University Press.

LeVine, R. A. (1990). Infant environments in psychoanalysis: A cross-cultural view. In J. Stigler, R. A. Shweder, & G. Herdt (Eds.), *Cultural psychology: Essays on comparative human development* (pp. 454–474). Cambridge, England: Cambridge University Press.

Levy, R. (1973). *Tahitians: Mind and experience in the Society Islands.* Chicago: University of Chicago Press.

Low, S. (1985). Culturally interpreted symptoms of culture-bound syndromes: A cross-cultural review of nerves. *Social Science and Medicine, 22*, 187–196.

Lutz, C. (1982). The domain of emotion words on Ifaluk. *American Ethnologist, 9*, 113–128.

Lutz, C. (1985). Depression and the translation of emotional worlds. In A. Kleinman & B. Good (Eds.), *Culture and depression: Studies in the anthropology and cross-cultural psychiatry of affect and disorder* (pp. 63–100). Berkeley: University of California Press.

Lutz, C. (1988). *Unnatural emotions: Everyday sentiments on a Micronesian atoll and their challenge to Western theory.* Chicago: University of Chicago Press.

Lutz, C., & Abu-Lughod, L. (Eds.). (1990). *Language and the politics of emotion.* Cambridge, England: Cambridge University Press.

Lutz, C., & White, G. (1986). The anthropology of emotions. *Annual Review of Anthropology, 15*, 405–436.

Manson, S., Shore, J., & Bloom, J. (1985). The depressive experience in American Indian communities: A challenge for psychiatric theory and diagnosis. In A. Kleinman & B. Good (Eds.), *Culture and depression: Studies in the anthropology and cross-cultural psychiatry of affect and disorder* (pp. 361–368). Berkeley: University of California Press.

Marsella, A., DeVos, G., & Hsu, F. (Eds.). (1985). *Culture and self: Asian and Western perspectives.* New York: Tavistock.

Mathews, H. (1992). The directive force of morality tales in a Mexican community. In R. D'Andrade & C. Strauss (Eds.), *Human motives and cultural models* (pp. 127–162). Cambridge, England: Cambridge University Press.

Mead, M. (1935). *Sex and temperament in three primitive societies.* New York: William Morrow & Mentor.

Mollica, R., Wyshak, G., & Lavelle, J. (1987). The psychosocial impact of war trauma and torture on southeast Asian refugees. *American Journal of Psychiatry, 144*, 1567–1572.

Myers, F. (1979). Emotions and the self: A theory of personhood and political order among Pintupi Aborigines. *Ethos, 7*, 343–370.

Ochs, E., & Schieffelin, B. (Eds.). (1987). *Language socialization across cultures.* Cambridge, England: Cambridge University Press.

Ots, T. (1990). The angry liver, the anxious heart and the melancholy spleen. *Culture, Medicine, and Psychiatry, 14*, 21–58.

Plutchik, R. (1980, September). A language for the emotions. *Psychology Today*, pp. 68–78.

Rosaldo, M. Z. (1980). *Knowledge and passion: Ilongot notions of self and social life.* Cambridge, England: Cambridge University Press.

Rosaldo, M. Z. (1984). Toward an anthropology of self and feeling. In R. A. Shweder & R. A. LeVine (Eds.), *Culture theory: Essays on mind, self, and emotion* (pp. 137–157). Cambridge, England: Cambridge University Press.

Rosaldo, M. Z., & Lamphere, L. (Eds.). (1974). *Woman, culture, and society.* Stanford, CA: Stanford University Press.

Roseman, M. (1990). Head, heart, odor and shadow: The structure of the self, the emotional world, and ritual performance among Senoi Temiar. *Ethos, 18*, 227–250.

Sartorius, N., Japlensky, A., & Shapiro, R. (1978). Cross-cultural differences in the short-term prognosis of schizophrenic psychosis. *Schizophrenia Bulletin, 4*, 102–113.

Scarry, E. (1985). *The body in pain: The making and unmaking of the world.* New York: Oxford University Press.

Scheper-Hughes, N., & Lock, M. (1987). The mindful body: A prolegomenon to future work in medical anthropology. *Medical Anthropology Quarterly, 1*, 6–41.

Schieffelin, E. (1983). Anger and shame in the tropical forest: On affect as a cultural system in Papua New Guinea. *Ethos, 11*, 181–191.

Shostak, M. (1983). *Nisa: The life and words of !Kung woman.* New York: Vintage Books.

Shweder, R. A., & Bourne, E. (1984). Does the concept of the person vary cross-culturally? In R. A. Shweder & R. A. LeVine (Eds.), *Culture theory: Essays on mind, self, and emotion* (pp. 158–199). Cambridge, England: Cambridge University Press.

Shweder, R. A., & LeVine, R. A. (Eds.). (1984). *Culture theory: Essays on mind, self, and emotion.* Cambridge, England: Cambridge University Press.

Simons, R., & Hughes, C. (Eds.). (1985). *The culture-bound syndromes: Folk illnesses of psychiatric and anthropological interest.* Boston: D. Reidel.

Solomon, R. (1984). Getting angry: The Jamesian theory of emotion in anthropology. In R. A. Shweder & R. A. LeVine (Eds.), *Culture theory: Essays on mind, self, and emotion* (pp. 238–254). Cambridge, England: Cambridge University Press.

Stigler, J., Shweder, R. A., & Herdt, G. (Eds.). (1990). *Cultural psychology: Essays on comparative human development.* Cambridge, England: Cambridge University Press.

Suarez-Orozco, M. (1989). Speaking of the unspeakable: Toward psychosocial understanding of responses to terror. *Ethos, 18*, 353–383.

Swartz, L. (1991). The politics of Black patients' identity: Ward-rounds on the "Black side" of a South African psychiatric hospital. *Culture, Medicine, and Psychiatry,* 217–244.

Titchener, E. B. (1908). *Lectures on the elementary psychology of feeling and attention.* New York: Macmillan.

Tousignant, M. (1984). *Pena* in the Ecuadorian Sierra: A psychoanthropological analysis of sadness. *Culture, Medicine, and Psychiatry, 8,* 381-398.

Vaughn, C., & Leff, J. (1976). The influence of family and social factors on the course of psychiatric illness. *British Journal of Psychiatry, 129,* 125–137.

Vaughn, C., Snyder, K., Jones, S., Freeman, W., & Falloon, I. H. R. (1984). Family factors in schizophrenic relapse: A California replication of the British research on expressed emotion. *Archives of General Psychiatry, 41,* 1169–1177.

Weisner, T. (1983). Putting family ideals into practice: Pronaturalism in conventional and nonconventional California families. *Ethos, 11,* 278–304.

Wellenkamp, J. (1988). Notions of grief and catharsis among the Toraja. *American Ethnologist, 15,* 486–500.

Westermeyer, J. (1988). *DSM-III* psychiatric disorders among Hmong refugees in the United States: A point prevalence study. *American Journal of Psychiatry, 145,* 197–202.

Westermeyer, J. (1989). *Psychiatric care of migrants: A clinical guide.* Washington, DC: American Psychiatric Association.

White, G., & Kirkpatrick, J. (Eds.). (1985). *Person, self, and experience: Exploring Pacific ethnopsychologies.* Berkeley: University of California Press.

White, G., & Lutz, C. (1992). Introduction. In T. Schwartz, G. White, & C. Lutz (Eds.), *New directions for psychological anthropology* (pp. 1–20). Cambridge, England: Cambridge University Press.

Wikan, U. (1990). *Managing turbulent hearts: A Balinese formula for living.* Chicago: University of Chicago Press.

World Health Organization. (1979). *Schizophrenia: An international followup study.* New York: Wiley.

Wundt, W. (1903). *Grundriss der Psychologie* [Compendium of psychology]. Stuttgart, Germany: Engelmann.

Conclusion

CHAPTER 11

The Cultural Shaping of Emotion: A Conceptual Framework

Hazel Rose Markus and Shinobu Kitayama

I n the initial chapter, we set out three far-reaching goals for this volume: (a) to outline the ways in which cultural processes organize emotional processes and emotional experience; (b) to outline the ways in which emotional processes and emotional experience foster and enhance sociocultural processes; and (c) to integrate cross-cultural descriptions of emotion within contemporary theories of human emotions. At its close, we believe that we can see some progress in all of these goals.

As a working definition, most authors here would probably not object to Rosaldo's (1984) definition quoted by Jenkins (chapter 10, this volume), which asserts that emotions are "self-concerning, partly physical responses that are at the same time aspects of a moral or ideological attitude; emotions are both feelings and cognitive constructions, linking, person, action, and sociological milieu (p. 304)." Building on this view, we suggested in the introductory chapter that emotions can be viewed as a set of socially shared scripts composed of various processes—physiological, subjective, and behavioral—that develop as individuals actively (personally and collectively) adapt and adjust to their immediate socio-cultural, semiotic environment. Emotions allow and foster this adaptation and they result from it (chapter 1, this volume, p. 5). With regard to culture, those contributors who directly discuss its definition converge on a view of culture as a distribution of both collective and individual meanings and their supporting practices.

From this currently emerging view of emotion and culture, emotions are not *just* private properties of the heart and mind, not *just* consequences of individual attempts to make meaning and adapt to their specific environments (although they certainly are this, as Ellsworth, Frijda and Mesquita, and Posner, Rothbart, and Harman lucidly instruct). Expanding the scope of focus, we can see that the physiological and neurochemical patterns that accompany private feelings can also be construed as the bodily elements of habitual tendencies of subjective emotional experience and expression, and that these habitual tendencies are themselves part of the vast repertoire of individual and collective social practices that make up a culture.

In the course of our conceptual efforts to join emotion and culture, we and many of the other authors in this book are questioning a set of commonly held distinctions. These include a distinction between the individual and the collective; a distinction between culture as "ideas and ideals" and culture as "practices and institutions"; and a distinction between emotions as physiologic, cognitive and affective states and emotions as social products and experiences. The question of why individuals experience particular feeling states has a variety of answers: physiological, cognitive, and sociocultural. One can see throughout this volume an explicit acceptance of this notion. Most of the authors reveal an effort to elaborate certain aspects of the construction and functioning of emotion without prematurely privileging their own realm of concern as the core or the really "real."

For the purpose of drawing together and integrating some of the theoretical assumptions and empirical findings from this cultural perspective, we have developed a framework (see Figure 1) to illustrate some of the processes and mechanisms involved in the cultural shaping of emotion. Here, we have attempted to diagram in a series of telescoping realities the interdependence between the seemingly external, public, political, and corporate, and individual reality and the seemingly internal, personal, private, and corporeal reality. What we were working to achieve here, as are many other cultural psychologists and psychological anthropologists (Corsaro & Miller, 1992; Holland & Valsiner, 1988; Schwartz, White, & Lutz, 1993; Sperber, 1985; Stigler, Shweder, & Herdt, 1990; Wertsch, 1992), is a dissolution (hence the dotted lines of Figure 1) of the hard and fast boundaries between the inner and the outer, the ideational and the material, the self and society. This diagram should help to underscore that many of the important differences among the theorists in this volume stem primarily from which segment of the collective-to-individual reality or individual-to-collective reality is lit up in their analysis of emotion and culture.

The theoretical model diagrammed in Figure 1 consists of several components. It assumes that habitual tendencies or ways of feeling, including predispositions for emotional responses, somatic experiences, or more intersubjective mood states, develop through socialization and enculturation, as individuals actively seek to accomplish a degree of adaptation to their own immediate, *individual reality.* The individual reality comprises a number of social settings (e.g., school, work, home, market place, etc.), which in turn are made up of, and shaped by, a variety of *sociopsychological processes* such as linguistic conventions, socialization practices, scripts for everyday behavior, as well as educational, religious, and media practices. These processes are called *sociopsychological* in that they are made possible and *real* by each participating individual's social behavior. At the same time, they are also cultural and collective and implicate what Durkheim (1898/1953) called *social facts,* those objective and external realities that can exist relatively independently of the wishes, desires, hopes, or plans of any particular one of those participating individuals. These sociopsychological processes, of course, are also historical products; they must have been created at some point in history and they must have been preserved in the culture for some reason(s). Here, we suggest that every cultural group has some key ideas that have been traditionally and collectively held in place and that are used to select and organize their own sociopsychological processes. These *core cultural*

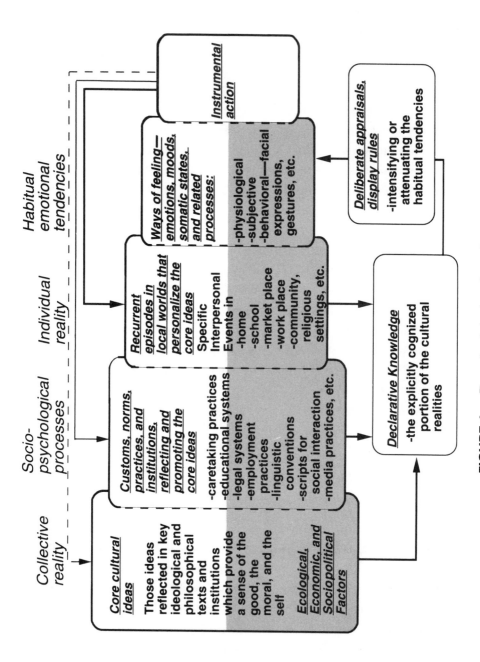

FIGURE 1. The cultural shaping of emotion.

ideas can influence the nature of the group's habitual emotional tendencies through constraining and affording particular, relatively culture-specific sets of immediate and everyday life realities, in which members of the cultural group are socialized or "trained" to think, act, and feel in a more or less adaptive fashion.

In addition to this process of transforming the core cultural ideas to individual psychological tendencies, two more processes are included in Figure 1. First, each individual's behavior may, in turn, cause changes in *both* the immediate social reality and, less frequently, the collective realities of the cultural group. This possibility is acknowledged by the feedback loops in the upper part of the figure. Second, we suggest that the core cultural ideas, sociopsychological processes, as well as the nature of local worlds, need *not* be explicitly encoded in each person's memory or cognitively and self-consciously articulated in the person's deliberated thought processes. For any given individual, cultural realities can exist independently of what he or she thinks or knows about. Parts of the collective and individual realities may be explicitly encoded or "objectified" in memory and, once so encoded, they may become objects of conscious and deliberate thought and, as such, they may organize more intentional forms of action. For example, one may explicitly and deliberately appraise implications of a friend's behavior, which in turn may lead to certain emotional behavior. This possibility is acknowledged in the lower part of the figure.

Collective Emotional Reality: Shared Views of How and What to Feel

According to Figure 1, the prevalent emotions of a given cultural group are simultaneously related to a set of collective understandings of what is a person, what is good or moral, to their supporting and sustaining practices, and to more individual phenomena like subjective affective states, facial expressions, and physiological responses. Under *collective reality*, we include cultural ideas and the ecological, historical, economic, and sociopolitical factors that afford or constrain these ideas. For example, the United States is a nation with a rich tradition of moral imperatives, the most well-elaborated of which is the need to protect the "natural rights" of each individual (Shweder, Mahapatra, & Miller, 1990). This core idea is rooted in several key ideological texts: the Declaration of Independence and the Bill of Rights, which protect certain inalienable rights, including life, liberty, and the pursuit of happiness. Throughout much of Asia, the prevalent ideological and moral discourses are and have always been quite different. There, one finds an emphasis not on natural rights, but on the inevitability and desirability of hierarchy, and on the achievement of virtue through the cultivation of the individual into a "social man" (Yu, 1992). This core cultural ideal is anchored in the works of Confucius and Mencius and finds expression in an array of economic, political, and social institutions.

As suggested by Menon and Shweder (chapter 8), the core cultural ideas may not be fully available to all members of a given cultural group. Their studies suggest, for example, that only some members of the Indian community of Oriya have full cultural expertise with regard to the meaning and consequences of the story of Kali, the central cultural icon. Other members appear to be unaware of the meaning of this powerful cultural symbol. Similarly, it would not be surprising to discover that many members of the collectivist and individualist cultural groups described by Triandis could not articulate the worldviews that seem to organize their feelings and their daily activities. Societal integration may well require that the foundations of the cultural models or schemas be largely taken for granted, and that their propositions be transparent or "go without saying" (Holland & Quinn, 1987). Such transparency may keep the core cultural ideas from being contested and challenged and thereby work to preserve the culture (Moscovici, 1993).

To indicate the possibility that aspects of a group's ideological commitments may not be available to all members at all times, we have shaded half of the box representing collective reality in Figure 1. The shaded segment here, and in the other sections of Figure 1, indicates what is represented cognitively. Thus, the core cultural values and ideals may be recruited and explicitly articulated in each individual's conscious awareness, and they may be used to organize psychological processes, but they need not be. Importantly, habitual emotional tendencies can develop independently of this articulated route of cultural influence. In this way, cultural ideas can cause differences in emotional tendencies even when these ideas and beliefs are not individually and cognitively encoded and elaborated in conscious awareness. Of course, cultural values and ideals are often encoded cognitively, but this analysis implies that for a given individual cognitive representations need not be central in the cultural shaping of emotion.

Sociopsychological Products and Processes: Transmitting the Core Ideas

The cultural ideals and moral imperatives of a given cultural group are given life by a diverse set of customs, norms, scripts, practices, and institutions that carry out the transformation and transmission of the collective reality (Kleinman, 1980; Miller, Potts, Fung, Hoogstra, & Mintz, 1990). These sociopsychological products and processes objectify and make public and "real" the core ideas of the society (Bourdieu, 1972; D'Andrade, 1984; Durkheim, 1898/1953; Farr & Moscovici, 1984; Geertz, 1973). Because the key cultural ideas are built directly into so many norms, practices, and institutions, it is unnecessary for every member of the culture to be able to articulate or reflect on the core cultural ideas. For example, in the United States, the idea of human rights as inherent and "God-given" is given force by an array of legal statutes protecting individual rights. In this way, the idea of the person as an autonomous, separate entity is reinforced and maintained.

Many chapters focus on one or another of the mechanisms of cultural transmission. Markus and Kitayama (chapter 4) draw attention to a diverse set of caretaking and schooling practices that develop a powerful association between feeling good and standing out from others (the cultural ideal of independence) among Americans, and a similarly powerful association between feeling good and fitting-in and seeing one's self as part of a relationship or as a member of a community (the cultural ideal of interdependence). In another example, Menon and Shweder (chapter 8) find that the powerful cultural idea of *lajya* as indication of harnessed anger is carried in many practices; most overtly, the message is transmitted in everyday discourse with the idiomatic imperative "to bite your tongue."

Wierzbicka (chapter 5) focuses exclusively on the role of linguistic conventions and scripts as well as on the lexicon and the grammar of language in creating the often seamless connection between emotion and culture. She forcefully argues that culture leaves an indelible mark on all aspects of the emotional process through the nature of the affective lexicon and specific meanings of emotion terms. In the words that cultural groups use to construct their feeling states, Wierzbicka finds clear lexical confirmation of significant differences in core cultural ideals. Moreover, she notes that the culturally authorized role of emotions, that is, a culture's attitude toward emotions, is reflected in the dynamics of everyday discourse enabling, in some cases, the highlighting, elaborating, and even the celebrating of individual feeling states. Americans, Wierzbicka notes, are encouraged to "feel something good all the time" and to behave as if one "felt something good most of the time." Other cultural groups, like the A'aras described by White (chapter 7), through their communication scripts, constrain private feelings and do not accord them such a significant role in the regulation of behavior. Instead, their emotional experiences are realized in the nature of the interpersonal atmosphere among group members.

Local Worlds: Living the Cultural Ideas

The third segment of Figure 1 represents the specific settings, circumstances, and situations of everyday life that make up an individual's immediate interpersonal environment, and in which particular customs, norms, and practices become lived experience. It is within the demands and expectations of these specific interpersonal, recurrent social episodes that people, often unknowingly, live out the core cultural ideas and values. Because people desire to locate themselves in social space and to know where they belong, who they are, and what to feel and think, they will immediately appropriate and construct *personal meanings* for their various sociocultural contexts (Shweder & Sullivan, 1990; Taylor, 1989). Because these meanings or construals of social situations are customized and *personalized* (e.g., Cantor & Kihlstrom, 1987), they are likely to be very diverse even within a single cultural group. Yet, at the same time, because they are also powerfully afforded and their range so constrained by the surrounding collective and individual realities of their respective cultures, systematic cross-cultural variations will likely be present as well.

It is here, in the course of specific interpersonal interactions, that some of the culture-specific tendencies of emotional experience are shaped. For example, in these specific and recurrent everyday social episodes, people come to understand, attend, and elaborate on their subjective affective states, or instead, to use these subjective affective states as cues to whether the atmosphere or mood between themselves and others is smooth or strained.

In the United States, men and women, African–American or European–American, Jewish or Christian, may share similar culturally organized ways of thinking about the self and others because they share a single, broadly defined cultural and sociopolitical reality. However, each person must *also* respond to a set of cultural requirements that are associated with being of a particular ethnic group, gender, religion, age, generation, region of country, and so on. So, in "feeling something good," an important American cultural imperative will be accomplished, but in the locally appropriate way. It is one's immediate interpersonal setting and its associated set of "scripts" and social conventions and language that will determine largely how and what is felt, and that will entrain the attentional, appraisal, physiological, and expressive processes described by Posner, Rothbart, and Harman (chapter 6), Ellsworth (chapter 2), and Frijda and Mesquita (chapter 3).

From this perspective, emotions, even for the most individualistic North Americans and Europeans, may be perceived as social, interpersonal products that are jointly and interactively crafted and held in place (cf. White, chapter 7). Cultural variation in these emotional tendencies is likely because the nature and frequency of social episodes varies considerably across cultures. For example, Americans may be likely to create settings that are designed to elicit and promote private good feelings, typically experienced as fun or happiness (e.g., a diverse array of parties, one for every conceivable occasion). As a result, many situations that have the production of happiness as their primary purpose may be present in American daily social life. Indeed, in the United States, it is appropriate, and often required, to ask "Are you happy?" or "Did you have fun?" in nearly any circumstance, and by the same token, individuals believe that it is their right to experience subjective happiness in many domains of life. By contrast, Japanese may not be especially inclined to structure interpersonal situations in which the goal is to "have fun." Japanese do have parties, of course, but it is possible to hypothesize that they are fewer in number and variety, and that their primary purpose is the production of a harmonious interpersonal atmosphere. A Japanese mother will rarely ask her child the equivalent of "Did you have fun today?" when the child returns from school.

Habitual Emotional Tendencies Reflecting the Core Ideas

As people respond, adjust, and chart their courses through the sets of specific, interpersonal episodes that make up their local worlds, episodes that have been shaped by norms, practices, and institutions supporting the groups's core ideas, a set of habitual emotional tendencies will develop. As a consequence, these emotional tendencies become the most individualized manifestation of the core cultural ideas. The nature of the emotional tendencies will be importantly determined by how a given event has been coded (see Frijda & Mesquita, chapter 3), and event coding (i.e., is this a personal insult, an affront to my family's honor, a magic spell, etc.) depends on a culture's salient or focal concerns. A person's attention will be "naturally" drawn by the focal events of one's culture; they cannot remain unnoticed. Thus, American feelings are particularly likely to be manifest and expressed in those interpersonal situations in which one's attributes or performance can be evaluated. Among the Balinese or the Bedouins, feelings will be manifest and expressed in those situations in which one's honor or status or dignity can be evaluated. What results is an *affective tuning* between the prevalent social episodes of a person's local world and one's prevalent ways of feeling.

The final segment of Figure 1 represents the person's "authentic" subjective feeling. As the chapters by Ellsworth (chapter 2), Frijda and Mesquita (chapter 3), and Jenkins (chapter 10) suggest, a person's emotional tendencies, even seemingly "natural" bodily relations to misery (e.g., war and job loss) will be locally situated, but they will also be individually crafted and fine-tuned. It is unlikely that any two individuals will have the same emotional experience to a given event. Even twins inhabiting the same local world will attend to different features of this interpersonal world, and thus the meanings that they achieve and the actions that accompany them can be quite divergent. The basis of this variability in emotional experience is the individual interpretive structures or schemas that have developed as a result of previous emotional conditioning, both conscious and nonconscious and of past efforts at meaning making.

In short, we have tried to summarize, in Figure 1, a general theoretical framework that views *culture* as a part of individual or psychological processes in general and of emotional processes in particular, and *emotion* as significantly enabled and shaped by cultural ideas, practices, and institutions. Rudimentary as it is, we believe that this figure begins to capture a consensual understanding of the close and intricate interdependencies between culture and emotion that have emerged and developed in embryonic form among the authors of this volume and among the many other participants of the emotion and culture conference of June 1992 on which this volume is based.

According to this analysis, many psychological and physiological processes of emotion may be best understood as participating elements or constituents of a wholistic and nearly seamless interaction between individual minds and cultural reality. Psychological tendencies to form particular sorts of appraisals or to act in one way or another may be best understood as enabled or afforded by the nature of recurrent social events and episodes of the corresponding cultural environment. In other words, these tendencies are shaped as a result of the person's active adaptation to the cultural environment. Similarly, regulatory processes of attention cannot be understood fully without explicit reference to a specific set of cultural practices in which these processes are embedded, to the cultural stimuli to which they are conditioned, and to the ways in which these practices and stimuli are coherently and meaningfully organized within the entire culture.

Thus, we believe that conceptual and empirical research on emotions can be furthered by acknowledging explicitly the possibility that the nature and functions of emotional processes may depend crucially on the characteristics of the particular cultural reality in which these processes operate. This would mean that any emotional process, for instance appraisal patterns or attention regulation, will have to be described and analyzed not only as constituted by more elementary component processes, but also as afforded, supported, and held in place by a set of cultural practices and institutions in which these processes are embedded.

Overall, we believe that this volume has made a convincing theoretical case for this cultural affordance or constitution of psychological and emotional mechanisms. When this general theoretical orientation is fully established, future research may be more specifically tuned to the nature of cultural conventions, practices, or institutions that directly afford and enable the specific aspects of emotional processes. Although many findings of this sort have already been available and reported in this volume, a great deal still remains to be done. It seems appropriate to end this volume with a call for a new generation of theoretical and empirical research focused on the subtle but powerful interdependencies between culture and emotion.

References

Bourdieu, P. (1972). *Outline of a theory of practice.* Cambridge, England: Cambridge University Press.

Cantor, N., & Kihlstrom, J. F. (1987). *Personality and social intelligence.* Englewood Cliffs, NJ: Prentice Hall.

Corsaro, W. A., & Miller, P. J. (Eds.). (1992). *Interpretive approaches in children's socialization.* San Francisco: Jossey-Bass.

D'Andrade, R. (1984). Cultural meaning systems. In R. A. Shweder & R. A. LeVine (Eds.), *Culture theory: Essays on mind, self, and emotion* (pp. 88–119). Cambridge, England: Cambridge University Press.

Durkheim, E. (1953). Individual representations and collective representations. In D. F. Pocock (Trans.), *Sociology and philosophy* (pp. 1–38). New York: Free Press. (Reprinted from *Revue de Métaphysique,* 1898, *6,* 274–302)

Farr, R. M., & Moscovici, S. (Eds.). (1984). *Social representations*. Cambridge, England: Cambridge University Press.

Geertz, C. (1973). *The interpretations of cultures*. New York: Basic Books.

Holland, D., & Quinn, N. (Eds.). (1987). *Cultural models in language and thought*. Cambridge, England: Cambridge University Press.

Kleinman, A. (1980). *Patients and healers in the context of culture: An exploration on the borderland between anthropology, medicine, and psychiatry*. Berkeley: University of California Press.

Miller, P. J., Potts, R., Fung, H., Hoogstra, L., & Mintz, J. (1990). Narrative practices and the social construction of self in childhood. *American Ethnology, 17*, 292–311.

Moscovici, S. (1993, Spring). The return of the unconscious. *Social Research, 60*, 1, 39–93.

Rosaldo, M. Z. (1984). Toward an anthropology of self and feeling. In R. A. Shweder & R. A. LeVine (Eds.), *Culture theory: Essays on mind, self, and emotion* (pp. 137–157). Cambridge, England: Cambridge University Press.

Schwartz, T., White, G., & Lutz, C. (Eds.). (1993). *New directions in psychological anthropology*. Cambridge, England: Cambridge University Press.

Shweder, R. A., Mahapatra, M., & Miller, J. G. (1990). Culture and moral development. In J. Stigler, R. Shweder, & G. Herdt (Eds.), *Cultural psychology: Essays on comparative human development* (pp. 130–204). Cambridge, England: Cambridge University Press.

Shweder, R. A., & Sullivan, M. A. (1990). The semiotic subject of cultural psychology. In L. A. Pervin (Eds.), *Handbook of personality* (pp. 399–418). New York: Guilford Press.

Sperber, D. (1985). Anthropology and psychology: Toward an epidemiology of representations. *Man, 20*, 73–89.

Stigler, J., Shweder, R., & Herdt, G. (Eds.). (1990). *Cultural psychology: Essays on comparative human development*. Cambridge, England: Cambridge University Press.

Taylor, C. (1989). *Sources of the self: The making of modern identities*. Cambridge, MA: Harvard University Press.

Wertsch, J. (1992). Keys to cultural psychology. *Culture, Medicine and Psychiatry, 16*, 273–280.

Yu, A. B. (1992, July). *The self and life goals of traditional Chinese: A philosophical and cultural analysis*. Paper presented at the International Congress of Cross-Cultural Psychology, Liège, Belgium.

Author Index

Subject Index

About the Editors

Shinobu Kitayama is currently an associate professor of psychology at Kyoto University, Japan. He received his PhD in 1987 from the University of Michigan and taught at the University of Oregon from 1988 to 1993. Dr. Kitayama has worked in the areas of emotional influences on attention and perception, cognitive processes in social judgment, and cultural psychology of self and emotion.

Hazel Rose Markus is a professor of psychology at the University of Michigan and a research scientist at the Institute for Social Research. Her research has focused on the role of the self in regulating behavior. Dr. Markus has written on self-schemas, possible selves, the influence of the self on the perception of others, and the constructive role of the self in adult development. Her most recent work is in the area of cultural psychology and explores the interdependence between selves and socio-cultural environments.